A Public Purpose

A Public Purpose

AN EXPERIENCE OF LIBERAL
OPPOSITION AND
CANADIAN GOVERNMENT

TOM KENT

McGILL-QUEEN'S UNIVERSITY PRESS
KINGSTON AND MONTREAL

© Tom Kent 1988
ISBN 0-7735-0649-7

Legal deposit first quarter 1988
Bibliothèque nationale du Québec

Printed in Canada

Canadian Cataloguing in Publication Data

Kent, Tom, 1922–
   A public purpose
   Includes index.
   ISBN 0-7735-0649-7
   1. Canada – Politics and government – 1957–1963.
   2. Canada – Politics and government – 1963–1968.
   3. Canada – Politics and government – 1968–1979.
   4. Liberal Party of Canada – History.
   5. Kent, Tom, 1922– I. Title.
   FC621.K46A3 1988   971.064'092'4   C87-090359-4
   F1034.3.K46A3 1988

The cartoons by Reidford on pages 43, 217, 253, and
373 are reprinted by permission – The Globe and Mail.
The cartoon by Duncan Macpherson on page 135 is reprinted by permission – The Toronto Star Syndicate.

Contents

Preface

Anyone who writes a book about public affairs centred on personal experiences is foolhardy. I had strong inhibitions about it, despite the urgings of friends. Hitherto, my writing has been of only one kind. The memoranda, editorials, articles, papers, speeches, even a small book, have all been directed to what should be done or not be done: by governments, federal, provincial, or municipal; by political parties; by the various other organizations – corporate, public service, and academic – with which I have been involved. They have been directed to policy, of one kind or another, at the time they were written.

Therefore, while this book is an account of personal experience, it is also directed towards aspects of the making of public policy that may be of interest, and perhaps of a little value, to people concerned about the politics and government of today and tomorrow. The relevance of experience is no doubt less than those who have it are tempted to imagine. There are, however, some wheels that seem to be in frequent need of reinvention. Some of the ideas that have been submerged or misshapen under the presure of events may be useful if they are lifted out and re-examined in the context of today's problems. I have written in the hope of making some contribution of that kind.

Nevertheless, the account is self–centred and therefore open, like all of its kind, to the risk of being self-serving. No one can pretend to be entirely objective about events in which he or she was a participant. I therefore emphasize that this book does not purport to be a history, which would have to be based on material from many other accounts. Public policies are the products of many minds. I simply took part in the collective processes that developed Liberal policies, remade the party in opposition, and conducted government in the Pearson period and in the first three Trudeau years. In order to be as accurate as I can on specific issues, I limit my account to those of which I had direct experience. That restriction of purpose is the only reason why this book makes little or no mention of many of the people who, as party workers, or politicians, or civil servants, contributed greatly to the public business of Canada in the eighteen years from 1954 to 1971. Such men as Paul Martin, Jack Pickersgill, and Mitchell Sharp are leading examples of many who played more important parts in the Liberal party and in the Pearson government than my references to them would indicate. Some have published their own recollections, different in emphasis from mine. Accounts from personal perspectives can be diverse without being necessarily in conflict. It is for the historians, not the participants, to piece together the full story.

I have not cluttered the book with footnote references, which would have given a false impression that it is pretending to be a history. Apart from what is already a matter of public record, there are only two sources. The main one is my papers. Many of these were memoranda to Mike Pearson; his method of work was quite often to return them with comment, either scribbled on them or given in discussion, so that the originals of some which were significant, for subsequent action or inaction, ended in my files rather than his. Now that the book is finished, my papers will be deposited in the Public Archives for scholars to examine if they wish.

The other source is, of course, my recollections. I believe that these are still accurate, but they have been checked as far as possible with those of the people still living with whom I worked most closely. The two who were centrally important, at different times, were Walter Gordon and Gordon Robertson. I was extraordinarily blessed in those partnerships, and this book has further increased my indebtedness. Both W.L.G. – in the year before his death – and R.G.R. read the first draft, corrected me on some matters, commented on many, and gave me wise advice. To the extent that this account is balanced and accurate, about the many matters in which one or other was involved, they are to be greatly thanked. The responsibility for errors of fact and judgment remains mine.

I am much indebted to the Institute for Research on Public Policy, which through its fellowship program provided the office services and other support without which the writing of this book would have been much more difficult. I particularly appreciate the encouragement of Rod Dobell, President of the Institute, and of Louis Vagianos, its former Executive Director. Three members of the staff of the Institute's Halifax office – Ruby Day, Donna McCafferty, and Janise Rae – shared the heroic work of converting my original scribble and subsequent amendments into word-processor text. Their accuracy, speed, and patience were exemplary, and I am deeply grateful.

I am also fortunate in my publisher. It was William Watson, Consulting Editor to McGill-Queen's University Press, who prodded me into writing the kind of book this is, rather than the less descriptive one that I had been considering. He was an incisive and perceptive critic of the draft, and was joined in constructive comment and wise advice by Philip Cercone, Executive Director of the Press.

My greatest debts are to Phyllida Kent. If we had not been married since 1944 there would not be this story to tell. I was engaged in the kind of life that demanded large sacrifices from our family and depended on her great understanding and strong support. The book is also partly hers in another sense. She has been the sharpest critic of the drafts, in structure and in detail, and the prime source of improvements that have made it more balanced, more precise and better written than it would otherwise have been.

PART ONE

Getting Defeated

Winnipeg editor gets warm reception in Ottawa

1 Coming From

This book is an account of involvement in public life, not an autobiography. The reader is entitled, however, to a brief explanation of where the author came from, how he happened to be where he was at the beginning of the account.

I was born in England in 1922. My parents were not well off. In the thirties all the mining and engineering operations in our Midlands town stopped. My father was out of work for a time, and it was only with the war that there was a general recovery. I was lucky to get a scholarship for secondary education, which was then not free and my parents could not have paid for. At first my best subjects were physics and chemistry, but interest shifted to history and literature, and through them to politics and economics. A combination of university scholarships made it possible to go to Oxford without parental expense. From there I was recruited into war-time intelligence service, for what has since become famous as "the ultra secret." This was the breaking of ciphers used in radio messages that the Germans believed to be entirely secure. In this way, the section in which I worked penetrated the secrets of the agents of the *Abwehr*, German military intelligence. My contribution to breaking ciphers was minor compared with the reward: it was this activity that brought my wife and me together.

It was also by the good fortune of acquaintanceships made in the ultra work that I was recruited, after the war, to the editorial staff of what is now *The Guardian*, then the famous *Manchester Guardian*. The editor, A.P. Wadsworth, who had a large influence on me, made the appointment in a typical handwritten note to the effect that they could give me some sort of introduction to journalism if I was so foolish as to want it. By 1950 I had the happy choice of becoming Assistant Editor of the *Guardian* or moving to London to the same position on *The Economist*, which, under the brilliant editorship of Geoffrey Crowther and with a star as bright as Barbara Ward, had become the internationally most important journal of public affairs. I left the *Guardian*, with regret, for the sake of the broader experience.

As part of that process, in 1951, I visited the United States for the first time, and added three weeks in Canada because the *Winnipeg Free Press* had invited me. I had become acquainted with some Canadian Ministers and officials who, when in London, by natural affinity liked to discuss the state of the world with *Guardian* people. Edgar Ritchie, then one of the senior people at the Canadian High Commission in London, used to joke that its dispatches to Ottawa were mostly copied from our editorials. Also, in the early postwar years the *Winnipeg Free Press* had a full-time correspondent in London, Frank Walker (later editor of the *Montreal Star*). We became friends, initially when observing the beginning of the first GATT conference in Geneva in 1947. After Frank had returned to Winnipeg, and had not been satisfactorily replaced, I became in 1950 a regular contributor to the *Free Press*. The first attraction was that it was an easy way to add to my income, but I became increasingly interested in Canada. I was, however, unprepared when the point of the 1951 invitation turned out to be that Victor Sifton, the owner of the *Free Press*, was asking me to become its Editor.

At the time, I declined. *The Economist* was close to the centre of public affairs and had the income to build on its position. One way in which Geoffrey Crowther liked to articulate his aims for the paper was that no one, from the Prime Minister or the Archbishop of Canterbury down, should refuse an invitation to lunch at *The Economist* – not because of the quality of the conversation, which could be taken for granted, but because the food was also so good.

Among Geoffrey's many shrewd measures was to move the offices of *The Economist* from the financial district to the "fashionable" West End of London. There he bought, for a song, an apartment building that had been damaged by incendiary bombs and renovated it, for offices, out of the war-damage compensation attached to it. In 1950 there were still older taxi drivers who responded with a knowing wink when one stated the destination, 22 Ryder Street, located in the corner between St James's and Jermyn Street. The prewar residents of its apartments were reputed to have included some of London's most expensive ladies.

Thanks to Geoffrey, I became by far the youngest member of the dining club that Keynes had started. Its membership of about two dozen was a careful mix of politicians, civil servants, City of London financial people, and professional economists. When I was admitted the luminaries ranged, at the extremes, from Harold Macmillan, then on his way to the prime ministership, to Lord Waverley, whom Geoffrey privately described as a monument talking; in his earlier incarnation as Sir John Anderson, he had been the wartime Chancellor of the Exchequer who first put some of Keynes's ideas into budgets. Apart from Geoffrey, the member who had most influence on me was Sir George Schuster, a City man who, as a friend of Sir Stafford Cripps, had somewhat bridged the gap between the financial establishment and the Labour government; I had worked for him, informally, when he chaired a government task force on reconstruction of the cotton industry.

The club met monthly in a room at Brown's Hotel that had a large, circular table which facilitated coherent discussion after dinner. Some members were still inclined to believe that most important innovations in economic policy were first explored at its meetings. The accuracy of this belief had varied with circumstances, and had certainly declined since Keynes's death. Still, for a young man not out of his twenties, the discussions were stimulating enough. They illustrate why I could not consider leaving the heady life associated with *The Economist* without savouring it more than I had done by 1951.

By 1953, I felt differently. The pleasantness of the life could not compensate for the lack of ideological roots. The postwar Labour government had been a great disappointment. I fully supported the great social changes brought about by the war and the postwar advances in the welfare state, but I disagreed strongly with Labour's continuing devotion to public ownership as a dogma rather than a device for special circumstances; above all, Labour's management of the economy had been very poor and the party's attitudes offered little hope that it would do better in future. The Conservative party was not an attractive alternative. With some of its younger MPs I was in agreement on many issues, as I was equally with a few Labour MPs and with my friends in the miniscule Liberal party. But on those issues the Conservative and Labour men were at odds with their parties.

The central issue was summarized at the time as "joining Europe." The tentative steps that led eventually to the Common Market were then being developed. I was convinced that this was the direction in which the future should lie. I could see no satisfactory recovery of the British economy without European union. My main prescription for a British government was that it should be taking the initiative for that union.

Governments of both parties were wedded to a different view. The Labour party could hardly have been more deeply imbued with a defensive, "Little Englander" sentiment. Most Conservatives were of the same mind.

The stimulating discussions of the company I was able to keep were no more than froth on the poor beer of postwar British politics. I could see no possibility of attitudes changing in time for Britain to have its hand in the building of European union. In fact, of course, a Conservative government did eventually take Britain into a Common Market already well established among the original six members. It was a classic case of the right decision made far too late. The British economy had gone too badly for too long to be rejuvenated in the way that it would have been as a partner in European union during the early postwar period.

In the 1950s I could see only a gloomy future for Britain. My personal prospects were good enough. I could reasonably entertain the ambition of becoming, while still relatively young, the Editor of either *The Econo-mist* or *The Guardian*. But I could see no great satisfaction in that if I were ideologically homeless, if my editorial position had to be one of constant-ly crying a plague on both your houses. And I could not see Britain providing the environment I would wish for my sons, the third of whom was born in 1953.

In contrast, I was fascinated by Canada. In 1952 I made a second, extensive visit, not only across the country but also, thanks to a bush plane of the Hudson's Bay Company, into the north. I found myself in close sympathy with ministers such as Douglas Abbott, Mike Pearson, and Brooke Claxton, as well as with the mandarins who were then at the peak of their influence. In the first few years of the 1950s I was privileged to meet the government of Canada at its best. Perhaps there was an element of the grass looking greener on the other side of the water; but after due allowance for that, it still seemed clear that Canada was a better society, and Ottawa provided a better government, than I knew in Britain.

Victor Sifton had left his offer open, and in the summer of 1953 I told him that I would now be interested. At his suggestion, we discussed it while I made a third visit, during the final stages of that year's general election campaign.

Television had not then lessened the political significance of news-papers, and the *Free Press* had had, thanks primarily to John W. Dafoe's great editorship, a unique importance among Canadian papers. After Dafoe's death in 1944, however, it had become stuck in playing old tunes; such variations and improvisations as there were on the themes did not reflect the former skill and power. Victor Sifton was realistic enough to recognize that the paper had lost influence, which was what he most cared about, and honest enough to admit, to himself and a few others, that he had mishandled the senior staffing in succession to Dafoe. He offered me a mandate to modernize the paper, and I accepted.

The move to Canada was made early in 1954, initially with no respon-sibility except to get acclimatized. In that I was generously helped by many people, but above all by Bill Lawson, a Manitoban by upbringing who was then chief of the research division of the Bank of Canada and later its Senior Deputy Governor. While my family was still in England, and I was spending most of my time in Ottawa, Bill gave me the hospital-ity of his apartment. That resulted in a wider circle of friends than would otherwise have been possible. Most important of all for my future work was the family relationship with Bill's twin sister and her husband, Gordon Robertson.

I went back to England in May, to help with the family's emigration to Winnipeg. In June we moved into the rambling house that went with the job. Grant Dexter, who had been an outstanding political correspondent and became so again, but who had been miscast in the editorial chair, returned happily to Ottawa. At mid-year, 1954, I started the job of editorship.

2 *Do as I Say...*

It was in 1954 that things began to go wrong for the Liberal party, which had been in office since 1935. That gave an element of irony to the timing of my immigration. The quality of government that I saw in Ottawa in 1951–3 had been one of the strong attractions of Canada. Soon, however, it turned out to be government in trouble.

That few people realized this quickly is no shame. It is inherent in the nature of political parties that when they are enjoying success they are insensitive to indications that the basis of their success is being eroded. And federal Liberals in Canada had special reason not to notice clouds when they were no bigger than a man's hand.

In 1953 they had handily won a general election that meant they would be in office without interruption for twenty-two years, from 1935 to 1957. The party could fairly be described as the most successful political organization in the democratic world. The Canadian economy had been greatly boosted by the war and now seemed to be on top of the postwar world. While that might be attributed largely to favourable circumstances, there was also justification for the world-wide view that the Canadian economy was extraordinarily well managed by its government. No country seemed to have fewer social and political problems. Even the English-French tension, real enough in the war, seemed to have relaxed, to the point indeed that a Francophone prime minister could declare, in the summer of 1954, that "Quebec is a province like the other provinces." Internationally, the country enjoyed a reputation and an influence quite out of proportion to the size of its population; and if that was made possible by economic strength, it also owed much to the skill and the internationalist spirit of the diplomacy headed by L.B. Pearson.

There was, however, one Liberal at least who in early 1954 saw that change in the party should come before long. He was the party's leader. On 29 March I talked with Mr St Laurent in the Prime Minister's office in the centre block of the Ottawa Parliament Buildings. His mood was reflective, fitting both his personality and the circumstances. He had

recently returned from an extensive tour of European and Asian countries, where he had been received in ways that underlined the high
regard in which Canada was held in the world community. It was therefore natural that the conversation should turn to international affairs and
hence to what was at that moment the commonest topic of world political gossip. Winston Churchill was aged to an extent that many people
saw as senility. Should he, would he, retire from the prime ministership
of Britain?

Mr St Laurent asked me what I thought. I was unbecomingly hesitant:
Mr St Laurent was seventy-two himself; and though he looked well
enough that day, I knew that he had not stood up too well to the rigours
of his Asian travel. I therefore replied that I perhaps had a prejudiced
view, since most of my friends and acquaintances in British politics were
comparatively young MPs; they all, irrespective of party, thought that Mr
Churchill ought to go.

Mr St Laurent was not hesitant: "Of course he ought; he should have
retired some time ago." He leaned back in his chair and though I was not
taking notes – this was a conversation, not a journalistic interview – the
gist of his reflections was unforgettable. I cannot after this interval claim
to reproduce his precise phrases or entirely to reflect the style that
helped to give Mr St Laurent his "Uncle Louis" nickname. But what he
said went something like this:

> Very few men in public life hold on to two truths about the decision
> to retire: it's the most difficult decision to make; and to make it cor-
> rectly you have to make it sooner than is necessary. It's the one deci-
> sion for which no advice is any help to you. All the people close to
> you have their own reasons for wanting you to go or wanting you to
> stay. You must make the decision alone. And therefore you must de-
> cide before it's really time, because if you wait for that, you have
> then lost the capacity to judge your situation objectively. You can't
> overcome the tendency to take an exaggerated view of your own
> role. I've seen that happen to so many people; I'm determined it
> won't happen to me. I feel in great condition now, but I won't re-
> main here for as long as I feel that way. I shall retire while I'm still
> sure that I don't need to.

The indication that he thus gave to me was not kite-flying. Our conversation was intended to be, and remained, personal and confidential. The
reality of his intent became known later, because he discussed it with his
closest colleague, C.D. Howe. His biographers, Robert Bothwell and
William Kilbourn, record that Mr Howe said later that in 1953, "I had an
understanding with our leader that we would both retire after a year or

two in office and give the new leader time to get organized."

It was natural to Mr Howe to think of the leader as getting "organized," but he went on to recognize (with the benefit of hindsight) that the problem was that "the Liberal dynasty had run out of ideas." The crucial task of a new leader, if he is the right man for the times, is to adapt government policy to changing circumstances. If he does so, a change of leadership part way through a government's term is the smoothest way for a party to be remade. It is the way that both King and Pearson made possible by the timing of their retirements, though in the second case the successor, inheriting a minority in Parliament and buoyed by the public enthusiasm for him, chose to call an election without bothering to organize in Mr Howe's sense. Mr St Laurent, by hanging on until electoral defeat in 1957, and Mr Trudeau, by hanging on until near the end of the government's term, so that his successor had little time in which to organize, destroyed the possibility of remaking the Liberal party in office rather than in opposition.

One lesson that I would draw most firmly from experience and observation is that there is need, in both the public and the private sectors, for a changed attitude about the length of time for which heads of organizations are expected, and expect, to occupy their positions. There is some truth in the Peter Principle that large organizations tend to promote people to the level of their incompetence. It is more generally true that the head of an organization was the right person for the job, or at least as good as any available choice, at the time of the appointment. But the requirements of the job often change more quickly than the person. The frequency with which leaders become obsolete has increased as change accelerates. We need to find ways of making it seem natural that heads of organizations should often serve for shorter terms than are now usually expected, and then move, whether it be sideways, down, or out.

The discussion with Mr St Laurent on 29 March 1954, was not in those general terms, but the specific moral was plain: prime ministers should resign at the peak of their powers, thereby giving their parties the opportunities of renewal in favourable circumstances. The irony, though I did not know it, was that Mr St Laurent had just then passed the point of decision that he had, in principle, discerned so clearly. He had been exhausted by his world travel, and the effects on his health were recurrent. Thereafter, short periods of activity alternated with prolonged bouts of inertia – not in the sense that he ever failed to perform conscientiously the routine work of his office, but in the sense that he sank into the indecision of apathy. In particular, he did not do as he had said. He did not make his intended decision to retire by 1955. And Mr Howe soldiered on with him.

The consequence was clear from 1955. The St Laurent government, which had been so sure of touch, stumbled under indecisive leadership. It began to misjudge both public opinion and the consequences of its own actions. As is usual in democratic politics, the decline was at first with a whimper rather than a bang, though by 1956 the pipeline debate reached that second dimension. The momentum of the Liberal system ensured that some important achievements were still recorded in domestic affairs, while internationally Canada, through Pearson's diplomacy, reached the peak of its contribution with the UN action to end the Suez war. Nevertheless, the government from 1955 on was marked by the misjudgments and arrogance that led to its electoral defeat in 1957.

The men who left the Cabinet in 1954 were not Mr St Laurent and Mr Howe but three of its younger members. One, Lionel Chevrier, returned to politics later. The others, Doug Abbott and Brooke Claxton, were two of the ablest ministers. Their loss, which was permanent, greatly weakened the government.

Claxton was a sagacious man of ideas; if he had stayed in the Cabinet he might have helped considerably to lessen the errors of the following years. Abbott was the strong man among the younger ministers. He had even been known to change C.D. Howe's mind. He was an excellent Minister of Finance. He had a charming capacity to carry his competence lightly and was sometimes in consequence underrated by people who were not politicians. Politically, he was both sensitive and sensible. If he had stayed he would have been my choice to succeed to the leadership, ahead of Pearson. While his sympathies were not quite as broad as Pearson's, he had an even clearer mind, a better understanding of most issues, and above all a greater capacity to make firm decisions and a stronger grasp of how to execute them.

Abbott and Claxton had personalities too mature to be overimpressed by the gratifications of power. Anyone who has been exposed to public life can understand the inclination of such men to go on to other, less demanding experiences. But they were relatively young men. A Prime Minister, or indeed a leader in other fields, cannot be content with those who want to stay. He must be concerned, above all, about who will succeed him. He needs to hold the Abbotts of this world, to persuade them that it is their responsibility to go on serving the public interest.

As far as I could discover, Mr St Laurent made no such attempt. He was deeply distressed to lose such colleagues. Indeed, Abbott in 1954 told Walter Gordon that Mr St Laurent had said that he wanted him (Abbott) to be his successor. But he did not press the point. It was typical of Mr St Laurent's courteous disposition that he accepted that his colleagues knew what was best for themselves and he should not stand in their way. That is not leadership, however. Letting Abbott and Claxton go was the first evidence, and in my view one of the most serious consequences, of the recurrent bouts of passivity that marked Mr St Laurent's behaviour from 1954 on.

This concern was expressed in the first editorial I wrote from Winnipeg. On 4 June 1954, the Abbott resignation was expected, though officially a month away. I hoped that he would be persuaded to stay. The editorial forecast the reasons – in economics and in federal-provincial relations – why life was going to get harder for the government, and pointed out that it was on the Minister of Finance, next to the Prime Minister himself, that the responsibilities of leadership, through harder times, would fall. The Cabinet had by no means all the strength it used to enjoy. Some of its members had grown old in office; and from others, easy electoral success had extorted a penalty. Mr St Laurent's problem was to put life back into his team.

In fact, Abbott's resignation resulted in the promotion of Walter Harris. At the time it seemed as good a choice as could be made from the available talent, but it proved to be a promotion beyond the limits of competence. Mr Harris never grew to anything near the grasp of the elements of public policy that distinguished Mr Abbott. His political skills were real enough but they were directed to minimizing trouble in the short run, not to recognizing the occasions when decisive action was appropriate. He remained, despite the importance of his new position, a member of what C.D. Howe used to refer to as the "Junior League" in Ottawa.

My hopes for something better were dashed by an early incident. When he became Minister of Finance, Walter Harris retained the role of Leader of the House of Commons which he had previously combined with the relatively minor portfolio of Citizenship and Immigration. Talking to him soon afterwards, I thought it polite to express some commiseration about the burden of the double job. His response, with apparent relish, was that really he had three jobs, since he was also responsible for the party organization in Ontario, and that took more time than either of the others. I was too amazed to think of any comment that would not have been explosive.

In fact, thanks to the senior public servants, the government's financial management did not deteriorate quickly. The economy recovered strongly from its small 1953–4 recession, and the Harris budget of 1955 was sensible. After that, praise became difficult.

For ten years after the war, Canada's economic policy had had three arms. One was the active interventionism of C.D. Howe, of which more will be said later. The other two arms were macro-economic policies of fairly "easy" money (symbolized by an almost unvarying Bank of Canada rate of 2 per cent) and a moderately "hard" fiscal policy – which Mr Abbott always somehow managed to represent not as taxing more than necessary or spending less than possible, but as the happy consequence of the buoyancy of the economy. The combination was a sound Keynesian prescription for Canada's circumstances, and it worked.

With Walter Harris at Finance, fiscal policy was somewhat relaxed. The more significant change was that, whether from lack of understanding, political calculation, or perhaps a combination of the two, Mr Harris deliberately distanced himself from the Bank and monetary policy. What had been the harmonious co-ordination at the centre of economic policy disappeared. The Bank – the governorship of which changed in 1955 from Graham Towers to Jim Coyne – became distrustful of fiscal policy, and understandably tightened monetary policy. By 1956–7 it was, if anything, overreacting. The short-term consequence was to intensify the recession that began to develop in 1957. The longer-term significance of the estrangement between the Finance Department and the Bank was, however, to start Ottawa along a path that contributed to the poor economic management of the Diefenbaker years and culminated in the Coyne affair of 1961.

Meantime, however, the Bank contributed significantly to one of the two major achievements of which the St Laurent government proved to be capable even in its declining years.

The tax rental arrangements between Ottawa and the provinces, which had originated in the war, were due to expire in 1957. There had to be some renewed or new system. The more constructively minded people in Ottawa were anxious to take the opportunity to establish some stable principle to deal with the basic fiscal problem of Confederation: the provinces are significantly unequal in their levels of income and employment and in the extent to which their jurisdictions include the headquarters, and therefore the profits, of corporations doing nation-wide business. Provincial governments therefore vary greatly in the level of revenues that they can raise by taxes on income and wealth. The Rowell-Sirois Commission had diagnosed the problem and proposed one solution, but it had been opposed by the richer provinces and set aside in the exigencies of the war. Circumstances were now more favourable, and various ways of implementing the Rowell-Sirois concept were suggested. The best that emerged was, indeed, a considerable advance on the Commission's proposal. Known at first as "Plan C," it was the brainchild principally of three outstanding public servants: Maurice Lamontagne in the Prime Minister's Office; John Deutsch at the Department of Finance; and Bob Beattie of the Bank of Canada.

In essence, the idea of Plan C was that the federal government would levy personal and corporation income taxes and estate duties but would remit to the provinces the proceeds of certain levels of these taxes. What would be remitted to each province would not be, however, the actual yield of the taxes in that province. Their average yield, per capita of population, would be calculated for the two richest provinces, Ontario and British Columbia, and remittances to the other provinces would be made up to the same level. This was "equalization," a way of ensuring that all provinces could afford roughly comparable levels of public services without the poorer provinces having to handicap themselves further by imposing substantially higher levels of taxation on income and wealth than the richer provinces needed.

Plan C was the first embodiment of the equalization concept. Its expression has since been broadened and sophisticated, on the whole steadily though with occasional slippages, and the principle is now accepted, and indeed embedded in the constitution, as the financial cornerstone of Confederation. But in 1955–6 it was an unfamiliar idea and the indecisive condition of the St Laurent government militated against its adoption. The three inventors of Plan C were friends of mine; I was deeply interested in the subject; and there was precedent for my involvement because John W. Dafoe had been a member of the Rowell-Sirois Commission. I was made privy to the plan and to the problems that its proponents faced.

There was strong opposition to Plan C from some senior officials of the Department of Finance. That would not have mattered in the old days. Doug Abbott would have made up his mind – I have little doubt that it would have been for Plan C or some ingenious modification thereof – and the officials would have fallen into line. But the Minister in 1955–6 gave no sign that he had a definite view. There was no line for officials to fall into.

The role that public servants play in policy-making is widely misunderstood. The idea that they should merely implement policy decisions, for which all the ideas have come from elected men, is nonsense. Government has never been so simple that it could be run that way, and certainly it is not today. We pay senior public servants to be the professionals in government and they would not be doing their job if they did not have significant influence on policy.

What they should not have, and as far as I have seen usually do not have, is decisive influence, *as long as the politicians are doing their job*. But for that the politicians in office – the Cabinet as it used to be or nowadays the key members of the Cabinet, given the expansion that has destroyed its collective decision-making capacity – have to be agreed on clear objectives. If they are, they will make the final decisions and the senior public servants will have, properly, influence but not power. It is only when the politicians do not know their own minds that officials fill the vacuum. They can then become decisive to policy, and that is often better than the alternative of indecision. In this respect, the weakness that needs correction is not in the government structure in Ottawa, but in the political system that results in politicians coming to power with too little definition of what they are going to do with that power. Much of this book is about the effort to ensure that the Pearson government was one that did know, and had told the electorate, what it would do.

In 1955–6 Walter Harris did not know what he wanted from the federal-provincial tax arrangements. I think his attitude to them was chiefly that they were a political hot potato and his inclination towards all such vegetables was to leave them alone if he possibly could. It was therefore clear that Plan C would be adopted as government policy only if the Prime Minister took responsibility for it, including the preservation of its integrity through the federal-provincial negotiations in which each provincial government would be trying to get something more favourable for itself. But Mr St Laurent was in no mood to do that readily. He would take on the task only if most of the Cabinet were persuaded not only that Plan C was the right policy but also that it was one where the government's success was of major importance.

That in turn was not easy, because the old habit of the Cabinet had been to defer in such matters to the Minister of Finance. To get a sufficiently strong Cabinet view without the prior leadership either of that Minister or of the Prime Minister would require a good deal of explaining of Plan C and persuading as to its importance. The proponents of the plan enlisted me as an unofficial assistant in the process. I talked with a number of ministers on whom it was thought that I could have some persuasive influence. Among them was one whom I then barely knew, a relatively recent recruit to the Cabinet, Jean Lesage. We had long discussions and I found him highly understanding. It was the beginning of a relationship that was of some importance in the remaking of the Liberal party and, later, of considerable significance in the conduct of the Pearson government.

The Cabinet and Mr St Laurent were persuaded; he handled the matter with a renewal of his skill and determination; the plan was legislated, intact in principle, in 1956, and began in 1957. It was a measure of the greatest importance to Canada, and my very minor role gave me experience that was useful later.

The other main legislative achievement of the late years of the St Laurent government was hospital insurance. In that case there was no doubt that the Minister responsible did his job. Paul Martin was the able and determined protagonist of hospital insurance and he was well assisted by his department and particularly by the skilful Deputy Minister of Welfare, George Davidson. They had to push hard against the doubts of Mr St Laurent and others.

For the *Winnipeg Free Press* hospital insurance presented a problem very different from federal-provincial tax arrangements. Paul Martin had for years been preparing the way by means of federal health grants, one of the last important measures adopted during Mackenzie King's prime ministership. Sensibly, the program financed the improvements in hospital facilities that were necessary before hospital insurance could be practicable. It was roundly attacked, however, by small-c conservatives, including the then editorialists of the *Free Press*. The objection was that the grants were avowedly designed as a step towards the complete health care plan that was Paul Martin's objective, but was at the time regarded as outrageously expensive by some of his colleagues, as well as by more rigid champions of small government.

The vehemence of the criticism continued to rankle with Paul, and in the second volume of his memoirs of *A Very Public Life* he protests that he "could not fathom how Tom Kent ... normally a liberal-minded man, could have sanctioned an onslaught on my efforts to lay a sound basis for health insurance." The fathoming would indeed have been difficult: by the time he came to reminisce he had forgotten that I was not editing the *Free Press* at that time.

The paper's previous position did, however, inhibit my discussion of the hospital insurance legislation in 1956. Newspapers, like other institutions, are continuities. There are limits to the speed with which they can change direction and the ways in which they do it. If they take strong editorial positions – whether they should do so at all is another question, which I am not discussing here – they cannot lightly reverse themselves and expect to be taken seriously. As with political parties, changes of mind should either be directly related to changed circumstances or be made gradually, with careful preparation of the ground for each step. It was impossible for the *Free Press*, given its past, suddenly to declare a glowing endorsement of hospital insurance. Unlike my predecessors, however, I did not want to criticize it on the basis of opposition to comprehensive health care.

I felt as strongly as Paul Martin that we should move to a system ensuring that no one went without needed care because of inability to pay for it. Paul was not, however, aiming to achieve that at once. The 1956 legislation would enable everyone, irrespective of income, to get "free" care in hospital, but it in no way helped people with low incomes to get medical attention outside hospital or to obtain needed drugs and other forms of care. I sought a means of moving in that direction.

The precedent to hand was the income tax legislation, which treated medical expenses up to 3 per cent of the taxpayer's income as a normal cost to which we may all be exposed, but allowed expenses above that level to be deducted from taxable income. The allowance, in that form, is indefensible, because it is highly regressive. Like almost all "tax expenditures," in the contemporary jargon, it benefits people more the better off they are. A person paying tax at a high rate may be relieved of a large proportion of medical costs above the 3 per cent level. A person or family on a low income, paying no tax or a low rate of tax, gets no, or little, benefit.

The *Free Press* in 1956 therefore espoused comprehensive health care in a form that stood the tax provision on its head: it proposed that a comprehensive government plan should pay all medical expenses over 3 per cent of the income of the person or family needing care. At the time, this no doubt appeared to Paul Martin and others to be no more than a diversion, avoiding a definite position on hospital insurance as such. There was no possibility of the government adopting the plan; the development of policy had already been too firmly set to hospital insurance. But, in my mind at least, it helped to point a way towards comprehensive health care; as will be shown later, it became relevant when a Liberal party in the remaking was considering its policy for medicare.

Hospital insurance and equalization in federal-provincial taxes were the major achievements of the last term of the St Laurent government. They were exceptions to the confusion and indecisiveness that otherwise invaded it. Mr St Laurent was as able as ever, when Maurice Lamontagne could stir him from his lethargy. To that we owe equalization, and also the creation of the Canada Council. The Unemployment Assistance Act of 1956 was a compromise measure into which a reluctant government was pressured by public opinion organized by the Canadian Welfare Council; its importance was that it prepared the way for the Canada Assistance Plan. Hospital insurance was achieved by a persistent Minister, thanks to provincial help. The way they came about does not, however, lessen the value of these last great measures of the twenty-two Liberal years. They were significant strengthenings of the fabric of Canadian society. A good many governments have gone out of office with less to their credit. Marginal voters, however, were not impressed. The government's troubles were far too conspicuous.

3 *The Press in Politics*

From 1955 onwards, the St Laurent government had an increasingly bad press, as politicians are wont to put it. Most politicians exaggerate, I think, the influence of the press on public opinion. They are themselves the most avid readers of newspapers, and nowadays watchers of TV news and public affairs programs. The consequence is a mutually-regarding relationship between the media and public personalities. The media feel important because they constantly see how much their subjects care, while the vanity of the subjects makes them take the media much more seriously than do other readers, listeners, and viewers. The mirrors of this relationship magnify, within the small world of active politics, the importance of the press. Thinking makes it so. In the large world one sees, time and again, that much of the public has a healthy distrust of media comment and makes its own common-sense judgment of people and measures. And that has been and will be greatly helped by television which, for all its faults, does give people a more direct and revealing view of the actors on the public stage than was available before the 1950s.

In that decade, however, television was new and the habits of mind of politicians still reflected the past in which "the press" indeed meant the daily newspapers. Certainly the politicians proved to be highly sensitive to the changed editorials of the *Free Press*. As I saw it, we were simply moving the paper's stance from its outdated, right-wing liberalism to a centre position in contemporary politics. Its comment became more direct and more relevant to current events. As the *Free Press* had been, if its editorials were related to the news at all, it was to the news of several days before. In my view, if there is a justification for daily newspapers expressing editorial opinions, it is to stimulate people to think more about public affairs, and arrive at their own opinions either by agreement or by disagreement. For that purpose, the comment should be as current as possible. I adopted the simple practice of going to the office early, with the rest of the staff, so that appropriate editorials could be written in the morning for the paper which went to press at lunch-time.

An incidental effect was that Victor Sifton, to whom Grant Dexter had looked for policy leadership, now read the editorials only after they were in type. We sometimes debated them afterwards, but not with rancour and always with detachment. As I illustrated earlier, in the case of hospital insurance, care was taken not to make sudden, blank negations of the paper's previous positions. We moved by steps, and were usually some way along a new road before it clearly culminated in a fundamental change of direction. Victor, on his side, played fair to our understanding and never attempted to impose his views over mine. The details of policy mattered less to him than his delight in seeing the *Free Press* get attention and have influence, as well as make money (which it had done before, but did increasingly). Above all, he relished the paper's involvement in political combats.

Of those, there were plenty. At the national level, they were more about governmental style than about the ideology of policy; my views were not far from those of most of the mandarins and of the younger members of the Cabinet. But in local and provincial affairs the situation was very different. When I went to Winnipeg its civic affairs were dominated by people who, whether their party labels were Conservative or Liberal, had few constructive ideas for the city. The provincial government was philosophically far to the right; worse, it was a cautious, narrow-minded government that was doing very little to promote the province's economic development. The *Free Press* became unmercifully critical.

This might not have mattered much if the oppositions had remained as somnambulant as they had long been. But in civic politics, Stephen Juba, a man from the wrong side of the tracks and therefore much distrusted in the Manitoba Club, took his opportunity to become, as it turned out, a long-lasting mayor. In provincial politics, Duff Roblin, who in 1954 became the leader of the minute Conservative caucus, was of a new generation and a "red Tory." There was no political ground to the right of Premier Douglas Campbell, and Duff plunged energetically to his left – that is, to the centre. The opposition view and mine therefore coincided on many issues. Duff astutely took full advantage of this. Lacking caucus strength and even the most modest research facilities, he found it convenient to base many of his speeches and questions on *Free Press* editorials and reports. Some Liberals soon professed to believe that the Tory caucus was in fact a morning meeting of Duff and me to plan the opposition for the day. The state of feeling was captured by one of my colleagues who, when I was going to a rare lunch with Premier Campbell, handed me a summary of his research on how to detect poison in food.

It was a little later that I returned from a visit to Ottawa to find the office adorned with a cartoon. Under the line, "Winnipeg editor gets warm reception in Ottawa," it showed me tied to a replica of the Peace Tower with Messrs Howe, Gardiner, Pickersgill, and Harris stoking the fire and war-dancing round it. C.D. Howe in particular appeared to be enjoying himself.

I was enjoying the controversies. Expressing opinions is not, however, the distinctive function of the media. That is to provide information, and to do it as accurately, fairly, and comprehensively as is practicable. I had been brought up in the journalistic tradition of which the best-known expression was the declaration of C.P. Scott, the famous Editor of the *Guardian*: "Comment is free, but facts are sacred." More precisely, the tradition was that firm editorial opinion must be combined with the conscientious independence of a powerful staff of reporters, identified correspondents, news analysts, and copy-editors. The *Free Press*, when I arrived, was very different. Editorialization had always been its main interest. Except on a few special topics, it was not greatly zealous about the quality of its news coverage and, retaining the traditions of strongly partisan journalism, had no inhibitions about using the news columns to support its editorial opinions. To change that was to me even more important than the modernization of the opinions.

Once a natural initial suspicion of the newcomer and his different ways had been overcome, there was enthusiastic co-operation from the desk and reporting staff. Thanks to growth in circulation and profitability, the business management of the paper was persuaded gradually to raise the salaries of the journalistic staff from what had been miserably low levels. We were then able to attract some bright additional talent. The *Free Press* did not become by any means a great newspaper. But by comparison with the past, its news coverage became considerably more comprehensive, more consistent, more investigative, and much livelier. Above all, the news ceased to be an instrument of propaganda.

The consequences were disturbing, to put it mildly, to many Manitoba politicians and others. That was true from an early stage in civic and provincial affairs, but the culmination came with the 1957 federal election campaign. Initially the news staff were inclined to expect it to be as boring and predetermined as 1953 and they had not entirely lost the mindset that the coverage would have to be favourable to Liberals or at least unfavourable to Conservatives and, even more, to the ccf. When it became apparent that the campaign had considerable news value, and that reporters really could be assigned to comprehensive coverage without partisan bias, the *Free Press* newsroom developed almost feverish enthusiasm. The reporter assigned to C.D. Howe's climactic meeting at Morris, Manitoba, which will be referred to later, had the help of almost a dozen other staffers who attended on their own time and spread themselves through the hall to pick up gems from the audience. The resulting report of the Minister's catastrophic discomfiture not only gained a national newspaper award; more immediately, it was the prize exhibit in Conservative committee rooms across the Prairies. The other side of the coin, of course, was the bitter indignation of the Liberal organization; as they saw it, by such reporting the *Free Press* betrayed its own.

In the midst of this tension I received a message that had a future significance I did not then appreciate. It was in a letter from a friend who had been having lunch with one of the campaigning Liberal ministers, the Secretary of State for External Affairs. My correspondent reported that Mike Pearson had told him, "with aplomb," of the "very stylish treatment given in your news pages to the rambunctious meeting which cornered C.D. Howe."

Fortunately the Pearson reaction was truer to public opinion than that of narrower Liberals. Victor Sifton, encouraged by the paper's growth in circulation, was stalwart in his support of the new style, though it involved him in a good deal of personal friction with some of his friends.

Though it cannot be proved, I like to think that it was the improvement in our information and analysis, rather than our more controversial editorials, that for a time restored the importance of the *Free Press*. It is true that it was, outside Manitoba, the editorial page that was read by a small group of opinion-leaders. But the editorials themselves had a good deal of information and analysis, and it was on the same page that we published the more analytical contributions of our own staff, particularly Grant Dexter's on national politics, and also the articles that I obtained regularly from some distinguished commentators. We had Isaac Deutscher on East-West relations, Norman Macrae of *The Economist*, for a short time L.B. Pearson, and others.

In Ottawa, a number of politicians and principal public servants had the page on their desks the morning after its publication. The whole paper was far too bulky for that, but in those days the Post Office's "air mail" provided – for, if I remember rightly, seven cents – virtually as fast service as couriers now do for ten dollars or so. For subscribers who wished, we tore the editorial pages from a bundle of copies, stuffed them into airmail envelopes, mailed them in the early afternoon, and they were regularly in Ottawa hours before the start of the next parliamentary day.

The kind of opinionated editorship I practised was in a long tradition. Both the role of television and the increased concentration of newspaper ownership have brought its usefulness into question. But in its time, extending into the 1950s, it was a significant element in the process of developing public policies in a free society.

4   *Howe's Canada*

The political controversies of 1955-7 were centred on the quintessentially controversial character of C.D. Howe. It is the nature of government that some kinds of infection spread quickly through the whole system. The St Laurent government's troubles became general, but the main ones all began with Mr Howe.

It is fair, therefore, first to say something about his qualities. C.D. Howe was an engineer, a builder. He had remarkably sound, far-sighted judgment on the benefits of projects for Canada, as well as a shrewd view of their costs. He was ingenious and determined in getting the projects he favoured off the ground. He had great capacity to generate in others the same enthusiasm and determination with which he worked himself. He had the first-class administrator's ability to delegate while his own ultimate responsibility remained unquestioned. He was, in short, a very unusual politician. His qualities served Canada extraordinarily well not only in the war but in the first ten years after it. For twenty years, from 1935 to 1955, C.D. was the right man for his time. There are few people in public life of whom so much can be said.

Thirty years later, it is not difficult to see what was wrong with that time. Until the 1940s, Canadian economic development had been slower than, given the potential of the country's resources, it could well have been; that was the price we paid for the brave venture of the National Policy, using a tariff wall to build an unnatural economy out of a continent-wide string of settlements. For the 1939–45 war Canada's resources were marshalled as they had never been before, and postwar circumstances gave us an entirely new opportunity to develop them further. Howe saw the opportunity more clearly than anyone and he had the determination, the skill, and the power to see that it was taken.

The problem was that, as an inevitable consequence of past slow growth, Canada was very thin in the required managerial and technical talents, the entrepreneurship and the venture capital. C.D. did all he could to entice, cajole, prod, even bully Canadian businessmen into the big projects he loved and rightly saw as necessary. But when the response was inadequate, as in many sectors of the economy it inevitably was, C.D. was not going to let that stop him. If the project was at all appropriate he turned to American businessmen, whom he encouraged and cajoled in much the same way as he did Canadians. He didn't see much difference. The colour of the dollars didn't matter to Howe. If it was Americans who had the dollars, and also the enterprise and technology we hadn't, then they were the people for the job.

In some cases, that is. There was nothing narrow, when he was on the track of a project, about C.D. While his philosophy was that of big-corporation enterprise, he had little hesitation about government undertaking a project if private capital was unsuitable or unavailable. To C.D., it wasn't socialism if it was C.D.

It would be, in my view, a highly unrealistic critic who found any serious fault with either the purpose or the method of any significant number of the Howe projects – either the ones for which he was directly responsible as public enterprises (Air Canada, Atomic Energy of Canada, Eldorado, the St Lawrence Seaway, to name only a few) or the much larger number of private projects which he in various ways encouraged, using to the full the prestige that the North American business world came to accord to him.

The policy issue that remains relevant today concerns not the individual projects but what they all added up to: on the one hand, a proportion of foreign ownership in the Canadian economy that may have been paralleled in some colonial economies but is unique to a country that regards itself as economically advanced; on the other hand, a degree of both public ownership and of government intervention in the private sector that was remarkable in Mr Howe's own day and that provided a precedent for considerably more in later years. The question is whether something important fell between these stools.

The Canadian economy has significant advantages: in its location; in its natural resources; in the educational standards made possible by its postwar prosperity and by the country's attractiveness to professional and skilled immigrants; in the sophistication of its financial institutions and the extent of its public infrastructure; in the moderation and stability of its politics. But these advantages have not led us to create many technologically advanced industries at an international level of efficiency, able either to sell abroad or to replace the products and components imported, particularly, by us subsidiaries in Canada doing business with their parents and affiliates.

Some smaller economies, with even less domestic market as a base and fewer natural resources, have been more successful in their development of manufactured exports for world markets. Such development could not be expected in Canada from most of the subsidiaries of us corporations. They came either for materials or components for their operations elsewhere, or to manufacture their established products for the Canadian domestic market. If they were interested at all in exporting from Canada to third markets, the products concerned were iron ore concentrates or similar, virtually unprocessed materials. There was no reason for them to develop in Canada manufacturing, or even further processing capacity, of the kind necessary to compete in world markets despite the level of labour and other costs in an advanced economy.

But if the us corporations were not to do this, who, in the Canadian economy as it was built in the postwar period, could do it? We had some strong, technologically advanced, Canadian-owned enterprises – the two steel companies in Hamilton were conspicuous examples – but they were not many and even their business strategies were usually directed to serving the Canadian market, beating imports on the lines in which they specialized, rather than seeking export markets.

There clearly was an impending problem. Ours was necessarily an open economy, with a high standard of living reflected in the volume of our imports of many products. We paid for them mainly with our exports of primary products. If the outcome was a deficit in the current account of our external transactions, augmented by dividend and other payments to foreign owners and by other service transactions, that did not make the Canadian dollar weak because there were offsetting imports of capital. But it required no great prescience to see that our extraordinarily strong position in the export of primary products was a feature of postwar circumstances that would not endure. As the rest of the world economy rebuilt and progressed, we were bound to lose some of our edge as a source of raw materials, and also to become less dominantly attractive as a home for US investment.

The mistake most of us made was not that we were blind to such future trends; it was that we assumed too easily that the growing sophistication of our economy would result in the development of new industries capable of exporting enough to offset the relative decline of the primary sector. That was what should have happened by the seventies. It didn't.

To blame Mr Howe for not having made it happen in the fifties would be an unrealistic hindsight. Since the economy was fully occupied, the only way to develop, instead, substantially more manufacturing, export-oriented and import-competing, would have been to suppress some of the projects of the Howe era. The times were not ripe for such a shift.

The fair criticism of Mr Howe is not that what he did was mistaken or excessive but that he took little interest in preparing the kind of social and entrepreneurial infrastructure that would have provided a more favourable environment in which Canadian enterprise and technology, oriented to world markets, could have blossomed later. The federal government in the fifties did very little for skill training, for industrial research, and for the universities. Many programs that were started later, in these areas and in various kinds of export encouragement and industrial development assistance, might have been more effective if they had begun before the 1960s, when they were rather desperate attempts to catch up with what other countries were doing.

In that sense, our difficulties in the eighties can be attributed in part to short-sightedness in the fifties. At a time when we were better placed than most countries to undertake the kinds of measures that fundamentally improve the development potential of an economy, we were not in the forefront. We were too content that our economy was growing apace to be bothered that it was with American capital and in conditions that were obviously bound to change.

The short-sightedness was not Mr Howe's alone but that of the government as a whole, of the business community, of the educational establishment, of the society generally. But Mr Howe bestrode government and the business community, at least, like a Colossus, and it can fairly be said that his over-bearing style strengthened the inhibitions against the consideration of longer-term problems. Anyone who doubted that, with

C.D. in charge, all was right with the Canadian economy was clearly an impractical ignoramus. I had a strong impression that one of the reasons why C.D. greatly disliked me was a paper I wrote for one of the British banks, which was fairly widely reproduced in Canada and the United States; it analyzed the Canadian economy of the mid-fifties under the title "The American Boom in Canada." I don't think he read it but I'm sure that the title was enough to make him angry.

Despite the regard I had for much of his achievement, C.D. and I were never able to communicate. John Deutsch, one of the most perceptive men of his generation, once explained the reason to me. "You are concerned with policies. What's a policy? You can't construct it, you can't see it. For C.D., it doesn't exist. The only realities for him are projects. And you don't disagree very much with his projects. So he can't understand you at all. He thinks that your criticisms must be nothing but ill-natured destructiveness."

The charge of destructiveness was a Howe favourite. Two incidents in our relationship are worth recording because they illustrate the kind of emotionalism that often takes hold of proud politicians in trouble. On one occasion in his office, banging his fist on the desk, he said to me: "I know you destroyed a government in England" (a grotesque exaggeration, of course, of my contribution to criticism of the 1945-50 Labour government) "and now you've come to try to destroy the government of Canada." Perhaps because he had been an immigrant himself, C.D. was more inclined than anyone else to seize on my come-lately status as a point of weakness. On another occasion, I was regaled by an amused senior civil servant, who had been the third person present, with an account of a conversation between Messrs Howe and Pickersgill, who was having his troubles in the portfolio of Citizenship and Immigration. They agreed that what was wrong with immigration law was that it hadn't kept Tom Kent out of the country. For Jack Pickersgill, a man of liberal mind, this was no doubt a humorous comment; but for C.D., I suspect, it was serious.

C.D.'s unabashed revelation of his sensitivity to criticism was shared by some of his colleagues. At that time, and even into the 1957 election campaign, the view of most observers – and it seemed, as far as one could judge, the dominant public attitude – was that the Liberals were invincible. I think that it was their private reaction to criticism, even more than their public actions, that made me feel that in fact the government had the smell of death about it. Ministers were unused to troubles, and the self-confidence they had built up was too massive to be shaken when troubles came. Those were dismissed as trivial. Rather than give serious consideration to the causes of the troubles and how to deal with them, ministers were simply affronted. They tried to rationalize away their discomfiture by inventing spurious explanations for it. Perplexity mixed with arrogance and indignation to create an emotional turmoil that affected most of the Cabinet.

There were exceptions. Some ministers, Pearson most notably, were untouched and detached. The Prime Minister retreated into his long periods of passivity. The net result was that few decisions were made and some of those that were made were bad. There was a spinning of wheels that dug the government, and Mr Howe in particular, deeper into trouble.

The first of the government's major disasters was the Defence Production Bill of 1955. Four years earlier, in response to the Korean war, Parliament had given to the Minister – Mr Howe, of course – the same kind of massive powers to intervene in the economy that had been used in the Second World War. In particular, firms could be required to make what the government wanted at prices fixed by the government. But such powers had been given for a fixed period of four years only. As Mr Howe himself had said at the time, they were special powers needed for an emergency and "should not be of a continuing nature."

They had now to be either abandoned or renewed. In an uncertain world, the government wanted them kept on the statute book. While the opposition would have made a ritual fuss, it is unlikely that there would have been serious objection if the legislation had been a simple extension of the powers for another fixed period, for four years or even longer.

And that would have been the legislation proposed, there is little doubt, if there had been a counting of heads in Cabinet. But over the years Mr Howe's dislike of having to make his case in Parliament had intensified; to him, it was a talking shop that wasted the time of a man of action. As he wrote to a friend at the time of one adjournment, "we got rid of Parliament this morning." So he decided to dispose of the matter once and for all. The Bill he proposed in 1955 was to make his draconian powers as Minister of Defence Production permanent. Mr St Laurent went along, and the Cabinet dutifully followed.

Mr St Laurent spoke himself, unconvincingly, at the beginning of the debate. Then he left it to C.D., and C.D. got no help from his colleagues except for the other veteran, Jimmy Gardiner. The opposition dug into obstruction. Mr St Laurent sat silent. C.D. had no argument except to insist time and again that he would not compromise with such a foolish opposition. The government looked worse every day the debate went on.

By 25 June 1955, I was sufficiently distressed about the defence production issue to write directly to the Prime Minister. I apologized that anxiety made me presumptuous in pressing advice on him, but I had to urge him that it would be wise to withdraw. A Bill making such powers permanent was wrong both in principle and in practical politics. It gave the opposition an issue highly favourable to them and "many friends of the government are, I believe, particularly troubled by it."

Mr St Laurent replied on 27 June: "I agree with you that it was a mistake to allow the Opposition to get such an issue but I do not agree that the Liberal voters are very much concerned about the outcome. It may be unfortunate that they should not be more concerned but they have such faith in Mr Howe that they are trusting more to men than to measures." It was a frank admission of Mr St Laurent's own unhappiness with the measure and a sharp confirmation of how inadequate he had become as a leader; it seemed to me also to indicate that he was far out of touch with opinion even in many Liberal circles. The letter concluded, however, with a pointer, clear enough though it was in double negatives, to what was to happen ten miserable days later: "That [the preceding paragraph quoted] does not mean that I am not grateful to you nor that all that is bothering you is not getting and will not continue to get serious consideration. With kind regards."

On 7 July Mr Howe declared in the House that he would not withdraw the Bill even "if the Government must still sit here until the snow flies," and then he went off for a weekend fishing trip with his friend Charlie Wilson, the US Secretary of Defence. The Prime Minister telephoned the Leader of the Opposition and invited him to draft an amendment to the Bill that would satisfy the opposition. Mr Drew sensibly proposed again to limit the Draconian powers to four years, Mr St Laurent agreed, and the Bill was passed before a furious C.D. came back from his fishing.

While the outcome was a victory for common sense, it had ill consequences. Mr St Laurent's prolonged indecision had meant that the eventual outcome was a humiliation for C.D. that would have been painful for any politician and was appalling for one of his temperament. The opposition, having tasted blood, was spoiling for more. Equally, when another battle was joined, Mr St Laurent and, this time, most of his ministers felt that they could not "let C.D. down" again; they had to stick with him to the bitter end. But for this, I do not think that the government could have let itself be driven to the extremities to which it sank in the pipeline debate of 1956, and the subsequent politics of Canada might have been very different. The further irony was that on the pipeline issue, unlike defence production, the government put forward, after a rational process of negotiation and political consideration, a good legislative measure; the error was entirely in the way it was presented in Parliament.

C.D. had been working for some years on the idea of a pipeline, following an all-Canadian route across northern Ontario, to move Alberta gas to use in central Canada. To him it was a nation-building project of the same kind as the CPR in its day. Just as in the nineteenth century it would have been cheaper to move freight north-south across the US border, and east-west by US rails, the all-Canadian pipeline was not a venture that private capital, left to itself, would choose. A line south of the Lakes was less expensive to build and gave access to more immediately remunerative markets. Again, nation-building was a defiance of short-run economics. A Trans-Canada pipeline could therefore be financed only with some government involvement. But for the Canadian economy, seeking development across its east-west breadth, the pipeline was an entirely sound project. It had not been long in operation before those who had said it should not be built were silent – apart, that is, from some professional economists who may still question, in academic journals, whether the CPR made "economic" sense.

Mr Howe was characteristically determined on the pipeline. With the St Lawrence seaway nearing completion, he relished one more great construction achievement before retirement. He negotiated, with mixed Canadian and American interests, long and hard. His first proposal, at the beginning of 1955, was turned down by Cabinet – this was before the Defence Production fiasco – and C.D. was driven to comment that the government had fallen into the hands of children.

He did not give up, however. He widened the scope of his negotiations and, in particular, brought in Premier Frost of Ontario. It was agreed that the northern Ontario section of the pipeline would initially be owned by a Crown corporation, with Ontario contributing part of the capital. It would be leased to the Trans-Canada Pipelines company and, when the whole operation was earning sufficient revenue, would be bought from the governments at cost plus interest.

This proposal was approved by Cabinet and announced in the Throne Speech starting the 1956 session. It was a reasonable scheme; if it had been all that was required, as C.D. and the promoters first suggested, there would no doubt have been strong criticism but there would not have been a pipeline furor. Towards the end of April, however, the rest of the story emerged. Trans-Canada Pipelines could not raise the money to build the Prairie section of the line in 1956. It needed a government loan for 90 per cent of the cost.

This faced the Cabinet with a new and very difficult decision. The *Free Press* editorial about it was published on 2 May, when the proposal was a matter of officially unconfirmed speculation. I was at pains to emphasize the difference between the new scheme and the earlier proposal for a loan guarantee, which would have provided an initial subsidy while leaving the company to unburdened enjoyment of subsequent profits. The new proposal was a short-term loan on tough terms; it had to be repaid – with 5 per cent interest, then not a low rate – before the company could make any money. If the loan was not repaid on schedule the government could take full ownership of the line.

In the editorial I reviewed other possibilities, with the obvious conclusion that there was no practical alternative that did not mean that the line on the all-Canadian route would be deferred for some time, if not forever. I supported the proposal, not knowing that the scheme that Cabinet accepted some days later would have an additional feature: there was to be a deadline (5 June) for passage of the legislation and to make that possible C.D. would move closure – the parliamentary procedure that shuts off debate at regular intervals through the various stages of Parliament's consideration of a Bill – as soon as the legislation was introduced.

That was on 14 May. My editorial on 15 May was headed "Foreclosure." The objection was not to closure as such. "Freedom of discussion in Parliament is not freedom to discuss indefinitely. There comes a point at which prolonged debate serves no purpose in clarifying public opinion and frustrates rather than serves the purposes of democracy." (Nothing in the whole subsequent controversy was sillier than Mr Diefenbaker's promise – never fulfilled – that a Conservative government would abolish closure.) But, I argued, closure was a procedure rarely used in the Canadian Parliament. It had to be regarded as an extreme measure, and to take it right at the beginning of the debate was "appalling. It will give many a Liberal bad dreams at night." The editorial commented:

> The Government has struggled for years with the pipeline. Mr Howe has made decisions, found that they did not work, and made new decisions. The cabinet has argued and negotiated and delayed. Eventually, out of all this confusion, there comes a Bill. And Mr Howe says in effect: 'Right, we've decided what is best for the country; time is short; whisk it through.' There is here something dangerously near the idea that the Government's thinking is enough, and that Parliament's argument in public, as the focus for popular thought and discussion, does not matter.

The direct effect, the editorial forecast, would be to change the whole nature of the debate. The issue of whether the pipeline Bill was a good measure would become hopelessly confused with the issue of whether or not closure should be applied. This was an inadequate prediction of the pandemonium that disfigured the House of Commons for the next three weeks. The opposition parties had skilful tacticians in the use of procedural devices, notably Stanley Knowles and Davie Fulton. Mr Howe made no pretence of understanding anything about Parliament. He was dependent on the help of colleagues more versed in political and parliamentary tactics. The two who were supposed to be skilled were Walter Harris and Jack Pickersgill, but on this occasion they were no match for their opponents. I would think it fair to say that the difference was not so much in ability as in motivation. Knowles and Fulton were men with deep feeling for Parliament and they were driven by a genuine sense of outrage. Harris and Pickersgill were on the defensive, trying to ride out a crisis of the making of the man who called them junior leaguers. The great Mr Howe of the world of business and administration was in Parliament an ungainly and, under pressure, bewildered beast. Anyone who admired his qualities had to mourn. Mr St Laurent sat silent and unhappy. The *Free Press* comment that I remember best was a Peter Kuch cartoon, in which – in reminiscence of events in Europe – we depicted Howe as a tank at which Knowles and Fulton were hurling stones, while Mr St Laurent stood in the rubble reading J.S. Mill on representative government.

The tank, of course, rumbled through. Despite all the opposition's procedural stratagems, closure served its immediate purpose and the Bill was passed only a few hours after Mr Howe's deadline. The irony was that the pipeline company then let him down. The point of the deadline was supposed to be that it was necessary in order that the line could be built across the prairies, from Alberta to Winnipeg, before the close of the 1956 construction season. The company turned out not to have the firm supply of pipe that was supposed to be its great asset. In the event gas did not arrive in Winnipeg until a year later.

There was another irony of the pipeline debate, of more long-term significance. There was very little discussion of the pipeline proposal itself. Thanks to the tactic of immediate closure, the primary issue was the role of Parliament. But the emotionalism of that issue made it easy for the opposition parties also to wallow, without effective challenge, in a second and spurious sentiment: anti-Americanism. By the mid-fifties there was beginning to be a good deal of uneasiness, particularly in Ontario, about the extent to which our economy was coming to be dominated by us corporations. The opposition parties rubbed vigorously on this nerve. To the limited extent that the pipeline itself was debated at all, it was portrayed as an abject sell-out to American interests. They were being blessed with Canadian taxpayers' money in order that they could exploit us. The Canadian Parliament was being strangled by closure in order to meet a deadline that these American interests had arrogantly imposed.

This was very unfair. As I suggested earlier, there was indeed by then reason for concern about the extent of us business in Canada. In effect, we were purchasing fast growth by neglecting to develop the Canadian entrepreneurship and technology needed for longer-term development.

But such considerations were irrelevant to the pipeline. If it had been financed with the loan guarantees Mr Howe originally proposed, the deal would have been over-generous to the company's owners, both Americans and Canadians. But in the form in which the arrangement was legislated in 1956, the involvement of some American capital in no way jeopardized Canadian national interests. Mr Howe could be criticized for indifference to the long-term weakness arising from too much American capital, but the pipeline was one of his projects in which a genuine Canadianism was paramount. That truth, however, was entirely submerged in the furor created by the government's method of proceeding in Parliament. It invited and deserved an all-out opposition that subordinated cool assessment of the project to a larger issue.

Such an experience inevitably had inhibiting effects on the St Laurent government during its remaining twelve months. An outstanding example was its reception of the report of the Royal Commission on the prospects of the Canadian economy.

The appointment of the Commission in 1955 had been a manoeuvre of the "Junior League" ministers, who got it past Mr St Laurent when C.D. was away. They were looking for new ideas on economic policy and chose for that purpose the best possible Commission chairman, Walter Gordon. I was highly critical of the Commission's preliminary report, when it was published in December 1956, and later of the full report. Though I would still make some of the same points, for the most part I subsequently came to think that my criticism had been wrong. In important ways the Gordon report pointed to changed directions that, if they had been adopted at the time, would have lessened the difficulties we have since experienced. But that was not to be.

C.D. had been opposed to the very idea of the Commission. He regarded an inquiry into Canadian economic policy as an inquiry into C.D. Howe, and there was no need for that. He was furious with some of the recommendations of the preliminary report and by that time, after all the buffetings the government had suffered, Mr St Laurent was in no mood for more of the worry that crossing C.D. would involve. No doubt there was some sense of guilt that he and the Cabinet had gone a long way with C.D. but let him down in the crises, not only on defence production but also, through their lack of parliamentary talent, in the pipeline affair. The Prime Minister was therefore quick to disavow the ideas for change that were expressed in the Gordon report.

The government was going to go on as it was. It would go to the country not with new initiatives in its platform, as some of the "Junior Leaguers" had hoped, but with the plea that all was well and would stay so as long as the electorate stayed with the old firm.

Though Mr St Laurent himself had his moods of doubt, for the most part there was extraordinarily little self-criticism in Ottawa at that time. In December 1956 one of the younger ministers calmly told me that as a democrat he was glad that the election was six months away; if it were being held then, the government might well win every seat but one, and that would be bad for democracy. I was dumbfounded.

5 The 1957 Election

The *Free Press*, of course, was merely one voice in the rising chorus of disapproval of the government that culminated in the pipeline debate. That was the biggest single factor in the 1957 defeat of the Liberal party. It epitomized the combination of the government's two main faults: its declining competence and its mounting arrogance. Both opposition and media critics tend to lessen their own effectiveness by making a fuss about every supposed example of bad administration or of the misuse of power. The public, I think, is more realistic. People know that politicians and public servants are human and are bound to make a good many mistakes. They also know that those with power naturally get a bit above themselves. But if the public is fairly tolerant either of some incompetence or of a measure of arrogance in its politicians, it loses faith when it sees a good deal of both together. And that was precisely what the government's handling of the pipeline displayed.

But if this was the national issue that hurt the government most, a second example of the same combination was even more decisive for voters on the Prairies. It was the subject of my most direct and extended confrontation with Mr Howe.

In those days public opinion in the three prairie provinces still meant, predominantly, farm opinion. In the early postwar years world markets for grain, at first supported to an important extent by relief and reconstruction aid, were strong. The farmers came to a prosperity that few had known before. Though city prejudices often created a contrary assumption, it was a prosperity earned by unsubsidized production. Canadian grain farmers did not receive the supports that were and are commonly given to farming in industrialized countries. In particular, they did not receive the support that the US Treasury provided to their opposite numbers south of the border.

The 1950s were not far advanced when the lavish US farm policy led to the accumulation of large grain surpluses. They hung over the market for a while and then the United States embarked on extensive giveaways. As a result, the commercial markets for Canadian grain were greatly weakened. The elevators were plugged; a large part of the crop had to be stored on the farms. In contrast to the economic growth of Canada as a whole, in contrast to the rising real incomes of most Canadians, prairie farmers in 1954 and in 1955 had 40 per cent less cash income than they had had in 1951.

It was a situation, one would think, to make any government shiver. But not C.D. Howe. Through 1954 and late into 1955, he persisted in denying that there was any serious problem. In doing so he seemed at first to be influenced by an old controversy. During the war the government had taken over the marketing of grain from the private trade embodied in the Winnipeg Grain Exchange. There had been no return after the war. All grain marketing was entrenched in the Canadian Wheat Board. That had the enthusiastic support of the great majority of prairie farmers, who identified the Winnipeg Exchange with their past miseries. But the government take-over was a sensitive issue in the business community, which encouraged the unfounded suspicion in the rest of the country that government marketing necessarily meant that somehow the farmers were being subsidized out of the country's taxes.

C.D., of course, had not been passive in his response. He had characteristically appealed to current experience: the good times of the late forties and beginning of the fifties proved that the Wheat Board was the right way to market. What, then, was the meaning of all the unsold wheat that by 1954 was clogging farmers' bins and machinery sheds and even piled on the ground? Mr Howe's response was to ignore, as long as he could, the existence of the question. To face it would be to admit that government marketing was not the security blanket it was supposed to be.

Wheat marketing had long been a subject of controversy between Howe and the *Free Press*. True to its "free trade" concept of liberalism, the paper had been the main champion of the Winnipeg Grain Exchange and had continued to attack the Wheat Board in every way it could. For me, this was an encumbrance to be disposed of. Pragmatically, I could see no point in continuing to fight a lost battle. In principle, I could see no merit in the case. It had nothing to do with the virtues that the market mechanism *can* have. When there is anything near a genuine market, with considerable numbers of buyers and sellers, without collusion on either side and with reasonably equal access to knowledge of what is going on, then the result will be the most efficient production of what people want, and can afford to buy, that is possible in existing social and technological circumstances. There can, of course, be market failures because, for example, technological or other changes in circumstances are poorly anticipated, or because of temporary but large distortions resulting from the herd-like behaviour of speculators. Some kinds of government intervention and regulation can lessen some of these weaknesscs. But by and large, market mechanisms are more efficient than any more centralized method of determining production is likely to be.

The provisos in that argument are, however, crucially important to the marketing of Canadian wheat, and indeed of many agricultural products. There are plenty of sellers – farmers – but many fewer buyers. In the postwar world, indeed, the buyers of Canadian wheat either were governments or were operating under government controls. In these circumstances there seemed to me little doubt that, provided it was at all well managed – and there was ample evidence that the Canadian Wheat Board was well managed – centralized selling would produce better returns to Canadian farmers than a restored Grain Exchange would have done. And if there had ever been any doubt about that, it was removed when the main competition became the giveaway program of the US government.

That was the opportunity. Arguments about what marketing method might be best in the long run had become irrelevant. For over a year *Free Press* editorials had simply ignored their one-time favourite topic. By September 1955 I felt able to take it up, in order to put it to rest. The effects of the US giveaway program had reached the point at which it was reasonable to plead that "the whole community of the prairies, without consideration either of politics or of other disagreements, should stand together." Specifically, "those who opposed the establishment of government marketing" now had a duty "to refrain from making any argumentative capital out of the fact that wheat marketing by government is not now going so smoothly as most of its proponents said it would ... No marketing method, government or free or anything else, will enable us to compete with giveaways. At this time, the Wheat Board marketing system is not on trial ... We have to do the best job we can with the equipment that the majority of people wanted."

This was the kind of editorial that made one section of opinion think that the *Free Press* had gone to the devil – or, as the most critical saw it, to socialism. C.D. never quite adjusted to what was, from his viewpoint, a change of the rules in the middle of the game. As long as the *Free Press* had been the Grain Exchange's champion, what it said about anything else connected with grain influenced only a handful of prairie farmers. C.D. had some justification for treating the paper's editorials with the contempt that came so readily to him. He did his best to sustain that attitude, though from the fall of 1955 onwards the positions taken by the *Free Press* became increasingly those of many prairie farmers and their organizations.

Mr Howe insisted otherwise, but his claims that nothing had changed, that prairie farmers both should be and were satisfied with his policy, began increasingly to sound – in the words of one editorial – "almost as remote from the farm problem as if he sat in an office in Timbuktu." It was at about this time that a Manitoba farmer was reported to have become so incensed with C.D. on his television screen that he fired at it with his shotgun.

The rising disagreement with C.D.'s stance concerned two main issues. One was how to deal with the Americans and the other was how to ease the immediate income position of the farmers.

On the first, Mr Howe's tactic was very quiet diplomacy: he and his officials talked to their us opposite numbers in private but made no public criticism. The us officials – as distinct from the politician, Secretary of Agriculture Ezra Benson – always charmingly agreed that the giveaways were bad policy but there was nothing they could do because the policy reflected the farm lobby's power in Congress. The public outcome of the quiet meetings was that Mr Benson could claim that the two governments were working together, with a minimum of friction, on the disposal of wheat surpluses. In the absence of public statements by Canadian ministers, there was no reason for anyone in the United States to know that the give-away program was hurting anyone. Prairie farmers were an interest group deeply affected by us policy that had no lobby in Washington.

I did not suggest that we should protest against the surplus disposal program as an unmitigated evil which the Americans should stop. That would have been unrealistic. I argued that, if we made our case publicly, plenty of Americans would see that surplus disposals that apparently were expanding without limit were bound to demoralize any normal commercial trade; every customer country would wait as long as it could to buy grain in the hope of first being given it. We should demonstrate firmly and plainly what this was doing to Canadian farmers who lived without subsidies. And we should therefore appeal to the United States to set a publicly declared limit to the monthly amount of its non-commercial disposals of grain. For that, I argued, it would be possible to enlist political interests in Washington as a countervail to the farm lobby.

Whether such a tactic would have worked is, of course, unknown. My argument was that it was the sensible course that was worth trying. But Mr Howe would not give it a try. He did eventually go so far as to admit that markets were "generally demoralized" by us disposal policy; but there was nothing, he argued, that could be done about it.

Whether or not that was true, the second and even more important issue remained: how to ease the immediate income position of grain farmers. While the farmers themselves understandably looked with some envy at the US system of massive subsidies and surplus disposals at the taxpayers' expense, they were realistic enough to appreciate that in Canada grain production was too large an element in the economy for a copy of the US system to be politically and financially feasible. Practical proposals came to centre on the much more modest idea of modifying the Wheat Board's payments system to provide cash advances for farm-stored grain. I put forward a detailed suggestion which would have meant that a then typical wheat farmer, with 150 acres seeded, would have been assured of minimum payments in 1956 of $2,250 for his 1955 crop. It was a very moderate proposal but C.D. would have none of it.

By this time he had more than ever taken the stance of the beleaguered politician for whom the world is divided only into staunch supporters and sworn enemies: either people had faith that, with him in office, all was for the best; or, if they criticized him on any point, it must be because they were trying to undo him at all points. Though the demand for cash advances was taken up not only by the farmers' unions and the Saskatch-ewan Wheat Pool but also by many other prairie organizations, even including some constituency Liberal associations, Mr Howe persisted in regarding it as somehow a plot against the Wheat Board and him. His message to farmers was reduced to one thing: an assertion that their problems weren't all that bad. "You look well enough fed," he said, poking the stomach of one farmer critic.

The political consequences of Mr Howe's latter-day immobility cul-minated in the Morris meeting, mentioned earlier, of the 1957 federal election campaign. The constituency was, on its past record, among the safest of Liberal seats. The incumbent had been an able Member of Parliament. Though relatively young, he had chaired the Commons' agri-cultural committee. Mr Howe, seeking to commend him warmly to his constituents, explained to them that the agriculture committee had members of all parties from all parts of the country and was liable to get all sorts of ideas. Their member had done a very good job of keeping it in line and seeing that it caused the government no trouble. At that point Mr Howe clearly had no idea that, for many of the people in the hall who normally voted Liberal, he was underlining the reason to prefer another representative this time.

The significance of the meeting was not that it was antagonistic – anyone who knew anything knew that it would be – but that in face of the criticism Mr Howe, so long the epitome of confidence, was bewil-dered and disorganized. He had come, he obviously thought, prepared. When a questioner began to talk about how little grain he had been able to deliver, Mr Howe interrupted: we should get the facts straight, and he had them all with him – a tabulation of deliveries at, he said, every elevator point on the Prairies. But after minutes of agonizing searching he could not find the point that the man on the floor was talking about.

Another interruption was even more unfortunate. Mr Howe stopped a man whose question was turning into something of a harangue: if he wanted to make a speech like that, he shouldn't come to a Liberal meeting but to one of his own party. The questioner responded that, as almost everyone in the hall except Mr Howe knew, he was the president of the Liberal association for the provincial constituency.

Eventually, as Mr Howe retreated from the platform saying, "I must be on my way," the Liberal candidate tried to undo some of the damage: "We don't claim that we're infallible." But it was too late to separate himself so far from Mr Howe. In 1953, he had received 66 per cent of the constituency vote. In 1957 he got 30 per cent.

Mr Howe's was the worst case of a politician whose success had eventually become an insulation from reality. But it was not different in nature from much of the Liberal campaigning of 1957. Mr St. Laurent opened the campaign in Winnipeg in late April. His manner, I commented, was that of "the chairman of the board of a successful corporation reporting to a shareholders' meeting." The government ran on its record with no apparent perception that it had become, since 1955, a tarnished record. As the campaign proceeded, and the evidence that all was not well could not be ignored, even Mr St. Laurent could do no better than to tell his listeners that they really had no choice; the opposition was fragmented into three parties that could not agree and no one of them would be strong enough to form a government, so the Liberals were sure to stay in office. So arrogant an argument could hardly have been better calculated, in the mood of the day, to irritate marginal voters, to make them swallow their doubts and vote for the Conservatives as the strongest of the opposition parties.

Late in the campaign Paul Martin was sent out from his western Ontario stronghold to try to repair some of the damage in Manitoba. When he arrived he called me from the airport to ask how I thought the election was going. I said that I didn't know about the rest of the country but on the Prairies the government would lose most of its seats. Paul professed surprise and disbelief and gamely assured me that all the reports from the rest of the country were favourable. He was, however, a politician who kept his feet on the ground. Over the next few days he made excellent speeches, but it was too late for them to matter. He called me again from the airport as he was leaving: "I see what you meant."

One of the reasons for the extraordinary complacency with which the

Liberals entered the campaign was that they greatly underestimated John Diefenbaker, who at the end of 1956 had succeeded George Drew as Conservative leader. It was an error to be repeated in 1963 and again in 1965, an understandable error for people immersed in the practice of government: Mr Diefenbaker never had any ideas coherent and precise enough to make the stuff of public policy; he was driven by considerations of a more personal and negative kind.

He had been elected party leader at an extraordinarily unimpressive convention, to the demonstrated anger of most of the Quebec delegates and to the unconcealed distress of the party's Ontario establishment; Premier Frost did not lift a finger for Diefenbaker in the 1957 election, though he joined the bandwagon in 1958. Almost the only distinction of the convention was a keynote speech by Robert Stanfield, then the new Premier of Nova Scotia. To the surprise of the press and of the delegates, he devoted quite a bit of time to foreign policy. Many Conservatives had vehemently attacked the role of Canada in the Suez crisis; they regarded Mr Pearson's famous initiative for a United Nations solution as a betrayal of Britain. Mr Stanfield, giving the first demonstration of his qualities of national statesmanship to come, quietly put aside such sentiments. The Suez affair was now "well beyond the time for recrimination." The moral of "that past and painful experience" was that "the test of being a good Canadian must be simply a man's devotion to Canada as a nation – a nation within the Commonwealth and within the United Nations." It was a brave speech that seemed to be barely noticed by the convention, but for me at least – I had never seen Mr Stanfield before – it was the beginning of a respect that grew steadily with the years.

For a decade, however, the leadership of the Conservative party lay with a very different man. Qualities of statesmanship could not be attributed to Mr Diefenbaker. In one respect, however, I disagreed with the Ottawa Liberals' estimate of him. I had listened to his oratory from platforms on the Prairies. Rationally, it was appalling; emotionally, it was superb. Mr Diefenbaker was the right man to catch the votes of many Canadians in the mood to which they had moved after too many years of the St. Laurent-Howe regime.

On the night of 10 June, when the election result was clear, my emotions were deeply mixed. It would have been inhuman not to have had some feeling of "I told you so." In taking views different from those of the majority of Liberals, I had been open to the criticism, and the self-doubt, that I was a young newcomer who did not understand Canadian politics. The most telling feature of the election results was the fate of the Cabinet itself. The prestige enjoyed by a Minister in his own locality normally helps him to do better than the party average. In this election Liberal ministers fared worse than backbenchers. Half the Cabinet,

Howe and Harris included, suffered personal defeat. The reasons, it was pretty clear, were those which had led me to the view that the government was destroying itself.

There were broader reasons for rejoicing. I began the editorial on 11 June:

> A Liberal is a democrat first and a party man afterwards. The disappointment of defeat therefore comes second to this: the democratic process works in Canada. During recent years many people have feared, with apparent reason, that it was not working well. They have said that in times of prosperity a government could get away with almost anything and a satisfied electorate would not turn it out ... But it was not so ... Across all the polling booths of English-speaking Canada on June 10 there lay the shadow of the pipeline debate ... the harsh brusqueness of the government's use of closure had firmly crystallized in the public mind a feeling that men so long accustomed to power had grown arrogant in their use of it.

But applauding the reasons for the movement of public opinion did not remove my distress and concern. I liked and respected Mr St. Laurent. And, bitterly though Mr Howe had disliked me and much though I had latterly disagreed with him, I still had great admiration for his achievements and the qualities that had earlier made them so many. If only Mr St. Laurent had retired as he had indicated he would, and Mr Howe with him, they would have gone down in history as men of great and virtually unblemished achievement. Two years too long, and they were going with reputations tarnished by latter-day errors and the humiliation of a misconceived election campaign. It would have been a hard man who did not need to swallow a lump in his throat.

Stronger than that distress, however, was my concern about the future. I would not have felt it if the Conservative party had then been led by Diefenbaker's successor, Stanfield, or by anyone with the qualities of some of the subsequent Conservative provincial premiers – Roblin in Manitoba, Robarts and Davis in Ontario. With any of these as the new Prime Minister, it would have seemed to me that the democratic process had worked positively as well as negatively, that not only had a worn-out government been rightly set aside by the voters but it had been replaced by one of normal competence which would have made some useful changes of policy.

The thought of John Diefenbaker as Prime Minister, however, worried me deeply. I recognized the force of his oratory but I could see no evidence and feel no hope that he was capable of leadership in the complex process of government. That was why I had written, before the

election campaign began, that despite all its faults, the St. Laurent government was still preferable to the alternative. And despite the errors of
the Liberals during the election, nothing in the Diefenbaker campaign
had provided any reassurance.

It was a concern by no means confined to non-Conservatives. Early in
the life of the Diefenbaker government, I was leaving the Parliament
Buildings late one evening and passed the office of a Cabinet Minister
who was at the door saying goodnight to some guests. He took me by the
arm. The party was over, he said, but I must come in for a drink with the
friends of mine who were still there – his wife and a couple I knew well.
We talked for a time, but it was clear that the Minister wanted to say
something to me privately. He arranged that the other couple would give
his wife a lift home while he drove me the short distance to the Chateau
Laurier hotel. In fact we drove round and round "Confusion Square," as
its traffic pattern then caused Confederation Square to be known, while
he unburdened himself of the advice he wanted to give me. Up to now he
had respected my political judgment. But he had heard that I was intend-
ing to support Pearson for the Liberal leadership. That was crazy.
Pearson was a decent fellow and he wouldn't be able to cope with
Diefenbaker at all. He would be eaten alive. Anyone with any sense at
all should see that Paul Martin was the right man for the Liberal leadership: then there would be a fair competition between two flannel-
mouths.

I reeled under the punch line but protested that he was being greatly
unfair to Paul. I agreed that as opposition leader he might be more adept
at dealing with Diefenbaker on his own ground, but he wasn't at all the
same kind of man. I intended to support Pearson not because I thought
anything but well of Martin but because I thought that, on balance,
Pearson would be the better Prime Minister – and Diefenbaker's mistakes, not the opposition skills of either Martin or Pearson, would create
that opportunity. The Minister was not convinced, and we parted in
friendly disagreement.

Such, from the beginning, was the internal condition of the Diefenbaker government. What was on the surface reflected, no doubt, the
genuine feelings of most of the Conservative caucus: they respected, and
indeed many adored, the man whose platform oratory had got them
where they were, and they loved his ability to tear opponents to pieces.
But others, and among them some of the ablest, disliked and distrusted
him, and they grew in numbers. At first, my friendships with some of the
ministers continued; they had been warmed by my criticisms of the
previous government and by the objectivity of the *Free Press*'s election
reporting, which was a departure and which meant, given the nature of
the campaign, that it was helpful to Conservatives on the Prairies. Later,

as tension mounted, relations of any intimacy became difficult, though as late as 1961, when I was moving to Ottawa to work full-time for the Liberal party, one Conservative Minister acted as a reference for my mortgage application. The personal relationships across party fences are not as bad as they must often seem from the outside.

Even Mr Diefenbaker was not, at first, entirely unfriendly. Soon after he became Prime Minister we had in his office a lengthy conversation, not of my planning, in which he seemed to want my opinion on some relatively minor matters of government organization. He then asked whether I thought that he should remain, as he was for a few months, his own External Affairs Minister. I learned later that he asked Pearson the same question. When I had made the obvious comment about the work-load, he said he agreed but he was determined not to appoint a Minister until he was sure that he had the very best person for something so important. (He was always sensitive about unfavourable comparisons on external affairs arising from Pearson's reputation.) What did I think of Sidney Smith, then the President of the University of Toronto? I said that, while it would be tough for anyone to be a newcomer at the same time to diplomacy and to the House of Commons, I thought Smith might have the necessary flexibility. I did not add that I would have been more impressed by the discussion if I had not known, from other sources, that Smith had already been approached. His early death was one of the misfortunes of the Diefenbaker government.

At the time, however, what the incident did was to confirm my impression of one of Diefenbaker's strongest traits. He was a perpetual actor, whether he was defending someone in court in his early days or delivering a political speech. He could not stick to a script but went with the floor, making whatever mental rearrangement of the situation would put him into a role that he thought impressive for the audience of the moment. The mental rearrangement had no necessary relation to reality. It was not a quality compatible with effective and responsible leadership of a government.

The errors that resulted were often particularly humiliating for anyone who saw Canada in the kind of role that it had played with Pearson at External Affairs. An early example was provided when, within a few weeks of becoming Prime Minister, Mr Diefenbaker went to a Commonwealth Conference in London and made an impassioned speech about his wish for more trade and investment coming to Canada from the Commonwealth and especially from Britain. It had been one of the complaints of the Conservatives in opposition that Liberal policies promoted trade with the United States and neglected trade with Britain. In office, Mr Diefenbaker began to talk about a shift of 15 per cent of our trade from the United States to Britain. The figure seemed to be plucked from the air. It may have sounded good to some Canadians, but it showed complete lack of understanding of Britain's problem.

The new Macmillan government had just made the brave decision to put economic realism ahead of the inhibitions that had stifled British economic policy since the war. It was seeking free trade with Europe. To that there was, however, much opposition within its own Conservative ranks; the critics – the ex-Canadian Beaverbrook vehement among them – unrealistically claimed Commonwealth trade as the alternative. Mr Diefenbaker's speech was a direct encouragement of the opponents of the UK government's policy, and they used it to the full.

A leading British Minister, Heathcoat Amory, came to Canada to sniff out the ground. We were acquainted, and I was asked to meet with him at the house of the UK High Commissioner to Canada. For anyone who knew the problem, what he had to say was inevitable. Diefenbaker had created a situation in which there was only one way for the British government to deal with the opponents of free trade with Europe. If the Canadian government talked, however vaguely, about a lot more Commonwealth trade, the British government could not respond with less than it was proposing in Europe. It had to suggest free trade between Britain and Canada.

What, Heathcoat Amory asked, did I think the Canadian reaction would be? I said that considerable segments of Canadian opinion would be delighted, but the government would be horrified. Free competition from Britain was the last thing that was wanted by the protected textile, footwear, electrical, and other industries of central Canada. If the British made that proposal they could be sure that the Canadian government would dive for cover; there would be no more loose talk from Ottawa about massive trade shifts.

The proposal was made, at a meeting of Commonwealth ministers at Mont Tremblant in late September. Amazingly, Mr Fleming and other Canadian Ministers were completely unprepared for it. The kindest thing to say would be that they stuttered like Grade Six boys suddenly required to perform in Grade Twelve. No more was heard of the 15 per cent trade diversion. The British were kind. They agreed to a face-saving plan for a Commonwealth trade conference, which was eventually held in Montreal in the fall of 1958. It was about as pointless a waste of taxpayers' money as there has ever been. I have seldom heard a politician be more critical of other politicians than was one of the British ministers of my acquaintance, Reginald Maudling. One evening during the conference, we speculated about what the Canadian ministers, led by Donald Fleming, imagined they were doing. The unavoidable conclusion was that they had no idea. It was a sad fall from the role in the world that Canada had played.

PART TWO

Remaking a Party

"We need a Braintrust"

6 Getting Involved

While I did not expect to remain a journalist all my working life, I had not contemplated, before 1957, that I would ever become involved in an active political role. If anyone had suggested it, I would have said that I had neither the right temperament nor the required talents. Perhaps I would have been correct. Three things, however, led me to an unexpected path. One was the concern about the quality of the Diefenbaker government that I have illustrated by incidents in its early performance. The second factor was pressure from friends in Manitoba. The third was the influence of Mike Pearson.

The pressure was first operative very quickly, and on an unlikely occasion. Shortly after the election, Jim Coyne, the Governor of the Bank of Canada, was married in Winnipeg. The reception was at the home of the bride's sister, Jean, the wife of E.B. Osler. The Oslers were among our closest friends in Winnipeg. (E.B. later served for a term as a Liberal MP.) The wedding guests were mostly the younger members of what might be called the Winnipeg Liberal establishment.

After the champagne had done its work, a small group of them got me into a corner. I was partly responsible for the defeat of the St Laurent government, they said, and the same thing was going to happen to the Manitoba provincial government, for the same reasons. I objected that they were inventing a scapegoat: the voters defeated governments, and the most that any commentator did was to articulate the feelings and views that were at work among marginal voters. All right: their interest wasn't in blame anyway, and they admitted that much of the criticism of the government had been valid. But I must admit that criticism was an easy game and what mattered now was the future. The Liberal party was in disarray, more hurt and disorganized than I knew. Its survival might be in question. Having articulated the criticism, it was up to me to help to articulate what should be done now. I said that I would be ready to give the new government as hard a time as the old one, harder if it was as bad as I thought likely. That, they said, wasn't good enough. The Liberal party had to be rebuilt by a new generation – these were relatively "young" Liberals – and I should not be content to pontificate from the comfort of an editorial chair. I should put my energies into working inside the party, to help to renew it.

This was like many conversations *in vino veritas*, but with the difference that it was promptly followed up. Within a short time I was responding to the invitation and working closely with the small band of Liberal activists. It was the easier because, in the context of the past of the *Winnipeg Free Press*, the involvement seemed entirely natural to almost everyone concerned.

I had doubts, though it was not as clear to me as it now is that a journalist should not be engaged in politics. Rightly or wrongly, the possible conflict of interest did not prevent me from taking the next step. The desire of the younger Manitoba Liberals for rebuilding was encouraging, but clearly not in itself of great importance. Manitoba was too small. No doubt there would be somewhat similar groups across the country, but there would also be Liberals clinging to the belief that the minority Conservative government was a mere hiccup in Canadian politics, that nothing unusual needed to be done before the electorate reverted to its loyalty to the old party that had served so well. If a renewal movement was to succeed, it would have to be helped to coherence and direction by the national leadership.

Mr St Laurent said nothing immediately about his future, but there was little doubt he would soon announce his retirement. The succession was the central issue. Among the Liberals who had been prominent under St Laurent and Howe, Abbott had had the best potential as a political leader. But by the summer of 1957 he had been three years on the Supreme Court. The field was now small. The serious possibilities were only Pearson and Martin.

Of the two, I knew "Mike" by far the better. Our outlooks on the world were very similar, with the result that editorial criticism had never extended to the foreign policy of the St Laurent government. Indeed, it was the Suez crisis that moved our relationship to something closer than the easy friendship that Mike had with countless people. Editorially the *Free Press* had reacted to the British and French action against Egypt much as he did. Many Canadian newspapers, however, were still inclined to see no possibility of wrong by Britain, and were therefore strongly critical of the Pearson diplomacy that produced the United Nations "peace-keeping" intervention. As a consequence, Mike particularly valued our support and found time to discuss the UN resolution even at the peak of his negotiating efforts, when I remember him red-eyed with exhaustion. I became a confidant.

That had two immediate results. First, it was on Mike's initiative that Hamilton Fish Armstrong early in 1957 asked me to write on Canada's new place in the world for *Foreign Affairs* – then very much the quarterly that embodied liberal Western thinking about the world. Mike was delighted with the article and no doubt many people in the diplomatic world interpreted it as an expression of his view. Though in fact he had not seen it before publication, the effect was to identify us rather closely in the minds of many "insiders." That was reinforced more generally when, promptly after the defeat of the St Laurent government, I arranged with him to contribute a series of articles on world affairs to the *Free Press*. The articles were syndicated in other papers, but the primary association was well known.

I was greatly influenced by the fact that our association had never been affected by my strong criticism of so many policies of the Liberal government. He did not hide his friendship when some of his colleagues regarded me as the enemy. The respect in which he and I were temperamentally most alike was that we had not come to politics by the normal partisan route. He had moved from the civil service, in which he had worked for Bennett as well as King, and had found Bennett the easier of the two. Equally, our primary concerns were with what public policies should be. We both saw the party process as the means by which these policies could be established, not as a competition for power irrespective of policy. We did not have the partisan feeling, the sense of being Liberal or Conservative or NDP first and forming opinions second, that is natural enough in people whose party membership is the route by which they have become actively involved in government business.

This was a critical factor in making me think that the Liberal party in which I could feel at home would be a party under Pearson leadership. The preference did not reflect a low opinion of Paul Martin, who has often been underrated. Intellectually he was Mike's equal and more; he had many likeable qualities; and he had political skills, both strategic and tactical, that Mike never learned. Later on, in opposition and in government, I found Paul a good person to work with. Even in 1957, it was obvious that Mike had comparative disadvantages. He had character traits that combined to make him, often, an awkward politician. In public he could veer between bumbling and hectoring in a way that cost many votes. So did the habit of quipping that seemed at times to cast doubt on his seriousness and sincerity. His knowledge of domestic issues was clearly inferior to Paul's. I took too little account of that, not anticipating how often, outside the areas in which he had already proved so competent, he would be uncertain and wavering. Later, and particularly in 1962, I sometimes wondered whether my view about the leadership had been correct. On balance, however, I thought and still think it was.

In 1957, in any event, the choice of leader seemed to me as clear as the decisiveness of the convention vote subsequently caused it to be regarded. There was one immediate consideration of overwhelming importance. Paul's strengths were reflected in the fact that he had already had a lengthy career within the Liberal party. He brought experience, but was it not to a large extent the wrong experience? He would come to the leadership with a baggage of associations, commitments, and loyalties which, I felt, would inhibit a process of thorough renewal in the Liberal party. He was a man for evolution when the situation called for greater change sooner. Defeat had created in the Liberal party a vacuum that could be filled only by new policies and with new people. Precisely because of his comparative detachment from previous partisanship, it was Mike, not Paul, who could best attract new people and formulate new policies .

That, right or wrong, was the decisive consideration in my mind, as I think it was for a good many others. Soon after 10 June, I had a long talk with Mike. It confirmed that we were in substantial agreement about the reasons for the Liberal defeat and that he fully accepted the implication of the analysis: that the political change ran much deeper than was indicated by the narrowness of the parliamentary result. I thought it best to press the point, and predicted that Diefenbaker would get a clear majority at another election before long. The Liberal party could then well disappear unless it was rebuilt with new policies and new people. That could be done but it could well be more than four years, perhaps eight, before Liberals were in office again.

I was relieved and impressed that this assessment did not deter Mike from talking about his own role. He had never planned a political career, or indeed aimed deliberately at any of the jobs he had done. They simply happened to him. Until now, he had vaguely thought that what would follow from External Affairs would be the UN or some other international role. But the election defeat had changed his outlook. It would have been different if the defeat had not extended to so many ministers. If most of them were still around, he might have honourably withdrawn from politics. But with the survivors so few "I'll have to stay here and work to rebuild the party. Even Maryon accepts that." (Mrs Pearson never had any liking for politics.)

I was, of course, delighted he felt that way, but the logic of his position was that he should seek the leadership of the party. He admitted the logic, but was not committing himself. At that point he had the good reason that Mr St Laurent had not resigned, and indeed did not do so until September. But from the discussion I felt fairly confident that the next leader of the Liberal party would be L.B. Pearson. Despite my fluttering doubts about commitment, friendship made it necessary to say that, if there was any personal way in which I could help him, he should tell me.

Some months later he did, in the way that was most easy to respond to. His award of the Nobel Peace Prize in October carried with it the obligation to deliver a public lecture at the ceremony in Oslo. It was his

nature to take that very seriously and with his characteristic self-depre-
cation he claimed to be in great difficulty: over so many years as a
Deputy Minister and Minister he had grown accustomed to having people like Doug LePan and Arnold Smith – distinguished members of the
External Affairs Department – to help him to write speeches. Would I
help him with this one? I was, of course, delighted to do so. With
characteristic cleverness, he had chosen as his first request for help
something that involved no problem at all for my newspaperman's conscience. We discussed an outline of the speech – it became "The Four
Faces of Peace" – and I wrote the economics part of it. A collaboration
could hardly have begun more happily.

Mike never did "seek" the party leadership in the sense in which we
are nowadays accustomed to such candidacies. He gradually let it be
known that he would accept if the party convention wanted him. In
contrast to Paul Martin, he did no campaigning and indeed had no kind of
organization until Walter Gordon, discovering this, improvised a rudi-
mentary one as the convention was starting. The expenditure on the
leadership campaign came to a grand total of $3,000. The mechanics who
now play so much part in the affairs of both major parties, and produce
expenditures of hundreds of thousands of dollars per leadership candidate, would no doubt regard it all as hopelessly amateurish. In the 1957
situation, at any rate, Mike's very lack of formal campaigning was
probably part of his strength. Certainly he had an easy victory. Perhaps
for some others, as for me, it was his tentative style that drew me
gradually into deeper involvement.

Meantime, in Manitoba, the conversation at the Coyne wedding was
followed up. The "Young" Liberals organized a convention for the fall
and asked me to deliver the keynote address. In hindsight it wasn't much
of a speech, but at the time it served some useful purposes. I defined a
Liberal as someone who believes that Canada will be best governed if it
has two or three terms of reform for one term of consolidation. The
defeat of 10 June was the way the democratic system should work. It was
not liberalism to want to be in office for the purpose that properly
belonged to Conservatives – "consolidation without reaction."

In Canada liberalism was in the leftward part of the political spectrum
or, as I preferred to call it, on the radical side. "The Liberal party is the
party of constructive change. That's the only basis on which it can make
its electoral appeal." Premier Campbell, who spoke later, voiced agreement at some length. No doubt he was not expressing his own feelings so
much as recognizing the approval that the audience had given to the
speech. Jack Pickersgill was Ottawa's man at the meeting. I had not
modified any of my criticisms of the St Laurent government and indeed
had summed them up by saying that the Tories had come into office by

putting on clothes that the Liberal government had mislaid. Nevertheless, Pickersgill was friendly and perceptive in his response. On both fronts, forces were being realigned.

The major part of the speech I recall with sadness. Thirty years later, it is still an item on the unfinished agenda of reform.

As an example of the measures to which a renewed Liberal party should put its hand, I discussed the taxation of corporations. Our market economy, I argued, is not working as it should. The primary reason is not, as is often alleged, direct government intervention. It is that we limit the effectiveness of market economics by tolerating and in important ways encouraging businesses larger than genuine market forces would produce. "The free economy is in danger of being destroyed from within, by the people whose idea of private enterprise is that more and more should be done by bigger and bigger corporations controlled by the new managerial elite." The tax structure has a powerful influence in this direction. It is why so much saving takes the form of undistributed corporate profits. They facilitate empire-building by investments that are not subject to the criteria of the market and often serve no economic purpose, while new and small enterprises that can spark and push development are inhibited by lack of capital.

If we are serious about market economics, the argument went on, there should be a corporate income tax only on the income (above some reasonable provision for liquid reserves) that businesses retain. Profits that are paid out to Canadian shareholders should be tax-free as far as the corporation is concerned. They should be fully and progressively taxed as personal income. One effect of such a change would be to make it much less easy for established corporate managements to incur costs in the spirit that government is paying for half of them anyway. The most important effect of all would be that saving would be in the hands of individuals, who would choose how to invest. A larger pool of capital would be available to new and smaller businesses. Established corporations would have to compete in attractiveness to investors before they could expand. Market forces would work better where they are most important – in influencing the directions of change, of adaptation and development, in the economy.

My views on taxation have, I confess, wobbled over the years. In retrospect, I think that this view in 1957 was essentially correct. If such a reform of the tax structure had been made, Canadians would have established more new enterprises and put more capital into new technology and into the refurbishing and expansion of existing small and medium-sized operations. More would have been spent on research and development in Canada. There would have been more searching for exports and more competitive production of some of the things that are now imported, particularly by the subsidiaries of foreign corporations. We would therefore have been better prepared for, and would have adapted better to, the changing economic circumstances with which by the seventies we were so conspicuously failing to cope. Less of our industry would have been outclassed by that of other countries, our productivity would have been higher, and our unemployment less.

This is speculation, of course, and even those who agree that tax reform would have been an influence in the directions I suggest may question whether the magnitude of its effects would have been very great. Anyway, the proposals were soon just water under the bridge. The Young Liberals cheered them, but that was that. In the Pearsonian style, the Deputy Minister of Finance was asked informally what he thought of my ideas. Mike was impressed by the answer. He reported that Ken Taylor said that I had made a very strong case and that he was personally favourable to such a reform direction. But it was not the kind of issue on which the Liberal party was then equipped to campaign, and subsequently Mr Diefenbaker took the tax reform issue out of political contention by appointing the Carter Royal Commission. It made an excellent report, but only after an inordinate time. Its proposals were not up for decision until we had moved into the Trudeau era of economic policy, and what finally came out – after long delay and uncertainty that for a time seriously inhibited investment and made us even worse prepared for the recession – was a feeble compromise.

However, the immediate significance of the Young Liberal speech was not reduced because its main proposal was to come to nothing. Its reception apparently impressed older politicians. A committee under the chairmanship of George Marler was set up to prepare for the policy discussions at the Liberal convention, which in January 1958 was to choose Mr St Laurent's successor. I was asked to be the Manitoba member of the committee. This was the crucial step in my move into active politics, though at the time I rationalized it as an "ad hoc" service, asserting in my letter of acceptance that it did not "involve any binding of the future views of the *Free Press*."

Shocked by electoral defeat, conscious that the party establishment had indeed got out of touch with public opinion, the convention organizers were sincerely concerned that the delegates should have a genuine opportunity to re-shape the party's policy. The convention was to have an elected resolutions committee and a remarkable amount of time, for a convention primarily directed to choosing a new leader, was to be provided for discussing policy resolutions on the floor of the full convention.

No one imagined, however, that coherent results could be expected to well up *ab initio* in the three days of the convention. Constituency associations and the various organizations within the party – university Liberals,

Liberal women, Young Liberals – were therefore solicited to propose draft resolutions in advance of the meeting. They did, in large numbers, but mostly close to the deadline. In theory, the task of the Marler committee was to consolidate these into drafts for consideration by the convention's Resolutions Committee, which could do as it wished with them. What emerged would go to the full convention for debate, possibly for change, and thus for adoption as the party's statements of policy.

In practice, of course, while the resolutions from the "grass-roots," and particularly those that arrived before the last minute, were genuinely taken into account, the consolidated versions largely reflected the discussions, over the preceding two months or so, of the Marler committee. And the Resolutions Committee in turn, while it conducted a good deal of vigorous discussion, ended up with resolutions that were mostly very close to the consolidated drafts submitted to it.

The composition of the Marler committee was therefore crucial to the operation. It was, on paper, about two dozen strong, though there was by no means full attendance at the meetings, which were held frequently in the second half of November, in December, and on every one of the last five days preceding the convention. George Marler was an excellent chairman, unassertive of ideas and admirably firm in getting business done. The former ministers were Jean Lesage (most important, from my viewpoint), James Sinclair, Paul Hellyer, and Jack Pickersgill. The MPS included Jim Byrne, a wise man from BC, Walter Tucker from Saskatchewan and my ally on Prairie issues, and Allan MacEachen; the Senators were, notably, David Croll from Toronto and Donald Smith from Nova Scotia. The "outsiders" included Maurice Lamontagne and me. We had various sub-committees, including one on "Liberal principles," which I convened. The most important was on "general economic policy" and brought together Lesage, Sinclair, Lamontagne, Byrne, and a few others, including me.

As always in such committee efforts, the main work fell on those who were readiest with their pens to write drafts: Lamontagne in French, me in English. We were close enough in thinking for it to be an easy partnership, and most of the more vigorous members of the committee were generally allies.

The resolutions eventually approved by the full convention, and proudly published as a booklet *New Statements of Liberal Policy*, were pretty much the same as the committee drafts. They began with the "principles" resolution, entitled "Liberalism for Progress." Its generalities established the stance that I thought was essential for the party's renewal. The second paragraph, in particular, stated the philosophy that was then needed to distinguish reform from right-wing liberalism: "Freedom is much more than a negative absence of restrictions. Freedom demands positive, unremitting effort to establish those political, social and economic conditions in which all men and women have the opportunity to develop their full stature."

From that base the statement asserted that Liberalism is opposed to privilege of all kinds:

> Liberal policies use the power of the state to ensure that a free economy will operate productively and vigorously, steadily and fairly, to the benefit of all the people. The Liberal party has always supported and promoted government action in all fields in which the public interest genuinely calls for public enterprise. It believes that outside these fields the fundamental role of government is to encourage the maximum possible release of individual energy and initiative ... Liberalism believes in equality based on the right of every individual to full opportunities in society ... To be real, these opportunities require full employment in an efficient economy. In order to abolish want and distress, society must insure the individual and the family against economic and social hazards. The high employment policies and the social security system established in Canada by the Liberal party must, therefore, be maintained and constantly improved.

And so on. It would be an exaggeration to claim that such generalities were solidly fleshed out in the more detailed resolutions. Certainly, however, there were some solid struts for a new platform. The commitment to high employment was made more specific, in terms of Keynesian economic management and "a nation-wide programme of economic development and public works." The development programs included promotion of research through government agencies, industry, and universities; integrated energy development; and development of northern Canada's resources. There were to be federal grants to municipal works, increased government sharing in the construction of low-cost rental housing, and a capital assistance fund for the Atlantic provinces.

In social security, there was to be "provision against major medical, dental and surgical expenses" which, combined with the hospital insurance that had been legislated, "would ensure that no Canadian would be financially crippled by illness." "Adequate" unemployment insurance would "be extended to those unemployed because of illness" – one of my favourite proposals. There would be "immediate consideration" of a national pension scheme, "the pensions to begin at age sixtyfive [as opposed to the seventy that was then applicable for old-age security] and to be based upon federal government contributions as well as upon contributions of employees, employers and self-employed." And family allowances were to be improved "with special reference to payment of the allowances for children remaining students until they attain the age of eighteen years."

Other resolutions included a program which I had particularly urged in *Free Press* editorials: "an extensive scheme of Canada Scholarships and Bursaries for university students" supplemented by interest-free loans for students. "The Liberal party believes that Canada must end the situation in which many young men and women are shut off, by lack of funds, from education that they have the ability and the ambition to use to the country's advantage."

On farm-stored grain, as indeed on a number of issues, there was a rather weak compromise: there would be "improvement" but the only specific commitment was that the government would cover actual storage costs, as if the grain were in the elevator. I was disappointed too by the vagueness of the reference to tax reform. Apart from the motherhood declaration that taxation would be according to ability to pay, it was agreed only that the Liberal party "will ensure that tax policies place no unnecessary restrictions on the opportunities open to competitive small businesses and enterprising individuals. It will encourage savings by Canadians for investment in the ownership and control of Canadian industries." That could be interpreted to cover the kind of proposal I had made, but it could have many other meanings.

The final two weeks, before and during the convention, seemed like endless days of discussion, drafting, negotiating, redrafting. Even so, a political convention always has its lighter moments. Bob Fowler was the draftsman of Mike's speeches. Late during the first evening he and Maurice Lamontagne and I were in his room at the hotel, discussing the draft of the nomination speech. We sat in the only three chairs in the modest room while Mrs Fowler reclined elegantly on the bed, reading a book. There was a loud knock at the door, and when I opened it Jean Lesage more or less pushed Premier Campbell into the room: "I told you I'd show you where the decisions are really made." Mr Campbell, gazing at the lady on the bed, looked like a respectable gentleman who had been thrust into a den of iniquity.

All this was back-room work, and "back-room boys" have since become the objects of much criticism and resentment in the Liberal party. Certainly there should not be a presumption that anyone has a right to take part in determining public policies if he or she has not been voted into the responsibility. The criticism can, however, be unrealistic. A political leader has to have help, and if it is to be effective the help must be of the leader's choice. The election of a leader is not of one person but, by clear implication, of some associates. As long as they have the leader's confidence, they exist by a process that is not less democratic for being indirectly so. A leader who proclaims that there will be no back-room boys (or girls) is playing to the gallery in an amateur production.

There are, however, legitimate questions about the back-room role. They relate not to its existence but to the issues of quantity and of style. Mr Pearson and Mr Stanfield and all who preceded them, in Liberal and Conservative parties, had very small staffs both in their personal offices and in the party organizations. With Mr Trudeau there came a new style, which Mr Mulroney has made more extreme. Not only has the number of senior assistants been multiplied; they have bevies of assistants in their turn.

This, of course, is part of the process that has made the prime ministership more like a presidency. That in itself cannot be dismissed as undemocratic. The United States is not less democratic because a vote for a president carries with it his choice of otherwise unelected Cabinet members and senior officials in their hundreds. The American system, however, also provides for the election of Senators and Congressmen who have, relative to the President, far more power than our parliamentary system gives to MPs, including Cabinet ministers, relative to the Prime Minister. The multiplication of staff around the Prime Minister can have only two possible effects. One is an inefficient duplication of work that, in the cabinet-parliamentary constitution of government, is the responsibility of ministers answerable to Parliament for their departments. The other effect is that the staff, and particularly the senior members of it who qualify as back-room boys, exercise power which detracts from that of the elected ministers. In practice the two effects, duplication and detraction, are mingled. Neither, of course, was Mr Trudeau's intent, but they happened and they have not been getting less. The direct impact is on the ministers and MPs, and they are among the leaders of their party in the constituencies and in its provincial structures. Resentment that back-room boys have taken over therefore spreads through the party ranks.

My impression of the Trudeau period – I cannot say that it is more than an impression – is that the power to shake and to fix which some back-room boys claim, or have attributed to them, is somewhat exaggerated. That may be especially true of claims and attributions when they are fostered as retrospective consolation after retirement to the Senate.

In the Pearson period of my experience, at any rate, back-room work had a different character. Certainly Mr Pearson delegated a good deal of responsibility to me, at some points in his leadership of the opposition and as Prime Minister. But, first, I was an individual; I was not operating with a staff. Second, it was a delegation for a clearly understood purpose; and the purpose was to fulfil the democratic process, not to override it.

In opposition, it was that the Liberal party should tell people clearly what it would do if they elected it; and in government, it was that we would do what we had said we would do.

This is the essence of democratic, representative government as I see it. More importantly, it is how Mike Pearson saw politics. Without that shared assumption, he would not have assigned the role he did to me. I do not think that I am deceiving myself in saying that I would not have accepted it on other terms. It was crucial to our relationship.

It turned out that the relationship with Jean Lesage was also of considerable importance. One of the incidental effects of work on the resolutions committee was that it greatly increased my respect for Jean Lesage and the understanding between us. Shortly afterwards I received from him one of the charming "My dear Tom" letters of which he was a master, thanking me "very deeply" for the "wonderful job" without which he did not see how "the Platform that we now have" could have been prepared. The collaboration had been "a real inspiration ... a great encouragement to keep on working restlessly for the Party." I was, naturally, pleased and, equally naturally, had no idea that our friendship would be significant for the work of the Pearson government.

At the convention, Mike was easily elected and in his acceptance speech warmly endorsed the policy resolutions. Most important was the consensus that they registered. Former Cabinet ministers and old political warhorses joined in attitude with the Young Liberals (a classification that included many people who would normally be thought to be in at least the early years of middle age), as well as with the idealists who wanted, above all, to back a Nobel prize winner against Diefenbaker tirades. The conservatism of the later St Laurent years had not dissolved completely away, but temporarily it largely disappeared underground. There was not breast-beating, of course, but the implicit recognition of past mistakes was clear. While due tribute was paid to the past, the new policies clearly expressed a shift of direction.

There was nothing remarkable about the policies. They embodied Canadian versions of the ideas that were in the air of a world where, for instance, Galbraith was just finishing the writing of *The Affluent Society* (it was published that summer) and Kennedy was preparing the presidential campaign that, in its expression of a new, forward-looking spirit, struck responses in many parts of the world besides North America. The Liberal Party of Canada caught up with the times. In doing so, it embraced new policies almost as soon as it was defeated. They were not cooked up just before election campaigns, by clever people in back rooms. The main lines of policy of the rebuilt Liberal party – conspicuously, the emphasis on employment, medicare, a national pension plan, but many others too – were adopted at the party convention of January

1958, and by as democratic a procedure within the convention as the processes of political parties ever produce. Those policies were reaffirmed and made more definite, at the National Rally of January 1961, by equally democratic procedures.

The policies did not, in other words, originate from the remaking of the party. In essence, they were already written when the organizational rebuilding took place. To a large extent, indeed, the new people who did the organizing came forward because they were coming to a body of ideas, for the better government of Canada, that they felt to be at once progressive and practical.

This is the central fact about the remaking of the Liberal party from 1957 to 1963. The process was not to regroup, reorganize, and, some time later, determine policies. The main lines of policy came first. They were the presence behind all the detailed work of opposing, reorganizing, finding candidates, building support. All that came second, not first.

The remaking of a political party cannot be achieved without the people who are party stalwarts because they were before, or their fathers before them; the people who like power and influence for the sake of power and influence; the people who are thinking about fees and appointments; the people who dislike or despise those now in office; the people with particular axes to grind. All such motivations play a necessary part in the work that goes into the political process. But for a party to move public opinion as it was to be moved between 1958 and 1962/3, there has to be a broader starting-point: a concept of what a new government will do, of the purposes for which the party seeks office. Without that, the mechanics of party organization are hollow. They will not engage the enthusiasm of volunteer campaign workers that is necessary to get out the votes, even of people who are by no means satisfied with the existing government. To move the country, there must be a belief that a change of government will result in positive changes for people. That there should be enough policy to sustain that belief is essential. The rest is housekeeping, necessary and important but secondary.

The housekeeping is likely to be more enthusiastic the wider the sense that people through the party have participated in its policy-making. For that, democracy and strong leadership have to be reconciled. The policies will not be realistic and coherent unless they are finally shaped by a very few people. The work of the Marler committee for the 1958 convention, and later of the working group that Walter Gordon established for the 1961 National Rally, is essential. But their work can be well done only if it is sensitive, and is seen to be sensitive, to the ideas of active party people across the country. This need is confused by the outdated habit of referring to "grass-roots" opinion. Postwar Canada had become, even by the late fifties, highly urbanized. To adopt ideas whose time had come was to become more urban than the Liberal party had previously been. There was no choice. Mr Diefenbaker's hold on the rural vote, outside Quebec, would not be quickly released. It was in cities and towns, initially at least, that the Liberal party could be rebuilt. It was their opinion leaders who must feel at home with Liberal policies. In that we were, I think, successful. The policies of the rebuilt Liberal party were not made at the grass-roots, but they were as close to the sidewalk as national policies are ever likely to be.

So, at least, I believed. I left the January 1958 convention thinking that we had started well. We had the foundation on which to build in comparative leisure. I did not know that during the convention a bomb had been planted that would blow this happy plan to pieces. Gallingly, I had been the one observer of the planting but had not recognized it for what it was.

7 *No Bigger Mistake*

In 1957 the Conservatives had only a few more seats than the Liberals. The balance of power lay with the CCF and Social Credit groups. But, of course, they did not want another election soon. It would be a decision for or against giving Mr Diefenbaker his chance, and the smaller parties were sure to lose votes however the main issue was decided. Equally obviously, the Liberals did not want another election before their new leader was chosen. By universal consent, therefore, no challenge was offered to the government in Parliament during 1957.

But what was to happen after the Liberal convention? In normal parliamentary practice, the new leader of the opposition would move "no confidence" in the government. Its first seven months in office had not been happy. There was already much of the sense of confusion that characterized Mr Diefenbaker. He had backed away from many of the things that, on the hustings, he had said he would do. The boom of 1955–6 had faltered badly. In the last few months of 1957 unemployment increased to an extent that was, by the standards of the time, drastic.

There were grounds enough for criticism and an opposition that failed to move no confidence, once its leadership was settled, would lose a lot of face and some public credibility. But the last thing the Liberal party could want was that such a motion should pass, causing dissolution and a general election. The party was not prepared for another campaign, and it did not require much realism about public opinion to recognize that Diefenbaker would gain more from the feeling that he should be given a proper chance than he would as yet lose from the mistakes he had made. The Liberal interest was that he should have more time to go wrong before people voted again.

There was much agitation, therefore, about whether or not to move no confidence, and the test was to come immediately after the Liberal leadership convention of 14 to 16 January. The following Monday, 20 January, was anticipated to be a "supply" day, the standard occasion for a no-confidence motion.

It was Pearson's nature that he was deeply concerned as to what, if he were leader, he would do. Indeed he was so concerned about it that Walter Gordon said to me, during the weekend before the convention, that unless the question was got out of the way Mike would go on worrying about it instead of doing anything to get himself elected by the convention. Accordingly, on Walter's initiative, Mike on 13 January met with Walter, Maurice Lamontagne, Bob Fowler, and me, theoretically to settle the issue. The four of us were quickly unanimous in our advice: defy the parliamentary convention, don't move no confidence.

Our principal reason was simple: Mike was not a man who could make a good job of pretending. An attempt at a "fighting" speech, ostensibly aimed at rallying the whole opposition to vote down the government, would be a flop. Further, Diefenbaker must be spoiling to call an election. A no-confidence motion would be playing into his hands. The government probably would be sustained by the smaller parties, but there would be bound to be things said in the debate that he could use as an excuse for dissolving Parliament and taking the issue to the public.

Anyway, the agreement among Mike's personal, as opposed to party, confidants was clear. He concurred. I accepted the task of preparing a barebones draft for the kind of speech that would be appropriate. Time was limited, because of the demands of the convention, and what I wrote in my hotel room late that night – or rather, in the early hours of 14 January – was a mere legal size page and a half of "possible headings for Monday speech." Its key phrases are reproduced here as they were hurriedly tapped out on the typewriter, without troubling about capitals or much about syntax and punctuation.

The structure on which we had agreed for the speech was that Pearson faced a dilemma about which he would talk entirely frankly. One side of it was:

> what country needs at this time is vigorous govt action, not the pause in govt action that an election campaign involves.

perhaps party opposite would like an election because has not capacity for vigorous action.

but canada needs vigorous action & to make it impossible – as general election in the critical two months would do – would be rash action with bitter taste for those hundreds of thousands of canadians, their wives and families, whose jobs disappeared while gentlemen opposite toured country engaged in talk & promises which they do with such grandeur, instead of responsible action in which they fall so short.

That was one side of the dilemma. To force an election would be against the national interest. But the other side was: "what can people of Canada gain by government staying? will it do what is needed?"

The notes suggested a brief analysis of the economic situation. We had had slight economic pauses in 1949 and 1954; but they were different, in dimension and in origin, from this time. In those years the economy slackened because exports slackened. This time they had not. The recession had been generated at home. With wise policy government could control it. But already it had been allowed to become much worse in dimension. The notes went on:

achievement of govt to date has been to restore to this nation the fear – fear of want, fear about jobs – from which liberal govt freed it.

problems already created for country by 7 months of tory govt will not be cured readily or easily.

government shows no sign of capacity to cure them.

believe we could cure them – based on experience – on lines of liberal resolution on economic policy.

but we could not start till two months from now and these are the critical months, months when only most vigorous and prompt action can prevent gathering of seasonal unemployment into mood of depression, of diminished confidence, which could carry country far down road of depression which we had all grown to think, under liberal government, country had left behind for ever.

Therefore, the argument continued, if the government did not now take the right action, it would not be long before the lesser evil for Canada would be for the opposition to force an election:

but before comes to that, appeal to gentlemen opposite to adopt liberal policies: ideas set out for them in our platform: glad to give those ideas to idea-less government. please act on these lines for people of Canada.

And so on. They were not speech notes to be proud of. That they could be interpreted as arrogant – the charge to which the Liberal party was all too vulnerable – could be excused only by haste and tiredness. The whole thing would have been scorned as a feeble cover for the Liberals' fear of an election. There were just two things to be said for it: it was better than any alternative we could think of; and it was vastly better than what was in fact done.

I gave Mike the notes on the 14th and kept the one carbon that, in my amateurish overnight typing, I had made. By then the convention had assembled, and I saw little more of him. He was at last busy asking delegates to support him, or at least making some of those who had decided to do so feel appreciated. I was immersed in the resolutions committee. But on the morning of the convention's second day, I made a hurried visit to him. He had done some rewriting of the Fowler draft of his convention speech, and had put in things that seemed to Bob undesirable. Maurice Lamontagne and I agreed with him on some points, and I was delegated to discuss those with Mike. I was doing so when Jack Pickersgill arrived.

Parliament was sitting while the convention was in progress and Jack was nobly holding the fort there, with a handful of MPs, while most were at the convention. He therefore had to hurry up to the House but there was an urgent matter, he said, that he must discuss first. I had to leave within a few minutes anyway. Mike said all right, he was sure the changes I wanted to make were OK, so he could see Jack if I would write them in and give the text to the secretaries for retyping. The Pearson "headquarters" at the Chateau were not lavish, and the only quiet place to do my editing was the bathroom. When I had given the speech to the secretaries and was rushing away, Jack was just going out of the door. Mike grabbed me by the arm and pulled me back into the room. "Jack's come up with a different idea about what to do on Monday. It sounds to me too clever by half. But we'll have to talk about it later."

We never did. By the end of the convention, on Thursday night, everyone was exhausted. On the Friday morning, before taking a flight back to Winnipeg, I called Mike's office to see if he was available for the discussion he had said he wanted. But, understandably, he was still exhausted and staying at home. I arrived in Winnipeg with a miserable attack of flu, and went to bed. I was still there on 20 January when Vic

Mackie, the *Free Press* reporter in Ottawa, telephoned to read to me the resolution that Mike had just moved in the House. It was a minute or two before he could convince me that he was not putting me on.

As I learned later from Mike, he had over the weekend discussed the Pickersgill idea with a number of the party seniors; he specifically mentioned St. Laurent and Howe. They had concurred in it, and he had decided to accept their advice over that of his amateur associates, as we were understandably regarded by many party oldtimers. Charitably one can say that his decision reflected the becoming modesty of inexperience; but his own first judgment had been far better.

Jack's idea was indeed too clever by half. The motion criticized the government in the manner of traditional no-confidence resolutions but, instead of aiming at the government's defeat, concluded that "in view of the desirability at this time of having a government pledged to implement Liberal policies, His Excellency's advisors should in the opinion of this House submit their resignation forthwith."

It was clever in the sense that it was the one kind of adverse motion that the smaller parties could not possibly vote for. It could not result, directly, in an election. It was also preposterous. It was a proposal that the Liberal party, which the electorate had voted out only seven months before, should now return to office without an election. It could not have more strongly underlined the things about the Liberals that people had become fed up with. It could not have more fully suggested that the convention and its resolutions meant nothing, that the Liberal leadership – including Pearson – had learned nothing, that they had lost all the instincts of democratic politicians and remained far out of touch with public opinion.

It was not even a good manoeuvre for its narrow purpose of barking without biting, of avoiding an election. The government was not defeated but Mr Diefenbaker was given good reason to ask for dissolution, to put the issue of confidence in his government to the ultimate test of public opinion.

A few days later Mike telephoned me. He had a commitment to speak in Brandon, Manitoba. In the late evening he would be flying back from there to Winnipeg, with a connection to Toronto and Ottawa. But there was a later flight onwards (at something like 3 AM; we were still in the era of night flights by piston aircraft). He wanted to talk to me and would stop over for the three or four hours if I could meet him.

I picked him up at the airport, drove him to my home, and settled him into an armchair with a drink of Scotch and a sandwich. He put his feet over the side of the chair and began: "I don't know if I'll ever be any good as a party leader but certainly no one ever started anything by making a bigger mistake." I reminded him that his own first reaction to

Jack's proposal had been the right one, and he responded that my draft would have been the right speech. He had realized that the other one was wrong as soon as he got to his feet, but it was too late to change and he had to go through with it.

He quickly came to the point. It was certain that Diefenbaker would dissolve Parliament almost at once. As soon as possible afterwards, would I come to Ottawa for a few days to draft the Liberal election platform? He knew my doubt about such a close party commitment, but what was required was chiefly to select, from the convention resolutions with which I had been so closely involved, those that could best be developed into more precise shape for the election platform. I could be sure that he would never hold it against me if I later exercised my right to differ from him. (I accepted that as true of Mike, though of very few people.) He knew now how weak in personnel the party was, and his need for my help, he said, was desperate. He had learned his lesson and would not be asking any of the oldtimers to be involved. Maurice Lamontagne would join me, of course, and if I agreed he would also ask John Deutsch (who had moved from the public service to the University of British Columbia) and Maxwell Cohen (of McGill) to lend a hand. Lamontagne and Deutsch were two of my best friends and, while I did not know Cohen well, it would be a compatible group.

That was the pitch, made with Mike's extraordinary persuasiveness in most one-to-one relationships. I hesitated only briefly, and it was as a committed man that I drove him back to the airport for the middle-of-the-night flight.

From here on, my relationship with L.B. Pearson is central to this account. It most often puzzled, and sometimes angered, our friends and associates. We had many viewpoints in common, but our temperaments were very different. In some respects our strengths and faults were complementary, but they could lead to misunderstandings when we were under pressure. From 1958 to 1961 Mike's relationship with me was probably not much different from that with other close friends, except that spasmodically he asked me to do more work for him. That was very small, however, beside the consistent and highly effective work of Maurice Lamontagne, who had a place in his office. And from 1960 on, Walter Gordon did by far the most valuable work of all.

Until the summer of 1964, when he suddenly aged, there was no sense that Mike was old enough to be my father: he was so extraordinarily young in spirit that, while there was no question about his seniority in status even more than in age, the relationship was a straightforward friendship until I became, late in 1961, the employed assistant. That did not cause much change of attitude, on either side, but it made our contacts so frequent that most of them had to be strictly business. Under pressure, we grew to need each other greatly, and to use each other without mercy. Mike's demands on my time and energy often seemed to be without limit. I reciprocated by pressuring him to be definite and firm on many occasions when his disposition was to evade and to waver, by pressing him to make decisions however much he wanted to put them off and watch a hockey or ball game on television instead.

For the full four years of 1962 to 1965, there was in effect an implicit understanding that, for the sake of the larger need, we could live with the ways in which we irritated each other. Perhaps we both found some relief behind each other's backs. Certainly Mike was free in grumbling to me about his ministers and other associates. I, however, breached the implicit agreement in our direct relations more than he did. As my wife once commented to him, he and she were the two people with whom I relieved the tensions of work by getting angry. But he was forgiving, and for eight years in all, from 1958 through 1965, we had an alliance that was perhaps almost as frictionless as was compatible with its being so close and active under so much pressure.

By December 1965 we had used each other as fully as, on both sides, we felt we could. There was no quarrel, simply an agreement that the time had come to change. Though I took the initiative, Mike was clearly of the same mind. Perhaps because we had never been such very intimate friends as he and Walter Gordon were, there was none of the ill feeling that developed from the separation with Walter and was made worse by the temporary realliance in 1967. During the remainder of his prime ministership, Mike occasionally breached the proprieties by consulting me about government matters outside the departmental responsibilities of a Deputy Minister. After his retirement our relationship was intermittent, but when we talked it was still with the same closeness, particularly about the issues of international development that became his major interest.

What we did not do was to review the past, except on one occasion in 1972 which turned out to be the last time I saw him. Our discussion then was partly about the troubles of the Trudeau government, and Mike went on to talk about our problems and successes. He concluded, typically, "Well, we didn't do too badly." I was out of the country when he died and, not having attended the funeral, had to write my condolences to Mrs Pearson. Generously, since she and I often competed for influence on him, she responded that she particularly appreciated the tribute because "you were very close to Mike." My letter had said, in part:

> The historic role of a man, is, I suppose, the magnitude of the effect that he has, directly and indirectly, on the lives of millions of people. In that sense, Mike is going to stand very large indeed in history. But

the quality of a man is perhaps more truly reflected in the nature of the direct effect he has on individuals ... As a politician, the distinctive, outrageous, wonderful quality of Mike was that he insisted on doing what politicians are supposed not to do – see both (or more) sides of a question. It was that which made unlikely people such as me work for him ... Mike completely changed my life from any course that it might otherwise have taken; and whatever the heats and indignations and frustrations of some moments, it was the greatest of privileges to work for him.

8 *The First Platform*

Parliament was dissolved on 1 February and on 3 February I sent a telegram confirming that the next day I would once again arrive at the Chateau Laurier for some days of intensive work. Maurice Lamontagne was on the spot throughout and we were joined by John Payne, a Winnipeg man who had been released by the Hudson's Bay Company in order to handle Mike's public relations for the campaign. John Deutsch and Maxwell Cohen came for shorter periods. Mike himself sensibly took a few days' holiday, at Walter Gordon's farm north of Toronto, to build up energy for the campaign. He joined us on the 9th. The main planks of the platform were released to the press on the 10th.

It was an intense effort in irrelevancy. There was little doubt, in my mind at least, that Diefenbaker was going to sweep the country, and nothing the Liberal party said would make any difference. But that was the short-run situation. I hoped that we were also preparing a way for different times. Entirely insignificant though it was at its time, the 1958 platform did set a style to which the Pearson Liberal party remained basically true, despite many waverings. It was very different from the politics of the later St Laurent years, of the Conservatives under Diefenbaker, of the Trudeau era, and more recently of the Conservatives under Mulroney.

The basic concept was that a party should seek office by telling the electorate as precisely as possible what it would do in office. There are obvious limitations to that concept. No one can foresee many of the circumstances with which a government is going to have to deal over a four-year term. Representative government therefore cannot be government according to a precise mandate. In large degree, it has to mean that the electorate chooses which of two or more groups, and especially which party leader, it trusts to make the best decisions about things to come. But how is that choice to be made? If it is only a judgment between personalities, all offering mere generalities about how they will govern, then representative government is not a process by which the people put any definite stamp on events. Their choice of representation is a random happening with very little predetermined relation to the way they are afterwards governed; public policy proceeds without significant democratic sanction.

There is democratic sanction only if the party has been definite about the major measures it will take if elected. While the resulting mandate cannot be restrictive of additional action in office, it should be clearly front and centre in the Cabinet's performance. Modern government is far too complex for a Prime Minister and ministers to do much serious policy-planning after they are in office. They are always too busy with the immediate. If they do not come to office with clear, comprehensive, realistic objectives, they will not formulate them afterwards. In many areas of policy, they will be the slaves of events, of lobbying groups, of officials who know so much more than they do, of opinion polls, of short-term calculations. Government will be little more than a hurried procession from ad hoc decision to ad hoc decision. It will have some purpose and direction, based on the prior wishes of a majority of the people, only if the Cabinet comes to office with what it will do, in at least some major areas of policy, already enunciated in its party platform. If it has been elected only by showmanship and generalities, whether it does well for the country will be more an accident than a reflection of democratic decision-making.

I should emphasize that all this refers to concept, not dogma. The degree to which a party platform can be rationally specific varies with circumstances. Certainly a democratic country, and particularly a country as large and diverse as Canada, cannot be well served by strongly ideological parties. But the problem is that our diversity, with the consequent necessity for parties to be somewhat loose alliances bridging regional interests, provides politicians with a rationalization for being excessively indeterminate about what they will do in office. Most are more comfortable the more vague they can get away with being. And since both the main parties, at least, tend to like the same rules of the game, the effect is as if there were a conspiracy between them to woo the electorate more with rival generalities and personalities than with definite directions in public policy.

It is a conspiracy against the national interest. It is one of the reasons why so many people with active public concerns have turned away from the party political process to press their concerns through the plethora of special interest groups. The lamentable consequence is that the competition for central power, through government, tends to be left too much to people whose interest is more in the power, and the perquisites it provides for some advertising agencies, contractors, "consultants", and lawyers, than in what to do with power for the public interest.

The circumstances of February 1958 called particularly strongly for precision in the Liberal platform. Precision would not do much to win votes, but it would do as much as possible to remove the albatross of the Liberal party's recent reputation. It would provide the maximum contrast with the Diefenbaker style and thereby prepare, to the limited extent we could, for a future in which people would see the hollowness of that style.

The platform was written in a sitting room that I had taken at the Chateau Laurier. We were serious and pressed for time, so that I can recall only two lighter moments. One was the expression on the faces of some gentlemen who passed my door at the moment when I was transferring bills from my wallet to the handbag of Mary Macdonald, Mike's executive assistant. What I was in fact paying for was the Scotch that she had kindly bought to help to make the Chateau's room service meals more digestible. Max Cohen did not share in the Scotch. My other recollection is of the mounting horror with which John Payne and I watched the rising tide of the Chateau's crème de menthe parfaits, which for Max seemed to be a more insatiable taste than ours for Scotch.

Our easiest decision was that we would go into precise detail about some measures to increase employment. The Canadian economy had experienced small downturns in the business cycle in earlier postwar years, but we were convinced that the 1957 recession would become something more – as, indeed, it did – unless prompt action was taken to stimulate consumer demand. The situation was right for Keynesian measures. The world economy was buoyant, Canada's external accounts were not in trouble, and the federal financial position was strong; thanks to the former Abbott policies, boom times had garnered substantial budget surpluses and reductions in the outstanding federal debt. The situation now called for tax cuts, as a quicker way to stimulate the economy than increased government spending. The economic case was bolstered because the tax cuts which would best increase spending coincided with our disposition to make taxation more progressive.

We proposed a cut of four percentage points in the rates on the first $3000 of taxable income, which in those days was the whole of the taxable income of most people. For the great majority the proposal meant a cut of about 25 per cent in their tax bills. It was supplemented by what we called the dowry plan: the basic exemptions of a married couple would be doubled, from $2,000 to $4,000, during the first three years of married life.

In addition to these measures to encourage consumption directly, we proposed to help small businesses by halving the corporation tax on the first $10,000 of profits and to encourage all business investment by accelerated depreciation on projects started in the fiscal year from 1 April 1958. We also proposed to abolish the 7 1/2 per cent special excise tax on cars.

Other employment measures included special grants to municipalities to cover the extra cost of construction done in the winter and acceptance by the federal government of extra expense in its own projects for the same purpose. For the longer term, there was to be a Municipal Loan Fund (to be established in consultation with the provinces); a special bank for export financing; changes in the National Housing Act to reduce the size of the downpayment then required for a house; special federal assistance for trunk highway construction; and establishment of a National Advisory Board on Economic Development and Automation, composed of representatives of industry, labour, agriculture, and the universities, which would help to plan long-term investment, training, and adjustment programs to cope with automation, and other measures for economic growth and employment.

Prairie farmers were promised modest support prices on grain (basis $1.50, No. 1 Northern at Fort William) and compensation for the cost of storage on farms. There was to be a new Farm Development Bank for agriculture generally.

For social security, we said that a new Liberal government would take three immediate measures: workers would qualify for unemployment insurance benefits because of illness, on the same basis as the benefits paid to workers who lost their jobs; unmarried women and widows would become eligible for old age assistance at age sixty instead of sixty-five; and family allowances would be paid to age eighteen for a boy or girl who was a student.

Figures were put to my favourite scholarship scheme. There would be 10,000 scholarships and bursaries a year, to the value of $1,000 and $500 a year respectively, and payable for four years. Loans for university students would be interest-free until one year after graduation and thereafter would carry interest at 4 per cent and be repayable within four years.

We estimated the costs of the definite measures. The tax cuts would reduce revenues by $400 millions and the extra expenditures in the first year would be about $100 millions. (They would, of course, cost more later, but we were confident of rising revenues with restored prosperity.) The immediate budget deficit – how small it seems now! – was the sound and realistic way to create jobs, create them quickly and naturally because the measures were designed to put more money into the hands of consumers. The program was not one of high-sounding promises but, we claimed, of precise, practical measures to which a Pearson government would be absolutely committed. It was a firm, responsible program for combatting the recession, for restoring Canada to economic growth, "in accordance" (we said to reassure the right wing of the party) "with the Liberal principles that have so often proved their worth to the public in the past." A case in support of that claim could be made. But, of course, while the platform was entirely in the spirit of the recent policy resolutions of the party, it was a large departure, both in its precision and in its policy content, from the recent Liberal stance in office.

On the morning of 9 February we discussed the draft with the leader. He was well satisfied, and John Payne began to put the main points into a press release. During the afternoon Mike telephoned principal members of the party to tell them what was to be in the platform. The earlier names on his list were the more activist-minded people – Martin, Sinclair, Lesage, and the like – and he reported enthusiastic endorsement. The responses changed somewhat as he went further. In the evening he called me again: he was particularly concerned because Senator John Connolly, who was to be campaign chairman, was unhappy about the platform. Could I come out to the house – or rather, to the Sandy Hill duplex that was then his home – so that the three of us could settle things? John Payne drove me somewhat dramatically through a heavy snowstorm, and the meeting sustained the tension. It was a battle that had to be refought many times during the following five years.

John Connolly made the orthodox politicians' case very well. It was unwise to offer precise policies. They would offend or frighten off some potential supporters and they presented the other side with targets to shoot at. An election campaign was much like a battle, in which the main effort was to attack and damage your opponent. We should concentrate on criticizing Diefenbaker and otherwise gain as wide support as possible by stating our own platform in generalities. That had always been Mackenzie King's method, and he had been the most successful Canadian politician. Even if we did decide that this time it was desirable to be more specific on a few points, we should introduce such planks in the platform one at a time and late in the campaign, when they would get more attention than they would as a package and when the other side would have less opportunity to criticize them.

My response, of course, was that the Liberals had lost in June precisely because people were tired of the old style. Diefenbaker had stood for something new. True, he had not been precise, but he did not need to be because the Conservatives had been out of office so long that, in the minds of most voters, they were unencumbered with old baggage. The Liberal situation was quite different. It would be a long time before generalities would again convince people that the Liberal party had anything constructive to offer. We were unlikely to win this time anyway, but if we wanted to renew the party and win next time we had to identify it with policy positions definite enough to make a public impact, in future if not in this election. That would not be achieved by bringing out policies one at a time later in the campaign. They would then be dismissed as the promises of desperate politicians, bribes to the electorate offered by men who didn't expect to deliver on them. We should state our platform comprehensively at the beginning and neither add nor subtract as the campaign went on.

In the absence of a clearly stated platform at the beginning, our criticism of Diefenbaker would be regarded as mere carping by people who didn't like being out of office for once. Indeed it would be counterproductive: after so many years of Liberal government many marginal voters wanted to give Diefenbaker a chance and any strong attack would create more dislike of us than distrust of him. That would be true however skilled the criticism. But in fact it wouldn't be effective criticism because that wasn't what Mike was good at. It wasn't his style. Everyone knew that. The convention delegates knew it when they chose him as leader. They had shown that they wanted new policies and a man who identified naturally with such policies.

Mrs Pearson was present through all this. She did not take part in the discussion but I knew that I had won when, as I was making the points about the Pearson style, I noticed him catch her eye and she nodded affirmatively. The decision was firm. The platform would stand as it was. The press release would be made tomorrow. John Connolly was graceful. He said that he recognized I might well be right and anyway he fully accepted Mike's decision and would do everything he could for the campaign on that basis. Over the following few years he and I often disagreed, sometimes strongly, but we did not quarrel.

John Payne and I slithered back through the snow and checked the final typescript of the press release. Going late to bed I reflected on how unexpectedly decisive the day had been. After this I would have to stand by Pearson whatever happened.

During the following seven weeks it would anyway have required a hard heart not to give Mike any help within one's power. The Liberal party organization, which had seemed so powerful, when built on the party being in office, had largely melted away. There was a desperate shortage of people to make arrangements and to produce campaign literature and materials. The effective use of television had not been learned. Winter weather added to the difficulties. Politicians then did not charter their own aircraft. Mike, struggling around the country by scheduled flights that were often delayed, to meetings that were poorly planned, worse organized and usually miserably attended, became a more and more pathetic figure as the certainty of a massive Conservative victory mounted.

During the winter evenings in Winnipeg I wrote notes for speeches by him and a few others and answered telephone calls from John Payne, who all too often was calling from somewhere where Mike's party had arrived late or been held up. But my main undertaking, at Mike's request, was to write both a short version of the platform, theoretically for wide distribution though there turned out to be no organization for that, and a fuller version to serve as a guide for candidates and other speakers. It explained the programs in more detail and the reasons for them and added the longer-term measures that we had not tried to put into the press release. Mike was quite as concerned as I was that, having been in the convention resolutions, they should not be ignored in what we had come to call "The Pearson Plan."

Thanks to the invaluable volunteer help of two other Winnipeg journalists, Jean Edmonds and Ellen Gallagher, the job was done in a week or so of long evenings and nights. On 26 February I sent off the texts to Ottawa and on 27 February took the morning plane to Saskatoon, carrying a copy and also an excessively long speech on Western agriculture. Mike was coming from the other direction, his flight was late, and he had an afternoon meeting, attended mainly by students from the University of Saskatchewan, which went on too long. He barely had time to read through the speech, over a hasty meal, before we drove through the inevitable snow storm to Rosthern, a small town north of Saskatoon, in Walter Tucker's constituency. The speech was badly delivered to a small audience of impassive farmers. It must have been close to midnight before we could settle back in the Saskatoon hotel to go through the extended platform document, but it was the kind of work for which Mike could summon up energy however tired he was. The next morning I telephoned a few amendments to Ottawa and felt that the job had been done with all reasonable speed, at least. It proved to have even less immediate influence than I expected. One sign of the strain and disorganization at Liberal headquarters was that the copies of "The Pearson Plan" that came back to me had some pages twice and others not at all. It was, I'm sure, little read and hardly used. Its significance is that the Liberal party's rapid recovery from 1958 to 1962 was not achieved by delay in redefining, positively, where the party stood. While details were refined later, in large measure the new policy of the Liberal party was adopted at once, in 1958, and carried through to the later campaigns and to government.

In 1958 Mike soldiered on through an increasingly hopeless campaign. He stuck to the program and, contrary to John Connolly's fears, the Conservatives did not try to find much fault with the proposals as such; they simply asked why, if they were so good, the Liberals hadn't acted on them when they were in office so long. That was the point that, in 1958, was bound to be effective whatever Liberals said.

Mr Diefenbaker got an additional opening when, late in the campaign, Mike was panicked into putting a gloss on the program. He said it would mean a "tax holiday." Strictly, there was nothing wrong with that. The proposed reduction in tax rates was to apply to the whole 1958 tax year. By the time it could be legislated, payroll deductions would have been made at the higher rates for half the year or more; new tax tables would therefore mean that most people had nothing to pay for some weeks. Nevertheless, bringing out that point late in the campaign made it seem like a new promise that was highly vulnerable to the charge of irresponsibility.

Like most people, I had every expectation of a large Conservative majority in 1958. I thought the Liberals would lose many seats, but not so many as they did in Quebec, and I did not anticipate that CCF members as outstanding as Stanley Knowles and M.J. Coldwell would be swept under the Tory wave. Unable to resist joining in the predictions of which journalists are so fond, I guessed 160 Conservative seats; I was not prepared for 208.

On the morning after I could offer, editorially, only Francis Bacon's consolation: "The good things which belong to prosperity are to be wished, but the good things that belong to adversity are to be admired." Mike's telegram to me was typical of the man: "I could not have been more grateful if the result had been reversed." In a later letter my consolation to him was that he had "salvaged all that was possible and good for the future ... With your leadership, we'll come out all right in time." That was, at the time, more hope than confident prediction.

9 Transition to Kingston

Reduced though it was to a mere forty-eight members, the conduct of opposition in the 1958 Parliament was the least of the Liberal party's problems. For one thing, the CCF had been even more cruelly cut down, in both the number and the quality of its membership, so that there was no challenge to the Liberal role as *the* opposition. Second, though the numbers were small, they included redoubtable parliamentary performers. Mike himself was never a very effective critic; he lacked the taste for it. But Martin, Pickersgill and Chevrier could run circles round most of the Conservative ministers. Above all, opposition in Parliament was increasingly made easy by the confusions, indecisions, and mistakes of the government.

For journalists, opposition is fun, and perhaps particularly fun for a newspaper proprietor of Victor Sifton's nature. Though he did not have the temperament to play a public role, his chief interest was in politics and his disposition was to be critical.

In the internal affairs of the *Free Press*, these were happy days. As a business it was doing increasingly well. Victor Sifton was delighted by my becoming a power in the Liberal party. It was a validation of his judgment in finding me to edit his paper, a restoration of how things had been in the great days of his father and Dafoe. True, the new policies of the Liberal party were rather different from those he had formerly favoured, but he was able to take the change in his stride. "I can live with those" was his comment to me on the convention resolutions and the election platform.

Editorially, involvement with the Liberal party created no immediate problems. I had no reason to write anything that I would not have written anyway. Nevertheless, uneasiness about the potential conflict of interest could not be shaken off. It was a concern less about editorial independence than about the integrity of the news columns. We might in fact avoid bias, but the suspicion of it would certainly be there.

During 1958, therefore, I began to think, indecisively, about a change of occupation. Having been trained in economics and involved in small-scale management at both *The Economist* and the *Free Press*, I had some hankering for inside experience of the larger world of corporate decision-making. The gentleman's understanding with Victor had been that I would plan to stay with the paper for a minimum of five years. This would end early in 1959, so that I could begin to consider moving. It was, however, an extraneous issue that brought me to a decision.

Harry Crowe was a professor at United College, then the struggling forerunner of the University of Winnipeg. While on a sabbatical leave, he wrote to a fellow professor a letter bitingly critical of the college and its administration. Somehow, the letter arrived, not in the hands of its intended recipient, but on the desk of the college principal. He was ill-mannered enough to read it, and ill-advised enough to take it to the college's board of governors. They were even more incensed, and forthwith fired Crowe.

It was an action utterly wrong on two counts: the reason for firing was an offence to academic freedom; and the evidence for firing derived from the illegitimate use of private correspondence. Nevertheless, there was a good deal of support for the college board. The governors of the University of Manitoba were not inclined towards public criticism of their opposite numbers at the junior institution. And the Chancellor of the University was Victor Sifton.

I therefore felt constrained to mute our editorial comment. It was firm in saying that Professor Crowe should not have been fired, but appealed for conciliation rather than denunciation of either side. Some of my friends understandably felt let down by this. Frank Underhill, whose own experience had left him with particularly strong feelings about academic freedom, wrote me a personal letter of pained and fiery complaint. I was not greatly disturbed. Victor was remarkable among publishers in having no outside business interests that could jeopardize the paper's independence. It seemed to me a small price to pay if his one public service activity, as University Chancellor, necessitated unusual circumspection about an issue on which, undoubtedly, I otherwise would have written much more strongly.

However, while I could compromise to this degree on the editorial page, the news columns were another matter. Our reporters had done a good job of digging out the facts of the Crowe story, but their independence of the "front office" was still fragile. Victor's naturally strong emotions were engaged on the side of the United College board, and as the Crowe affair boiled up, with intense feelings on both sides, he found it increasingly irksome to leave the news staff to handle as they thought best the plethora of facts, assertions and statements and the many vehement letters we received. Also, Dick Malone, his assistant on the business side of the paper (and subsequently the architect of both the building and the downfall of the short-lived FP chain of daily newspapers from Montreal to Victoria), became heavily engaged as adviser to the United College board in its troubles. They both wanted to tell the news staff how to do its job. As long as I was present this did not matter. The staff would resist attempts to pressure them behind my back. But it was proved that, as I feared, outside involvement had a price. I returned from a brief absence to find that someone had buckled under pressure; unfair priority had been given to the college administration's side of the story.

This concerned me not only in itself but also for its larger implications. What would happen on some major political issue if I was away in Ottawa working with the Liberal party? There could well be "front office" pressure that the staff could not resist. Our news columns could revert to being instruments of propaganda. I might be powerless in the particular situation, but I could not escape responsibility; it would seem that I was misusing the paper because of my political involvements.

I am not quite sure what I would have done about the particular situation if it had not been for a friend, Sam Freedman (later Chief Justice of Manitoba). At a social gathering the next evening he remarked to me in his measured tones that "this is not the *Free Press*'s finest hour." That seemed to crystallize my feelings. On New Year's Day, 1959, I told Victor that I was going to leave. He was deeply distressed, the more so when in turn each of the two most senior members of the staff declined, in the circumstances, to take my place. One of them came to tell me that the proud Victor had broken down and wept: things had been going so well and he had thoughtlessly messed it all up, for the paper and himself and me. I did the only reasonable thing and agreed to remain as if nothing had happened, for up to the middle of the year if necessary, to give time for restructuring.

Victor facilitated this. It was typical – his reputation as a hard man with money reflected his public appearance more than his private behaviour – that he promptly took an initiative I did not ask for, and made a generous financial arrangement for the interim period. The conclusion of my relations with the *Free Press* was, however, sad. Victor Sifton did not find a successor to his liking. For some time he hoped, according to Grant Dexter's comment to me, that I would change my mind. Great as was my regard for Grant as a journalist, I would not be sure of his objectivity on such a personal matter. In any event, Victor did not approach me directly and I did not contemplate staying. After some months he decided to do what perhaps he had always, with part of his nature, wanted; he took the title of Editor himself. The consequences were not good. Victor was temperamentally unsuited to the role, it was not the way to get good work from others, and the tension told. He died two years later. Meantime, the *Free Press* had largely reverted to its earlier style and policies.

As long as I was working with Victor, we got on well. After I had left, however, he became bitter. He was too realistic not to know that the influence of the *Free Press*, about which he cared most, had diminished. My role in the Liberal party, however, continued. According to Mike

Pearson, to whom he talked, it was the contrast that angered Victor. Shortly before his death he even appealed to Mike to sever connection with me; I was, an amused Pearson informed me, "very dangerous." That was, as Mike pointed out, hard to reconcile with Victor's attitude at the time of the 1958 convention and the subsequent election. But with Victor's death I regretted that I had not tried to mend a relationship that had been important to us both.

For a year or more after moving from the *Free Press*, I concentrated on a new and enjoyable job in business, with Montreal as headquarters. The company of which I was a vice-president, Chemcell, controlled on behalf of Celanese Corporation extensive industrial operations in Mexico, Venezuela, and Colombia, as well as plants in Alberta and Quebec and plants and logging operations, both coastal and interior, in British Columbia. The President was Max Mackenzie, who had been Deputy Minister to C.D. Howe in the great postwar days to 1951. He became a friend from whom I learned much. Other close associates included, as scientific adviser, C.J. Mackenzie, former Chairman of the National Research Council, and the very able T.N. Beaupré, later Chairman of Domtar. Pearson and I kept in touch, but it was a quiet period in the Liberal party. In retrospect, that was a pity. The work of formulating strategy and refining policy would have been better done if it had been begun earlier instead of being compressed almost entirely into 1961. But in 1959–60 the corporals' guard in Ottawa could keep itself busy enough with day-to-day issues; public disillusionment with Diefenbaker was as yet far from the point at which people thought seriously of the enormous Conservative majority melting away in one term; understandably, if unwisely, leading Liberals were not yet in the mood for constructive thinking about what their next government would do and how it could be achieved.

By the summer of 1960, therefore, I was becoming concerned. The situation as I saw it was set out then in a lengthy letter to Jo Grimond, MP, a Scottish friend who had become the leader of the minute British Liberal party. He had sought my comment on a draft statement of policy that he was considering, and I reciprocated with a statement of my own viewpoint at the time. Since that was the background to much that followed, it may be helpful to quote part of the letter. It discussed, among other things, the state of the Liberal party and the need for Mike to make a clear statement of his philosophy and general policy, "which would provide a rallying-point for all the people who want to be liberal reformers but have little guidance as to what that means in the 1960s."

In Canada it is necessary to explain why the Liberal today, without being any less concerned about freedom, would much extend public expenditures on education, health (including medical insurance and sickness benefits), housing and urban renewal. This has to be combined with a national policy for securing more equality among our still very diverse regions. There have to be sound policies for broadening the economy and raising employment levels; for increasing our trade and improving our payments balance; and for giving Canadian defence and foreign policy a satisfactory role in the world.

Primarily, I would say that Liberals need to shift the emphasis of their thinking a good many notches (in our case) towards egalitarianism. That's essential if we really want to regain the radical role that, in Britain, Socialism has muffed and that here is at the moment hopelessly spread among individuals rather than parties. We have to show that we really do want to create a much more equal society. And I would emphasize, too, a more skilful society (more "educated" having rather an odour to it) – which is not only of obvious importance but can have, I think, considerable political appeal.

Indeed, the emphasis on the need for greater human skills, for the maximum use of our brainpower, perhaps helps as much as anything to clear away our nineteenth-century hangover about economic liberalism and gladly accept the more collectivist framework of contemporary economics and administration; the Liberal policy is not to wring our hands over the way that science and universal education are taking the world, but to insist that this necessary collectivist framework can and should be fashioned in such a way as to broaden, not narrow, the individual initiative and responsibility that will be more rewarding to individuals who are more skilful, who have more security and who live in a more equal society.

I discussed with Mike the idea of a statement of political philosophy and policy identified with him personally. As usual, he was receptive to the idea; but it did not come to anything. The kind of things I had in mind were written only in the course of 1961, and then not as personal Pearson statements.

In the summer of 1960 Mike was more interested in the idea of the Kingston conference of "liberally-minded" people. In the form in which it started, it was not new. A similar proposal had first come, as far as I know, from John Connolly. He had written to me about it only a few days after the 1958 election. The precedent in his mind was from the time when Mackenzie King was in opposition and the Port Hope conference, under the sponsoring spirit of Vincent Massey, was held in 1932. In his letter John Connolly suggested a fairly small gathering, "some 50 or 60 people." It was to be an identified party meeting, though informal in the sense that people would be invited because they had ideas rather than because they held positions in the organization. The purpose would be an extensive discussion of Liberal attitudes and policies. It was assumed that the conference would be private, not an affair open to the media.

Like so many ideas, this would have been a good one if it had been implemented at the time proposed. In 1958, or perhaps more realistically in 1959, such a conference might well have provided a helpful push towards an earlier exposition of what the new, Pearsonian Liberal party stood for. To restore a party's credibility in the public mind, after the kind of rejection that had been given to it in 1958, is necessarily a gradual process. If the work of making clear policy statements had begun early in 1960, instead of only during 1961, it seems to me probable that considerably more people would have known, by the time they voted in 1962, that the Liberal party really did stand for something they liked.

However, the idea of a renewal conference lay dormant in 1958 and 1959, and what was actually done in September 1960 was a response to different circumstances.

In the meantime, I returned to an active policy involvement in quite another way. June 1960 saw the "Quiet Revolution" election in Quebec. I played no part except to vote, but of course was as elated as anyone by Jean Lesage's triumph. Shortly afterwards, on 7 July, I received a letter from the new Premier, asking me to call him at 9 AM the following Monday, when he would be at the Windsor Hotel in Montreal and would have time to discuss something he wanted to ask me to do. It turned out to be that I should spend some days at Maison Montmorency, the Dominican retreat house near Quebec City of which Father Georges-Henri Levesque had become the Superior when Premier Duplessis had insisted that such a dangerous radical must be removed from the deanship of social sciences at Laval University.

The reason for the mission was that a federal-provincial conference (in the Diefenbaker years a much rarer event than it has since become) was scheduled for later in July. Jean Lesage wanted to make it the occasion for him to state the outlook of the new Quebec and its role in the Canadian confederation. Remembering our collaboration on federal-provincial issues in earlier years, he wanted me to help prepare this statement. Maurice Lamontagne would also be at Maison Montmorency. The importance of the location was that Lesage and some of his ministers (he attached particular importance to René Levesque and Paul Gérin-Lajoie) could come there in the evenings and discuss the content of the statement.

The plan was carried out with the efficiency that, for some years at least, characterized the Lesage government. It was an extraordinarily stimulating experience, for three reasons: an incidental one was the opportunity for leisurely discussion with Maurice Lamontagne of federal affairs and particularly of our respective papers for the Kingston conference; a second reason was the wonderful personality of Father Levesque; most important was the exhilaration of contact with the able and progressive government that, after so many sterile years under Duplessis, Quebec was now to enjoy.

Since I was not capable of writing in French, my contribution to the work was only to draft a few paragraphs in English and to act as a sounding-board for the other participants' ideas. I can therefore be uninhibited in praising the results. Lesage dominated the federal-provincial meeting and I believe that his main statement, prepared at Maison Montmorency, has stood up well to the test of time as an expression of the viewpoint of many of the people in Quebec who for the past quarter century have been concerned that their own twentieth-century society should be fashioned in the context of a co-operative Canadian federalism.

This was also the time when in New Brunswick the Liberal party, under the new, reform-minded leadership of Louis Robichaud, replaced the Conservative government. It was under the influence of such events that at the beginning of August, writing again to Jo Grimond, I became optimistic: "I now think that if we can put ourselves in a good policy stance, there is a very good chance of achieving the large turnover required to give a Liberal victory in the next general election." That changing mood affected many Liberals and did much to shape the Kingston conference.

Few events in Canadian politics have been as thoroughly misunderstood. Because it was originally billed as a "thinkers' conference" it was regarded as the source of new Liberal policies. It was not. It produced no ideas, subsequently embodied in the 1962 platform, that had not already won party acceptance, in principle if not in detail, in the 1958 resolutions and platforms. What it did do, because it was diverted from the billed intention, was to make the media and the public more aware of those ideas. By 1960 the media were paying attention, whereas in 1958, understandably they were not. For that reason, Kingston was indeed important. Unfortunately, however, its format and its content conformed to the original design. As a result, it included some discussions, particularly one for which I was responsible, that did political harm.

Earlier in the year, I had discussed the planning of the conference in some detail, particularly with Mike and with Mitchell Sharp, who agreed to organize it. The timing was to be early in September, and there seemed to be complete agreement on three points. First, the party organization as such would have no role; indeed, one of the merits of Mitchell as organizer was that he could use the resources of his corporation office in Toronto for management details. Second, those invited would be people who accepted the description "liberally-minded" but might have affiliations with other parties or none. Third, since the purpose was an uninhibited exchange of ideas, the conference would be entirely private; while a few of the participants might be journalists, such as Michael Barkway, Jeanne Sauvé and Jean Edmonds, they would be attending as sympathetic people of ideas and there would be no reporting.

On that basis, I agreed to contribute a major paper on social security, as did Maurice Lamontagne on economic policy. Mitchell was afraid that some of the contributions would be fairly bland (and he was right) and he therefore particularly asked me, and no doubt Maurice, to make sure that ours would provoke discussion. I readily made that promise, in the belief that it related to a private conference. I also did what was asked, as standard routine for a conference in the "academic" spirit, and completed my paper in plenty of time for advance circulation to the participants.

I then went abroad for a family holiday, and returned just in time to drive from Montreal to Kingston with Carl Goldenberg and John Payne. We had a cheerful reunion dinner with old friends, and then I discovered what had happened while I was away.

The literature about the conference had accorded with the planning discussions. The letter of invitation, signed by Mitchell Sharp for the organizing committee, emphasized that this "study conference on national problems" had no official connection with the Liberal party, and that "to ensure an atmosphere of complete freedom of opinion and discussion ... [we are] planning to hold our meetings in private."

Two things changed. The original invitation list was fairly short, but many more people asked to come and in the end some 200 were accepted as "liberally-minded thinkers," which of course meant that most were listeners and the "study session" concept was greatly diluted. Second, the press applied pressure. The conference was taking place just after Labour Day, before the end of the silly season when political journalists are desperate for things to write about. And by this time the Diefenbaker government was generally perceived to be in trouble. The journalists naturally wanted to make as much as possible of the political significance of the conference, and on that basis they demanded the right to be present. Mike became frightened about charges of concealment. At the last moment he buckled to the pressure. I found, on the evening before the conference started, that journalists were to be allowed to attend and report the papers presented to the conference.

I was furious, for two reasons. First, the late change gave an impression of having been caught out. Opening the conference to the press suggested that it really was, and had always been intended to be, a conclave of the Liberal party. If that had been true, it should have been organized very differently. The "study" topics should have been planned to lead to conclusions relevant and practicable for party policy. They were not. Looked at that way, there was much about the conference that was amateurish. But, having gained admission, the press naturally looked at it that way. It made better copy if it was seen as a party occasion, in truth directed to party policy, which the press had virtuously succeeded in uncovering. I could not blame the journalists for that.

But I did blame Mike. The moral is one that I have had to draw all too often. People responsible for running organizations, and people involved in politics more than most, have to recognize that there are strict limitations to the extent to which they can permit themselves the luxury of changing their minds. Often, if they are realistic, they will recognize that yesterday or earlier they made a decision that would have been different if they had then known what they know today. Quite often the best course is then to change the decision. But quite often also, if a series of actions based on the original decision has already been taken, the lesser evil is now to stick with the original decision.

It would have been far better, in 1960, never to have planned Kingston as a closed "study" conference. That would have been all right in 1958 or 1959, but by 1960 there was too much journalistic interest in the Liberal party's policies. By then it would have been better to plan a sizeable and avowedly public conference, open to the press. But that had not been the plan. The last-minute change produced the worst of two worlds.

I had not been angry with Mike before. I should emphasize that I did not feel that I had found feet of clay. That came some years later, with his treatment of Guy Favreau and Walter Gordon. Until 1964, at least, there was nothing basically wrong with the way Mike stood on the ground. What I did feel, for the first time at Kingston and on some subsequent occasions, was that there was a weakness at the knees.

My second reason for anger was that the change of plan was a breach of faith with the people who had prepared papers on the clearly defined basis that they were intended to stimulate off-the-record discussion. For many, the change did not matter; the papers were, as Mitchell had feared, bland enough anyway. But for two of the speakers, and as it happened the two who were closest to Mike, the change did matter.

Maurice Lamontagne, in his excellent paper on economic policy, took a Galbraithian view of administered prices in parts of the private sector and on that basis made the case for a governmental price-review process in such areas. It was a good subject for discussion among economists but it was not developed as a policy proposal for a party conference. It was not central to the main points of the paper. It was, however, gold for commentators well aware of the fears in some quarters that the Liberal party was becoming "socialist." As a result, most of Maurice's paper was given far less attention than it deserved, while the most controversial point was emphasized out of all proportion.

My own case was even worse, as will be explained later. When I found that the rules for the conference had been changed without notice, my first impulse was to walk out. I was dissuaded by Walter Gordon. He sympathized with my objections to the change in the nature of the conference. But with his usual calm rationality he pointed out that, since I had virtuously prepared my paper in advance, it had already been circulated. It might not be the paper I would have written for a public occasion, but for good or ill I was stuck with it. Today was too late to withdraw. Indignant though I was, I had to recognize the force of the logic. I decided to swallow my anger and stay.

Once the conference had become public, mine was the paper that was bound to attract most attention, because it was more closely related than others to bread-and-butter political issues. Moreover, it was at the cutting edge of what, at least in the minds of most political commentators, was then the central issue for the future of the Liberal party. The CCF was in the process of turning itself into the NDP. It hoped to broaden and modernize its appeal to the point of replacing the Liberals as the alternative to the Tories.

After the slaughter of 1958 that did not seem to be an impossible dream. Liberal parties had disappeared in other countries. The emasculated Canadian party – with, as many people saw it, a charming but ineffective leader – could well be squeezed to nothing between Diefenbaker's populist Conservative party and a "new" party, with the anticipated strong leadership of Tommy Douglas, that could appeal not only to traditional trade unionists and much of the western farm vote but also more broadly to the increasing numbers of young, white-collar and prosperous blue-collar, urban voters. Whether this happened would depend chiefly on whether the Liberals or the NDP made the better impression with their economic and social policies. In 1960, however, the media still had the mind-set of the 1950s; the strength of the Canadian economy, subject to only minor blips, was pretty well taken for granted. Anyway, economic issues were underemphasized by political commentators, if only because in those days very few understood them. The cutting issues were therefore largely identified with social policy.

My paper had not, however, been written with calculations of party strategy in mind. It was designed for the kind of private, "intellectual" gathering that Kingston had been supposed to be. The title – "Towards a Philosophy of Social Security" – summed it up. A good deal was devoted to my favourite theoretical theme: freedom is not just the absence of constraint but, equally, the opportunity to act. For anyone except a hermit, the opportunities of the individual depend on the society in which he or she lives. In contemporary society, with all the interdependence that is inherent in advanced technology, much of what we can do, as consumers as well as producers, is not individual but collective. We have to make the decisions about it as a society. That is to say, a good deal of our consumption necessarily takes place through the expenditures of government. In this sense – not in the socialist sense that government should own the means of production – freedom for the individual does not lie in pushing back the increased role of government. If we are concerned that people as a whole, not privileged groups, should truly enjoy more freedom, we have to make more collective provision to protect people against poverty-inducing disasters and to make positive opportunities accessible to all. In short, the philosophical position was one that at the time might have been most readily identified as Galbraithian.

From that position, I proposed an agenda for the directions of development to which we should give priority. A reasonable period to plan for was eight years, on the grounds that one should aim for two terms of progressive government against each one of conservative government – which was my way of identifying my liberalism without expressing more partisanship than I felt. The agenda had eleven items:

• Medicare, which I defined as protection against financially crippling costs of illness. Government should pay the individual's medical bills on a sliding scale related to income: all or virtually all at the lowest income levels, a declining proportion at higher incomes.

• Sickness insurance: that is, there should be the same level of income-maintenance for sick people as for those who are unemployed for other reasons.

• Reshaping of unemployment insurance, to make it also a protection against disaster. A sound system would not be much concerned with short-term unemployment. Initial benefits (say, for two months) could be at a token level. But instead of benefit entitlements running out, if unemployment is prolonged, there should be a social obligation to provide a high level of income maintenance, subject to willingness to accept job mobility and undertake training; these conditions would be tough if general unemployment levels are low, but subject to realistic relaxation as and when unemployment becomes more severe.

• Extensive employment training.

• Regional development, because it is economically wasteful and socially disruptive to require so much mobility of people that substantial communities quickly decay. Government should moderate adjustments by public investments and inducements to move some jobs to where the workers are.

- Major investment in the renewal of urban cores.

- More public housing for rent, in order to facilitate mobility. It should not, however, be subsidized, except where it is necessary to the removal of slums as part of urban renewal schemes.

- Better schools, smaller classes, more and better paid teachers (this was 1960!) in the public school system.

- Equality of opportunity for university education, approached through national scholarships and backed by capital expenditures on improving university facilities.

- Rather than "the blanket of bigger pensions and family allowances for all" (which I did not regard as priorities), a concerted effort greatly to enhance social services and especially "hard-case" social work. This would involve federal assistance not only to provinces and municipalities but also to voluntary agencies.

- "World welfare": foreign aid as we then knew it was, I argued, only a small step towards "the world-wide welfare economy that is to come." Rising expectations in Asia, Africa, and South America were "the most fundamental of all the revolutionary changes now taking place in the fabric of our societies." To assist the economic progress of the Third World was the most profitable investment the richer countries could make, because it was the essential basis for a secure world for us all to live in. I suggested that Canada's aid might also be a direct benefit to us, because it could help us to build to an economic scale some of the manufacturing industries essential to diversify our employment. But whether we achieved that or not, "a good deal more Canadian tax money will have to go, and should go, to aid for the under-developed areas of the world."

I pointed out that this was an agenda for Canadian government as a whole, federal, provincial, and municipal. The required federal-provincial negotiation and co-operation was a subject for a discussion of its own. I did not see Kingston as the occasion for building a federal political platform.

Looking back now, one cannot see anything remarkable about the proposed agenda. Its items were little more than indications of directions that were in fact followed, without much controversy, in the sixties and seventies. What Kingston produced was pretty tame stuff. But it was billed as a "thinkers' conference," a rare event in Canadian politics; the media were eager for anti-Diefenbaker straws; and speculation about the coming Liberal/NDP struggle made good copy. Politicians are prone to follow media assessments, and in this instance academics have had reason for the same inclination; they have a natural bias towards believing that a conference of "thinkers" has formative importance.

If a party needed such a gathering to give it ideas, it would be broken down beyond any hope of rebuilding. Access to ideas is the least of the problems of politicians of any competence at all. The real problem is to identify the ideas that are right for the times and the party's role in those times; to develop them into policies that can be brought home to marginal voters as ones that will be significant, desirable improvements for them and for the country; and to mould those policies into a general party stance that people can find credible.

All that is an undertaking that can be performed only by people within the core of the party. It requires, certainly, that they be open to ideas and perceptive of those whose time is near; it requires knowledge of the way government programs operate; it requires political talents, including the ability to present ideas and policies in simple, straightforward ways; it requires an ability to make decisions at the right time, which is the talent least frequently combined with the others. The process may be assisted by consultation with experts and "thinkers," perhaps by small, private conferences of the kind John Connolly had proposed. But it is quite unrealistic to suppose that a gathering of hundreds of heterogenous "thinkers", talking in the glare of media publicity, can contribute anything to the process.

I do not mean that a conference of the Kingston kind should not have been held. It showed that the Liberal party was alive and kicking. But it would have done so much more effectively, and without its ill side effects, if from the beginning it had been conceived and planned for that purpose, not converted to a media event at the last moment.

Writing as I thought for a different conference, I was dissatisfied when I had expounded my analysis and philosophy of social security, described an agenda of priority measures, and written the obvious general comments about the financing of those measures. They should not be implemented, I argued, faster than could be financed at the level of revenues that an acceptable structure and level of taxation would yield in a fully employed economy. That was not, for the short run at least, a bothersome restriction. The economy was operating well below capacity, but even so the federal deficit was not very large. It seemed to me that the realistic rate of implementation of the measures I was proposing would create financing requirements little if any greater than the buoyant revenue from existing tax levels in conditions of full employment and economic growth. I was in favour of reforming the tax structure, for the sake of both fairness and economic efficiency, but to do so was not critical to the agenda with which the social security paper was concerned.

I was tempted to stop there. Certainly I would have stopped if I had known that Kingston was to be a public conference. But in the circumstances at the time of writing, I was dissatisfied. Mitchell Sharp's fear that the papers would be too bland was going to be proved correct. For "thinkers" there was nothing very novel about my philosophizing, and the agenda added little to what I had written before. To fulfil my promise to be controversial, something had to be added. And the logical addition was more discussion of taxation.

At that time I had temporarily, and to my subsequent regret, put aside the idea of restructuring the corporate income tax to induce the distribution of profits to shareholders. In the absence of that, I did not think that the personal income tax should be markedly more progressive. (This was before it was perverted by the tax shelters created in such profusion during the Trudeau years.) I therefore argued that, if more revenue was needed, there were two more acceptable ways to raise it.

One was to abolish the rather ineffective succession duties that were then levied and to replace them by a substantial inheritance tax. This should not be levied on transfers between spouses, and orphans under the age of twenty-one should also be entitled to some relief. But all other inheritances and gifts should be subject to a tax on the recipient, levied on the lifetime amount received. There would be a reasonable exemption level – I suggested $100,000 – but above that quite a steep, progressive tax.

This was not calculated to endear me to the richer friends of the Liberal party, and the second proposal was more radical. If corporations were going to continue to reinvest large undistributed profits, then government should at least lessen the bias of the tax system towards large corporations by limiting the privilege of businesses virtually to decide for themselves what expenses could be deducted from profits to determine taxable income. I identified the conspicuous target, in the sense of the perquisites for owners and executives commonly undertaken in the spirit that the government was paying half anyway, and which substantially lessened the real redistributive effect of the personal tax structure.

More important than this conspicuous consumption, however, were the levels of promotion, merchandising, and advertising expenditure. For the economy as a whole, they were largely wasteful; they would not be undertaken on anything near the same scale in the genuinely competitive conditions of economic theory. In the real world they were inflated by the calculation that half of them came out of taxation, not net profit, and in real terms they were a diversion of talents that could be more productively employed. I suggested that expenditures on the service of selling were as appropriate for special taxation as alcohol and tobacco. The simple way to do it would be to set limits to the degree to which such expenditures, notably advertising, were recognized as deductible expenditures in arriving at taxable profits.

That was certainly controversial, though it was not lighthearted on my part. As much now as then, I think these are serious topics for discussion. Certainly we would have, in my view, a better society if large inheritances and gifts were substantially taxed. And I think it at least likely that we would have a more innovative and genuinely competitive economy, with the scales less weighted in favour of established corporations, if there were limits to the tax recognition of promotion and advertising expense in relation to other costs.

But such suggestions, whatever their worth in the long run, were appropriate for the Kingston conference that I had thought I was writing for, not the conference that was. They were fine for controversy in academic circles; they were not ideas whose time had come politically. Much more preparation within the world of ideas would have been required before the advertising proposal could sensibly be suggested at a public conference that was being linked by the media to the development of a party platform.

The consequence was inevitable. Controversy was indeed stirred, not in the conference itself but in the media. It is the nature of the mirror world of journalism that the media pay exaggerated attention to anything that particularly concerns the media, and most – nowadays, in Canada, an average of about 80 per cent – of the total revenue of daily newspapers comes from advertising. I could hardly have made myself a greater heretic, condemned in editorials across the country. More importantly, the attention given to the advertising tax, as it was labelled, inevitably meant that my social security agenda got much less attention than the media would otherwise have given it – attention which from most of the journalists would have been, I have no doubt, warmly favourable.

Most important of all was the consequence for Mike Pearson. The two Kingston papers that attracted most attention were those of two of his closest associates; and both were open to the criticisms, from the viewpoint of unideological, practical politicians, that we were naïve idealists, and that we were, in the eyes of the business community, dangerous radicals if not socialists. The second point did not bother me much, but the first was deeply offensive to my pride. As a journalist, I had thought that I could be interested in ideas while recognizing which were practicable. It was ironical that, when becoming involved in politics, I should have been trapped into what was bound to appear, to all but the few who knew the story, as a lack of the basic understanding that politics is the art of the possible. Mike had an off-the-record session with the press at Kingston. He said (some of the journalists told me; I was not present) that mine was "the most intellectually brilliant" paper, but that was no consolation for the confusion of purpose that, I felt, had marred it and the conference.

There was, however, a positive side. The most immediately significant reaction was that of William Mahoney, Canadian National Director of the Steelworkers, who attended as the tough spokesman of English-Canadian trade unionism. (Jean Marchand was present from Quebec.) Mr Mahoney amended his prepared text to praise my paper and say "if the Liberal Party ... comes up with a policy that implements the program outlined by Mr Kent, this could well be a place where the aims of organized labor and the aims of the Liberal Party could coincide."

Walter Gordon was more forthright. He came across to me after the social security session saying, "I must shake the hand that has strangled the New Party before it's born." There was, of course, some wishful thinking in the comment, but the handshake was the beginning of an alliance that never afterwards faltered. To that point Walter and I had been suspicious of each other as competing influences on Mike. I had been critical – too critical, as I noted earlier – of his Royal Commission report, and had seen him as too much a Bay Street man. He had reciprocated by seeing me as an old-fashioned liberal.

At Kingston we recognized that we had been wrong about each other, and thereafter occasional disagreements never shook our friendship and co-operation. I shall have much more to say about that, and in the process will explain my assessment that the Liberal party as it was remade by 1962 was more the party of Walter Gordon than of Mike Pearson. It was unfortunate indeed for Canada that this did not remain true in 1963 and in the government that followed. Among all the people in public life that I have known, in Canada and elsewhere, there is none for whom I have such unstinted admiration and deep regard as for Walter Gordon. In opposition and in government, he was consistently outstanding in many things: in his wholehearted devotion to the public interest as he saw it; in the openness of his mind; in his intellectual honesty; in the quickness of his perceptions; in his humanity and good humour; in his ability to concentrate on essentials; in his quiet determination to get things done; in the efficiency of his working procedures and organizational methods; in his calmness equally in triumph and adversity; above all, in his courage. He could make mistakes, of course, but never was there anything mean or narrow about his attitudes, his judgments or his decisions. His place in Canadian history will be far larger than he was given credit for at the time.

Other personal contacts at Kingston also proved to be of future importance, in particular with Claude Morin, then a professor at Laval. Our papers were very different in style but they were philosophically compatible. That would not have been so if we had been discussing the comparative roles of federal and provincial governments, but we were not. The compatibility of purpose for government taken as a whole stood us in good stead when, a few years later, we were negotiating intensively with each other on behalf of the governments of Canada and Quebec.

10 *Rallying*

Though it would have been much better if it had been planned to be what it turned out to be, the Kingston conference had important benefits. It was sufficiently different from most party political processes to generate considerable enthusiasm among many participants and to stir the interest of many more people. It inspired a widening of the group of new activists within the party and had some energizing effect on the party's surviving establishment.

In particular, Kingston, because of both its virtues and its faults, stimulated interest in the idea of a National Liberal Rally, an official party gathering to discuss policy, to be held in Ottawa in January 1961. Paul Hellyer was appointed chairman and did a remarkable job of organization for a meeting that turned out to have over 2,000 participants. The Rally marked Walter Gordon's formal entry into politics. Despite his close friendship with Mike and his strong concerns about public policy, Walter had reservations about partisan identification. He did not want to become committed without reasonable confidence that the Liberal party was capable of adopting and carrying out policies with which he was comfortable. In the course of the summer of 1960 he resolved his doubts. More perhaps than anyone, he took heart from the Kingston conference and plunged enthusiastically into the role of chairman of the Rally's policy committee.

His first step, a few weeks after Kingston, was to gather a small group to do preparatory work on the policy statements. This time, of course, there was no question of privacy. Indeed, unlike most meetings of political parties, the Rally was to be completely open: the press could sit in on all the policy committees as well as the plenary sessions. Resolutions were invited from all units of the party, and they arrived in the hundreds. Systematic preparation was necessary if the resulting output from so large a three-day meeting was to be other than chaotic. Walter solicited advance work from a number of individuals, but the core group settled down to be Walter, Maurice Lamontagne, Bob Fowler, Maurice Sauvé, and myself.

The resolutions were to be divided into subject areas, for each of which there was to be a committee at the Rally. The advance task was to prepare what we called a "working paper" for each committee. The hope was that these could be seen as composite drafts, embracing as much as possible of the substance of the "grass-roots" resolutions that could be expected, but at the same time avoiding large inconsistencies with party policies as they had been previously declared. The freewheeling discussions of so large a conference were bound to result in resolutions containing more timber than could be incorporated in a party platform. But the preparatory work made it possible both to moderate the number of parochial or clearly impracticable suggestions that emerged, and, also, to ensure that the large body of resolutions that was the Rally's output – in the end, thirty-nine pages of single-space typing – was, by political standards, coherent.

In structuring the Rally, the basic decision was how to divide up policy issues into topics for committees. That would do much to determine the flavour and direction of the resolutions. The core group readily agreed to have separate policy committees on the three social policy issues that we regarded as priorities: health; the skilled society (that is, vocational training and university scholarships); better homes and towns (that is, housing and urban redevelopment). There was a general grouping for "other social security." Economic policies were also well subdivided among committees on unemployment, fiscal and monetary policy, trade, small business, and so on. In all, there were, in the end, twenty-one committees.

The preparatory group first met in late October; from then to Christmas, meetings and drafting work pretty fully occupied my weekends. We had long discussions that were not less vigorous for being generally harmonious. Most of the writing fell to me. The reward for the work was that a good number of the points to which I attached priority proved to fit with the predominant sentiments of the delegates to the Rally.

Most important was the "Plan for Health," which got top billing. It promised comprehensive medical care, including drugs, to be financed from general federal taxation rather than the regressive device of a premium. In the interval after the Kingston conference I had thought of what seemed and still seems to me a satisfactory way of achieving what I had been looking for since the discussion of hospital insurance in 1955–6: that is to say, a way of making health services universally available but subject to a financial control that enables medical priorities to be respected. The ready availability of service should not mean that the quality of care where it is most needed may be diluted because resources are diverted to attend to the minor or non-existent ailments of people who tend to overuse a "free" service. The financial restraints commonly adopted or suggested – forms of co-insurance, partial but fixed charges, extra billing by doctors – are flawed. If they are high enough to be a restraint for people with middle and large incomes, they become an impenetrable obstacle to some of the care, and particularly to preventive care, genuinely needed by people on low incomes.

My objective was a financial control better adjusted to ability to pay. The proposal – warmly approved by the Rally – was that government would pay all doctors' and druggists' bills but would make a return of the total, for each individual, which would then be included on his or her tax form as an item of income. The effect would be, of course, that people with low incomes – below the taxable level – would get all their medical attention without cost while richer people would pay the proportion that is "fair" by the standards embodied in marginal tax rates.

The merits of this depend, it should be said, on two riders about the tax system. First, there would have to be adequate arrangements for forward averaging, so that a person who incurs heavy medical costs does not thereby have his or her deemed total income, for tax purposes, increased by more than some ceiling proportion in any one year. Second, the tax system would have to be effectively progressive; it must be free, as it was in 1960 more than it is now, of devices that enable some people with large incomes to remove much or all of those incomes from the taxable category. The fairness of all social measures depends on the structure of the tax system.

Subject to those riders, I think that this part of the Rally plan had very great merit. Unfortunately, as I shall discuss later, it was lost in the confusions of politics. Four years further on, when we came to medicare legislation, the complexities of federal-provincial relations submerged any such form of financial control.

At the time, satisfaction with the resolution on health was paralleled by the Rally's adoption of the proposals that I labelled "The Skilled Society." They asserted the principle of ensuring that "no young men and women are shut off, by lack of funds, from education that they have the ability and ambition to use to their own and the country's advantage. Liberalism requires equality of opportunity, and therefore education at all levels should be free." As one step to this objective, the scholarship and loan plans of the 1958 election platform were reaffirmed. On vocational and technological training, the resolution declared that "large extensions and improvements" were "a government investment that deserves higher priority than it has yet been given." We were more specific than before. "A new Liberal government will set up a Canadian Vocational Training Organization" to help provincial governments with "financial assistance, expert advice and specialized organization for establishing technical and vocational training courses." Most importantly, there would be an incentive for retraining, particularly for the unemployed, "by guaranteeing to them an adequate living allowance during the training period."

Many of the other resolutions – on "Better Towns and Homes," on immediate measures against unemployment, on longer-term economic policy ("A Vigorous and Expanding Economy"), on the limitation of election expenses and their payment from the treasury – were also highly satisfactory in the form in which they were passed at the Rally. The victory of the party's progressives over its conservatives was as complete as I wished. Indeed, I found myself at the end concerned that too much had been committed.

Ironically, the issue on which I fought a losing battle at the Rally was one on which I wished to limit the proposals for social security. In the Kingston paper, while admitting that pensions were in need of improvement, I had excluded any major early steps from my agenda, on the argument that they were a lower priority than medicare, scholarships, training, and urban renewal. The "working paper" from our preparatory group reflected this view. Its only specific proposal for pensions was that the qualifying age for the old-age assistance then available would be lowered from sixty-five to sixty for widows and spinsters. Many delegates to the Rally wanted much more. The compromise wording that eventually emerged was: "The pensions presently available to many older persons are inadequate. This deficiency can be remedied either by a direct increase in monthly payments under the present Old Age Security system or by a new contributory scheme, if this can be worked out with the approval of the provinces on a sound actuarial basis. A major objective that should be given high priority is to lower the starting age of old age pensions to 65." It was a vague statement but it was to have large implications for future policy and for my work in particular.

However, the one Rally resolution that contained the seeds of major future controversy within the Liberal party concerned defence. The preparatory group had ducked this issue; we asked that the "working paper" drafts on foreign policy and on defence should come from Mike himself. The Rally delegates, however, were boisterous. Defenders of a careful position had a hard time, but they maintained direct communication with the leader and the resolution that was eventually passed had been given his specific approval. On the most emotional issue, nuclear weapons, there was a somewhat contorted compromise. On one hand, it allowed for the possibility that "Canadian forces under NATO command" might possess "nuclear weapons solely for defensive tactical use" provided that the weapons were "under exclusive NATO control, not that of any single member state."

The emphasis on NATO – which Mike, in reflection of his original ambitions for it, always thought of as an organization for international co-operation as much as a military alliance – enabled this to be squared with a firm "anti-proliferation" statement. This was the other hand: "A new Liberal government therefore should not acquire, manufacture, or use such weapons either under separate Canadian control or under joint US-Canadian control." In other words, the Bomarc missiles in Canada should not be armed with nuclear warheads. It was on this that Mike, two years later, was to change his mind and thereby make, in my judgment, a major mistake.

At the time the Rally was a triumph. The delegates went back to their constituencies full of enthusiasm for a Pearson government and rising hope that it would indeed replace, at an election within a year or so, what more and more people, and particularly younger urban people, were coming to see as a government that was ineffective or worse. Activists began to prepare for the election, looking for able candidates and building organizations. A very strong group, centred in Toronto, included such people as Royce Frith, Dan Lang, Keith Davey and David Anderson. They were greatly aided by Walter Gordon's involvement. My old friends in Manitoba were also hard at work, with Joe O'Sullivan and John Lamont taking the lead in organization. Enthusiasm was perhaps at the highest pitch in British Columbia, where John Nichol and Hugh Martin were leading personalities.

Because the Liberal party has been so successful in winning elections and governing Canada most of the time, it is commonly regarded, not only from outside but by close observers and even by participants, as a powerful organization with unlimited powers of recuperation; when it suffers setbacks it will always make a quick comeback. The remarkable recovery between the 1958 and 1962 elections is taken as an outstanding example, and no doubt gives heart to those struggling to recover from the comparably crushing defeat of 1984.

I suspect that in fact the strength of the Liberal organization in the early 1980s was the same as it had been in the 1950s. That is, it was based almost entirely on the holding of power. When power was taken away, the organization turned out to be almost non-existent. The financial backers and the lawyers and others who had profitably combined their business with political work disappeared, with few exceptions, into the

woodwork. Of the ministers who had lost their seats, only the youngest –
Paul Hellyer, who had been in the Cabinet for a mere four months –
returned to active politics. The remaking of the Liberal party was mostly
the work of people who had previously had minor roles or none at all.

Mike Pearson, it is true, had been a Minister but he had come to that
from the civil service and before 1958 his involvement in party work had
been minimal indeed. Walter Gordon – who was the chief remaker – had
had no previous involvement in party politics at all. There were a few
important old hands in Parliament, and some elsewhere, but very many
of the candidates and principal workers of the 1962 campaign were either
new to the party or had before been very junior in it.

There were surviving organizations of a sort, at Ottawa, in the provinces and in the constituencies, but most of them were mere shells. They
became organizations again only as new people took them over. At first
that happened with painful slowness. The takeovers did not begin to be
numerous until 1960; they became a flood during 1961. Only in form was
the process one of renewing and strengthening continuing organizations.
In substance it was the building of a new organization, by new people,
from the ground up. It was not until the 1962 election campaign, and even
more after that near success had indicated the probability of another
Liberal government soon, that the faithful few among the people of the
fifties were rejoined by the many who had been on the sidelines. Some
commentators have written as if there was an army of Grits who, after
1958, laid themselves down to bleed a while and then rose up again as the
same army. That illusion was given some semblance of reality not only
by the continuity of the paper structures but, even more, by the reap-
pearance of many of the old soldiers in 1962. But when they reappeared
they were no longer captains. Some assumed, as their right, a degree of
eminence which always results in the appearance of deference by others.
In truth, however, their roles were generally those of armchair quarter-
backs whose talk was listened to only among themselves.

Canada is too diverse for such generalizations to be stated entirely
without qualification. In the renewal of the Liberal party, Ontario made
the running. Somewhat later, the takeover by new people was almost as
complete in British Columbia, New Brunswick, Manitoba, and Alberta.
Nova Scotia was slower. In Newfoundland, the Liberal party was and
remained the Smallwood party, and it was not until 1963 that its federal
representation took on a changed character. In Saskatchewan also, for
different reasons of provincial politics, the change was slow and never
complete. Above all, in Quebec, where the old organization was on
paper stronger than anywhere else, very little change was achieved until
after the shock of the Créditiste surge in the 1962 election, and there was
not a thorough takeover until 1965.

These diversities complicated the remaking of the Liberal party of Canada, but in no way altered the nature of the process. Ontario's dynamism quickly reinforced the change at the centre, and that in turn fostered the takeovers in other provinces; the significant differences were in timing and, of course, in the electoral results. The dominant characteristic of the rebuilding, however, was a large change in personnel. And most of the new people, particularly the most energetic, became enthusiastically involved because the party offered, from the beginning of the process, a worthwhile goal: not just to throw the existing government out and gain power, but positive ideas as to what a new Liberal government would do with its power.

The most innovative expression of the enthusiasm originated in the Toronto group. It was "Campaign College": a series of seminars for candidates and principal constituency workers. The content provided a good balance of why and how, of the case for a Liberal government and the practicalities of campaigning: organization, budgeting, managing time to attend to priorities, advertising, projecting on television. I was asked to contribute the opening paper on issues.

In the spirit of the project, the title was "How to present and stick to national issues." At most of the college sessions this paper was presented by Royce Frith, and he did it with enormous verve. In effect, it was a statement – though without, at the time it was written, official endorsement – of campaign strategy, and is therefore summarized here in some detail. The starting point was: "Good election planning means separating out, from among all the potential national issues, those that are good for us. The party that is likely to win in the election is the party that succeeds in establishing *its* issues – the ones that are to its advantage – as *the* dominant issues in the minds of the voters."

To do that was a matter of timing and of concentration. We should get in early with at least some of our issues, to get them established in the public mind and put opponents on the defensive. Second, we should resist the temptation of politicians, particularly in the heat of an election campaign, to hammer away at anything on which they think they have the advantage: "Campaigning means winning votes, not arguments." Therefore, "the only issues that matter, rationally, are those that a significant number of voters regard as important enough to influence the way they vote." We shouldn't waste effort on other issues, however good the case we could make. And we should recognize, realistically, that there were some issues on which the other parties had a good case and all the argument in the world wouldn't alter that; rather than be drawn into elaborate debate, we should stick to short, simple comments which would play down, as far as was practicable, the relative importance of such issues.

Within this framework, the paper discussed the possible issues. Mr Diefenbaker had been saying that *the* issue would be free enterprise versus socialism. We should treat that as irrelevant. Canada had and would have a mixed economy, responding to our particular Canadian needs, and few votes would swing on the basis of abstract ideologies. In the same spirit, we should campaign against the NDP only in those few constituencies where its strength made it our main opponent. Nationally, the issues were Liberal or Conservative. Our program, "not anything the New Party offers, says or threatens," was the alternative to continuation of the existing government.

I then turned to the basic argument within the party. "Some Liberals would have us concentrate pretty completely" on criticizing the Conservative record and say little about what we would do. I accepted the truism that governments largely defeat themselves and the Diefenbaker government had by now gone a long way down that road. But it did *not* follow that "a campaign of criticism of the government will in itself get out the votes for us. It isn't only governments that people get fed up with. They can dislike opposition parties too ... It's not so very long ago that people got mad with us, decided we'd been there too long, had become remote, inactive, arrogant, etc. And since then they haven't quite known what to make of us. We've seemed pretty mixed up."

Floating voters were therefore rather cautious about accepting our criticisms of the government. They were disappointed in it, but they didn't think it had done as badly as Liberals said. If we attacked it fiercely for everything under the sun, people wondered whether it wasn't just the angry fault-finding of "outs" who badly wanted in. We were liable to be seen as "carping and unprincipled critics. And that people don't like." Mr Diefenbaker had caught this with his criticism of Liberals "spreading doom and gloom for profit." It was a good line. "There's no way of arguing an answer. If people feel that it applies to what we're saying, it will stick and it will hurt us badly. The only way to handle this one is not to let it apply."

None of this meant, of course, that the Conservatives were not to be criticized. The question was how. We should criticize what *had* happened to the country, pointing particularly to unemployment, but we shouldn't make dire predictions about the country going further to the dogs. The spirit of the criticism should not be that the Tories are doing something and it's shameful; instead we should start by saying what the country needs and that we would do it, *then* attack the Tories for not doing it or doing something opposite.

"In sum, attacking the government's record isn't enough of an election issue for us. The national issues we choose should be positive Liberal policies: what we will do. Our criticism of the government must be based on those policies and won't be effective without them."

The rest of the paper followed obviously and does not need summary because it simply identified, from the Rally resolutions, the policies for national development, employment, health, and education that should be given priority as *the* issues.

To state this strategy was all very well, for party activists. For nearly two years, as things turned out, it was the approach that Walter and I had to go on repeatedly urging, with fluctuating degrees of success. The constant worry was whether the party as a whole would follow it.

In all that he said to me and to Walter, and no doubt to some others, Mike appeared fully to endorse the strategy and policies on which we and the other activists were working with the full backing of party sentiment, as it had been demonstrated at the Rally. But for several months afterwards Mike seemed to go into a personal slump. The enthusiasm in the constituencies, and particularly among Walter's collaborators, was not matched by any sense of clear policy, of decision-making and organization-building in Ottawa.

Few if any of Mike's speeches provided a coherent reflection of the strategy that he had apparently endorsed. When he was in good form he seemed unable to resist quipping attacks on the Conservatives, of the kind that some politicians can make amusing and use to win support, but which from Mike somehow did nothing but cast doubt on his seriousness. While he spoke in favour of the main policies approved at the Rally, he often wrapped them in so many words that his support seemed guarded and, worse, their impact on public opinion was blunted. Above all, he appeared unwilling or unable to act on the proposition that criticism of the government should be tied to positive Liberal policies. The reason, I think, was not lack of intellectual conviction on the point but his temperamental difficulty in putting his personality into the role of critic. Unfortunately, since an opposition leader at that point had to do a good deal of criticizing, the practical effect was that he gave the impression of an all-over-the-lot, carping critic.

Some of his colleagues made it worse. A particularly unfortunate example related to the exchange rate of the Canadian dollar. The Rally resolutions had been quite forthright in championing moderately more expansionist financial and monetary policies and had criticized the Conservatives for policies that produced too high an exchange rate. But when later in 1961 the rate began to fall, instead of seizing on this as a belated conversion to sensible Liberal policy, Mike's wandering comments were of the "view with alarm" kind, while Jack Pickersgill beside him tore up a dollar bill. I almost tore out my hair in frustration that we should so much help Diefenbaker's "doom and gloom" charge to stick, as it clearly did with quite a lot of voters.

This criticism has been stated from the viewpoint of the party's activists. Among them there was a bit of despair and a lot of quiet grumbling about Mike's lack of leadership.

To this day, I am not sure what was the relative importance of the various factors that inhibited Mike as an opposition leader. One certainly was that he was never comfortable in Parliament. Leading the opposition there imposed on him a strain that was exhausting. Partly for that reason, and with the conviction from which he never escaped that what was hard for you was good for you, he tended to concentrate too much on parliamentary affairs. In 1961 they included the drama of the Coyne affair, which he handled very well. But the price was that parliamentary preoccupations encouraged him to put off thinking much about the election campaign, which anyway held no relish for him.

Of comparable importance, probably, was the pressure on Mike from the people who did not like the policies embodied in the resolutions of a Rally that, deliberately sensitive as it was to sidewalk opinion, was seen as having moved the party leftward. In fact it had done little more than confirm the 1958 move; but now Liberal policies were seen as mattering.

Though their voices had been extremely muted at the Rally, the business establishment and the more cautious and conservative elements within the party reacted afterwards. Mike was subjected to many appeals to slow down, if not to stamp on, the alleged move to the left.

The result was that nothing happened, for most of 1961, publicly. Behind the scenes, Walter and I and others were working to refine the Rally resolutions into an agenda of government, with more precision and practical detail, with a setting of priorities and some rounding out to make a coherent platform. Others, still further behind the scenes, were working to obscure the Rally resolutions.

This was often described, and indeed thought of by the participants, as a struggle between the "left" and "right" wings of the party. The reality was more complex. It is true that there always were within the party people of conservative mind who did not want Canada to have, for example, medicare; their numbers increased, though not to any extent their importance, as former Liberals returned to activity. Throughout, however, the ideological conservatives were mostly people not actively engaged in politics; many were the business "friends" of the party, those whom I used to call "the men who come to lunch." They were a nuisance, because they worried Mike Pearson and wasted time for many of us, but there was never much danger that they would succeed in staying to dinner, in getting measures such as medicare taken out of the program.

The real battle was fought in more pragmatic terms. There were some important active politicians who would have privately preferred that the Liberal party had never expressed itself in favour of medicare, but they never suggested that we should switch to being against it. Their plea was that we not say of medicare that its time had definitely come. Within party conclaves, as distinct from at the lunch table, the struggle was therefore conducted not as an ideological debate but as a difference about the most effective electoral strategy: whether we were more likely to win if we were precise about our policies or if we were vague. The debate between John Connolly and me in Mike's sitting room in February 1958 was replayed, with variations, time and time again.

The correct classification, as I saw it, was not into ideological "left" and "right" wings, but into "doers" and "drifters." That is, the difference was between those who wanted power in order to do certain things, for which popular endorsement must therefore be obtained by means of a definite election platform; and those who thought that the Liberal party could and should return to power by demonstrating the faults of Diefenbaker, with whom people were fed up, and it could then best govern by deciding what to do in its wisdom as it went along.

That was the battle of which I was at the centre. Its tensions were illustrated by the reactions to a speech I made in Winnipeg in April 1961. The occasion was the leadership convention of the provincial Liberal party, now in opposition. To my great pleasure, it elected Gildas Molgat as provincial leader in succession to ex-Premier Campbell. Seven years earlier, when new to Winnipeg, I had thought that a very dull Legislature contained two able, younger members: Roblin on the Conservative side, Molgat on the Liberal side. A Manitoba in which they were the contenders for power was a province which had at last moved into the postwar world.

While my sympathies were not secret, I was not involved in the provincial leadership issue, but I had been asked to be the speaker at the session set aside for federal issues. The speech was an exposition of the principal Rally policies, but with an emphasis adjusted to the audience in one of the more conservative parts of the country: I emphasized what I considered to be the realism and "soundness" of Liberal policies for employment and health care in particular. Some of my Ontario friends objected afterwards that I had given far too much impression of caution.

But I also had a letter from Jack Pickersgill. Judy LaMarsh, who had been at the convention, had told him that the speech had been "very well received." Jack, while saying that "your thesis is one I accept almost without amendment", went on:

The only aspect of the matter that worries me is the public relations aspect, not of your speech itself but of the presentation in general of the thesis it embodies. It is a nice problem to calculate how much novelty the public will digest and still give a political party the half plus one of the public support without which ideas remain ideas and not practical policies. I think the Rally in January gave a lot of our normal supporters a good deal of nervous indigestion. The problem is to provide a reasonable amount of sedation for them without dulling the appetite of others who prefer stronger meat.

That was a fair statement of the problem. My quarrel was with the solution to it that Mike adopted. Essentially, it was a tactic of postponement: to soft-pedal the controversial policies for the time being. Mike wrote to me about the Winnipeg speech with typical warmth: he thought it was "exactly right, with the proper balance between the extremes of Liberalism. I hope you will not mind if I borrow shamelessly from it in the weeks ahead." But he did not.

I think that Mike was always clear in his own mind that, when it came to the crunch of the campaign, and afterwards in government, he would follow the declared policies of the party. Certainly in government he did. Contrary to a widespread impression, Mike could at times be unscrupulous, with his friends more than his enemies. Nevertheless, I am quite sure that in 1961 he would not have encouraged Walter and me and others to stick our necks out as far as we did if he had contemplated for one moment the possibility of chopping them off later. No doubt he calculated that if he maintained enough evasiveness to avoid confrontation with the party conservatives during 1961, it would afterwards be too late for them to stage an effective protest. They would be caught up in the campaign preparations even if they were unhappy at heart, and afterwards in government he would be fully in charge. In the meantime, avoiding confrontation gained for him a somewhat quieter life than he would otherwise have had.

In my view, however, he paid a heavy price. For too long he appeared to the public as an unconstructive, even whining, critic, a role that he played badly; he did not leave himself with enough time to establish momentum as a man with things to do that he believed in and the public liked. In return, he gained nothing except a lessening of tensions that would in any event have been minor. His position as party leader was at that point invulnerable. People who differed from his decisions could grumble, as the activists were doing then and the party's conservatives did later, but they were in no position to rebel and few would depart.

Some of the politicians were afraid that an activist strategy would involve a loss of campaign contributions from the establishment. I doubted that. Since I never had any direct contact with political fundraising, my impressions of it are that and nothing more. Business corporations seemed to me to look at the two main parties chiefly as Ins and Outs. They disliked the goodies for the unwashed, as they saw them, that all politicians offered in order to get elected. Their donations were a reflection less of ideology than of personal associations plus an estimate of which party was more likely to win and, to a lesser extent, which seemed less managerially incompetent. In this last respect the Diefenbaker government by 1961 scored very low.

Accordingly, it seemed to me that, while the adoption of an activist strategy immediately after the Rally might temporarily give some contributors pause, that effect would be fully made up by a more rapidly growing belief, in the media and among the public, that the election could produce a change of government. That was likely to have a stronger positive effect on the willingness of business to contribute to the Liberal campaign than any negative effects of the fear that a Pearson government would be to the left of the uncertain position of the Diefenbaker government.

Even if this assessment was incorrect, I went on to think, any net shortfall in funds would be far less important than the propaganda and organizational benefits of an early start in establishing our campaign platform. Mine was not, I should repeat, a closely informed view, and I might not have been so definite about it but for one thing: Walter, who knew what I did not about funding, had the same view.

I do feel personally confident in a more general comment about election spending. While there obviously is a minimum below which an effective national campaign cannot be mounted, it is lower than the parties generally aspire to; and spending much above that level is a crutch for lame politicians. The kinds of electioneering that cost a lot of money are often escapism for candidates with little idea of what, other than office, they are campaigning for. I have seen many indications that the "spectacle" aspect of campaigning pleases such politicians and their supporters far more than it influences people's voting. I am not disputing that a "normal" level of expenditure – what is "normal" varying with time and place – is necessary to effective campaigning. But the marginal effectiveness of spending more than an opponent is usually small and, if there is obvious lavishness, can even be negative.

Mike and I discussed election expenditures in the sense that we both favoured, in the interests of democracy, legislation of the kind that the Pearson government later introduced, to limit expenditures. But we never talked specifically about the funding of Liberal campaigns and I do not know whether concern about it was a factor in his caution about policy. My guess is that it was not.

But in 1961 the caution, from whatever mix of motives, was real. The consequence was that there was very limited use of the opportunity that existed in 1961 to get the policy stance of a renewed Liberal party firmly established in the public mind. If what was done in desperate hurry during the last six months before the campaign had been started eight months earlier, immediately after the Rally, its effectiveness would have been considerably enhanced – quite possibly, in my view, to make the difference between just failing and succeeding to upset the Diefenbaker government in 1962. That might-have-been speculation has little point now, but at the time the fear that an opportunity was being lost had much influence on my activities. It made me intensify my own involvements and particularly the alliance with Walter Gordon, as the man who was central to putting the necessary energy and organizational skill into the catch-up effort that would be required.

The first chance to move came when the illness of James Scott made the position of National Director of the party vacant. On Walter's initiative Mike agreed to the appointment of Keith Davey in May 1961. It was a major step, because everyone – led by Keith himself – recognized him as Walter Gordon's man. Though Walter at this point had no formal responsibility or authority – he was not named Chairman of the National Campaign Committee until late in 1961 – there was, from the moment of Davey's appointment, no doubt that Walter was going to be the major force in planning the campaign.

Our spirits were further raised when, soon afterwards, another Gordon idea was accepted. That was the creation of the Leader's Advisory Committee. In theory it was a formalization of the previously haphazard meetings of the leader with his principal parliamentary colleagues, identified by their being former ministers: Martin, Pickersgill, and Chevrier. The group had been strengthened, thanks to a by-election, by Paul Hellyer, and John Connolly represented the Senate. Whether he and Mike's two assistants, Maurice Lamontagne and Allan MacEachen, attended a meeting seemed to be largely accidental; the meetings were sporadic, ad hoc affairs summoned at short notice.

The Leader's Advisory Committee added some extraparliamentary people: Walter, Keith Davey, Bruce Matthews (the party treasurer) and, a short time after its beginning, myself. The fact that he and Bruce Matthews had to come from Toronto, and I from Montreal, helped Walter to insist on regularly scheduled meetings, roughly every two weeks. While Mike was of course the chairman, Walter was vice-chairman and Keith secretary. That meant that Walter organized the business. For some nine months, until the start of the 1962 campaign, the committee was in effect the central authority for the party. It created a measure of planning and organization, eventually even of coherence, that had been entirely lacking and certainly could not have been established by anyone less clear-sighted, determined, and skilful than Walter Gordon.

Though the essential foundation of ideas had been laid from 1958 onwards, the actual rebuilding of the Liberal party was done in 1961, unfortunately for the most part not until the second half of the year, with the formalization of party policy and of a campaign strategy, the recruitment of able candidates for Parliament, and the establishment of dedicated organizational groups in most of the country. It was all done, thanks, essentially, to one man: not L.B. Pearson, but Walter Gordon.

It is true, of course, that Mike chose Walter. The opportunity to do what was done, by Walter and all those of us who worked with him, was given to us by the leader of the party. Initially we would have been powerless without his authority. Most of us were involved because we had started from the belief that Mike Pearson was the Member of Parliament who could best be Prime Minister of the kind of government that we thought would be best for Canada. Mike never lacked friends and he would in any event have asked the help of many of us who were politically interested. In those days, when parties did not have anything near the staffing they do now, it would have been almost entirely spare-time help. And, left to him, the volunteer relationships would have been one-to-one. A great deal of good work would have been done and Mike would have applied himself, devotedly, to making use of it all. But it would have been virtually unstructured. Mike's capacity for organization was minimal. He would have overstrained and confused himself, by trying to cope with more than any man could, before he tried to develop a plan and a structure that enabled all the energies and talents willingly available to him to be deployed coherently.

He would not even have pressed Walter to substitute for him in these tasks, if Walter had not decided for himself that the job was necessary and he wanted to do it. Mike would have asked me, and I would have agreed, to do a lot of policy development work; but without Walter I would not have been asked to give enough time to it until far too late, and there would never have been scope for the essential communications within the party.

Walter's role was therefore crucial even in the policy area of political activity that most engaged Mike's interest and in which I would have done some of the same work, though less efficiently, without the alliance with Walter. In the recruitment of candidates and the building of organization, Walter's role was dominant. Keith Davey did the detailed work as Walter's very able agent.

For the 1962 campaign, Keith was extraordinarily the right man at the right time. He was essential to the balance of an otherwise rather blood-less team. Expressions of emotion and enthusiasm, whose flow is necessary to political organization, did not come easily to such people as Mike,

Walter, and me. Appropriately for a man whose passion was to watch professional team games, Keith was, as Walter aptly put it, the cheer-leader of the party. He was not, at this time, the man behind the bench. That was Walter. But good cheerleading was important to the success that the 1962 campaign achieved.

I should emphasize that the Keith Davey referred to in this book was young, and different from the man who came to be known as "The Rainmaker." After the party gained office in 1963, he had too little to do. To his great credit, he had no taste for the management of patronage with which some organizers busy themselves. At that time he also had little understanding of policy and of government operations. In 1964 and 1965 the outlet for his great energies was to think and talk about the next election. He developed a fervent belief that the Prime Minister should take the initiative in calling an election which, Keith claimed, would yield the Liberal majority in Parliament that had been missed in 1963. He talked about this, not only to the party organization but also to the press, as if it were virtually, perhaps entirely, certain that the Prime Minister would do as Keith thought he should. It was primarily this talk that created the state of expectations which, as will be discussed in later chapters, eventually led to a campaign that failed.

In the Trudeau years, Keith moved to greater responsibilities. His maturing was indicated by his senatorial inquiry into the media, which had lasting significance. But neither his role in 1962–3 nor his disastrous 1965 manipulation would have led me to predict his subsequent reputation as a rainmaking political operative.

An early decision of the Leader's Advisory Committee, under Walter's generalship, was to assign to me, at the beginning of July 1961, the welcome task of drafting a "pre-campaign strategy." It could be done quickly, as Mike, Walter, and Maurice Lamontagne knew, because it would be an adaptation for a slightly wider group of the "Notes on Election Strategy" that I had already written and they had seen.

At this point we were greatly helped by another of Walter's initiatives. At the suggestion of a New York friend of Bob Winters, he made contact with Lou Harris, who had been responsible for the opinion surveying that had so large an influence on Kennedy's presidential campaign. Walter, Keith, and I met with Harris and were much impressed. He established a Canadian subsidiary and became our pollster. Because public opinion polling has since become so much more influential in politics, I should emphasize that Harris was brought in only after Liberal party policy had been determined through the Rally, and indeed after Walter and I had formulated our main ideas about priorities and strategy. Polling provides important information, but we did not see it as a substitute for purpose and judgment in steering a political course.

What Harris showed us was that the dominant opinion about the government was that it was not much good, but equally definitely people were not very critical of Diefenbaker personally. He was still held in considerable regard, as a sincere and direct man. The Liberal party was not very well regarded; it was considered to be too negative and partisan. Pearson had not made a strong impression. People who had an opinion tended to think him vacillating and indecisive. Most importantly, the surveys showed that the issues that most concerned people were employment, economic activity and income security.

Lou Harris did his own statistical analysis of the answers to the survey questions, discussed their significance with his three contacts – Walter, Keith and me – and wrote his report. Walter presented it to Mike, and in summary form to the Leader's Advisory Committee, as the word of the expert. Some did not like it, but they could not refute it. The strategical conclusions were obvious: a negative campaign, particularly criticism of Diefenbaker, would not win the election; it could be won by a positive campaign, clearly identifying the Liberal party with policies for employment, economic growth, medicare, and pensions. This was precisely the activist position, but it ran very much against the instincts of some of the established politicians, whose chief preoccupation was to find ways of attacking their opponents. We would have had much more difficulty in getting assent to a positive, policy-based strategy if we had not had the surveys to support it.

My "Notes on Election Strategy" had been, like most of my discussions and correspondence with Mike since the Rally, a test of our relationship. They had been firmly and frankly critical of what I saw as the negative elements in his speeches and television performances – too little about Liberal policy and too much criticism of the government unrelated to, or even in some cases inconsistent with, the policy adopted at the Rally.

The criticism was, I think, within a constructive framework and friendly in tone, but very few people would have taken it in as good part as Mike did. I complained that virtually nothing had yet been done – by the leader, by other parliamentary spokesmen, or by the Federation – to make the party's Rally positions known, understood, and accepted as positive policies. All the emphasis had been on criticism of the government. The paper argued in harsh detail "why negation won't work," pulling no punches about the public view of the Liberal party as by 1957 it had become in office, of the style of parliamentary opposition that the survivors from that regime had sustained, and of Mike's ineffectiveness. There followed the warning that, while we were at the point in the life cycles of governments when their popularity was usually low, it was likely that doubtful voters would tend to come down on the government side as electioneering got into swing; this was the more probable because for the next twelve months we were likely to have slightly improving economic conditions; Diefenbaker was still a considerable campaigner; and outside Quebec, the Conservatives were much better organized than we showed any signs of becoming. "In short, as things now stand we're not going to win."

The next section of the paper made the case that the only way to regain the initiative, to make the floating voters over most of the country feel that a Liberal government could again lead the country constructively, was to identify the party firmly with positive policies on the Rally lines. The point had come at which the leader must give a firm instruction on the priority Liberal policies to be emphasized, on the criticisms of the government that could be made on that basis, and on the criticisms that shouldn't be made. This document must have the full authority of the leader behind it. It must ensure that the central group all talked the same language. We were at the point where the leader must take full command: anyone in the central group who didn't like everything about the document must make up his mind to accept it fully, nevertheless, or retire from the scene. No one (including the leader) could afford to waste emotional energy on doubts about the fundamentals of the strategy decided on.

It was in knowledge of this viewpoint that Walter had manoeuvred a mandate from the Leader's Advisory Committee for me to draft a strategy that could command a consensus. What emerged after I had submitted a first draft, and then redrafted in the light of committee discussion, did not in all respects go as far as I would have wished, but, as a document formally approved by the committee in late July, it was a substantial step forward. I will not summarize it in any detail here, because the central points were the same as those made in earlier papers and memoranda, though I did get special pleasure from persuading the committee to endorse the sentiment that for ex-ministers, and others closely associated with Ottawa, the basic thought with which to wake up every morning was "People will vote for us as we are, not as we have been." The basis of the campaign must be what a new Liberal government would do: "We can cure unemployment, we can get the country back to work, get things moving again. We can raise incomes. We can provide a health plan, university scholarships; we can improve life for older people by housing, health care and better pensions; finance better public services through a municipal loan fund and urban renewal grants; improve the tax system to encourage expansion." These policies had to be simply and strikingly stated, and criticism of the existing government must be based on them. The criticism should be that the government was not doing what the country needed and we would do, rather than a regurgitation of old controversies.

With this document the party leadership had at last established, on paper, at least, official guidelines for the campaign, and Keith Davey quickly transmitted them through the developing party organization. By now, however, it was not in the campaign at the constituency level, in most of the country, that I was afraid of our being ineffective. Whether voters took Liberal policies seriously, whether they believed that we would do what we said, depended very largely on whether they sensed that the party's leader meant it and could do it. Since 1960 I had been periodically urging that Mike should write a personal pamphlet setting out party policy as his. When the campaign strategy was approved, I tried at the same time to emphasize again the necessity of making his personal commitment plain, in emotional as well as intellectual terms. The notes that I prepared for a discussion with him, on 25 July 1961, were in part:

> You have to say – simply, warmly, directly – what you want to achieve in the government of Canada. You have to say what that means for Canadians. You *are* talking to 'my fellow Canadians' and you are talking about 'vision.' Those are the phrases that suit Diefen-baker's personality. They don't, thank heavens, suit yours. But they are simply his versions of the right fundamentals. There are other versions. There was Roosevelt's, there was Churchill's, there was Kennedy's in the last campaign. There must be Pearson's.
>
> You have to talk to people about where we should be going. You have to talk about things as they matter to people ... These speeches ... are far harder than an intellectual exercise, a policy statement, or a refutation of the other side. It's no use attempting them unless you have attitudes you feel deeply about, policies that you believe would really make life different for people for whom it should be different.
>
> I know that you do. But most people don't. The public hasn't got a positive impression of you.

The notes went on to make some detailed suggestions as to how Mike could improve his television performance, but the only definite outcome of the discussion was a request that I write a synopsis for the election platform, which I did by 14 August. He responded with a slightly edited version of it on 30 August. Walter, to whom I sent a copy, responded with a long letter of more constructive comment. The synopsis, however, was just that: a skeleton with very little flesh, and at that point I could not make time to do more.

The most important writing done then, in the summer and early fall of 1961, was Walter's: his book, *Troubled Canada*. He sent me drafts of the key sections as they were written, but I had few comments. The approach and style were distinctively Walter's. There was a terse analysis of the national situation and an admirably clear exposition of things to do about it – which, though the Liberal party was not mentioned, happened to be substantially the policies adopted at the Rally. Some of the media dubbed *Troubled Canada* the new Liberal Bible. Undoubtedly it greatly helped many people to understand Liberal policies and expound them in a way that won converts. As a result, most Liberal candidates for the first time said much the same things across Canada.

By late summer the sense of so much to do and so little time to do it was acute. One of the handicaps of an opposition, compared with the government, is of course that it has to guess at the date when the election will be called. The timing that could be considered normal was June 1962 – that is to say, after a term of four years plus the months required for a campaign in the spring rather than in the winter weather through which candidates had had to struggle in 1958. But during 1961 there were constant alarms that Diefenbaker would go earlier, because of his troubles and because we were obviously unready. It was not, however, easy for a government with Diefenbaker's majority to give a publicly respectable reason for an early election. I think it was contemplated. There was no other rational explanation of the decision to dismiss Jim Coyne from the governorship of the Bank of Canada rather than wait for the expiry of his term only a little later.

The intention seemed to be to make Coyne the scapegoat for the failures of economic policy, and the calculation was that Mike would fall into the trap of supporting Coyne. If so it didn't work, primarily because of Coyne's extraordinarily determined, courageous, and skilful conduct of his refusal to resign. Mike was also at his best in his handling of the affair, avoiding identification with Coyne's views while maintaining his right to the public hearing that was given by the Senate. When Coyne resigned as soon as the Senate had rejected the Bill to dismiss him, the possibility of an election issue collapsed; the Gallup Poll, indeed, demonstrated wide public sympathy with Coyne. Diefenbaker and Fleming had so mismanaged it all that the Governor of the Bank had been put into the role of the courageous underdog attracting natural public sympathy.

When that crisis was past, the "old pro" Liberal politicians became disposed to the theory that Diefenbaker would indulge his tendency to procrastination and the election would be postponed to late in 1962. If we pressed ahead with urgent preparations we would run the danger that propagandists greatly fear, of peaking too soon. It was Walter Gordon who, in face of the alarms of both an early and a late election, firmly insisted that we should stick with the probabilities: the only way to do detailed, coherent planning was to assume a June election, and if it turned out differently make the best adjustments we could. His judgment could not have been better.

In this context I had to make another personal decision. My involvement had reached the point where it was natural that I could be thought of as a possible candidate for Parliament. My friends in Winnipeg, led by Joe O'Sullivan, had indeed been suggesting for some time that I return; they were keeping the attractive constituency of Winnipeg South open. Keith Davey, who by temperament regarded the thick of an election battle as the natural place for any friend of his, was prolific of suggestions about available ridings. His favourite for me was Kingston, where he thought that I could get the nomination and the chances of winning the seat were good. (It was in fact won by Ben Benson.)

I had, however, several inhibitions about standing for Parliament. Deeply committed as I was to trying to bring about a Pearson prime ministership, I still had a lingering reluctance to adopt a long-term partisan label. More importantly, perhaps, I knew that my instrument was the written word and, while I had become reasonably happy in small meetings and on TV, I had no illusions of prowess as a platform orator. Also, deeply as I had been involved in the country's affairs for the past six years, on public occasions I was self-conscious about being a relatively new Canadian with an English accent. Further, I had a young family and, though financial motives had never dictated my career decisions, to expose them to the high risks of an MP father was perhaps to go too far.

From this mixture of motives, I do not think that I would in any event have been a candidate in 1962. But if there was any doubt, Walter Gordon removed it. He insisted that it was essential that I be in Ottawa. Our common concern was to lessen the damage caused by slowness in establishing and articulating the party's platform. We both thought that the best that could be done, in the limited time now available, was to produce policy literature in unusual volume and detail. If it was simple and clear as well as definite, it could enhance the effectiveness of candidates and other party workers as propagandists. It would help to create in the media a stronger awareness of our positive stance. And it would provide a coherent basis for campaign advertising.

It was more, however, than I could do, quickly enough to be at all effective, in my spare time. And, in Walter's view, no one else was going to do it or even to share the burden effectively. The need was for me to work full-time, starting as soon as possible – which would still be only about six months before the start of the campaign in April, for a June election date. Also, if I went to Ottawa in the fall, I could be more effective in other ways: to help to make what was said and done in

Parliament closer to the strategy; to improve Mike's speeches and especially what he said on TV; to develop the strategy as the election approached; and, Walter argued, be ready in the actual campaign to travel with Mike, write policy statements and speeches, keep the travelling show in line with the strategy.

We could not have a discussion so important to my future without taking our hair down. Walter and I were both concerned about Mike's indecisiveness as leader of the opposition. Was our belief that Mike would be a great Prime Minister surviving this experience? He would be much more comfortable in office than in opposition. But leading a government was very different from conducting its diplomacy. Would his lack of organizational capacity not be a fatal handicap? Walter's answer was that overcoming that handicap was what he and I were for. Mike would indeed be a great Prime Minister provided the role was, using the analogy of the business world, that of chairman of the board. In that he would be superb, provided there were people close to him to provide the necessary organization and management. He, Walter, would have to play the main executive role in government just as he was now doing in opposition.

This was not said from immodesty, of which Walter was incapable, or from ambition of the self-regarding kind. It was simple realism. Mike could not be an executive, it was not essential that he should be, but someone had to do it for him and the only person with the necessary status whom Mike would trust was Walter. But in the structure of government it would be a difficult role and it would work, Walter suggested, only if he had help. There had to be someone to see that the central resources for program formulation and administration were effectively directed to the policies to which we were committed. I could play that role as his Deputy Minister in Finance, if I preferred, but the job could probably be done more effectively from the Prime Minister's Office.

It was an intriguing design, but all that mattered then was to sustain faith that the creation of a Pearson government was worth working for. If it was, the logic of moving to Ottawa that fall was irrefutable, whatever it might mean for me later. I do not think, however, that Mike himself would have proposed it without Walter's insistence. Mike was ready enough to ask people for help, but not for too much.

His inhibition had, I think, two distinct sources. One was pride; though he was by no means unaware of his own limitations, he did not like to feel heavily dependent on help from any one source, even – as it turned out – Walter. Second, and no less important even though it was a contradictory element in Mike's complex personality, was a reluctance, mixed from modesty and humanity, to ask sacrifices of people. Without

Walter's initiative, he would certainly have asked me to work full-time with him during the actual election campaign. That could have been done by taking a leave of absence from my well-paid job. It would not have exposed me to the risk, as well as substantial immediate financial sacrifice, involved in taking on an eight-month task and uncertainty thereafter. But it would also have been a far less useful service to him and to the party. Perhaps the real point was, in the last analysis, that Mike's lack of a sense of organization made him unaware of that.

However, on Walter's prompting, he did in late August propose that I join him as soon as possible. I was sorry to leave Max Mackenzie and a life that was comfortable as well as interesting, but by now the call of the trumpet was too strong to resist. The description of my job was about the clumsiest ever invented: "Special Consultant to the Leader of the Liberal Party and to the National Liberal Federation." John Connolly, as President of the Federation, objected not to the appointment but to not having been told about it until it was publicly announced. Even Walter Gordon was not capable of safeguarding against every detail of disorganization.

The title, however, served its purpose. It was Mike's way of indicating a broad mandate without using words like policy and strategy that would have exacerbated the distrust felt by the party's conservatives. The assignment was clear enough to the people chiefly concerned: it was to get the strategy and policies into operational shape and provide the words to support them. I started work on 1 October 1961, for what turned out to be ten years in Ottawa.

II *Preparing an Election*

I went to Ottawa in the belief that, because of the strength of 1954–7 images and because of its internal tensions, the Liberal party in opposition had not given people an accurate impression of what a Pearson government would be. The task, in the presumed seven or eight months from 1 October to polling day, was to change the impression of an indecisive party still weighted by some of the faults that had resulted in its rejection in 1957 and 1958. That had to be replaced, in as many minds as possible, by a clear picture of the government with firm, progressive policies that I thought Pearson, with Gordon in particular at his side, would provide.

The transformation, if it came, would be made by Pearson and 264 other candidates. My job was to provide the words that might make their efforts more coherent and more effective. The writing agenda that I set, for the six months until the presumed start of the campaign, had two items of special importance.

First, there was to be a booklet which would state all the declared policies of the party, as precisely as possible in the firm language of "what a new Liberal government will do." This was to be designed primarily for candidates and other active campaigners, though it might also have some direct influence on the press and on opinion leaders generally. By putting all of the policies inside one cover I hoped to do all that could be done to make the campaign coherent across the country. There was also a secondary purpose in my mind, which I discussed only with Walter and a few others: if the election was won, such a booklet would be a more useful reference than a collection of leaflets and statements in speeches; it might be more effective as a pressure on the party in office to do what it had said it would do. In the event, after the 1963 election, it did serve that purpose quite well.

The second major item was a series of small leaflets on particular programs and policy areas. Together these would cover most of the material in the main booklet; but whereas that was to be primarily a reference source for the converted, the leaflets were to be propaganda. They were to be short and plain enough to be widely distributed as campaign literature. They had another value which seemed to me important. I knew that, realistically, the booklet could not be finally approved and printed until late in the six-month period – until the start of the election campaign was close. The leaflets, however, could be produced in a series – eventually there were 16 of them – at intervals of a week or two starting in November. I therefore hoped that they could help to create a better impression of the party before the election campaign began.

In those days, the Liberal party's staff was the minimum required for organizational work. Mike had two assistants in his own office, Maurice Lamontagne and Allan MacEachen, and Maurice had done a great deal of writing for him. But by late 1961 both were busy getting ready to run as candidates for Parliament. They were not replaced. In consequence, the pamphlets and the booklet were a very small part, in volume if not in importance, of all the words – several hundreds of thousands – that I wrote between 1 October 1961, and the end of the campaign on 18 June 1962. Most were written for Mike, as speech texts and notes for television appearances. The extent to which he followed them varied from minimal to close. On television, in particular, it was frequently, though not universally, minimal. Speeches as delivered were usually closer to the texts, or at least to their themes, though the positive points tended to be blurred by circumlocutions and qualifying phrases and Mike usually threw in some criticisms of Mr Diefenbaker and his government which had been shunned in the texts.

Most ghost-writing, I suppose, involves a high level of frustration. With some audiences, when he felt at ease and particularly in small meetings and when he was not being reported, Mike could be highly effective. But on the hustings and on television his inhibitions usually took hold. They made him seem uncertain and imprecise in making his positive points, and his awareness of this often led him to try to offset it in his criticism of opponents, which became too strident to be effective. I learned to be fairly philosophical about what happened to the speeches in delivery and, in the campaign, to circumvent it to some extent by providing the press with advance texts of key parts of the speeches, which the journalists were usually happy to use as the basis of their reports rather than wait for added words. Even so, I doubt that I could have tolerated the frustrations of speech-writing if that had not been subsidiary to the main activities of campaign planning and to the satisfactions of writing the associated stream of policy memoranda and strategy papers, as well as the booklet and leaflets and, later, the campaign literature and advertising derived from them.

One leaflet was a concession to the orthodox politicians who put more weight on criticizing the Diefenbaker government than on saying what a new Liberal government would do. The title I used for this purpose was *The Wasted Years*. The leaflet consisted essentially of two charts. One projected the trend line of growth in real gross national product as it had been from 1947 to mid-1957. With it were plotted the actual GNP figures, which from 1957 to 1961 fell well below the previous trend. The area between was shaded. It represented the difference between our actual production, in the past 4 1/2 years, and the production we would have had if the economic growth of previous years had continued. At 1961 prices, it was $14 billions. That was nearly $800 worth of goods and services for every person in the country. For a family of four, it was over $3,000. And the loss has been getting bigger every year. In 1961 alone it was about $5 billions. That was the 14 cents on the dollar of a national income then under $37 billions. It was $100,000,000 a week; nearly $600,000 for every hour of every day; nearly $10,000 every minute.

The second chart similarly projected the 1947-57 trend line for employment and compared it with actual employment in 1957-61. By late 1961 the widening gap had reached 300,000 jobs. These were "the jobs we lack," jobs that would have existed if economic growth had continued since

1957. They were the human costs of "Canada's wasted years, the years of Tory talk instead of action, of mismanagement instead of purposeful government."

That was indeed an oversimplification, and I am perhaps being defensive when I emphasize that those of us who were responsible for Liberal policy in opposition were not so stupid as to think that the particular kind of boom which Canada experienced up to 1956 would go on. "The American boom in Canada", as I had characterized it, reflected special postwar circumstances. We knew that the Canadian economy would have to undertake major adjustments, and in designing our programs the objective of facilitating those adjustments was as important, in the minds of Walter Gordon and myself and others, as the objective of securing greater social equality. We thought – and certainly I continue to think – that, far from being in conflict, the two objectives were mutually reinforcing through a balanced mix of policies.

In retrospect, I think that we underestimated some of the obstacles to adjustment. But that was not apparent during the sixties. In the early part of the decade the economy recovered from the recessionary phase of 1957–61 and continued to perform quite well through the period of Pearson government. It was only with the turn of the decade that there began to be clear reasons to fear that, in a changing world, we were missing the boat. Some of the external shocks – notably those originating in the oil industry – were on a scale that nobody anticipated. Moreover, it was hardly possible in the 1960s to foresee that any Canadian government would respond to changed circumstances with the extraordinarily vacillating mix of inappropriate and incoherent policies that marked the Trudeau period. Though there were indeed emerging difficulties that could be diagnosed in the sixties, the extent of our economic deterioration was the product of a combination of ill fortune and misjudgment in the seventies.

In 1961, therefore, I did not have to stretch my conscience very far to produce the *Wasted Years* leaflet. By the standards of political propaganda its over-simplification was modest. And it served well the internal party purpose of pleasing the people to whom the "what we will do" leaflets were less appealing than I thought them. Many candidates used it more vigorously than most of the other fifteen.

Those others were all in the positive vein. The general format was to discuss an area of policy in some hundreds of words, and then to state in point form "what a Liberal government will do." The concluding refrain was that "The Liberal party has, for today's problems, the answers that are progressive, realistic and responsible."

It was fundamental to the strategy that the leaflets, with one exception, were not designed to break new ground but simply to make more definite, for the public and hopefully later for a Liberal cabinet, the policy positions identified at the National Rally. Nevertheless their importance as official party statements, particularly when put in the form of declarations of future government action, made it necessary that each leaflet be formally approved by the Leader's Advisory Committee. That involved a good deal of discussion, and resulted in compromises that took the edge off a few of the proposals.

The exceptional, and therefore most contentious, leaflet was the one in which, under the title of *Purpose for Canada*, I tried to set out the fundamentals of economic policy-making through consultative planning. This was going beyond anything articulated in previous policy statements, and I therefore worded the first draft with considerable care. In particular I defined planning as innocuously as possible: "Liberals believe in planning in the sense that it is the government's duty to be far-sighted; they believe that government should provide the conditions in which all our enterprises – public and private – can exercise foresight for the successful running of their own business." Nevertheless, there was an uneasy feeling, on the part of some members of the committee, that the leaflet would somehow commit them to more than they wanted. As a result, whereas the draft referred to "the planning task" and therefore the establishment of a "National Economic Council," in the final version this became an "Economic Advisory Council" which was "to help" the government.

The issue here was not the primacy of the Cabinet, which was not challenged in the original proposal. It was the power of the departmental bureaucracies, especially that of the Finance Department. Much is made nowadays of the self-serving role of bureaucracies in the governmental process. In my experience the strongest champions of bureaucratic influence have been members of the Liberal political "establishment." This is not, of course, universal; contrary things are sometimes said and there are some dissenters in practice as well as words. After some years in opposition there might well be a thorough change. But in the 1960s many leading Liberals had long been accustomed to, comfortable with, and greatly dependent on the senior public servants. The National Economic Council as I envisaged it would have created more direct, representative, and thoughtful connections between government and the other major actors in the economy, in business, labour, farming and the professions. The real significance of the compromise that, in the 1962 leaflet, reduced it to an advisory council "to help" was that it then could not be a serious competitor to the bureaucracy in influencing the decision-making of ministers. That, unfortunately, was the rock on which the Economic Council of Canada foundered after we had created it in 1963.

Another lost battle concerned medicare. The Leader's Advisory Committee would not follow the National Rally in accepting the concept that the most equitable way to maintain the appropriate kind of financial discipline was to treat the cost of the services provided as an addition to taxable income. The main objection voiced was that, even though the imputed additional income would be taxed only at the individual's marginal rate on his other income – that is, nil for people below the taxable level and at low rates for most others – it would not be fair and practicable for middle-income people requiring really expensive care. My answer was that the additional tax could be spread forward over a number of years, on a formula limiting the proportionate addition to tax in any one year, and with forgiveness of any liability outstanding at death. The counter-argument was that this made the scheme too complicated and hard for people to understand. I said that it would not be as bad as many other complications of the tax system (then, and even more so since).

The real concern, I think, was presentational: that the scheme could be attacked as giving with one hand and taking with the other. It seemed to me that the plan would not be difficult to describe in a way that a large majority of people would understand and accept as eminently fair and practicable. But I did not convince the doubters.

In the end the leaflet adopted the categorical approach. Medical services would be provided without charge to all children up to the age of sixteen, to "the unemployed" and to "most retired people." "All other Canadians" would be covered for doctors' bills "above a low annual cost." It was a poor set of words to describe proposals that were, in my view, both administratively unsatisfactory and unacceptable, because of the anomalies involved, to public opinion. My consolation was that we had at last got the commitment to the principle of medicare quite firmly embodied in Liberal policy. I was confident that, when we came to implementation in government, something better than the categorical approach would have to emerge from the process of negotiation with the provinces that was in any event required before the details of the plan could be firmly established.

Apart from these two points – the National Economic Council and the structure of medicare benefits – the drafts of all the leaflets and, more importantly, of the platform booklet survived the processes of the Leader's Advisory Committee without significant change. There was sometimes lengthy discussion, but it ended in no more than minor changes in wording.

Three factors made this possible. One was that Walter Gordon was as convinced as I was that the party's policies should be stated definitely and should be in line with the Rally resolutions. Where I anticipated difficulties I discussed with him in advance how we could deal with them. Walter was not a man to waste time niggling over minor points of wording and he trusted my draftsmanship. Our firm alliance was crucial to the committee discussions.

Second, though the committee embraced considerable philosophical differences, Mike's skilled chairmanship made its proceedings consistently good-natured. People pressed points only if they both felt strongly themselves and sensed that they had significant support. In this atmosphere the draft had a great deal going for it.

Even so, however, the process would not have been so smooth but for a third factor. While I wrote the drafts, I took care to be able truthfully to say that each reflected a good deal of consultation with people in the party who were knowledgeable of the topic. By this time I had extensive contacts with party activists in Ontario and the western provinces. In Toronto, on Walter's initiative, there were special working groups on medicare and on pensions, with which I was in close consultation. The pension committee produced recommendations in great detail, which were the basis for the original version of the Canada Pension Plan. In Quebec my personal connections were considerably less close, but Maurice Sauvé was extremely helpful in arranging consultations.

The Atlantic provinces were another world, where contemporary ideas of participation seemed as yet to have made, at least within the Liberal party organization, little impact. On any issue Jack Pickersgill stood ready to make an authoritative pronouncement of regional opinion, if not immediately then after he had put in a telephone call to Premier Smallwood. Mike did all he could to promote a second opinion from Allan MacEachen, but the effect was muted by Allan's cautious nature.

Despite the geographical variations, the consultation that went into the writing of the leaflets and the booklet was extensive. I was greatly helped by the small staff at Liberal headquarters, in particular by Paul Lafond. Other people in Ottawa were important advisers, notably Gordon Blair on constitutional and legal points. Most of the consultation, however, was by telephone, rather than meetings and correspondence. Even so, it meant that this writing took an entirely disproportionate amount of time, compared with all the speeches and memoranda and, later, campaign material. But it was the foundation of all the rest. Romantically, perhaps, I saw myself as the agent articulating a consensus of liberally minded people on what government should do in the 1960s in Canada. I think we were a sufficiently broad group to respond sensitively to the felt needs of a very large number of Canadians. The responses – the government programs we proposed – were certainly the result of careful thought and discussion over a period of years.

The introductory section of the booklet – "The Liberal Programme: General Election 1962" was printed over the signature of L.B. Pearson. While far short of the personal political statement that I had earlier hoped we could present, it was pregnant of the spirit that drove Mike as Prime Minister:

> Its purpose is to give the voters of Canada a clear statement of what they will be doing if they entrust the country's affairs to a new Liberal government. That is the basis on which we ask for your support … The proposals that we put before you are not election promises, cooked up for the occasion to attract support from this group and that. They are nation-wide policies developed during four years of careful study and intensive discussion among Liberals all over the country … This is the programme of action that I believe will serve the best interests of all Canadians. It is what we will do.

Mike Pearson was not only sincere in this as a statement of his intentions at the time. I think that is true – despite increasingly widespread cynicism about politics – of most of the statements of most politicians, at the moment the statements are made. Where Mike was different was that during five difficult years in office he continued to hold to and act on the same intentions.

Getting to the point of his saying "what we will do" had been slow and on some points, such as the financial provisions for medicare, was still left weakly imprecise. But once he had told the electorate what he was going to do it became for him a genuine commitment. As Prime Minister he was conscientiously determined to carry out the program. In this respect nothing could be further from the truth than the widely accepted view of Pearson as a weak man. The reality was more complicated.

A bill of criticism can easily be drawn up. Mike was weak in many of his dealings with people. His dislike of giving offence often made him evasive. Many of the issues that come before a Prime Minister are outside the range of established policy, and on those he was often indecisive. He could not organize, and the effect of disorganization was to intensify his tendency to become, under pressure, confused and vacillating. That, of course, can happen to anyone who carries heavy and complex responsibilities; but most manage not to show it too clearly. Mike, however, had very little art of concealment. When he was confused or uncertain it was usually all too obvious. He thereby greatly multiplied his own difficulties in the rough business of politics.

But, while such points can be made in criticism, they are much less than half the truth about Mike's strength and weakness. The proof is in the performance. The Pearson government did what he had said it would do. It would have been easy for a minority government to find excuses for postponing much of what had been promised. That, indeed, was what many ministers in the Pearson Cabinet wished. Almost every measure in the program was viewed with something from dislike to doubt by at least a few ministers. I don't think there was any item, taken separately, on which dissidents would have been in the majority, but the normal processes of bargaining could easily have produced agreement to set aside a considerable number of the proposed measures – if Mike's determination had been in doubt.

It was not. Despite all the difficulties that the government encountered – many of them, it must be said, of its own making – he soldiered on. His flexibility was that of the reasonable man who is prepared to modify details when that is necessary to achieve the main purpose. He was entirely firm in the resolution that the essentials of the program for which he had come to office should be implemented. Though the Pearson weaknesses were publicly damaging and privately distressing, though they made life in office greatly harder on him and others, they were superficial to the man, and to the politician a burden that he carried bravely.

To him it was always clear that the results were what mattered. To get them he was heavily dependent, because of his lack of organizing ability, on others. But they could not have been effective without the resolution that he gave to the program objectives. That is why his prime ministership achieved so much, why he made far more mark on Canada than have many ostensibly stronger men, with more aggressive personalities and more popular skills.

It is because of Mike's dogged resolution that the Liberal platform is of more importance, historically, than the media, understandably cynical about election promises, treated it as being. Some journalists did, however, relish the leaflets. In March 1962, after the flood of them had piled up, one of the wittier of my friends in the parliamentary press gallery wrote to me:

> Dear Tom: On checking over your most interesting series of pamphlets, The Liberals Have the Answers, I cannot seem to find the one on the Sons of Freedom Doukhobors. I hesitate to attribute this to any slip up in your office and am inclined to attribute it to the unreliability of the mails under the present Administration. As the subject intrigues me, I would be most grateful to receive this pamphlet by return post. Yours, Maurice Western.

The fourteen leaflets on the "what a Liberal government will do" theme dealt in a more explanatory style with the major areas of policy declared in the platform booklet. The exception was defence. It was included in the plan for the leaflets, but Mike proposed that he should write the draft himself. It was no surprise that, with all the demands on his time, he never produced it. Paul Hellyer, Walter and I all tried our hands at short drafts to get him started, but nothing came of them, and in the end the external and defence policy part of the main platform document was the only printed statement. Mike approved my draft of that with minor qualifications.

Of the "policy" pamphlets, two have already been referred to: *Health Care As Needed* (that is to say, medicare plus income insurance in the sense of eligibility for unemployment benefits in illness) and *Purpose for Canada* (that is, consultative planning through an "Advisory" Economic Council). The programs set out in the other twelve included a long list of measures for full employment ("the first aim of a new Liberal government"); "full equalization" in federal-provincial taxation, with compensation for opting out of established programs and contracting out of new shared-cost programs; family allowances beyond sixteen for students; university scholarships and loans; job training with allowances; a Municipal Loan Fund; broadened contributions to urban renewal; capital for rural development; increased construction of low-rental housing; a federal labour code, including minimum wage; extended unemployment insurance coverage; the Canada Pension Plan; increases in old-age security and in assistance and disability allowances; deficiency payments for grains; underwriting of crop insurance; capital for agricultural co-operatives; encouragement of marketing boards; improved price supports, research, and marketing information for farmers; regional development through an area rehabilitation agency, tax incentives, capital grants; rigid limits to election expenditures and federal payments to them; a voting age of eighteen; political affiliation on ballot papers; a non-partisan commission for constituency redistribution; no revocation of citizenship; a national flag; bilingualism in federal documents; "steady" immigration related to employment opportunities; independent review of immigration decisions; and a series of measures to provide "a better break for the Atlantic Provinces."

There were two leaflets outside this pattern. One, as noted above, was a denunciation of economic performance under the then government: *The Wasted Years*. And finally there was, in *The Issues before Us*, an attempt to express the spirit of the whole program in a way appealing to both the left and the right wings of the party. The consensus achieved within the party was at that point real, if uneasy. A few sentences will illustrate the balance:

As a nation we can use only what as a nation we produce. Progress depends fundamentally on economic growth, on expanding production.

Liberal policies – for full employment, for a medical care plan, for scholarships, for pensions – will make sure that national expansion works fairly, to improve opportunities for all Canadians.

The tragedies of poverty and despair which still disfigure our democratic society – especially among the aged, the blind, the disabled, the mentally ill – can be removed.

For all these and many other necessary reforms, the Liberal party has constructive, responsible, practical policies of progress.

The party consensus embodied in the 1962 platform was achieved with a great deal of work, far more than would have been necessary if Mike had determined that it be done earlier and been more decisive about what he wanted. But for its achievement in the end his personality was crucial. In the crunch, his diplomatic skills were superb. He was extraordinarily skilled in making diverse people feel that they had all been listened to and in deploying his critical resource – the respect in which he was held – to just the extent necessary to get acceptance without resentment. At that stage, the production was beautiful. The only trouble was that the product got to market too late. Party workers did not have the literature in time to use it as effectively as they could have done. As a result, many voters went to the polls without having been enough exposed to the Liberal program to recognize it as credible.

There had been a prerequisite for Mike's role in the final stages of settling the election platform. He had become convinced that the individual policies were desirable and practicable. His integrity required that he also feel assured that the program as a whole was realistic. There were voices, from the right of the party, to tell him that it was too big, that it threatened the Canadian economy with ruin because it would require either tax increases or large budget deficits.

In coping with such arguments Mike was handicapped by the distinctly non-numerative cast of his mind. Like many people who are brilliant enough in other respects, he could not hold magnitudes in perspective. Much as he trusted Walter, simple assurances were not enough. It became my responsibility to produce figures that – in the unintellectual terms in which, under the pressures of the approaching campaign, my friends and I thought of it – would "get the conservatives off Mike's back."

I had excellent help from a number of business economists and statisticians. The memorandum on "Financing of a new Liberal Government" pointed out that "the technique is essentially the same as is used in preparing pro forma cash flow statements [in business] ... the calculations are no less arbitrary than those from which industrial corporations make their major investment decisions." There were assumptions as to how timing of the implementation of all the program measures would be spread over a four-year government term beginning (we hoped) in June 1962. On that basis the extra expenditures arising from each program were calculated for each of the four fiscal years beginning in April 1963. Many of the estimates could be precise, but a few had to be guesses. In such cases I put the increases in costs on what seemed to be the high side. For example, we knew the existing private and insured expenditures on medical care, but how fast would increased utilization of doctor's services raise the cost of medicare? I allowed for a 50 per cent increase in the two years relevant to the projections. The costs of existing programs were also projected, of course, with allowance for a general increase of 2 per cent a year in real terms, as well as for specifically committed changes.

For the revenue calculations, it was assumed that the objective of returning to previous "full" employment levels would be achieved halfway through the government's term, in the second half of 1964, and that this would involve in 1963 and 1964 increases of 8 per cent in real GNP (the same rate of increase as in 1955 and 1956). For 1965 and 1966 real GNP increases of 5 per cent were assumed. The incentive reductions in corporation tax, included in the program, were assumed to be effective from 1963 on, but the tax structure was otherwise taken as unchanged for the purpose of the projections.

The bottom line was that in fiscal 1963–4 (with the economy still requiring stimulus) there would be a budget deficit of some $116 millions (compared with $800 millions then anticipated for 1961–2) and thereafter surpluses rising in 1966–7 to what then seemed to be the astronomical level of about $1.2 billion (in 1961 prices). In other words, all the promised program could be implemented, with, in conditions of full employment, a wide margin available to be used as government then thought appropriate – for a budget surplus and debt reduction or for a balanced budget after tax cuts and/or additional expenditures. The program was "financially sound."

It must be admitted that, in stating the conclusion so strongly, I was taking advantage of the fact that politicians rarely think more than four years ahead (and that not very often). The fiscal case that I projected for the mid-sixties was validly, if roughly, estimated and indeed proved to be close to the reality. If I had been pressed – which I was not – I would have had to admit that the projection could be misleading in the sense that this happy situation might not last long.

The factor that seemed to me entirely clear was that the provinces should and would gain more fiscal room; which meant, unless total taxation was to increase significantly, that the federal government would have to yield the room. My estimate of extra federal payment to the provinces was a 70 per cent increase in three years, which seemed a lot but was really too little. Further, while the cost estimates of the new programs were as realistic as I could make them for the four years, those were the early years of programs which in some cases would have inherent expansionary tendencies. Manpower training, in particular, was an example of a program which in my view should, and probably would, develop strong momentum.

On the revenue side, while I had little doubt that the projected GNP increases, and therefore revenue increases at existing tax rates, were attainable in the four years of presumed Pearson government, I would have hesitated to forecast the continuation of such growth rates in the seventies. I do not mean that I anticipated either the extent of the economic slowdown or the increases in expenditures that created the federal fiscal constraints of the later Trudeau years. My point here is simply that our calculations at the time were devoted to establishing the soundness of the specific programs to be initiated in the following four years. We were not claiming to foresee either the kind or the level of program initiatives that would be appropriate for subsequent governmental terms.

The memorandum on the financing of the program served its purpose. It satisfied Mike and his immediate associates that there was no intellectual basis for the right wing's pleas that the program should be, at least, soft-pedalled in favour of greater reliance, in the campaign, on attacking the Diefenbaker government on grounds more to its right than its left.

Intellectual conviction, however, was one thing. Emotional attitudes were quite another. I don't think Mike ever entirely overcame the feeling, rooted in his upbringing, that a deficit was immoral. I had encountered the same feeling earlier, among people in Winnipeg, and had dealt with it by means of editorials propounding that sound financing did indeed require balanced federal budgets: that is, budgets designed to produce revenues equal to expenditures if the economy was operating at full employment with stable prices. That seems over-simplified now, but in the conditions of the fifties and sixties – when we had a working international monetary system, buoyant world production and trade, virtually no supply shocks, no serious inflationary expectations and a smoothly working internal financial system – it was a satisfactory way to express sensible economic strategy in a practicable policy guideline. It had subsequently been articulated, in his 1955 budget speech, by so conservative a Liberal as Walter Harris. We got it into the National Rally resolutions – "a new Liberal government will so manage its affairs as to balance its budgets at full employment levels" – and it was of course stated in the 1962 program booklet and the full employment leaflet.

But the establishment of this view on paper did not mean that it penetrated into minds schooled in other traditions. The conditioning of many Liberals led them to attack the deficits of the Diefenbaker government (in conditions of considerable unemployment) as the road to hell and to imply, at least, that a Liberal government's first concern would be to pull the country back from damnation by balancing the budget whatever the state of the economy. For Mike, in some moods, such emotional influences were stronger than his intellect. It was necessary to fight battle after battle to save the whole policy structure from being exposed to ridicule by inconsistencies.

In early December I developed, from the "pre-campaign" strategy of the previous summer, a preliminary document on strategy for the campaign itself. Winning the election meant making enough people sympathetic to us and getting those people into the polling booths. The second was a matter of organization. The first depended on the strategy that the document propounded once more and was again approved by Mike and the Leader's Advisory Committee. I expanded it into a speech, with the detail required to appeal to the practical politicians, and during January delivered this to the National Liberal Council, to the campaign committee (which was at last set up in December, with Walter as chairman) and to meetings of candidates, many of whom had by then been nominated.

Yet even at this stage, difficulties in propounding the program consistently were far from over. Though its opponents had no real strength in the party, they could talk to Mike and worry him. We discussed this problem frankly and many times. My note of a Saturday lunch with Mike alone, on 10 February, reads: "We talked a lot about Left and Right in the party. He emphasized his job of bringing the Right along. That's fine. But I emphasized that the value of our programme depends on getting it known and accepted, and this takes time. It can't be done in the campaign. We're late already. He accepted this and agreed I should send two pamphlets to the printer on Monday." Those were almost the last, and the decision was for me the operational purpose of the lunch.

By this time the other flank also required protection. Now that there seemed to be a chance of our winning, new people were turning up – including Hazen Argue, coming from the NDP – and producing ideas that they wanted to add to the program. I was in the position of a conservative turning them down, because – as Walter and I constantly emphasized – our mandate was to flesh out the policies that the party had adopted at the Rally or, in many cases, as long ago as the 1958 convention. We must be able honestly to present the program as one that had been carefully and responsibly developed over the four years and it would be made less convincing either by subtraction or by addition, even of proposals that were in themselves good. But it seemed that the closer the election came, the more people there were who did not share our belief in the virtue of consistency.

As late as 12 March I was explaining to one of the principal officers of the party, as tactfully and patiently as I could, why I would not add to the program a commitment to reducing the national debt (the debt of 1962!). It was even necessary to deal, less patiently, with memoranda from people who harked back to 1935 and thought that we should model our campaign on what Mr King did then. That apparently meant that we should concentrate on attacking Mr Diefenbaker.

Perhaps the most depressing incident of all, because of the timing, was a lunch on 6 April with Mike and two of our candidates. One complained that the greatest problem he faced in his constituency was that he was tarred by association with Walter, who was seen as "very left-wing." Our main appeal should be the promise of "fiscal stability" as opposed to "spendthrift" programs. The other candidate argued that, rather than say much about specific policies, we should dramatize Diefenbaker's weakness: "tell people that today there just isn't a government." Mike to my amazement said little, even to defend Walter to whom he owed so much. He preferred, I suppose, that there should be a debate – of some heat – between the candidates and me. Fortunately, after they had got their woes off their chests, they eventually came round to somewhat more acceptance of the program and strategy.

By this stage it was too late, in any event, to produce a different program or a revised strategy. The critics of them were not only weak numerically; they never produced any consistent alternative. The nagging debates were a heavy drain on time and therefore a strain, I think, on Mike's nerves – certainly on mine – but they were much less important than they seemed in the heat of the day. A coherent party position had been established and protected from the attacks on the flanks. We were almost ready to campaign.

Talk in Ottawa was now much less important than what was happening in the constituencies. Thanks to Walter and Keith and their associates, many strong candidates were in place. Enthusiastic organizations had been developed, in most constituencies as well as at the provincial level. What mattered in Ottawa was not argument about policy but the actual planning of the campaign, allocating the finances, putting out the literature, writing the print advertisements, scripting the TV commercials.

Such work moved into high gear in March, since we were sticking to the presumption that Parliament would be dissolved some time in April for an election day in June. Increasingly, it was a little more than a presumption. The government clearly had not put together a legislative program that would make a continued session a better take-off for a later election. Further, dissatisfaction with Mr Diefenbaker was already strong enough for us to get what seemed to be reliable intelligence from

Conservative sources: they recognized that the momentum was with us and thought they would do better the less time they gave us to complete our preparations.

Maintaining security is a special problem for political parties. It is characteristic of politicians that many are compulsive talkers, and some even suffer from an irresistible urge to tell journalists all that is in their minds. Campaign preparations are bound to become partly known to opponents. The important thing is not to help them to anticipate further moves by exposing the reasoning behind your campaign planning. Yet risks have to be taken. As the campaign comes close, it is essential to morale that a good many party workers should feel themselves to be insiders who know how it is going to be won.

In March, therefore, I wrote a short version of a campaign strategy document, in a form in which no great harm would be done if a copy did get into unfriendly hands. I have no reason to think that this happened, though with Mike's approval the paper was distributed to key people across the country.

The burden of the paper was, of course, that the campaign had to concentrate on convincing undecided voters that we were a good alternative to a bad government, and the main way to do so was to talk simply and directly about what a new Liberal government would do. There followed the now familiar sermon about resisting the temptation to be sidetracked into arguments with opponents. What was wrong with other parties was the simple fact that they had not done or could not do the things the country needed, for which the Liberal party had firm programs.

No doubt, in the heat of the campaign, many candidates honoured this strategy as much in the breach as in the observance. But I think it helped to give more coherence to the campaign than there would otherwise have been, even though many of the leading Liberal speakers still in practice wasted a good deal of their energies on criticisms of the Diefenbaker government that pleased their supporters but did not win new votes.

Later in March, I prepared a short version of the main platform document. This was to be the principal piece of campaign literature. Because of its fold-out form, we called it the concertina. It had a message "To All Canadians" over the signature of L.B. Pearson, on the theme: "We need new policies for new times. The Liberal party has such policies ... This programme is what a new Liberal government will do."

Otherwise, the concertina was a terse statement of the main points of the program, in the form "A new Liberal government will ..." There were critics of this as campaign literature. They complained that the pamphlet tried to say much more than "the ordinary man" would pay attention to. Though advanced as "practical politics," such arguments seem to me to smack of intellectual arrogance. Certainly many voters are influenced chiefly by some particular grievance or some incident, some politician's phrase or some slick advertisements on TV, and will not bother with any wide-ranging statement of party policy. But the degree of susceptibility to particulars is not fixed. It varies with the broad impression of credibility that a party has given. A good pamphlet can influence that impression, even in the minds of people who do no more than glance at it. It is not wasted even if the proportion of people who read it carefully is limited; and that proportion is anyway higher, I think, than is supposed by those politicians whose own interest in the policies of government is less than their desire to be in power.

Preparation of this pamphlet was closely followed by work on the advertising copy for the campaign. At this point we were well served by Maclarens advertising agency, especially by George Elliott. He and I worked harmoniously together to write, in a few days at the beginning of April, the print advertising and scripts of radio and TV "spots" for the main national campaign.

Meanwhile, with Walter's leadership, Keith's energy, and the enthusiasm of a growing number of volunteers across the country, the work of organizing for the campaign progressed well. Few people are immune to their own propaganda and we began seriously to think that, despite the magnitude of the government majority to be overcome, we could win. Except that, as much else became encouraging, the party activists grew increasingly concerned that Mike was the weak link in the chain.

Skilled professional coaching produced only slight improvement in his performance on television and his speaking style remained, from most platforms, ineffective. All too often the reaction of some listeners to his speeches, as well as many viewers of television, was doubt whether he meant what he said. That showed up clearly in the opinion surveys. Ironically, it was Mr Diefenbaker, the actor-orator, whose sincerity was much more accepted by the public. I attributed much of the blame to training in a diplomatic world where a clear, blunt statement of intentions was regarded as amateurish and ineffective, not to say uncouth. Intellectually, Mike knew that politics was different, but the inhibition was there and produced a hesitancy that was crippling both to platform oratory and to television presentation.

There were others who were more critical; complaints that Mike was "weak" intensified. Some of the professional communicators talked about changing his image, and there were journalists who took up such talk. Mike did in consequence make some superficial changes, such as abandoning bow ties. But nobody who knew him well thought Mike could be other than himself. The concern of his friends was not that Mike should be different but that on public political occasions he should be more the man we knew in private. We never found out how that could be done, though at times we told ourselves that there was some improvement.

The alternative remedy we did conceive did not prove to be much good. It was to emphasize "the Pearson team" – the high quality of many of the people who were running as Liberal candidates. In the process we no doubt encouraged some excessive ambitions for high ministerial office, but I doubt that we had much other effect. Many candidates made good speeches, but media attention was inevitably concentrated on the leaders. And Mr Diefenbaker, with the kind of negative political skills that came so easily to him, turned the "team" idea to his own purposes.

He saw Mike as a weak politician and treated him with contempt. His oratorical denunciation was directed more vehemently to the men around Pearson, who were identified for his purpose as the five "bureaucrats" – Walter Gordon, Mitchell Sharp, Maurice Lamontagne, Bud Drury and me. It was no good objecting that at that point I had never been a government official. I was singled out for special attention. I was "the leader of the leader." And where was I leading? To socialism. This was allegedly demonstrated by means of carefully selected bits from the Kingston paper.

I was sorely tempted, for a heated moment, to reply in kind by releasing the letter that a Conservative premier – Duff Roblin – had written to me about that paper. It had begun: "I think your paper on social security is simply splendid." I do not mean that, in a long discussion of details, Duff unreservedly committed himself to agreement with everything in the paper. He was too good a politician for that. But the warmth of his letter would have made it impossible for Diefenbaker to go on attacking me as a socialist evil-doer. However, as Walter, with whom as usual I discussed the problem, put it: you don't allow Mr Diefenbaker's kind of political tactics to provoke you into embarrassing a friend. I ignored the attacks and Mike was never any good at defending me or the others. Fortunately, the evidence of the opinion surveys, supporting common sense, was that anyway it was a non-issue. It was a mark of the government's poverty of ideas that Mr Diefenbaker was apparently going to present the election issue as a choice between socialism and him. There were no signs that this cut any ice at all with marginal voters. Reporters on the Diefenbaker campaign tour later told me that, when the Prime Minister launched into his denunciation of me and my socialism, which he did from platforms across the country, even the faithful simply looked puzzled; after all, except in Manitoba, few of them had ever heard of Tom Kent before.

But if Mr Diefenbaker's line was electorally ineffective it was none the less successful, as he no doubt calculated, in heightening tensions within the Liberal party. There were people ready to tell Mike that it was confirmation that he was giving too much power to Walter and me. And, while Mike had a self-deprecating style, at heart he was proud enough. He would have had to be insensitive indeed to be entirely immune to being represented by the Prime Minister of Canada as the mere tool of others. The fact that he never could debate successfully with Diefenbaker made the latter's contempt hurt the more.

While neither Mike nor I would have admitted it to the other, or perhaps at the time to ourselves, Diefenbaker's characterization of me as the leader made it impossible for our relationship to be quite as easy as it had been. We respected and trusted each other enough to enjoy a friendly equality of discussion that yet did not challenge his seniority in position and in age. If he readily granted me primacy in matters of economics, numbers and literary style, I equally readily respected his far greater experience and his superior knowledge of many matters and of people. But it was a delicate relationship to be subjected to Diefenbaker's public distortion.

It was hardly possible for Mike not to have moments of feeling that he was too dependent on me and, while he did not do anything to correct it, wishing it were not so. By reaction, I had moments of feeling that he did not show an appreciation corresponding to how much he asked of me – "exploited" me, as Maurice Sauvé frequently said. For 99 per cent of the time our relationship did not change, or changed only to the extent that was inevitable as my position in the party changed, with broadening contacts and particularly because of the increasingly close association with Walter. The number of occasions when Mike and I rubbed each other the wrong way was still small, for so close a relationship and under so much pressure, but they were less few than they would have been if Diefenbaker had not identified a potentially sore spot and pressed on it with his gleeful skill in such enterprises.

For example, Mike's sensitivity about the relationship was at work in one of the few disagreements about campaign planning. Walter was adamant in the view that, as he put it with characteristic bluntness to us both, I must write all Mike's speeches. That meant travelling with him throughout the campaign. Mike demurred. He agreed that I had to do the speech-writing. But, he argued quite unrealistically, much of what was required could be done without being on the campaign tour all the time; I would need also to spend a good deal of time in Ottawa, to keep a hand on policy decisions at headquarters. His sense of this need was, I am sure, genuine. He had a well-based concern about the kind of stunts that, in the heat of campaigning, party enthusiasts were liable to get up to, and he thought that I could control them. But I doubt whether he would have given so much weight to this consideration if he had not also had an unstated concern that my constant presence with him during the campaign, which of course would be particularly apparent to the accompanying journalists, might be taken as confirmation of Diefenbaker's charge.

As was usually the case, I agreed with Walter. The lines of the national campaign had already been thoroughly planned. Though he had his personal contest, as a candidate in Toronto, to attend to, Walter was perfectly capable of ensuring, with Keith Davey's able lieutenancy, that the plans were carried out. No doubt, as the campaign developed, matters would arise that the three of us needed to talk about. But we communicated easily and were accustomed to doing it tersely. There was no doubt in our minds that any genuinely necessary consultation could be done entirely adequately by telephone. It was on the leader's campaign tour that there would be the greatest need to sustain both the reality and the appearance of firm decisions quickly made and clearly articulated. I could be most useful if I was on the spot, not only to write speeches but also to ensure in other ways that the campaign strategy was kept as clear and coherent as possible.

Walter, as usual, got his way with only a small compromise. I would travel with Mike most of the time, which in practice meant – by Mike's wish as much as anyone's, when it came to the week-by-week decisions – almost all the time.

I spent the end of March and the early part of April adding to the program "literature" as much other material as could be written in advance: a basic speech on the issues of the campaign; a letter from Mike to armed forces personnel; messages to identified groups (Indians, university students, Eskimos, and so on); statements on topics identified with particular interests (small business, municipal development, immigration, and the like). We got the preparation of a speaker's handbook, which had been contracted out to a retired party official, into something like final shape, and supplemented it by arranging for the writing of actual model speeches for candidates. Keith's communications arrangements were well worked out. Though it had all been more rushed than it should have been, we began to feel that we were ready.

What was expected happened on 17 April; Mr Diefenbaker announced the dissolution. Polling day was to be 18 June. There was one item in the plan that required immediate implementation. We had agreed that Mike should at once challenge Diefenbaker to a TV debate. We did not think it likely that he would accept: the precedent of the Nixon-Kennedy exchanges was then too fresh in every politician's mind. But the challenge was genuine in the sense that we felt fairly confident that in the conditions of a TV debate Mike could be more impressive than Diefenbaker, at least in comparison with the expectations of viewers who were marginal voters. It seemed to be a no-lose move, whatever the response.

We were concerned, however, about the tone of the challenge: it should be serious, convincing and without bravado. Walter and Dick O'Hagan and I spent some time on 18 April writing the following statement by Mike:

> In this general election we will all be sharing together in deciding the direction we want Canada to take in the next four years. We have serious problems in this country. We must cure unemployment, we must get our economy moving and keep it moving vigorously. What the government does in the next four years will settle the pattern of the future for us all.
>
> These problems need the fullest and frankest public discussion. Today, television provides one of the most important ways to discuss public issues as widely as possible.
>
> I therefore think that these should be a television debate between Mr Diefenbaker and myself. I trust he will agree with me that this would help the electorate and ought to be done.

Mr Diefenbaker declined the challenge, with an ill grace that made us feel that he was more on the defensive than we had dared to expect. Certainly the immediate issue of the challenge helped to create a valuable sense, in our organization and in the media, that we had the initiative. Perhaps we exaggerated that because we were so relieved that we had been right, thanks to Walter, to key our planning so firmly to a June date.

But a campaign cannot be so well organized that people do not become jittery as the moment to start approaches. Doubts and second thoughts expand to occupy all the time available. I was soon caught up in meetings and in telephone calls across the country. The pursuit by journalists preparing background stories began in earnest. There were also a few essential personal preparations. I bought extra shirts, since hotel laundries would be no use on the many stops when we would arrive in the evening and leave early the next morning. More importantly I bought, as the party's property, a tin trunk and stout padlocks. This was to serve as my mobile filing cabinet. Keith Davey christened it "the think locker." It became part of the priority baggage which at each overnight stop was rushed, with the help of a van that the local organization had waiting, from the aircraft to hotel rooms.

Our federal election campaigns, extending over virtually two months, are too long. Such an interval between the dissolution of one Parliament and polling for the next was entirely reasonable when the only way for political leaders to travel round the country was by whistle-stopping trains; when candidates depended on horses to get around their constituencies; and when, apart from the contacts that this travelling produced, people had to rely almost entirely on newspapers for their political information. But now that national television is the main medium for campaigning, and travel is by air, there is no reason why a campaign should take longer than the three weeks or so that has long been common in more densely populated countries. In the era of the computer and social insurance numbers, voter lists could easily be kept in a form in which they can be readily updated. There would be no difficulty whatever in abandoning the clumsy process of voter registration for each election, which is now the only excuse for the length of the campaign.

The only beneficiaries are the political parties, in the sense that each hopes to use a long campaign to put up a better smokescreen than the other. Despite what they proudly claim, neither government nor opposition wants to depend more than it can help on the record, on what it has done since the last election. Those performances are what the voters have in mind, in some broad impressionistic way, before the campaign begins. The objective of the politicians in the election campaign is to overlay such impressions with personality appeals, propaganda, promises, and denunciation of opponents.

The long campaign period enables the party organizations to be cranked up for such tasks, above all to expose the leader to a maximum of favourable publicity. It is likely, to say the least, that the voters who choose most wisely are those who stick to their comparative impressions of the parties' performance since they were last up for election. But the long campaign enables the parties to do their best to establish images over performance, personalities over policy.

That is the usual character of election campaigns. In 1962, however, our objective was different. The problem as we saw it was that the true picture of what a new Liberal government would be had not been drawn in time to have its full effect during the pre-campaign period. We owed it to the electorate to make up for this as best we could, taking advantage of the long campaign.

One of the primary decisions in the campaign planning, therefore, had been that we would start early. We recognized the risk that the campaign would, in consequence, peak too soon, that before it was over Mike and many others of us would be too exhausted to perform effectively. Nevertheless, an early start seemed to be an essential compensation for the failure to get our policy clearly stated long enough in advance. If we used the first week or two effectively, we could considerably increase the extent to which our position was registered, at least in the minds of the media, as creating the campaign issues. If we had started only when Mr Diefenbaker did, it would have been no time at all before Mike and others were putting much of their energy into criticizing his promises and attempting to reply to his invective. The importance of establishing our issues outweighed the risks of an early start.

Accordingly, the Pearson campaign party took off for the first time on 25 April.

PART THREE

Getting Elected

A little travelling music, Maestro

12 The '62 Campaign

We had decided that, since Premier Smallwood's fiefdom was the province in which the national leader's role was of least importance, we needed to visit it only once and could do so early; and on the way sufficient deference could be shown to the four seats of Prince Edward Island and the historic role of Charlottetown, which was therefore the first stop of the Viscount, chartered from TCA (as the national airline then was). It was a happy choice. The PEI countryside provided an environment in which Mike felt at ease. At rural meetings during the day he shook hands and cracked jokes as if he enjoyed campaigning. The painful stiffness of 1958 seemed to have quite gone. And in consequence, in the evening at Charlottetown, he delivered the opening campaign speech confidently. It was a very successful day. It also gave me a very gentle introduction to what I was to discover to be an increasingly tense part of my job: fending off the politicians and businessmen who wanted this or that promise on a local issue to be added to Mike's statements.

The next morning we flew to Stephenville, to be welcomed in great style by Premier Smallwood, and on to Deer Lake. From there the official party was a cavalcade of cars to Corner Brook, but I adopted what was to become almost a routine practice: with the secretaries I went ahead to the hotel to get the final speech text typed for Mike and a partial text reproduced for the press. I was never much good with a typewriter. Most of the speeches were typed by the brilliant secretaries from my scribble. Our party was small, and I had to be proofreader as well as draftsman. There was rarely time for any second thoughts.

As also became routine, there were telephone calls – with Walter and Keith quite often, but also increasingly, as the campaign warmed up, from a variety of people with questions, information, or suggestions. It was usually necessary to have a discussion with Mike before the evening meeting. When Mrs Pearson was travelling with him, as she did most of the time, they often took a pre-meeting meal in their hotel room. When he was alone, we often saved time by making the meal the occasion for our discussion. In either event it was usual to have a drink after the meeting. For Mike, this was a moment to relax before he went to bed reasonably early. For me, it was the time to get him to make decisions about the next day. He admitted the need but, in his tiredness, resented it. Increasingly, as the campaign wore on, though at first reluctantly, my solution was to make the decisions and tell him the next day. In any event, I usually stayed up much later, for talks with the local people and the press, telephone calls and writing.

In Corner Brook the talking solved what to me had been the mystery of the day. Premier Smallwood had been followed everywhere by a group of silent men, who stood out from the environment because they all wore black Homburg hats, in most cases one size too large. I could not think that Joey needed a security guard, but could not see what other role they might have. When the Premier had gone to bed and they had drinks in their hands, all became clear; they were Ministers in Joey's Cabinet and as such knew their place. A closer acquaintance that I made on the Newfoundland trip was Ed Roberts, then a highly precocious law student and impending politician. He subsequently became a Newfoundland Minister, but of a very different stamp. Besides the most voracious reading habits, he has one of the sharpest minds I have encountered in politics, and his early public exposure matured him into a man of unusual wisdom. It was the beginning of an abiding friendship.

The Corner Brook meeting was a local success, but a disaster in terms of Mike's campaigning. Theoretically, Joey introduced him. In practice, Joey made what would by any standards be considered a long speech. It was, of its kind, superb: a devastating denunciation of Diefenbaker and all his words and works. It was impossible for Mike to provide anything but an anticlimax. At his best, he would have been dull for an audience roused by Joey's oratory. Knowing that, he tried to be briefer than a main speaker would normally be, but in the process had difficulty in connecting up parts of his text and wandered ineffectually into substitutions that were almost as long as the deletions.

The following day Mike was taken by helicopter to Grand Falls and on to a short meeting at Gander airport, where we rejoined the Viscount and flew to St John's. Joey had learned his lesson. At that evening's meeting his introduction was just that. Mike's relief was so great that he spoke very well. In our discussion afterwards he gave ready agreement to an unusual number of items – texts and details of the tour plans for the following week. I then went, with Jack Pickersgill and others, to a party at the home of Don Jamieson, then the radio and TV expert who had earlier agreed with Walter and me to supervise the production of TV shows in which short statements by Mike would be interwoven with film footage of his campaign tour and speeches. It was a Newfoundland party that ended close to dawn. Fortunately the next day was Saturday, with no obligations except the long flight back to Ottawa. Mike was going to Washington for the weekend, to a dinner for Nobel prize-winners given by President Kennedy.

On the Monday morning, we flew to Toronto and there, at a press conference at the airport, made the official release of the platform booklet and "concertina." In a sense it was a great moment: the formal commitment of Mike and the Liberal party to the policies for which some of us had fought so hard. As an occasion it was, of course, anticlimactic. I hoped that I was not indulging in wishful thinking when I interpreted that as a measure of success: the press took the platform calmly because it was what they knew it would be. The flow of leaflets, speeches, and briefings had prepared them for it all. That did not mean, unfortunately, that we had got our position adequately known to the electorate before the campaign started. But at least the press knew and to a degree understood our policies. The reporting of them the next day, and subsequently, was satisfactory enough.

That afternoon we went to the studio of Bob Crone. I wanted to see at firsthand the difficulties that even so skilled a film-maker had in getting Mike to relax. We experimented with me sitting just off camera; Crone hoped that the familiar face to talk to might help Mike to be more his natural self than he could be looking at the camera lens. It didn't work.

Back at the Park Plaza Hotel, Mike, Walter and I wrestled with a classic campaigning problem. Our energetic BC campaign committee wanted Mike to make, in Vancouver the next day, a commitment that a new Liberal government would provide federal funding for a Coliseum project for which there was allegedly great popular demand. I was strongly opposed. It was indeed a platform policy that we would provide extensive additional financing for municipal projects; this was one of the major instruments for "getting the economy moving again." We could refer to locally popular projects as ones that *could* be supported under this program, if the municipality and province concerned gave them priority. But we should not go further. I had, of course, a double argument; part principle and part pragmatism.

Two of our most important claims were that as a government we would be good managers and we would work co-operatively with the provinces. We could not honestly believe that ourselves if we campaigned in a way that cluttered us with commitments to particular projects chosen according to their popularity in electorally key areas rather than assessed according to priorities either for our objective of increasing employment or in relation to the preferences of the provinces.

That was not in dispute, in principle, but of course we all three recognized that, to make it relevant to practical politics, we had to become a government by winning the election.

My second, pragmatic argument was that, while a specific commitment might win some votes in the area where it was made, if we did such a thing in Vancouver so early in the campaign, we would be pressed to similar promises across the country. And in that case the favourable effects, in this spot and that, would be more than offset nationally by the damage that would be done, in the minds of marginal voters, to the picture we had been trying so carefully to create of a party that would govern in the general interest, constructively, responsibly, firmly. A trail of promises across the country would dissolve such solidity as we had so far achieved for the idea that a Pearson government would be different; it was a tactic that would rightly encourage people to stay with Diefenbaker.

Mike and Walter wanted to agree; the only real differences were that Walter was even more exposed than I was to the pressures from our local organizations; and Mike, though less exposed, had by temperament greater difficulty in saying no. We therefore had to talk for some time before agreeing that Mike would express his sympathy with the project and say that it was the kind that could be given federal support under the policies proposed by the Liberal party, but he would not make any precise commitment.

That evening Mike was to speak in the York West constituency, at the nomination of the popular Toronto hockey player Red Kelly. He recorded in advance, for wide distribution, the part of the speech that dealt with Diefenbaker's feeble response to the challenge of the TV debate.

The following morning, May Day, we took the scheduled TCA flight to Vancouver. Mike made some appearances during the day there. The secretaries and I flew on to Victoria, where unexpectedly we were met by Jimmy Sinclair, later best known to the Canadian public as the father of Margaret Trudeau. He had been an important ally in the preparation of the resolutions for the 1958 convention, but his reason for taking the trouble to meet us in Victoria was that the secretary who worked particularly closely with me during the campaign, Pearl Hunter, had been his secretary when he was Minister of Fisheries in the St Laurent Cabinet. We had lunch, and he and I talked while the evening speech was typed. It was reassuring to find him enthusiastic about the platform and the campaign plan.

Afterwards the three of us went back to the airport to meet Mike's plane. It was a good thing we did, because there was not otherwise much of a reception. But the evening meeting was all right. Afterwards I got the agreement of Ray Perrault, the provincial party leader, to a statement prepared for the next day on an important BC issue, the Columbia River power treaty with the United States. Later on in the evening Mike accepted it, and we talked with leading BC Liberals. I found most of them like-minded, and that evening a number of acquaintanceships began to develop into friendships that were to be important the following year.

An aircraft, a DC6, had been chartered from Canadian Pacific for the next leg of the trip. No decision about further chartering had been made, partly because we were all concerned about finances and partly because Mike had a healthy inhibition about the élitism of chartering one's own transportation. But it was the only way to conduct with any efficiency the kind of travel across the country that our objectives required. The decision to continue the charter for the rest of the campaign was made easier by the helpfulness of the crew that CPA provided. Any lingering doubt was removed when the Conservatives chartered a sister aircraft for Mr Diefenbaker.

For the next six weeks "The Empress of Honolulu" became for me the nearest thing to a home. The press occupied most of it. The first-class compartment, at the rear of the propellor aircraft, was enough for the small official party, even after the next-to-last seats on one side were taken out and replaced by a desk, so that I could sit at the very back and write in comfort and relatively undisturbed as the plane made its many long flights. When there were stops for Mike to make brief daytime appearances at smaller places I often stayed behind on board and continued to work. One way or another, most of the remaining writing for the campaign was done in the aircraft.

On 2 May there were short stops in Kelowna, Cranbrook, and Lethbridge, on the way to Calgary. There I had a number of phonecalls to catch up with and decided not to go to Mike's evening meeting. It was a lucky decision, because it meant that I was ahead of our accompanying press corps in receiving the news from Ottawa: the Finance Minister, Donald Fleming, had announced a major devaluation of the Canadian dollar to 92 1/2 cents US

Obviously such a decision would have been taken, particularly during an election campaign, only out of absolute necessity; the official exchange reserve must have been drained by a major run on the Canadian dollar. What such spectacular events chiefly demonstrate is the herd-like nature of financial markets. They do not occur, however, without an element of truth in the underlying perception of greater economic difficulties than had previously been recognized. Nothing the government said would be able to alter that. Its campaign for re-election was based on the claim that all was well with Canada and getting better. The devaluation would certainly increase public scepticism. It was, from our partisan viewpoint, pure gold.

But even gold can be squandered. Sitting in my hotel room after the phone call, I was concerned as well as elated. It was not difficult to imagine many of our speakers going far too far in shouting disaster for the country. They could give Mr Diefenbaker an opportunity for which his skills were perfectly suited, an opportunity to present himself as believing in and fighting for Canada while Liberals aided and abetted hostile foreign financial interests.

It was essential that Mike react to the devaluation immediately and firmly. He should be very clear that it demonstrated the government's mismanagement of the economy and that it would hurt all Canadians through higher prices for things that came from other countries. But he should also be careful not to cry "wolf," nor to call foreigners to aid, as I was afraid he might be inclined, by arguing that it was respectable world opinion which had seen through Mr Diefenbaker. That was true enough, and in the following weeks surprisingly many Liberals said it, but it was not good politics.

I hurriedly scribbled a statement that seemed to me appropriate; got a taxi to the suburban location, in a riding it was thought we had a chance to win, where Mike was speaking; and managed to arrive just before the end of the meeting. It was possible to whisper the news to him before any of the journalists caught up with it. We discussed the situation in the car on the way back, he approved the statement, and we were able to reproduce it for the press party almost as soon as they got back to the hotel. It was not a masterpiece either of logic or of literature, but it served its purpose:

> The devaluation of our dollar to the arbitrary level of 92 1/2 cents is a confession of the complete failure of the present government's economic policies ...
>
> So-called stabilization at so unconvincing a figure as 92 1/2 cents cannot restore confidence. Confidence has been destroyed by the government's mismanagement of our economic affairs ...
>
> The consequences of this mismanagement are already being paid for by the Canadian people – by those who are without work and by those who no longer enjoy the progress in living standards which we had before 1957. Now further ill-effects will be felt by all Canadians, in higher prices for what we buy in the stores and in mounting uncertainty about our economic future.

The next day we flew to the difficult territory of Saskatchewan. Mike and the main party got off the plane in Yorkton and he was taken to a meeting there, on to Melville to another meeting, and then for a long car journey to Weyburn, the centre of the constituency that Hazen Argue had represented for the NDP and was now contesting as a Liberal. Pearl Hunter and I took the plane on to Regina, finished the speech for the evening – mainly on prairie farm policy, of course – and then drove to Weyburn to meet Mike over a meal. The meeting was large and Mike handled the speech well. Ross Thatcher, the provincial Liberal leader who had been known to describe me as a communist, was elated enough to tell several people after the meeting that he had revised his opinion of Tom Kent.

We drove back late to Regina. This was the time when the NDP government of Saskatchewan had bravely introduced medicare but was encountering strong resistance from the doctors. I thought it essential that Mike should not be in Regina without making a statement on the Liberal medicare plan, but he was exhausted by the punishing day that the Saskatchewan party organization had given him. We were due to leave at 10 AM the next morning, after a coffee reception.

Encouraged by Dick O'Hagan, the press secretary, I for the first time took the risk that became necessary on increasingly frequent occasions as the campaigning progressed. I wrote the statement and late at night had it reproduced, ready for distribution to the press, without Mike having approved it. We met at 8:15 AM He liked the statement but attached to its release the condition – entirely sensible in the political circumstances – that Ross Thatcher must first see it and approve. Fortunately, I was able to get hold of him at once, and in his new mood he thought it "bloody good."

The release was made before we flew on to Winnipeg. It affirmed the principle that "all Canadians should be able to get health care at the time they need it, without the anxious fear of bills they cannot afford to pay." The Liberal plan was national and would provide comprehensive care. It would "be worked out and carried out in full consultation and co-operation with the provinces." And – the dig at the Saskatchewan government – it would "deserve and receive the cooperation of the medical profession." There was more detail, and the confident ending: "I am sure that the Liberal plan will work well for both the public and the doctors. It will be a great step forward in social purpose, achieved in a Canadian way for the benefit of all Canadians."

In Winnipeg, the schedule arranged for Mike was again hectic, with two daytime speeches and an evening one at the nominating convention for the Selkirk riding. The speech notes for Manitoba put the main campaign themes into a distilled form that we used repeatedly in the following weeks:

> The issue in this election is the contrast between what the country needs and what it's getting ... unemployment, lower real incomes. These have been the wasted years. The present government tells you that things are fine. Their standards are too low for Canadians. We can set ourselves higher standards ... The Liberal party has the program that will make things better ... cure unemployment, greater security, better opportunities ... The Liberal program has been care-

fully worked out ... sound in principle, up-to-date, positive. The program is backed up by the quality of Liberal candidates across the country ... We can do much better. With a Liberal government, we will do much better.

Into that oratorical framework I fitted details of one or more of the policies, according to their appropriateness to the locality, and more specific criticisms of the government's lack of performance on health care or pensions or employment or whatever was the policy area being emphasized that day. For a while the variations were enough to sustain media interest and the momentum of the campaign. As it turned out, however, I underestimated the difficulties of keeping such momentum through all the weeks of the campaign.

I had no idea of that, however, on the evening of 4 May. Walter phoned with advance news of the latest Gallup Poll, which was very encouraging. And we were emboldened by the devaluation to take a plunge about which we had hesitated: to produce other specific evidence that the realities of the economic situation, known to the government, made nonsense of its election claim that all was well and getting better. The common view among economists and in business was that, while some recovery from the recession was taking place in 1962, it would not be strong or prolonged; by 1963 unemployment would be increasing again.

While the resources of Liberal headquarters did not run to anything that could be called a research capability, it was widely known in Ottawa that government economists had prepared employment projections for the Gill committee. That was an enquiry set up because the existing unemployment insurance system had been put into disarray by the recession. Its fund was depleted. The committee was to recommend what should be done about it. To do so, it naturally sought a careful estimate of the problem to which the future insurance system must be addressed – that is, the amount of unemployment. We had a copy of the projections.

In 1961 unemployment had been 7.2 per cent of the labour force, then a horrendous figure compared with the 3.4 per cent as recently as 1956 (the last year, as we liked to say, before the Conservative government). The official projections were that the rate would fall to an average of 6.0 per cent in 1962 but then rise to 7.3 per cent in 1963 and to 7.7 per cent in 1964 – which then meant a staggering number, by the standards to which we were accustomed, of well over half a million people out of work.

From Winnipeg we flew to Sault Ste Marie and I incorporated the unemployment projections into what could, I think, fairly be called a strong speech delivered there. It contrasted Mr Diefenbaker's rhetoric with his government's indecisions and lack of action, with the fact that national income per person had declined by 3 per cent, unemployment had greatly increased and, according to the government's own economists, would increase further to the appalling number of 535,000 in 1964.

What was the Prime Minister doing about this prospect? How could he claim that the Canadian people had never had it so good? "Are the Tories satisfied when, in this country, we have hundreds of thousands of people out of work? They talk about an upsurge and they are forced to devalue the dollar. They talk about national development ... Let him [the Prime Minister] tell us what he is going to *do* about it. He doesn't have to debate with me on television in order to tell us – though I think that debate would be the best way. But any way would be better than the government's failure to be honest with the Canadian people." The meeting – on a Saturday evening – was small but enthusiastic and the speech got good play in the press. It threw the other camp into some confusion. One prominent Conservative objected that we must have "stolen" the projections from confidential government files, while the Minister of Labour denied that any such projections existed; they were a figment of Mr Pearson's imagination. Mr Diefenbaker, as always more politically canny, could do no better than to try to defuse the issue; Mr Pearson was "forever finding reports," his challenge about this one was as "meaningless" as others, and no such report had ever come to his (Diefenbaker's) attention, "directly or indirectly."

Mr Diefenbaker was, throughout the campaign, more successful with this kind of obfuscation than we should have allowed him to be. None of us on the Pearson team was much good at infighting. Mike was particularly inhibited by the attitudes of an old civil servant. The secrecy that governments like to attach to such documents as the unemployment projections has become an outdated and counterproductive style of administration, but it was the one in which Mike had been brought up and he had no stomach for persistent, hard-hitting use of a document that had been "leaked" to us.

Under prodding from Walter he did eventually return to it, and put the obvious direct questions to Mr Diefenbaker: "It is now more than two weeks since I revealed the main predictions contained in the study prepared for the Gill committee. Has Mr Diefenbaker now seen the study? If he has not seen it, why does he not lift the telephone and ask for a copy? I am sure he can get one. Why is he trying to make this a hidden report?" But the Sault speech had been made on 5 May and it was then 23 May. The impact through the media was negligible compared with what it could have been if we had hammered home the forecast of higher unemployment when we had the advantage of surprise.

From the Sault, Mike moved on to his northern Ontario riding for a couple of days. For me this meant some time in Ottawa, meeting with

Walter, Keith, and Alastair Fraser (who was responsible for the detailed planning of Mike's tour) and scrambling to catch up with paper work and telephone calls. The tour group reassembled in Toronto, at the Park Plaza Hotel, on the evening of 8 May. Mike, Walter, Don Jamieson, and I met to plan television programs and Mike and I to discuss the speeches of the next two days. The main ones, at Hamilton and St. Thomas, seemed to be successes. Between, on a lovely day, we drove through southwestern Ontario with numerous stops at places such as Port Dover, Delhi, and Tillsonburg. In this territory Mike was at his best, delivering excellent little speeches. It was an exhilarating experience before we plunged into what quickly proved to be the tension-ridden low period of the campaign.

This involved a number of forays to Quebec and the Maritimes. The first, to Sherbrooke, Iberville, St Jean, and points between, was tension-ridden not only because of the sense of inferiority induced by our inadequacy in spoken French (Mike's was poor enough; mine was negligible) but even more because of the local organizational style. This meant that too much was attempted, everything was late, between meetings we were driven at speeds that induced continual quivering, and – worst of all – what should have been Mike's short intervals to relax and collect himself were invaded by candidates feeling entitled to bring their bevies of organizers to the leader's hotel room.

My strongest impression of these two days was the extraordinarily forceful oratory of Yvon Dupuis, but the sensations that come back even now are the green Cadillac in which I was driven and the near nausea of the journey, late at night, from St Jean to Dorval with an escort of Quebec Provincial Police screaming their sirens and taking us at what felt like a hundred miles an hour even through red traffic lights. It was a style that I had forgotten about until, twenty years later, I began to visit Africa and see the way in which the presidents and prime ministers of new republics feel it necessary to travel. By comparison, the short flight to Ottawa felt like being on solid earth.

The Sunday and Monday morning were a round of talks, telephone calls, and hurried writing, enlivened by a meeting at Stornoway at which Lou Harris made a presentation, brilliantly adjusted to Mike, of the findings of his survey. We should stick to a few main issues that were established in the minds of marginal voters, favourably from our viewpoint. Unemployment was the most important. We should not introduce new issues. All this was music to my ears. Mike was impressed by the performance. My concern was whether he would carry the tune in his head.

Afterwards we flew to Bagotville and drove to Chicoutimi and Jonquière. The meeting was poor, but I was cheered by a telephone call from Keith: Diefenbaker had spent most of his first CBC free-time TV performance replying to the "wasted years" phrase. In my interpretation, that was evidence that our strategy was working: we had created the main issue – if only we could stick to it.

The next day we moved to New Brunswick, flying to Chatham, driving to Newcastle, Bathurst, Dalhousie and back to Bathurst for the night. It was friendly territory and in the text of the evening speech I tried to hammer home the principal theme: "The main issue in this election is the need to make sure that every Canadian has worthwhile work to do." When we arrived at Halifax airport the following day our campaigning was three weeks old and we had been in all ten provinces. We released a statement noting this and underlining the theme:

> There is plenty of work waiting to be done in a great country such as ours. A new Liberal government will be determined to create the climate in which our economy will grow. In an expanding economy we can do what we need and pay our way; budgets can be balanced; taxes can be limited; the dollar will not be subject to panic devaluation. I believe that the Liberal party has the programme that will enable people to get back to work; that will free people from fear of chronic unemployment; that will get the business of our country, our finances and our currency into order. That is the election issue ...
> The wasted years will, I believe, be succeeded by the worthwhile years.

Mike was driven to Truro, New Glasgow, Antigonish and Port Hawkesbury. I took the plane on from Halifax to Sydney, to finish writing the speech for the next night, then drove to the Port Hawkesbury meeting, which was crowded and enthusiastic and at which Allan MacEachen, on home ground, spoke well.

The next day we flew to Greenwood, from where Mike was driven (often, he complained, at 80 MPH) between stops along the Annapolis Valley. I flew on to Yarmouth, to catch up with telephone calls and do more writing. Mike was too tired to do much good at the evening meeting. The next day's agenda did not improve matters: we flew to Mont Joli, Rivière-du-Loup and Rimouski. It was then that we began to gain some sense of the mood in Quebec. The disillusionment with Diefenbaker was complete but it was not matched by any great rekindling of enthusiasm for Liberals. The party's organization was not in at all the shape that our Quebec colleagues had led us to believe. Though I cannot claim that I then foresaw the Créditiste successes that were to come, there were obvious grounds to doubt whether the Liberal gains in Quebec would match the confident predictions. Late that night, as we flew back to Ottawa, Mike was not only tired but disgruntled.

I was equally so when, the next afternoon (Saturday), Dick O'Hagan and I watched a screening of the TV commercials that had been prepared by Maclarens. Some, we decided, were so poor that they had to be scrapped. On the Sunday there was much discussion with Mike, particularly about his role in the free-time television broadcasts in French. We eventually agreed on a plan in which most of the talking would be done by others but he would do a little. I made the necessary arrangements with the French scriptwriters. But, among a mass of phone calls at home that evening, there was one to say that he had changed his mind and would not do French TV at all.

My confident guess was that Mrs Pearson had persuaded him that he need not do so. I understood what was no doubt her concern, that he not exhaust himself. The problem about his wife's influence on Mike, which was great, was not that her advice was generally bad. On occasion it was, in my view, very bad, but for the most part it was no worse than most advice. The trouble was that her opportunity to express an opinion often arose only after Mike had already supposedly made his decision, and her instinct was to disagree. The result was that he was often nagged. Worse, Mrs Pearson could never accept that, as I noted earlier, it is crucial to leadership to recognize when the lesser evil is to stick to a decision once made, even if you soon regret it, rather than induce the demoralization that is so easily created if subordinates find that they cannot rely on a decision as final.

In this case, I was especially concerned about the change of mind because our relations with the Quebec campaign organization were already fragile enough. I could hear the word of it spreading like fire, another example of the weak indecisiveness for which Mike was already being criticized – often, of course, unfairly, as an excuse for what were in truth other peoples' mistakes. The next morning I did one of my stormings up to Mike's office and told him that the campaign was going wrong because he was not making firm decisions, looking ahead, defining who was responsible for what. It was not altogether fair, but Mike took the criticism with his usual good grace and I felt better for getting it off my chest. The upshot was, as so often, a compromise: he did some French-language TV, less than we had planned the previous day but enough for the call to the scriptwriters not to have to be cancelled.

It was therefore with some renewal of enthusiasm that I put the finishing touches to the main weekend product: "Campaign Strategy – The Home Stretch," a memorandum to all candidates and provincial organizations. Opinion surveys showed that "the issues most in the minds of those voters who are *tending* to move to us are of two kinds: (1) full employment and expanding industry; (2) rising prices and the need for better order in our national finances." Candidates and propagandists were urged to concentrate on those issues. "The Liberal programme would, above all, create jobs, get industry growing again, restore order in our financial affairs. All our major policies can be related to these central objectives."

The paper then dealt in some detail with the main items of debate and Conservative claims and criticisms, stressing always how to handle them positively and the necessity of treating the government not as wicked but as weak – "sterile in ideas and feeble in action." And so on. Mike approved it, to go out at once, and also a much shorter statement that we released to the press on 22 May – four weeks before the polling date:

> I have today written to all my 264 fellow-candidates in the Liberal
> cause. I have told them how clear I think the issues in this election
> are ... The Liberal programme will create the million new jobs
> needed for Canadians in the next four years. With this programme
> ... real income per person will increase, as it did until 1957, instead of
> falling as it has done since 1957. With this programme, we can restore
> confidence. The dollar will not be subject to panic devaluation,
> brought about by the mismanagement...

Etcetera. At this point, I was still a believer that we could win.

We flew to Toronto on Monday afternoon, 21 May, for a day and a half of filming for television, interviews with journalists – for which I had prepared notes on questions and answers that Mike might try to get across – and planning meetings. In those Walter and I, especially, agreed that while the campaign had run down, there were ways of putting renewed life into it. The task was not made easier by the very gruelling itinerary that had been prepared for the next three days: first, eastwards to such places as Whitby, Port Hope, Cobourg, and Trenton; then a flight to Sudbury and an evening meeting at Elliot Lake; back to Sudbury and on to Timmins, Earlton, and Kirkland Lake; then to North Bay, Chalk River, Deep River, Pembroke, Barry's Bay, Renfrew, Almonte, and Carleton Place and thus eventually to Ottawa. I wrote advance speech notes and press releases and decided, with Mike's agreement, that I could be better occupied without this journey.

On Wednesday in Toronto Walter and Keith and I got the latest Harris opinion survey. It confirmed that the trend towards our gaining support had slackened, not because there was anything wrong with our issues but because we were not getting them across effectively. In part, it seemed to us, this was because Diefenbaker's skill as a campaigner was beginning to show. We agreed that Mike should challenge him more directly.

The first good opportunity for that, however, came to nought. The next day it was reported that Diefenbaker had denied the existence of the unemployment projections we had used. I phoned Mike to urge that he should not only reply sharply but should also release our copy of the projections to the press. But for that Mike's training as a civil servant was too strong; he would not agree to the release. It was a sad case of not calling the other player's bluff. The first decision to use the figures implied, in my mind, willingness to publish the document if its existence was denied. If we did not do so, we lost our opportunity to demonstrate, on the most important issue, how far the government's rhetoric was removed from reality. I found myself remembering the warning of the Conservative Minister who had told me in 1957 that Mike would be no match for Diefenbaker.

By the Saturday afternoon Walter, Keith, and I were ready to go to Stornoway to put to Mike a number of suggestions that we hoped might reinvigorate the campaign. We had the backing of the opinion survey which clearly showed that a positive stance, firmly expressed as a challenge to Conservative vagueness, would swing marginal voters. I had prepared a sharp statement that we proposed – and Mike agreed – to release for the Monday morning papers and radio:

> At the beginning of the election campaign, I proposed that the Prime Minister and I should debate the issues before the country on television and radio.
>
> The Prime Minister refused.
>
> After reading what he said in his television appearance last Friday, I understand why he refused to debate with me.
>
> The government's election appeal is based on claims that would not stand up for one minute if we discussed them face-to-face.

One was Diefenbaker's claim that "we have done our part to raise the general standard of living in Canada," another that the economy was in a "recession" when he took office and now was enjoying a "boom." We demolished these outrageous assertions with simple statistics. The average standard of living – real income a head – had fallen by 3 per cent during the government's life. When it took office 177,000 Canadians were out of work; the current number was 485,000. Our statement concluded: "The public will understand why the Prime Minister will not enter a debate, in which he would be faced with the facts."

The second decision that Saturday afternoon was to introduce a new element into the speech that Mike would make in Winnipeg on the coming Monday. I had prepared a list of questions that he should put to Mr Diefenbaker. "If the Prime Minister won't face a television debate, perhaps there's at least some second-best way of presenting the issues as clearly as possible ... I therefore have an alternative proposal for him. Will he answer some questions that I put to him? He can answer them before one of his own audiences. That will be easier for him, perhaps, than doing it with me on television." Ten detailed questions, designed to show the state of the economy in hard facts, were then listed. "In order to avoid any doubt, I have earlier this evening sent a copy of these questions by registered mail [that was a Keith Davey touch] to the Conservative headquarters in Ottawa. I don't want to hurry him. Three nights from now ... I will be speaking in Vancouver. I hope he will answer my questions before then. In any event, I will answer them myself in Vancouver."

The third decision made that afternoon was that in Vancouver Mike would also make a public pledge that as Prime Minister he would either cure unemployment or resign. It was with some elation that afterwards Walter and I had a drink at my home before I drove him to the airport.

On Sunday I completed the details of the statement and speech, took them to Mike, and got his warm approval. My phone calls that day were buoyant and it was in great good humour that Keith and Dick O'Hagan and I worked on organizational plans for the next week or two. On Monday we flew to Winnipeg, to a good reception at the airport and an enormous and enthusiastic crowd at the meeting. The speech seemed to me to go very well; far more importantly, it delighted the key Liberals in Manitoba, many of whom had been fairly cool towards Mike. Their enthusiasm on this occasion combined with old friendships to make me stay far too late at a party and even to be so foolish as to smoke, in defiance of my normally strict loyalty to a pipe, the two excellent cigars that were considered to be appropriate congratulations. The joy was not restricted to party spirit. At an early breakfast the next morning with the four key Manitoba organizers, the subject they wanted to discuss was which of the candidates would be the best Minister from Manitoba in the Pearson Cabinet.

We then flew via North Battleford to Edmonton and a fairly successful meeting; the next day to Whitehorse – where there was a great cavalcade of cars, and a moose barbecue for lunch – and to Prince George for the evening; the next day via Abbotsford to Vancouver. Jimmy Sinclair was at the airport, to drive us to the hotel and talk, and I had some difficulty in getting the speech text and press release through the final stages of production as well as getting some script notes to Mike in time for a late-afternoon TV show.

The evening meeting felt like a triumph. The BC organization was in fine shape and the hall was filled beyond capacity long before the meeting began. I would not have got in, even by the back door, if I had not remembered that I happened to have a credit card of Mike's in my wallet, and with that was able to convince a commissionaire that I belonged. Mr Diefenbaker had not replied to our Winnipeg questions, so that Mike gave our answers, designed to lead to the punch line: "The first need is to get rid of this government." The rest of the speech was a terse statement of our main theme, including the commitment that "if we do not get rid of chronic unemployment ... my work will be over. But I don't expect either to fail or to resign. I am confident that a new Liberal government can clear up our disordered affairs." In Vancouver, at any rate, it seemed to go over well.

The next day we made the long flight to Port Arthur – it is hard now to remember how slowly piston aircraft travelled – and a large and enthusiastic meeting where again the speech seemed to go well. We arrived back in Ottawa late that Friday night (1 June) to the last weekend for paperwork and planning. On the Monday we did television filming in French and then flew to Toronto and drove to Galt and Kitchener, where, in addition to the meeting, we did more television filming, in English.

The next day we went to a series of Ontario towns, with the main speech in Walkerton. It was a sharpened attack on the government's record; with it went, at last, the release to the press of a copy of the actual table of unemployment projections as prepared for the Gill committee. Mike had eventually and reluctantly consented.

The following day Mike was in the London area, with an evening speech at Strathroy. I drove to Toronto to meet with Walter. It was apparent, despite the government's denials, that in May, after the devaluation, there had continued to be a heavy drain on the foreign exchange reserve and we wrote a statement about it for the press. Walter, Keith, and I planned the final TV shows with Don Jamieson and then met with Lou Harris to hear the findings of his latest opinion survey. They were moderately encouraging but once again indicated the need to be tough in our statements on unemployment, financial mismanagement, and devaluation. I wrote a message on those lines to go from Walter to all candidates, and was then driven back to London in time to brief Mike on the Harris report. After the Strathroy meeting we drove to Sarnia for the night.

The next day there were various meetings between Sarnia and Windsor but I went directly there to catch up with the speechwriting that I had not been able to do the previous day. In Windsor, Paul Martin's territory, there was plenty of Liberal ebullience, but perhaps for that reason Mike was strained as well as tired. His speech was not well delivered.

On the following day, 8 June, we flew from Windsor to Halifax, which provided a long time to write. In preparation for the destination we gave the press a release that the Halifax candidate, Gerry Regan, had phoned to ask me for. His constituency needed reassurance that it was not true, as Conservatives were saying, that a Liberal government would have no use for the Canadian Navy.

In Halifax, after the inevitable discussions and telephone calls, and after checking that Mike's meeting was full, I went to sit at the back of a rival (and not full) meeting at which Donald Fleming was the speaker. As usual he went on far too long, for the most part in a poor defence of the government's record, but even with his limited oratorical skills he scored a great success on one point: apparently Premier Smallwood had forced the Rotary Club in St John's to cancel an invitation to Fleming, as Minister of Finance, to speak to them on devaluation. It was a glorious opportunity to denounce Liberal arrogance. The nostalgia of the pipeline debate was in the air, and the audience responded.

I was deeply worried. The last thing we wanted at this stage of the campaign was to have all our careful building of a new Liberal party sullied by this kind of recollection of the regime that the electorate had rejected in 1957 and 1958. After talking inconclusively about it to Mike, and attending a press party at which the conversation confirmed my fears, I eventually set to work on the telephone and tracked down Jack Pickersgill at some remote point in Newfoundland. By then I was waking him in the early hours of the morning. He was inclined, as I feared, to make light of the matter but in the end agreed that some corrective action was needed. He promised to have Mr Smallwood issue that day an invitation to Fleming and Sharp to debate devaluation on a Newfoundland platform or on television. That was done, and I think it at least helped to defuse what could have been a seriously damaging issue.

From Halifax we flew – on Saturday, 9 June – via Trois Rivières to Quebec City. The morning began with a news report of a Conservative gaffe that made up for the Smallwood problem of the previous night. Alvin Hamilton had said he favoured a 90-cent exchange rate for the Canadian dollar; he and some other ministers had argued in Cabinet for that rather than 92 1/2 cents. It was an amazing statement from a member of a government, a breach of Cabinet solidarity on an issue on which it is most important for a government to maintain a solid front to the world. In fairness to Mr Hamilton, it made sense in the context of the way in which the Prime Minister, Mr Fleming, and other "orthodox" ministers (Alvin Hamilton could never be accused of orthodoxy) were themselves talking on political platforms. They were claiming so fervently that devaluation was a deliberate measure of which they were proud, a great thing for Canada, that anyone could be forgiven for thinking that some more of it would be even better.

It was probably this talk, more than Mr Hamilton's indiscretion, that encouraged the expectation of further devaluation which, as had to be revealed after the election, was draining the foreign exchange reserve at what became again the speed of crisis. Mr Fleming, of course, was compelled meantime to try to stem the tide, contradicting Hamilton and declaring that the 92 1/2-cent rate was "definite and final."

"What a way to run the country! ... We could not ask for a clearer example of why we believe we can do better." I wrote a statement on those lines and we had it typed during flight and given at once to the press.

Mike's speech in Quebec City, delivered entirely in French, was a considerable strain for him, but the crowd was large enough to mask any direct impression of the disappointment that the Quebec results were going to turn out to be. We stayed on at the Chateau Frontenac for Sunday, partly to give Mike a little rest but mainly to do the filming of the final TV appearances of the campaign. Don Jamieson and Bob Crone joined us for that. There was, as usual, an unfortunately distracting incident. Unlike the provincial leaders and parties in English-speaking Canada, Premier Jean Lesage and the Quebec provincial Liberals were keeping some distance between themselves and the federal campaign. That seemed natural enough in Quebec politics, but it was open to misinterpretation elsewhere. Mike therefore asked Maurice Lamontagne to invite Jean to come to see him at the hotel, but on Sunday morning the Premier called me to say that he wouldn't do that. He would, however, be glad to give a small reception for Mike at his home that afternoon. Mahomet and the mountain!

I passed on the invitation. Mike was not keen but said he would call Jean back. Some time later I got another call from a now angry Lesage: Mike had not responded and it was getting to be short notice at which to invite other people. We agreed that, to serve the political point, the guests should include the Liberal candidate in the federal constituency in which Jean lived. I couldn't find Mike and Jean called again. I stuck my neck out and committed Mike and myself to coming to the reception, for which Jean had compiled a short list of other guests. Eventually I tracked Mike down and by this time he seemed relieved and happy with the plan.

The reception was in fact a pleasant and appropriate affair, with Jean the very gracious host, and it enabled us to issue a press release that prevented serious allegations of a rift. When he was criticized in the

Quebec Assembly for involving himself in federal politics, Premier Lesage replied very satisfactorily: "I am a Liberal. Mr Pearson is a Liberal, and no one will prevent me from having in my home a great Canadian who will be the next Prime Minister of this country." The right result had been achieved, but once again only after an unnecessary expenditure of time and emotion.

With the TV filming behind us, we entered the grim last week of the campaign. For the Monday we were in New Brunswick, with a noontime meeting in Saint John and the evening in Moncton. The speeches were not strong. By this time Mike was very tired. And there was another factor: he was deeply troubled by the financial "crisis." It was clear that, with the help of Mr Hamilton, there was little confidence that the 92 1/2-cent exchange rate could be held. Companies were switching funds to US dollars and it was a safe guess – indeed, in the financial community it was known – that there was again a heavy run on the Canadian foreign exchange reserve.

I saw no reason why that should affect our policy. The market was overreacting, essentially because the election had brought home to it what we always knew – that the Diefenbaker government was in a mess and managing badly. The country was not going to be ruined. If we were in office we would probably float the rate again, and it might temporarily drop to 90 cents or less, but we weren't in an inflationary situation and a temporarily undervalued exchange rate would do no great harm while we put our policies to "get the economy moving again" into operation. The crisis, if it could be called that, reinforced the need for the economic policies we were proposing. There was no basis whatever for thinking that it undermined the country's ability, over the four-year term of a government, to put in place the other measures to which we were committed.

Mike could not give a counterargument, but he was troubled at heart. He could not shake off the conventional wisdom, so conveniently preached in business circles, that any kind of weakness in the currency was evidence that we could not afford more government spending. His conscience therefore told him that he must be "responsible." That couldn't mean that at this late stage he withdrew the policies. It meant that the way he spoke of them injected an increasing sense of caution. He used my texts, but his circumlocutions and his inflexions subdued them. In a sense, they fell between two stools and it might have been better if at that stage I had left him to speak only in generalities. I'm not sure. Certainly we did not end the campaign strongly, with the clarion calls for what a new government would do that I had aspired to.

In Moncton Mike also did a TV show with all the province's candidates, masterminded by Charles McElman (later Senator). He wanted to involve Mike in specific promises about local projects, to which I objected. It was on such matters that the issue of "responsibility" was real, but Mike's concern about it did not prevent him from leaving that kind of confrontation to me. In the end the program didn't go too badly, with hard commitments avoided, and McElman and I made peace of a sort.

The next day we were in Montreal. The speech, in mixed French and English, included a comment on the recent Gallup Poll, according to which the undecideds were down to 9 per cent and of those who had decided we had, nationally, 44 per cent against 36 per cent for the Conservatives. I was anxious not to boast that this meant that we would necessarily get more seats. What it did confirm was that "the Conservatives can't win." But the result could be a weak government: "The Conservatives provided weak government when they had more than 200 seats in Parliament. It would be weaker still if the effect of the election were to leave them just clinging to office. That is the kind of disaster from which we have to save Canada."

It was, however, from the organizers in Montreal that I learned, later that evening, of the reasons for doubt. They had begun to be aware of the Créditiste upsurge. They did not think that Maurice Lamontagne would win in the old Liberal bastion of Quebec East.

The next morning we cavalcaded through Mount Royal and other Montreal ridings, then flew to Trenton and drove to Kingston. There Mike used notes that were strongly worded, particularly on unemployment and the government's statements about it. The crowd was enthusiastic, but this was a seat we were going to win. By this stage in an election campaign, even more than earlier, those who come to meetings are almost entirely the converted, and their responses are no indication of how, if at all, marginal votes are still being influenced.

The next day, Thursday, we flew to Toronto and a massive meeting. There were various excitements. Khrushchev had issued a statement attacking the Canadian government, in a way that could be interpreted as an intervention in the election on our behalf. We issued a very short condemnation of his statement as arrogant, clumsy, inexcusable, and irrelevant. Later we discovered that a telegram had gone from Conservative national headquarters to all their provincial headquarters and Cabinet ministers:

> Most important all candidates stress significance Khrushchev's attempt to intervene in the election stop Facts are now clear K is trying to prevent re-election of the Prime Minister ... The Canadian people are entitled to be fully informed on the sinister background of this foreign intervention stop It would appear to be a prime responsibility of every Conservative candidate to fully inform electors in his

or her constituency often and emphatically in the next forty-eight hours stop

The man who most conspicuously followed this instruction, in winding up his campaign on Friday night, was Donald Fleming. He said that Khrushchev was "deliberately interfering" because he wanted to ensure the election of L.B. Pearson. "The man the Russians want is ... the man who would rather be red than dead." On the Saturday we issued an indignant rebuttal of this "vicious attack": "I will let the record speak against Mr Fleming's slander ... my record ... includes the honour of having been twice vetoed by the Communists for the highest office at the United Nations. It is sad to see a Minister of the Crown descend to such depths of smearing." But of course by that time the campaigning was over for the media and the rebuttal could not offset whatever damage had been done to us by this dirty tactic.

The second excitement in Toronto was that the government released the latest figures for unemployment. They had been rushed out ahead of the normal time, no doubt for election purposes. Since they were the May figures, they could be claimed to show a substantial reduction in the number of people out of work. In fact the reduction from April to May, I quickly calculated, was identical with the average of recent years. The figures did not indicate any improvement whatever in the state of employment. I inserted a page on those lines into Mike's speech for the evening but unfortunately – as happened all too easily – he mislaid it in the course of shuffling his notes on the podium. We put out a special press release instead, and I doubt that the difference mattered.

However, no one could stay involved in an election campaign unless he or she was capable of becoming so caught up in it that every minute move comes to seem important. On the Friday morning Mike and I engaged in a prolonged argument about the tone of his wind-up speech, which was to be delivered at an open-air meeting that evening in Brantford. He felt that to be philosophic and "statesmanlike" would be most effective. I felt that it was already obvious, to anyone who was going to be influenced by it, that he was more philosophic and statesmanlike than Diefenbaker. If there were votes still to be won, they were those of people who doubted either that he had the qualities of decisive leadership or that he was down-to-earth enough to perform on the so-called "bread and butter" issues that were of most concern to marginal voters. I wanted a hard-hitting speech on the main themes, on unemployment and the government's failures.

As usual, the speech as it was made had some of both strands and so was somewhat too long. But a large crowd received it enthusiastically, and we were all cheerful as we drove to Mount Hope airport near

Hamilton, for our last flight in the chartered aircraft. At Ottawa we said good-bye to the crew, who had been endlessly patient as well as efficient, and received a great reception from well-wishers who had come out to the airport late at night.

During the weekend Walter telephoned, and we shamelessly congratulated each other on our efforts while reconciling ourselves to the likelihood that we would not get a majority, though we still saw ourselves as probably having more seats than the Conservatives. We agreed that a minority Liberal government might not be a bad result; the need for NDP support might make it easier, not more difficult, to get our program implemented.

It was not to be. On Monday evening I watched the results with Mike. The Atlantic provinces produced some gains for us, but not what we had hoped. The Quebec returns made it clear that we were not going to get a majority, not because the Conservatives had held their seats but because so much of the turnover, outside the Montreal area, had been not to us but to the Créditistes. In Ontario we gained virtually all that we could sensibly hope for, but the results from the Prairies were poor and from BC only moderate.

By any normal standard we had achieved a massive swing, with the Conservatives cut from 208 seats in 1958 to 116. The NDP, with 19 seats, had not proved to be stronger than the old CCF had been before the 1958 sweep, and was well behind Social Credit, with its 30 seats almost entirely from Quebec. It was chiefly this Créditiste strength that had saved the government. It still had sixteen more members than we had. Diefenbaker would not be able, I felt sure, to make any solid alliance with the minority parties, but he could rely on their reluctance to face another election soon to enable him to stay in office.

We wrote a short, and I hope dignified, statement which Mike read on television and at a press conference. The campaign was over and we were still in opposition. I went to the inevitable party at the Chateau Laurier and, having drunk rather more than I should, home by taxi.

13 *All Good Men ...*

The end of the campaign did not bring the relaxation that, having failed to win, we might have expected to enjoy. Devaluation had not stopped the flight from the Canadian dollar. Losses from the exchange reserve in fact became even worse in the days following the election. On the Tuesday we were only guessing, but I suggested to Mike that a foreign exchange "crisis" would come quickly and urged him not to take it as seriously as it would be represented. It might mean that the government would have to borrow substantially from foreign sources and the IMF, in effect substituting those obligations for private foreign capital withdrawn from Canada. The Canadian economy was not so weak that we had to fear the kind of disaster that would oblige a responsible opposition to support the government in "saving the country and the dollar." It was not our business to talk about the seriousness of the "crisis." We would help more by taking it calmly. We should treat it as a consequence of mismanagement by a government in which the country had lost faith and which would soon be replaced through another election. Therefore Mike should not let the situation induce him to pull his punches in criticizing the proven deceitfulness of the government's claims and pronouncements during the campaign, in exposing its ineptitude as the cause of the trouble.

In the following few days I found this view shared by Walter and by most of the others to whom I talked, including the former Governor of the Bank of Canada, Jim Coyne. But it was apparent that Mike was not entirely convinced, and on the Saturday he told me that he had been visited by an emissary from Diefenbaker, in the person of the then Governor of the Bank, Lou Rasminsky, to plead the seriousness of the crisis and urge support for the emergency measures to be announced on Sunday (24 June). Though he was not specific about it, it was clear from Mike's manner that he had responded to the call for all good men to come to the aid of the country, not of the party. He had made some commitment, if not to actually supporting the government's measures, at least to not criticizing them directly.

The inevitable borrowing to bolster the exchange reserves had indeed more Draconian accompaniments, obviously conditions of the borrowing, than I, for one, had expected: a heavy tariff surcharge on imports, reduction to a nominal $25 of the duty-free allowance for people returning from abroad, and a 6 per cent Bank rate (at that time a horrendous level).

We were all agreed that we should not make detailed comment in response to the bare announcement of these measures, made that day without explanation. But I thought we should demand information and take the opportunity to do a little knife-turning in the government's self-inflicted wounds. My draft was very different from Mike's own. He asserted that "Canada is in trouble," that the difficulties were deeper and more fundamental than the flight of capital and pressure on the exchange rate, that the situation was "too serious for political partisanship or manoeuvring." He would have effectively committed "the full support of the Liberal party" to the emergency measures. If the statement had been made, Lou Rasminsky would have gone down in history as a Governor of the Bank who had a critical influence on the course of Canadian politics – the last thing he would have wanted.

Fortunately, other opinions that Sunday evening were closer to my draft than to Mike's and we ended by making no substantial statement at all, only a few sentences that said nothing. The next day Mr Diefenbaker saved the Liberal party from crisis and Mr. Rasminsky from historical embarrassment. His television address to explain the emergency measures was sufficiently full of evasions and partisan digs to make Mike angry and neutralize his sense of commitment to bipartisanship.

On the Tuesday morning he accepted, with virtually no modification, a statement close to the one proposed to him two days earlier. It did not commit us to support the government's measures but to judge them, when they were explained in Parliament, by what was best for the country. It said that there was no occasion for pessimism or panic. "I have no doubt that we will succeed in overcoming present difficulties. But we will do so by facing facts without distortion. We will do so as and when the government manages our affairs with wisdom and foresight."

My diary that day – the 26th – recorded "the crisis is over." In a sense, it had been a storm in a teacup. What we said about the emergency measures would not necessarily have mattered for very long. The subsequent performance of the Diefenbaker government provided plenty of other issues for effective attack. The real point lay not in the particular issue but in the factors behind the difference of opinion. Walter and I and the other activists were concerned that Mike's initial attitude would be the beginning of a trend that would emasculate the positive commitments of the party platform.

We had established the program when the party was weak and the people who cared were therefore for the most part the people to whom policy matters, as distinct from the people whose interest in politics is to be close to the levers of power in government. Now we were still in opposition, but with a vast difference from 1958–61. The government might not survive for very long and the common presumption was that the Liberal party would move on to victory. A good many people formed or rediscovered their active attachment to the Liberal party after the election. They were mostly conservative in the ideological sense but, since they could not voice opposition in principle to policies to which the party was thoroughly committed, their appeal had to be for caution – usually expressed as "responsibility" – in implementing measures such as medicare.

Mike was deeply sensitive to appeals to "responsibility." It was not just that diplomacy had taught him that often the way to get as much as possible done is to fudge opinions. The Methodist inheritance, a sense that there is a positive virtue in dealing with difficulties by tightening your belt, was often at war with his uncertain grasp of economic realities.

Therefore, while he was never a pushover for the men who came to lunch, he was always teetering on the edge. The fear of the party activists was that the post-election revelation of the financial "crisis" would tilt the balance. Indeed, in a gloomy moment on the Thursday after the election, Walter talked to me about resigning his newly won seat: in the post-election situation the conservative forces within the party would come out on top, our platform would be largely abandoned, and there was no point in staying involved. That was, fortunately, a very temporary mood, perhaps reflecting exhaustion from the election campaign rather than objective judgment. Within a few days Walter was back in fighting form. But the concerns that his depression reflected were going to recur through the rest of the year.

In the short run, we were cheered by the assembly of newly elected Liberal MPs in Ottawa on 27 June. That was hardly surprising. A great many of them were, in effect, Walter Gordon's people. The mood of the caucus was most definitely to attack the government and, for the most part, to be more rather than less specific about the program that in the campaign we had offered as the alternative to Diefenbaker's postures and platitudes.

It was an expression of the views of most of the caucus, as much as my own, when in a later memorandum I put in stark terms the argument that, if we supported the government's emergency program, we would indicate to the public that, when the chips are down, the two old parties are much the same. The smaller parties would press this point for all it was worth, without having to risk an immediate election. They would argue that the country indeed needed real change – almost two-thirds of the electorate had voted against the government – but the Liberals were showing that they didn't really stand for such change, whereas the NDP (or Social Credit) did. To prevent this we must "go into the session determined to fight the government all the way. We must work without hesitation to bring it down at the first possible moment."

The alternatives – either supporting the government or "just being indecisive" – were not only bad party politics. They would be a disservice to a country that needed a stable government to deal firmly and constructively with its problems. There was no possibility of Diefenbaker doing so. Our immediate task was to replace him, and our democratic duty was to use the parliamentary process to the full in order to achieve that purpose. The memorandum concluded with some hyperbole: "This is as clear, fundamental and crucial a political test as politicians ever face. If we wobble on this, the historians will say that we didn't know our business and failed ourselves and the country. If we wobble on this, we don't deserve to win and we won't; we might as well shut up shop now."

Such conclusions could not be reached without wondering whether partisanship was drowning intellectual honesty. I was never of the school that thinks that the duty of an opposition is to oppose, period. But there are situations in which the only way democracy works is for the opposition to fight the government for all it is worth. I thought then, and still think, that we were in such a situation.

At the end of June and in the first half of July, however, a smaller matter required attention: the campaign in the Stormont riding, where polling had been deferred because of the death of a candidate. Everyone was tired, and the internal tensions had some inhibiting effects on the campaign. In the end we won, though by a disappointingly narrow margin. It brought our number in Parliament to just a hundred.

I was having my own doubts about whether I should stay so actively involved in politics, but decided that the immediate aftermath of the campaign was not the time to leave. At least there should first be an effort to rebuild the arguments for a positive strategy in the new situation. The start of this process was an analysis of the 18 June voting. For speed, I did that first on the basis of the Canadian Press returns available a few days after the election. The Chief Electoral Officer's figures were not available until some weeks later. The differences did not significantly change the analysis, but for convenience I shall here quote from the final version of the paper, "Implications of the Popular Vote." The analysis was of voting for the four significant parties – PC, Liberal, NDP and Social Credit (which in 1962 meant, particularly, the Créditistes in Quebec). The votes for other candidates were so very small in 1962 that they could be ignored.

The Conservatives' loss of support on 18 June had been massive. Their popular vote had fallen from 3,910,000 in 1958 to 2,868,000, from almost 54 per cent to 37.4 per cent. By contrast the Liberal party's decline from 1953 to 1957 – from an election it had won comfortably to one in which it had been defeated – was from 51 per cent to 43 per cent of the total vote for the four parties.

There were two reasons why in 1962 the Conservatives had nevertheless survived as the largest party. The minor factor was that the rural vote had been much more loyal to the Conservatives than the urban vote and, particularly because there had as yet been no redistribution following the 1961 census, rural votes were considerably overrepresented in the

House of Commons. In consequence, though we had nosed just ahead of the Conservatives in total popular vote (the margin was a mere 4,000), they had more seats.

The major factor, however, was the strength of the two smaller parties. The decline in support for the government, plus the increase in the number of voters, meant that in 1962 there were in total 1,460,000 more votes for the three opposition parties than there had been in 1958. Of these, Social Credit garnered 707,000 additional votes (48 per cent), the Liberals 409,000 (28 per cent) and the NDP 344,000 (24 per cent). There was no lack of disillusionment with the Conservatives, but we had not won because, in round figures, "out of every four additional votes against the Tories, Social Credit got two, we got one, and the NDP got one." Of course, 1958 had been an extraordinary election, but there was not much consolation for Liberals in comparing the 1962 results with the more "normal" voting in 1957: on that comparison, the Social Credit vote had increased by 449,000, the NDP vote by 328,000 and the Liberal vote by only 76,000.

These figures showed that in 1962 the two-party system was less entrenched than at any other time except, perhaps, at the peak of the Progressive movement in the early 1920s. I analyzed how the total vote for the four parties had been distributed among them during the postwar years. In the elections of 1949, 1953 and 1957 the combined vote for the two smaller parties had varied between 16.5 per cent and 17.6 per cent of the total. In 1958 it had slumped to 12.2 per cent, but in 1962 soared to 25.2 per cent. One voter in four had turned to the "non-establishment" parties.

Moreover, the nature of those parties had changed. In the 1950s Social Credit had been virtually entirely a western Canadian splinter party and the CCF (NDP to be) predominantly so. Now SC had come to mean, predominantly, the Créditistes of Quebec. Their significance could best be seen by breaking down the Quebec analysis between the Montreal area and the rest. In the first the Conservative vote had slumped from 1958, the minor parties had made most of the gains in votes but were still too small to win seats, and a very slightly increased Liberal vote had been sufficient to yield gains in representation. But in the fifty-four Quebec ridings outside the Island of Montreal, the story was entirely different. The Conservative vote had melted from 678,000 in 1958 to 393,000 but the Liberal vote had also declined substantially, from 607,000 to 482,000. The NDP vote was negligible in both elections. The Créditistes had come from virtually nothing in 1958 to 501,000 – that is, slightly more than the Liberals.

The Grit/Tory, two-party system had remained the political pattern in the Atlantic provinces, on the Island of Montreal, and in some of rural Ontario. But in the rest of Quebec the Créditistes were the most popular party and in British Columbia that title belonged to the NDP. Also, in much of urban Ontario and in substantial parts of Saskatchewan and Manitoba, the NDP was comparable in strength to at least one of the old parties.

The memorandum drew the conclusions from this analysis in blunt terms:

> A continuation of the opinion trends evident on June 18 would be most unlikely to produce a majority Liberal government. Suppose, for example, that in another election the Conservatives declined from their existing 37.4 per cent to the 31.8 per cent of the vote that they held in 1953. This is a highly optimistic assumption. Nevertheless, it would not yield a clear Liberal victory if the extra opposition votes were distributed between the parties in the same proportion as was the Conservative loss of 16.5 per cent of the vote between 1958 and 1962.
>
> In that case, the Liberal share of the vote would rise from 37.4 per cent to 38.6 per cent and the other 4.4 per cent, out of 5.6 per cent lost by the Conservatives, would go to the minor parties ... There are only 25 seats that we would gain from this movement of votes. We would not get a clear majority.
>
> The conclusion is as clear as arithmetic can ever make it. We will not form a majority government unless we do better, relative to the minor parties, than we did last time.

The policy implications were equally clear. The voting analysis confirmed what had been strongly indicated to us by the opinion surveys before and during the campaign – but on which we had not acted with sufficient consistency and resolution. The case against the Tories had been made effectively, but not the positive case for voting Liberal. We underestimated the extent to which marginal voters, disillusioned by the Tories, would remember that a few years ago people had become tired of the Liberals.

To us it seemed all too natural to ask, after the mess the Tories had made, for a "return" to Liberal government. But that was out of tune with the feelings of many of the voters. They saw our campaign as largely the usual plea of the "outs" against the "ins." We talked about the days before 1957 in a way that entitled the public to think that our party was still in the hands of people who regarded those as the good old days. Since the public had not forgotten, we must not forget that they turned sour in the end. The argument continued: "As our campaign enthusiasm mounted, the public saw Liberals of past distinction out in front in numbers that covered up much of our 'new look'. This fitted our own mood and, irrationally, boosted our own morale. But it did not impress the marginal voter. On the contrary, it confirmed him in his belief that the Tories and we are pretty much Tweedledum and Tweedledee, engaged in a fight that means little to the public."

Now the only way to counter the NDP and Social Credit was to make our policies clearer, to show that they were new and that we were determined about them. The need for this positive strategy stood out with unquestionable clarity from the analysis of what happened on 18 June. Without it, there was no basis whatever for thinking that another election would give us forty more seats (as were needed for a parliamentary majority).

The argument seemed to me unanswerable, and I cannot recall it being openly disputed by anyone whose primary interest was politics. But I was not so naïve as to think that it would be consistently acted on. There were too many people whose attitudes and habits of thought were different. Mike was not very good at arguing with them; he had too much difficulty in making any case that turned on arithmetic.

I therefore decided to approach the conclusion by another route as well and wrote a second long memorandum, primarily for Mike, though it was also read by Walter and a few others. The clumsy title was "Strategy: The 'Left' or 'Right' Aspects." Mike was delighted with it, describing it as "a great State paper." The phrase was that of a public service historian, which in his thinking he often was, and it was kinder to me than it was accurate, particularly if the greatness of a document should be judged by its influence on events. But it was, I believe, an accurate portrayal of the condition of Liberal thinking in 1962. More importantly, it analyzed forces that are permanently in play within any Canadian party striving for a consensus within itself that is a sufficient base for gaining majority support from the national electorate.

Though the labels were then so conventional that they were unavoidable in the memorandum, the worn-out words "left" and "right" were not much help in analyzing the differences of view that must be reconciled within the Liberal party. The abiding issue was how definite or how vague we should be in the expression of our policies, rather than what the policies should be.

Underlying such a debate there were, of course, differences of ideology, fortunately covering a range rather than concentrated in two opposed wings. Instead of examining them as generalities, however, the memorandum discussed sixteen issues that agitated party debate, and on which it was possible to identify fairly distinct views as between those who wanted our positions to be definite and those who wanted to be vague. Though the details change with time, questions of an essentially similar nature are likely to be crucial for any opposition party that sees power within its reach. I therefore reproduce, in abbreviated form, some examples from the memorandum. On each issue, I stated first the view of those who were disinclined to be definite (A) and, second, of those who thought that we should be (B).

What is wrong?

A The main charge against the government is mismanagement of the nation's business – through lack of understanding, indecisiveness, confusion, playing politics. We should hammer intensively at these faults.

B The main charge against the government is neglect. It's been weak and inactive, and therefore it hasn't got results for people. Most Canadians have become worse off than they were in 1956. Unemployment has become severe, and will remain severe until a Canadian government adopts policies for the 1960s which are sharply different from Tory policies.

Management

A Our main plea should be that we would clear up the mess and provide better management.

B We will clear up the mess, and better management is an essential adjunct to good policies. But its role is secondary, not primary. Politically, you can't sell better management *in itself*. To claim it can only arouse old feelings about Liberal arrogance. What we have to emphasize is our policies. People won't believe we're cleverer, better managers, etc. because we tell them so. They'll make up their own minds on that, from what we do and what we say about the things that affect them.

Criticism

A Our propaganda should be heavily concentrated on exposing the government's faults.

B The negative case against the government must be driven home sharply and briefly. To dwell on it, at the expense of positive statement, won't move any votes; on the contrary, it stirs up feelings against the arrogant Liberal belief that only Liberals know how to run the country.

Confidence and Growth

A Confidence has been destroyed among businessmen and investors, Canadian and foreign. We should attack the high spending, high taxes and budget deficits which have led to devaluation. We should promise to balance the budget and hold down spending.

B Confidence was gradually undermined by years of slow-down in our economic growth. Having finally snapped, it must of course be restored. But the methods used must be compatible with the early stimulation of growth. The main Liberal claim is to policies that will cure unemployment and get production increasing quickly, so that Canadians can become better off year by year. That is the real basis for business confidence. We can't at the same time attack budget deficits *as such*. They're the symptom of trouble. Our promise is that we will achieve full employment; and *therefore* we will balance the budget.

Full Employment

A While we must promise to reduce unemployment, we should commit ourselves as little as possible to the meaning of full employment and to the specific methods by which we could reduce unemployment.

B We will cure unemployment, in the sense in which full employment means that no man who is adaptable enough to take a training course need wait long for a job. Asserting our ability to cure unemployment is, however, of little value. To carry conviction and win votes, we must say "how." A few principal policies for economic expansion must be simply and clearly stated.

Promises

A We should minimise promises of welfare benefits. They are unsound economics. They are poor politics because people in general have become distrustful of promises and a considerable number have become positively hostile to the idea of spending more tax money for social security.

B Local and sectional promises are often irresponsible and of dubious political value (though Diefenbaker did pretty well with some of his in the last campaign). But most of the voters we can win do want social progress. We won't win them by asserting in general terms our concern for the welfare of "the ordinary Canadian." A few main policies for social progress – to improve educational opportunities, to make good health care financially available to all, to ensure that everyone has access to adequate contributory pensions – must be set out definitely enough to be accepted as serious policies we really mean.

From such analysis of viewpoints, the memorandum concluded that our 1962 campaign had been neither one thing nor the other. It had tried hard to be both.

Where did we go now? No one could seriously propose that, for another election soon, we could make any significant ideological move from the consensus position established, at least on paper, in the printed 1962 policy statements. The only issue was how definite or otherwise we should be in campaigning next time. I summarized the arguments, and especially the conclusions of the statistical analysis, and ended: "The range of differences discussed here is – in policy, in what a Liberal government would do – pretty small. But in strategy, in practical politics, the differences are crucial. They mean greatly different impacts on the marginal voters who will give us victory or hold it from us. One way – by being more definite, firmer in our policies – I think we can win; the other way, we can't."

I suspect, however, that the main reason why the activists got their way, for the most part, was not the force of this argument. It was that we were more determined; in the last analysis, we were interested in a successful election campaign *only* if it produced a government with firm policy commitments.

14   *Organizing Opposition*

Gradually over the summer of 1962 I came to the decision – it was formalized by mid-August – that I should stay for another election. Mike could hardly have been warmer in requesting it. He was influenced, no doubt, by Walter's wishes. More encouraging, in a sense, were the urgings of some of the long-time politicians – Paul Martin particularly, but also ones with whom I had more frequently crossed swords. Less flattering, but intriguing, was the information that some of the more significant of "the men who come to lunch" had also opined that it was important that I stay.

In the previous nine months I had become more conscious of Mike's weaknesses as an opposition leader, but I had also encountered the Diefenbaker government at closer quarters. On balance, my belief that it was important for Canada to have Pearson instead of Diefenbaker as Prime Minister was strengthened rather than diminished. Friends divided into two schools of thought about my future. Some thought that I should stay in Mike's office between the elections but arrange to run in a "good" constituency the next time. I was not disposed to that, for the same reasons as before. The second group of those who offered personal advice thought that work with Mike during the campaign would again be necessary but in return I should get from him a promise that, if he formed a government, he would promptly arrange a by-election and put me into a senior Cabinet position. I had little doubt that Mike could be persuaded to agree to this in principle, though whether it would be an unqualified promise on which he could be relied to deliver I was not so sure. The question was in any case academic for me. I had come to Ottawa to do a job in opposition, and I was not disposed now to attach a condition to doing it. What happened to me after a successful election could be left to be decided then. Once or twice, in relaxed moments, Mike discussed the possibilities, but always in a desultory way and without any sense of creating commitments on either side. I felt things were best left like that.

The purpose for which I did want to use my bargaining power, in the summer of 1962, was to get some more effective organization into the operations of the Leader of the Opposition. I plunged heavily into that, on the basis of plans worked out with Walter, and Mike consented.

The starting point was that we now had not only a much larger Liberal caucus but one with many more talents. It seemed important that we be organized to make effective use of those talents from the moment Parliament was in session. To do so was essential to the morale of the new MPs and, through them, of the party organization across the country. It was also the way to use the session to strengthen the public impression that we were capable of running the government better than the incumbents. And, above all, it was the way to bring activist forces more effectively to bear on policy and strategy decisions.

In July Mike signed a letter to all the MPs, asking each to identify the topics in which he or she would like to specialize. For illustration I attached a list of twenty-seven topics into which public business could be divided. Almost all the replies were gratifyingly detailed and a great variety of interests were indicated. I had to put together an enormous jigsaw puzzle and in the end we set up thirty-nine "working groups" of MPs. Each had a convener and, generally, six or so other members, though a few were considerably larger: health, for example, was fourteen strong. Most members belonged to three groups and a few to more, but except for Jack Pickersgill no one was the convener of more than one.

The work was well spread. The members of each group were asked, on its topic, to review existing Liberal policy statements and consider how they might be sharpened or otherwise improved; to familiarize themselves with the relevant department of government and on that basis to prepare a dossier of events and issues which would provide useful material for debate and questions; to examine government measures, actual and anticipated; to prepare speeches, motions, questions, and private members' bills.

This activity had, of course, to be co-ordinated, more effectively than could be done at full caucus meetings. One danger was that the excitements of parliamentary business would absorb too much of the attention of members, and especially of the front bench, to the neglect of the work of influencing public opinion and preparing the way for the next election campaign. As a safeguard, it was agreed that the old Leader's Advisory Committee should be replaced by two main committees of caucus. One – with Lionel Chevrier as chairman, Jack Pickersgill (the real force) as vice-chairman, Allan MacEachen as secretary – was the House Tactics Committee. It was concerned with day-to-day parliamentary affairs, and was assisted by a three-member group to help MPs to prepare parliamentary questions and to screen them and smooth out their flow.

For the second committee I proposed the label "strategy," but it became the Planning Committee. Paul Martin was chairman, Walter Gordon vice-chairman, and I was secretary. The last was somewhat anomalous, since I wasn't a member of caucus, but that seemed not to bother anyone; by unanimous vote, I was asked to attend all caucus meetings. The nine other members of the Planning Committee included Donald Macdonald, Maurice Sauvé, John Munro, and Paul Hellyer. Our task was to try to ensure that what was done and said by MPs, in the House and outside, was directed as effectively as possible to the policy and strategy for another election. The most formal part of the process was that we held joint meetings with the working groups for such key topics as health, industry, finance, and monetary policy. The informal part was that I kept in close touch with the conveners of the more significant groups and indeed became in effect a member of some of them.

I do not know whether such an organizational structure would be of much use for an opposition party over the normal four-year term of a Parliament. That was not its point. We wanted another election soon, and the organization was designed to try to make the parliamentary session as much as possible the springboard for an early and successful campaign. As far as I could tell – and it seemed to be the virtually unanimous opinion of those involved – the way we worked was right for that purpose. The opening of Parliament was 27 September, and it was my hunch that, if at any point from October on we could have gone straight from the session to polling, without the intervention of an election campaign, we would have won a comfortable majority. The campaign made it another story.

The new organization involved a considerable change in my operations. I had as much contact as ever with Mike, but I was no longer his man in the way that I had been before; I was working with the caucus and party organization as a whole. It was invigorating. Relations with the new MPs were easy. Many of them had viewpoints close to mine and had come into politics for similar reasons. Those included a high regard for Mike and faith that he would be a good Prime Minister, but there was also widespread concern about his tendencies to vagueness and indecisiveness as opposition leader. From that perspective I was regarded as a good influence even by those who were not otherwise particularly sympathetic.

Even more important was Walter's close friendship. His prestige in the party was then at the peak that was sustained until June 1963. There was no question of a rebellion against Mike's leadership, but Walter's close relation to him was for activists the reassurance that a Pearson government would be what they hoped for. By the same token, others deeply disliked Walter's influence on Mike. They no doubt hoped to combat it more effectively once the Liberals were in office, but meantime they had nowhere else to go. Even if the party was more Walter's than Mike's, they still thought that it offered less bad government, at least in efficiency, than Diefenbaker provided.

I kept a room at the National Liberal Federation's office on Cooper Street and did most of my writing there, where I continued to have the assistance – as in all subsequent jobs in Ottawa – of the greatly talented Pauline Bothwell. But now I also had a small office in the centre block of the Parliament Buildings and spent much of the long working day there; at that location Pearl Hunter divided her secretarial attentions between Allan MacEachen and me. The routine was broken by trips to Winnipeg, Montreal, Kingston and, more frequently, Toronto.

In Manitoba Gil Molgat, as leader of the provincial party, and other friends kept in close touch. It was the only province where I was involved not only in policy issues, but also in organizational matters which elsewhere were entirely the business of Walter and Keith. Some personality problems in the campaign organization there were dealt with satisfactorily, but I failed in the most ambitious project. That was to persuade Steve Juba, the highly successful mayor of Winnipeg, to be a Liberal candidate in the next election. He was not disinterested in the national stage, and I think he could have been persuaded if he had been confident of Liberal strength in the next election. But he had an acute sense of political feeling on the Prairies, he regarded Mike as a poor politician, and he thought that the Liberal party in Manitoba had no chance of revival unless it promptly got rid of the conservative old-fogeys who were still, he argued, far too powerful.

In Montreal and Kingston my meetings were mostly with business, economist, and journalist friends to discuss policy issues. In Toronto there was more variety. Along with Walter and Keith and on one occasion Mike, there were meetings with Lou Harris about his opinion surveys; they could hardly have provided stronger evidence in support of an activist strategy centred on our program. There was also a rerun of the Campaign College, which had been so successful in the previous preparations and which we planned to use even more extensively next time; I contributed a revised version of the paper on how to handle national issues, which Royce Frith again delivered in great style.

There were meetings, too, with Bob Crone on television filming, and discussions with the various people, mostly in the Toronto business community, who with redoubled enthusiasm were now developing working details for programs such as the health plan and the municipal loan fund, as well as developing suggestions to make our proposals for industrial expansion more precise. I also met frequently at that time with Bill Macdonald, then on his way to senior partnership in the McMillan, Binch law firm. He was a loner rather than a participant in the Toronto group, but he had a highly active political mind; for some years from 1961 onwards he was one of the ablest and most supportive people with whom to discuss policy and strategy. Our views were then close.

The volume of correspondence increased considerably. More Liberals across the country, as well as the new MPs, offered opinions on which they wanted comment and asked for explanations or enlargements of policy statements. At the same time, Mike's appetite for memoranda was not diminished.

In theory, the Liberal position was largely settled. We were going to stick to the platform and pursue an activist strategy. That was the basis on which Walter was reappointed Chairman of the National Campaign Committee and on which I agreed to stay and to take on the functions with the caucus. In effect, we were treating the 1962 election as one battle of a war – a battle in which we had made large gains – and there was no reason to change the campaign strategy. Mike reaffirmed it in a major speech in Toronto on 18 September: "We do not need to spend much time in the coming campaign in exposing and discrediting Mr. Diefenbaker and his government. That has been done, by us and by them. We must spend more time in stating, in clear, concrete and simple terms, what we stand for." But while that decision appeared to be clear, the strategy would be acted on with some consistency only if it was continually related to developing events and to particular issues. In consequence I wrote, through the balance of 1962 and in early 1963, a great variety of memoranda and letters.

The organizational plan for the caucus working groups was supported by analyses of the lessons and errors of the recent campaign and was followed with detailed suggestions about machinery for the session and the campaign, including draft job descriptions for the principal people involved. Mike agreed that those expressed what was needed, but – as Walter, with a cynicism bred by experience, had predicted – he never issued them to the people concerned.

A more effective memorandum, because it visibly bolstered Mike's willingness to attack the government's "emergency" measures, set out in some detail "what we would have done if we had gone into office on 19 June." But he worried me by asking also for a memorandum on how we would have avoided the emergency. I pointed out that this was not a question that we should recognize as such, because the exchange crisis was a mere tip of an iceberg, a consequence of policies over the previous five years that were greatly different from ours.

A more substantial – at least, a much longer – memo was a "Preliminary Paper on the Presentation of Liberal Policy for the Next Campaign." We must make more impact with the positive part of our campaign than we made last time, and to do so we must stick to the existing platform. "We must look like a party that knows its own mind. Changes in policy, however desirable in themselves and however well-intentioned in fact, would be widely interpreted as weavings motivated by electoral calculation ... The extra sharpness of our campaign therefore has to come not from policy changes but from the way we present policy."

The improvements I urged were of two kinds. First, the program as a whole should be made more definite in order that it be taken more seriously. This involved drawing up a timetable for the way in which the items of the program would be divided over the four-year term of a government. The concentration at first would be on measures to get industry moving and employment increasing; the second phase would be particularly concerned with the longer-term measures to strengthen the economy; and the third phase would be when the major social programs took effect. Examples of the first were the municipal loan fund, reduced interest rates, tax incentives and the area development agency. The second phase included such measures as vocational training (with supplementary unemployment benefits), family allowances beyond age sixteen, university scholarships (to be effective, on the assumption that the government was formed in early 1963, for the 1964–5 academic year), activation of ARDA programs, insured mortgages for existing homes, the beginning of tax reform, negotiations to reduce tariffs and creation of the Economic Council. The third phase included the pension plan (to be effective January 1965 – I was optimistic by a year), the first stage of medical care (effective, I suggested, January 1966!), reform of unemployment insurance, the limitation of election expenses, reducing the voting age to eighteen, and so on.

With such a timetable, the cost estimates that I had prepared earlier in the year, but which had not been used, could be refined and, at the beginning of the new campaign, made public. They would show that, with the program spread in this way over a four-year term, it would all be comfortably financed on the principle of balancing the budget in conditions of economic growth with full employment. We would stop talking, as Mike and others had tended to do in the latter part of the 1962 campaign, about medicare *when* the economy improved. We would talk about medicare by January 1966, confident that by then it could be financed.

Of course, I did not seriously expect Mike, or other politicians, to swallow this proposal whole. Reluctance to be publicly so precise, to be "tied down" as they would put it, is too engrained. There is, indeed, a solid core of reason for that reluctance: government has to cope with unforeseeable contingencies. But there is also a good deal of convenient rationalization, making the uncertainty of the future an excuse not to do the hard work that makes it possible to be as definite, about some measures at least, as the electorate of a democracy is entitled to require.

My hope was that, by means of the planning exercise, the party would become more definite and confident about the program than some of the older politicians were disposed to be. During the parliamentary session in 1962 and early 1963, with the younger MPs as allies, the effort had a fair amount of success. During most of the 1963 campaign, with victory supposedly in our grasp, its effects largely evaporated until, late in the campaign, Mike in desperation returned to precision in the special and unfortunate form of commitments for the "sixty days of decision"; on that I will comment further in its place.

I had more success with the second, and major, proposal of the "preliminary paper." It was that, while we should make the platform as a whole firmer and therefore more credible, it was even more important to select, from the program, a few main points on which to concentrate our propaganda fire. In my now familiar language, "They must be policies that are simple to explain; policies that can be brought home to people; policies about which ordinary people will feel: 'that really would make a difference.' About these policies we must be specific, definite, firm."

The government having increased Bank rate to 6 per cent under its emergency program, I suggested that we should be specific about lowering interest rates. I argued (*ad hominem*) that in the great postwar days to 1955, with Abbott at Finance and Towers as Governor of the Bank, Canadian economic policy had been one of monetary "ease" (symbolized by a low and unchanging Bank rate of 2 per cent) combined with a fairly "hard" budgetary policy. It was only after the change of personalities in 1954–5 that there was a switch to a relatively softer budgetary policy and tighter money. "We were right before 1955 and wrong afterwards ... 'Tight' money is a matter of degree, and the degree is relative to what is happening at any moment in the us, rather than an absolute. Nevertheless ... it can be said that – unless and until Canada's position in the world economy changes greatly – the right policy mix for Canada is one that involves relatively lower interest rates than we have had since 1955, with less emphasis on monetary policy and more emphasis on budgetary policy as the instrument for avoiding over-expansion of demand."

We should most vigorously attack the current monetary policy and, with a commitment to lower interest rates, give sharper definition to the proposals to facilitate industrial expansion by such measures as reconstruction of the Industrial Development Bank. We should emphasize the provision of long-term finance for co-operatives and improved farm credit. We should particularly emphasize the Municipal Loan Fund; we should talk about it in terms of the municipal improvements, at low interest rates, that "come home to people" – sidewalks and storm sewers, streets and buses.

We should also, the memorandum argued, put more emphasis than we had on the proposal to extend family allowances beyond age sixteen, perhaps even, I suggested, up to twenty-one if the dependent remained a student. In conjunction with this, we should say more about our university scholarships and student loans, as well as about vocational and technical training. We should talk a lot about medicare, and to do so effectively must be more definite about some of the details of the proposal. Again, we should say more than we had about our housing proposals – extended grants for urban renewal, increased construction of low-rental homes, and mortgage insurance for existing homes. Finally, I suggested that we could put substance into our farm policy proposals (including improved credit and ARDA activation) and vigorous measures (including financing) to encourage production and marketing co-operatives.

This was a mixed bag, and the purpose at that stage (September) was not to settle on specifics but to try to get a vigorous discussion of priorities during the few (as we hoped) months before the government fell and the campaign strategy had to be in final form. I presented a first version of a strategy paper to a meeting of the national Campaign Committee on 25 September. It started from the evidence of opinion surveys. People were looking for change, for action to meet the country's problems, of which employment was identified as the greatest concern. But the public impression of what we stood for was still blurred. The NDP and, in Quebec, the Créditistes therefore presented a strong threat to us based on the case that we were not much different from the Tories.

The answer was not to increase attention to the minor parties by arguing directly with them. It was to put forward the positive action that we would take as a government, in contrast to the failure of the Tories. The most the minor parties could do would be to continue to help to keep the Tories in. For an alternative, the country needed Liberal action. We could win a clear majority provided that we made what a Liberal government would do, in definite ways, the election issue for marginal voters.

One member of the Campaign Committee objected quite fundamentally to the paper; he thought that we ought to talk more about the need for retrenchment. He did not win support. The upshot was that I would have discussions with the leader and assembling caucus and, in the light of those, prepare a paper for distribution to the organizations across the country. Those discussions did not change the approach. When I wrote a first draft on 29 October, the progress was in grouping "Liberal action" into six main points. Three were the policies "to get Canada moving in high gear" – "new jobs, new industry, better jobs." These were: the municipal loan fund; more plentiful credit (there was opposition to saying, directly, lower interest rates) plus tax incentives and adjustment grants for industry; and the "youth" measures – family allowances, scholarships, student loan fund and vocational training. The three groups of social policies emphasized health care, pensions, and "the family farm."

Mike endorsed all this, but had difficulty in reflecting it in his own speeches. A few weeks later, when we came to the first of the new series of "Nation's Business" television broadcasts, he decided to use the occasion to speak on the recent Cuban crisis. I was not opposed to his taking up a major international issue, but his script was of a kind to appeal to diplomats but not to the Canadian public. Its language was largely "officialese" and it offered nothing of leadership. To add insult to injury, he included a minute or two about domestic affairs that was so general – indeed vacuous – that it could only put people off.

Worst of all, he explained his lack of definite policy by arguing that the opposition should be given confidential defence information. I commented in a short memo:

> I can't see any value in pleading to the general public that you should be let into defence secrets in order to make up your mind. Other

people have to struggle to make up their minds anyway. Personally, I think that the idea of secret hearings is entirely contrary to the proper functions of a parliamentary committee in our system; but even if that is not accepted, and you want to argue for it in the House of Commons, I still suggest that a national television broadcast is not the occasion to do it.

Mike, as always, took the bluntness in good part and modified the script considerably, but it was still a sadly ineffective television appearance.

There was, however, some progress. The Nova Scotia Liberal party was holding a convention during the first weekend of November and Mike was to make a major speech. He wrote his own draft and I was cheered that it was a firm exposition of our policy on the lines of the draft strategy paper, though parts of it were in somewhat contorted language. He was in a buoyant mood and cheerfully accepted translation of the more important points into plainer words.

A major test of the application of the agreed strategy came just after the Halifax speech. November fifth and sixth were to be the occasion of a supply motion, giving us the opportunity to move a non-confidence amendment. By this time there had been no difficulty in deciding what it should be: a frontal attack on the core of the government's "emergency" program. We used plain words that would make it as difficult as possible for the NDP and Créditistes to support the government: "This House is of the opinion that the emergency austerity program of tariff surcharges and tight money, introduced on June 24th this year, should be stopped at once."

Mike introduced that amendment on the afternoon of the 5th. He spoke well. Then the Social Credit party, desperate to avoid an election, made its move. The titular leader, Thompson, proposed a sub-amendment, to add to our amendment the words "and replaced with a policy of debt-free money and constructive proposals to foster balanced domestic economy and balanced international trade." The calculation, of course, was that no other party would vote for debt-free money, so the government would survive on the first vote (the sub-amendment) and Social Credit could then use our having voted against their wording as a rationalization, of sorts, for voting with the government and defeating our amendment.

There was a meeting in Mike's office later that afternoon and the feeling, particularly Mike's own, seemed to be that we had to let the Social Credit ploy work; we couldn't vote for the sub-amendment. But no firm decision was made. I had dinner with Walter and later talked alone with Mike; he appeared to have made up his mind that we couldn't vote with Social Credit.

I sat up late to write a memo arguing that we should. We could have no quarrel with most of the wording – "constructive proposals," etc. The only sticking-point was "debt-free money." That was indeed Social Credit gibberish. I attached to the memo a "technical" appendix pointing out that all money in a sense is debt; it quoted from Keynes's *Treatise on Money*: "We can draw the line between 'money' and 'debts' at whatever point is most convenient for handling a particular problem." To talk about debt-free money was meaningless, but it would be equally meaningless to talk about debt-laden money – which presumably was what we were in favour of, if we regarded voting against debt-free money as an obligation of principle.

I concluded that, behind their meaningless jargon, what Social Credit really wanted was more money, lower interest-rates. We agreed with that. "In present circumstances, we are in favour of easier money. We favour it, of course, only to the point of wisdom in monetary expansion ... We no doubt disagree [with Social Credit] as to where the point of wisdom comes. But that isn't spelled out in their amendment. And therefore there's nothing in the phrase 'debt-free money' that we can conscientiously vote against."

This could be, and was, criticized as logic-chopping, but the point of the appendix – that there was not a fundamental issue of principle – was made. The question was one of political strategy, with which the memo itself dealt. The basic fact of the situation was that the government could be defeated in the near future only if we and Social Credit voted together. Whenever that happened, on whatever issue, Conservatives would say that we did it out of a lust for power. What else could they say? And what did it matter, given that their survival to that point had depended on Conservatives and Social Credit voting together? If we got an election, the voters wouldn't be bothering about the House of Commons manoeuvres either way.

They would be choosing between the Conservatives and us as the government. They would be less likely to vote for us if time had passed by, if the government had survived for a while because we had refused to vote with Social Credit when it was opposing the government in its sub-amendment. That would merely make us look weak and foolish. We would have thrown away part of our present advantage.

The only real argument against voting for the sub-amendment was that we might do it but not defeat the government; that is, it would survive with NDP support. But that would make the NDP look very weak indeed. Their troubles, and those of Social Credit, wouldn't be over with the sub-amendment. There would still be a vote on the main amendment. Social Credit would look foolish indeed if, when we had voted with them on their sub-amendment, they switched and voted for the government – for the austerity program – on the main amendment. The NDP would either have to vote with the government, for austerity, a second time, or else switch and vote with us – showing that they were so afraid of an election that they voted against the government when and only when they could do so safely, without defeating it.

Early on the Tuesday morning I got copies of this memo to Mike and to the people who were to meet to help him to make the decision – Messrs Gordon, Martin, Pickersgill, Chevrier, MacEachen, and McIlraith. We assembled at 11:30 AM. Chevrier put the case against my memo. There was, he argued, a matter of principle; and the party in Quebec was not ready for an election. The second point was correct enough, and what mattered to Chevrier. But it made his first point ineffective and it influenced no one, because we all thought that nationally our advantage lay in an early election. We doubted whether time was the decisive factor in determining whether the party organization in Quebec pulled itself out of its disarray in face of the Créditistes.

As a result Chevrier got no support except to the extent that Allan MacEachen, sitting on the fence, seemed to lean somewhat to voting against the sub-amendment. Gordon, Martin, Pickersgill, and McIlraith had all come to the view that we should vote for it, so we were five to one or two. Mike would obviously have been happier if it had been the other way, but he was impressed by the unusual alliance of the activists – Walter, Paul and me – with Pickersgill and McIlraith. He did not make a formal decision then, but at 2 PM, before the House met, there was a caucus and the general feeling was the same: vote for the sub-amendment.

In the House, there was another complication. Despite the supposed secrecy of caucus, the NDP had no doubt learned how the Liberals had decided to vote. David Lewis announced their move: the NDP would vote with the government, against the sub-amendment. As a result, at another Liberal caucus at 6 PM, there was considerable sentiment against voting with Social Credit when it wouldn't bring the fall of the government. But Paul Martin and Judy LaMarsh turned the tide with excellent speeches, and Mike concluded firmly: vote for the sub-amendment. As he, Walter, and I ate sandwiches for dinner in his office, and I scribbled notes for Paul to use in the final Liberal speech of the debate, Mike showed the strength and determination that was almost always his once a decision had finally been made.

In the upshot, of course, the government survived by eight votes on the sub-amendment thanks to NDP support. On the main question it was saved by support from Social Credit, though with some split: there were several abstentions and two Créditiste members broke ranks to vote with us. Though we subsequently took some flak, not all of it from outside the party, for "supporting Social Credit," there was no doubt in my mind that what we had achieved was of decisive, favourable importance.

Hitherto we had been talking to ourselves in proclaiming that the government could not long survive. With until then apparently solid Social Credit support, with the NDP's clearly desperate concern not to face another election soon, and with a widespread presumption that Liberals and Social Credit – or, to be exact, Quebec Liberals and their deadly enemies, the Créditistes – could not vote together, there had been no reason to think a parliamentary defeat of the government probable soon, and there was at that point no expectation that its internal strains might become so great that it would call an election without being defeated. Many observers, as well as most politicians outside the Liberal party, had thought that our talk of an early election was to keep our courage up; indeed, many wondered whether it was a sham, doubting that we really took it seriously ourselves.

From 6 November, the mood was different. The Conservatives no doubt began to hear, as we and journalists did, reports of Caouette rebelling against Thompson's leadership of Social Credit and talking about an early election. Indeed my impression, from the contacts I still had with some of them, was that it was then that many Conservatives, including some in the Cabinet, began to feel that the smell of death was on a Diefenbaker-led government. That was the precondition for the falling apart of the government that followed over the next few months. Anyway, as we had a drink with Mike late on 6 November after the vote, Walter and Paul and I and even Allan MacEachen were in an optimistic mood, and at the caucus the next day the morale of our MPs was high.

It was certainly different for the members of the smaller parties. They had been uncomfortable before. Now it became clear that the strain on them was beginning to tell. I tried to capitalize on the situation by means of a short memorandum, "The People Should Judge," that was incorporated into speeches by Mike and others:

> On June 18th, 63 voters out of every 100 cast their ballots for candidates opposed to the present government. The result is an unstable Parliament of minorities, in which the government is surviving precariously only by getting the temporary support of the smaller parties. These parties are really opposed to the government and all it stands for. When they support the government, they are merely playing for the time they want in order to get ready for another election. Parliament is therefore always on edge. No one knows what will happen ... The government is barely making even a gesture towards long-term plans. It is not giving leadership to the country. It

does not have a constructive programme of action. Ministers are just struggling to survive day-by-day. They are always looking over their shoulders to the minority parties. But constructive action is urgently needed for the country. The Liberal party therefore believes that it is in the national interest to have this unstable Parliament of minorities dissolved. The issues before the country should be taken back to the people to decide.

In the new mood our policy statements became, for a time, firmer. The caucus working groups were producing results. For employed people and their spouses, the medicare proposal had been, imprecisely, to "cover doctors' bills above a low annual cost." It was now agreed to specify that doctors' bills would be covered above a maximum of $25 per person per year for people of working age; all care would be free for children up to the time they left school and for people over the age of sixty-five.

It was not the plan I would have chosen, but it was a reasonable compromise among a lot of opinions and we had removed the worst of the obscurity that had been the greatest problem in the previous campaign. The economic programs were also strengthened by proposals to set up a Department of Industry (instead of leaving industrial policies as an offshoot of Trade and Commerce) and a National Development Corporation; the latter was a particularly favourite idea of Walter Gordon's, and at the time it had strong support in the party.

It was also decided to publish a special issue of *The Canadian Liberal*, for which I would write a summary platform statement under the heading "What We Stand For." It tersely listed most of our major policies under six headings: New Industry, New Construction, Opportunities for Youth, Square Deal for Farmers, Health Care for All, A Secure Old Age. It was distributed in December and, as things turned out, was widely used as campaign literature. In the newly aggressive spirit, we also decided to take an earlier initiative than before on the challenge to a Diefenbaker-Pearson debate. We wrote to the CBC asking that they include it in their plans for television during the next campaign.

In November, I also did a second draft of the "preliminary campaign strategy" paper. It was eventually distributed just before Christmas, as was also a memorandum asked for by the planning committee of caucus: an outline of points that MPs should make in speeches and interviews during the parliamentary recess. That was an unprecedented step towards gaining coherence for our party position.

Meantime, the business of Parliament floundered miserably. The government had clearly got to the state of being virtually unable to make the simplest decisions and of wanting to bring as little as possible before

Parliament; ministers didn't know or couldn't agree what to say, and anyway were afraid that anything they did might increase the risks of Créditiste defection and hence parliamentary defeat.

Though the government had promised, under the shock of the "emergency" in June, resolute new measures for the economy, the only idea that got even to the point of conception was a Bill to establish a "National Economic Development Board." That it got so far was, I suppose, the outcome of the one way in which Diefenbaker had been able to attempt, after the election, to strengthen his government. That was to appoint Wally McCutcheon to the Senate and the Cabinet. The product was, however, feeble. The Bill would give the proposed Board no significant role or powers.

Paul Martin and I decided to make a major attack on it. We developed a series of detailed amendments that would convert the Board into an instrument for indicative economic planning. The NDP would have to support the amendments, and on a number of points Social Credit would find it hard to support the government. We had some trouble in our ranks, from an unusual source. It was a mark of the new mood that Walter was beginning to think as the next Minister of Finance, and in those days the stance of the Department of Finance was still that it held a monopoly in all matters of economic policy. As I noted earlier, it was automatically opposed to any Economic Board or Council with substantial powers, and Walter felt that Paul was poaching on his territory.

There was a confrontation, at first somewhat angry. Paul and I agreed to a few compromises on our original wording, but not ones that appreciably reduced the role that we envisaged for the Board. Walter protested afterwards that I had "put it all over on him." I reminded him of occasions when I might have said the same about concessions to him, and neither our friendship nor our co-operation suffered at all. The whole thing came to nothing, of course, in the sense that, with the dissolution of Parliament, the Bill died on the order paper without having come to any final vote. But the amendments were extremely useful later; I was able to use much of their wording to secure quick drafting of the Bill to establish the Economic Council of Canada, which was among the earliest measures of the Pearson government.

A more fundamental development of Liberal policy took place in mid-December. To my knowledge, the first Liberal to seize on the idea of a Royal Commission on Bilingualism and Biculturalism was Dale Thomson, then a young academic at McGill. An Albertan by origin, a man of broad sympathies and sharp political understanding, he had been of considerable help in the 1962 campaign. Early in December he talked to me and wrote a highly perceptive memorandum on the next campaign in Quebec. The proposals included, besides the Commission, measures to turn the Ottawa-Hull district into a real national capital area in which people of both languages could feel fully at home.

The bilingual issue was fanned at that moment because Donald Gordon, as President of the CNR, made some very unwise remarks about no French Canadians being qualified for senior management positions on the railway. Maurice Lamontagne seized on the Commission idea and wrote an outstanding speech for Mike. The opportunity to deliver it came with a debate on interim supply on 17 December. There is no doubt that it contributed to the improvement in our Quebec vote between 1962 and 1963. It put heart into some good candidates, such as Guy Favreau. Its implementation was of abiding importance. The Laurendeau-Dunton Commission was set up very soon after we gained office. The government's acceptance of its main recommendations, giving equal official status to the two languages, was of critical, direct importance in Quebec. Perhaps even more importantly, the report was of decisive value in articulating and encouraging changing attitudes in English Canada; if those changes had been longer delayed it is unlikely, I think, that the federal attachment in Quebec could have survived through the moods and tensions of the 1970s. Maurice Lamontagne's contribution to Canada, in this and many other ways, has not had the acknowledgment it merits.

Though little had been done in the session to date, Parliament went into a lengthy Christmas recess. The government had obvious reasons to want that. I thought we should very strongly resist it, but we did not. Other reasons for concern were revived. We had made some progress but it seemed that whenever we did there was immediately a new outburst of hesitations. The closer we looked to power, the stronger the pleas of the people whose stock phrase was that we should be "responsible." By that they meant always that we should hedge about our policies and usually also that we should not be so combative in Parliament. Their advice was, in other words, that we should stop doing the things on which our greater likelihood of gaining power depended. But they did not see it that way and nor, consistently, did Mike.

I had begun to think about a revision of the general platform document, "The Liberal Programme" of the 1962 election. Everyone agreed that we could not change it in any substantial way. I was concerned, however, to make it more definite where we could – for example, by putting into the health proposal the $25 that the caucus working group had decided on, instead of leaving the amount uncertain. Also, I thought that, without changing the content, the exposition of policy could be improved by some reordering according to priorities. The 1962 document had been put together in a great hurry, and it would benefit from polishing of the language. What was involved was, in total, a fairly easy task, provided it was done at a time when day-to-day pressures were not too overwhelming. The parliamentary recess provided that opportunity, and – it was to be hoped – the last one. If the revised document was to serve its proper purpose in a campaign early in 1963, the work had to be done now.

I found Mike reluctant to agree. He was not ready to make up his mind on the caucus medicare proposal. While he fully accepted that our platform had to be essentially the same as in 1962, and we would indeed do everything possible to implement it in office, he was concerned as to whether we would seem irresponsible if, in the circumstances now, we emphasized its comprehensiveness, or (despite what we had already done in *The Canadian Liberal*, and indeed in many of Mike's speeches) decided too early which policies should be given star billing.

To me, this meant that we would go into another election campaign without much of the planning and preparation necessary for success. The policy stance would probably be all right in the end – I thought at the time, though one decision by Mike was shortly to prove me wrong. In December my concern was that the exposition of the program would again be too hesitant and too late to win all the credibility among voters that it merited. The planning being done in the organization across the field, under Walter's leadership and Keith Davey's direction, would be hobbled by indecision at the centre.

This was depressing, but we decided that the only thing to do was to treat it as a temporary mood and go ahead with all the planning and preparation we possibly could. A few days before Christmas Walter wrote to the campaign committee, saying that they should work on the basis that a general election between the end of March and some time in May was the reasonable prediction. Later, on 23 January – two weeks before the House was in fact dissolved – we agreed to plan on the basis of a specific election date, and chose 8 April. It was more luck than anything else that made us right to the day.

Mike's mood was perhaps partly explained by the talk that was going on at this time, in some business quarters, about replacing him as leader by Bob Winters. It was, of course, utterly unrealistic talk but it indicated the kind of sentiment that came to the surface when it seemed that the distrusted Diefenbaker was virtually out of the way at last and it was possible for people who fancied themselves as power brokers to think who they would really like to have as Prime Minister.

It was my job, as I saw it, to keep plugging away at firming and expounding our policies. In one memo to Mike I tried to deal head-on with the issue of "responsibility" in relation to the medicare plan. Obviously we should not be irresponsible. The question was how to be responsible. There were two ways. One was to say that while insurance against sickness had been a declared Liberal objective for forty years, in

Mike's view the nation's finances were not yet strong enough to make it possible. True, a Liberal government had put forward a medicare measure in 1945, but it had been rejected by the powerful provincial premiers, Drew and Duplessis, and in Mike's view they had been right. It was also true that he had promised a health plan in the 1962 election campaign, but he had not anticipated either the country's economic difficulties, shown in the foreign exchange crisis, or the strength of doctors' opposition, shown in Saskatchewan. Therefore a health plan was not now a firm Liberal commitment.

While I disagreed with it, that would be a responsible position. It seemed to me equally responsible to stick to what we had said, with the extra detail that the caucus had proposed. A new Liberal government would implement a health program. It would not be one of the early measures, because it was a complicated one to work out. Other details would be settled after careful consultation with the provinces and the doctors. But they would be settled and implemented before the end of the first four-year term of a Pearson government.

I could see no way in which that could be regarded as less responsible – as distinct from, in some people's minds, less desirable – than the first alternative. It had the additional merit of consistency. What was both inconsistent and irresponsible was to keep the health plan in our program but say little about it and shroud it in a fog of vague reservations, which couldn't be tied down as conditions but seemed to give us an out if we ran into some kind of trouble. That was the effect of the evasiveness which had crept into the 1962 campaign. It might have been motivated by a sense of responsibility, but it was nothing of the kind and it would not be in 1963. It was evasion, period, and politically it achieved nothing: it took the steam out of our campaign without genuine reassurance for the people who didn't want a health plan.

That memo was successful in getting the slightly improved version of the plan, as proposed by caucus, into the program. It was not successful in getting Mike to say much about medicare during the campaign.

My main effort to combat what I saw as a weakening of will was a memorandum written over the New Year holiday. Perhaps because the writing was therefore less interrupted, it was a more complete and more polished memorandum than most I wrote at that time. Mike took it very seriously; he discussed it extensively with me and asked for further notes on some points. The few other people to whom I gave or loaned copies – Walter, Paul Martin, and some of the "activist" MPs, as well as friends such as Pauline Jewett – expressed themselves in warm agreement.

It was a long memorandum, but much of it consolidated points already referred to and does not need summary here. The operative theme was that the native hue of resolution had been sicklied o'er, not by the pale

cast of thought, but by taking fright when faced with the certain consequences of our own decisions.

In the summer we had apparently made two firm decisions: to attempt
to bring about an election as soon as possible, and to extend the movement of public opinion in our favour by telling people more clearly what
a new Liberal government would do. We knew that we would be accused of irresponsibility, in face of the country's financial "emergency,"
and of lusting for power. It was ineffective criticism, but we had taken it
seriously enough to inhibit our actions. We had willed the ends but not,
consistently, the means. Our parliamentary tactics had been haphazard.
We had talked a lot, and often well, but we had not set ourselves to use
the main lever for the government's defeat in a Parliament of minorities –
to force as many divisions as possible on significant issues.

We had not done better in getting our policy across to the public. The
platform of 1962 had simply given firmer shape to the ideas favoured by
most delegates both at the 1958 convention and at the 1961 rally. The party
leadership had nevertheless been inhibited by lack of confidence in its
own program, by resistance coming from the wings of the political stage.
The range of choice about policy was small, but we had been a long time
about it.

We had not got our policy across to the public because we had been
slow, and now we were still behaving as if we had doubts about it. The
need was "to stop worrying and second thoughts; and therefore to be able
to strike the emotional spark – the feeling for a better, greater Canada to
which a new Liberal government can head the march – that will count
most of all."

The memorandum went on to suggestions as to what, if self-doubts
were set aside, should be our tactics in the resumed session of Parliament,
and it concluded: "Are we or are we not set firm in the strategy of
forcing an election soon? Have we or have we not determined to push
aside the pressures and inhibitions that have applied such powerful brakes
to the publicising of our policies? In both these questions can be answered yes, there is nothing to worry about; there is only work to do. If
they can't be, I don't know where we go; nor, I suspect, does anyone
else."

15 *The Nuclear Error*

In fact, we were about to go in a new direction, to almost everyone's surprise. In once again urging Mike to be firmer in the exposition of policy, I was this time promptly hoist with my own petard. What I had not anticipated was that he would in the process make a change in policy. The topic was in the area dearest to him, our external relations. It was the equipment of Canadian forces with nuclear weapons under American control.

At the National Rally the predominant sentiment had been strongly against acceptance of any nuclear role for Canada. The eventual resolution was toned down as a result of intervention on Mike's behalf, but it asserted that a Liberal government would withdraw from an interceptor role in NORAD (an agreement concluded early in the life of the Diefenbaker government); we would stop using our defence resources on "interceptor fighter squadrons or on Bomarc missiles" (installed in Canada under NORAD and designed for nuclear warheads).

The resolution stated equally firmly that Canada should not "acquire, manufacture or use" nuclear weapons either under Canadian control or under joint US-Canadian control. It left open the possibility of Canadian forces in Europe having nuclear weapons, provided they were "solely for defensive use," provided that NATO forces were "strong enough in man-power and conventional equipment to make nuclear weapons use unnec-essary to repel minor incursions or attacks," and provided that they were "under exclusive NATO control, not that of any single member state."

The 1962 program was a moderately faithful reflection of this attitude. The reference to NORAD was dropped. Willingness to participate in a collective NATO "nuclear deterrent" was stated with fewer qualifications. The key point – "the defence policy of a new Liberal government will not require Canada to become a nuclear power by the manufacture, acquisition or use of nuclear weapons under Canadian or American control" – was retained, though it was hedged fore and aft with qualifi-cations inserted by Mike. It was our policy "on the basis of present information," and a Liberal government would "reserve the right to examine each new development in the light of its over-riding responsi-bility for the security of the Canadian people."

In less formal pronouncements Mike was blunter in stating his own anti-nuclear sentiments. As late as November 12, 1962, he circulated to caucus the model letter that he was using in replying to correspondence about the nuclear issue, which said: "May I assure you that I do not believe that Canada should accept nuclear arms under national control by herself or by the United States. On the contrary, I have consistently argued that the nuclear club should not be extended."

A little earlier, in the aftermath of the "Cuban crisis" in October, he had been on the verge of making a speech for which I had written notes. I wanted him to suggest that this was a critical moment for a major diplomatic initiative. For the big powers that would mean negotiating a process of disengagement to reduce tensions at the points of sharpest conflict – then Cuba, Berlin, and Turkey. The contribution that the smaller nations could make was to stop the extension of nuclear weapons. Canada was well placed to take the initiative because it was a country of good repute and the one country that had early had the capability to produce an atomic weapon and decided not to do so. We should propose at the UN a firm self-denial ordinance of all non-nuclear powers, that they would not manufacture, acquire, cause to have on their territory, or use any nuclear weapons either under their own control or under the binational control of themselves and another power. This declaration by the smaller powers would give substance and permanence to any relief of tensions negotiated by the big powers.

The notes ended by pointing out that, for Canada, the non-nuclear declaration would free us to adopt the defence policy we ought to have but did not – a highly mobile conventional force which would give substance to our diplomacy by providing a military arm of real importance in brush fire situations, and especially for United Nations action.

Mike expressed himself in full agreement with this attitude – indeed, my notes merely made more specific the lines of thought along which we had talked together – and his statement in the House on the Cuba affair reflected much of the argument of the notes. But he decided, presumably after talking on the telephone with some of the international players with whom he maintained contact, that this was not yet the moment when a proposal for a major initiative would be most effective. The implication at the time was that he would do it later, but the moment he thought right never came. Events of a more domestic kind intervened.

On 1 November we had a lunch to discuss defence policy. Pearson, Drury, Gordon, and Hellyer were all present, and there was general agreement that nuclear weapons for Canada served no useful purpose. But shortly afterwards a Canadian delegation went to a NATO parliamentary conference in Europe. Our members talked particularly with Canadian army and air force officers and were much moved by their sense of humiliation and frustration: our forces were useless because their equipment assumed tactical nuclear weapons but they were not getting them.

The MPs, and particularly Paul Hellyer, came back convinced that Canada was becoming a laughing-stock, and worse, because we were reneging on our commitments. Whether or not we should ever have taken on the role we had within the NATO forces was no longer the point. Having made the commitments to our allies we should carry through with them. It was the opposition's job to see that the government stopped wavering.

Such sentiment was reinforced by the fact that the Canadian government had been conspicuously the last among the Western allies to express support for the United States in the Cuban crisis. The anti-American streak in Diefenbaker was of the kind that comes to the surface at testing moments, and was reinforced by his personal dislike of Kennedy. It was well known that there was deep division within the Cabinet. The Minister of Defence, Harkness, felt as strongly as Hellyer now did about Canada's commitment, and there was little doubt that a majority of the Cabinet would go along with him. But a few were opposed and the Prime Minister, as so often, was indecisive.

In this situation there were some MPs who thought, with Hellyer, that we should try to force the issue, but they were a minority. The commoner view was that it was the government that had made the nuclear commitment, whereas we as a party had an equally long-standing commitment against nuclear weapons on the terms on which they would be acquired. Therefore we could not do better than let the government stew in its own juice.

My guess was that by the time we came to office the immediate decision would have been made for us. The forces in favour of carrying through with the nuclear commitment were of the kind that usually wear down resistance within the Ottawa decision-making process. I did not believe that Diefenbaker's reluctance had any deep ideological basis, and it would not last much longer. The less we said meantime the better, because whatever we said was unlikely to produce much gain in marginal votes. There were more useful things for us to emphasize as the election issue.

Mike thought otherwise. All his interest and training led him to worry, not so much about the nuclear issue as such but about its significance for the Western alliance that he had helped so much to fashion. That was underlined when the retiring NATO commander, General Norstadt, visited Ottawa with the clear public message that Canada was letting down her allies.

It became clear, by the time Christmas was over, that nothing I or anyone else said would dissuade Mike from making a major speech on defence. I concluded that the sooner it was done, and I hoped out of the way, the better, and after further discussion with him drafted speech notes on 7 January. I emphasized that "We have, in Canada as in many other countries, a long tradition that in external affairs and in defence we try conscientiously to keep to a minimum the arguments between government and opposition." This was increasingly necessary because the only defence was now collective defence, and allies must be able to assume that the commitments we made in pooling our strength with them were commitments of the country; they would not disappear with a change of government.

The existing government had accepted for Canadian forces roles within the alliance, both in Europe and in North America, that required nuclear warheads as armament. That was true for our strike-reconnaissance aircraft in Europe, our "Honest John" artillery, our interceptor aircraft in Canada, and the two Bomarc missile bases. But we had not agreed to even the preliminaries for arrangements to make those warheads available. "The result is a major and serious gap in the defence arrangements of NATO. We said that we would assume a particular responsibility in collective defence, but we are not in fact doing so."

We had no right to back away from our commitments by our unilateral decision. "The issue in defence policy is how the free world can best make itself secure; it is then for Canada to work out, with her allies, how she can best make her proper contribution to that collective security."

We could well doubt whether Canada's most useful contribution to collective defence was the existing role, requiring tactical nuclear weapons. "There are very strong political and military arguments for concentrating the awful nuclear power in the hands of the countries that already possess it while the rest of us make our contribution through really effective conventional forces." A full reassessment, by the alliance as a whole, was urgent. If it confirmed that Canada could play an effective non-nuclear role, our commitments could properly be changed by agreement. "But they cannot honourably be changed by our unilateral decision ... Either we must do what we have said we will do or we must agree that there is something better to do, and switch accordingly to a different and effective defence policy. Those are the only two alternatives. We cannot rest in any third way of indecision."

It was not a heroic stance but it seemed to me frank and fair in the circumstances and to be consistent with what we had said in the past. It provided a line of action that a new Liberal government could undertake promptly and sensibly. It would probably result in our taking tactical nuclear weapons, but not before there had been an honest exploration, with our allies, for an honourable alternative. It was also entirely in the spirit of what Mike had said in all the discussions in which I had taken part, with him alone and with others. I gave him the notes but heard no more. Normally he followed one of two procedures. Often it was to return my notes with some pencilled comments, which I found a way to incorporate. On other occasions, when he wanted to make more substantial changes, the notes were re-typed, in whole or in part, as a second draft which was sent to me for comment – which usually meant a very short further discussion and minor amendments to make the final version.

On this occasion he did neither of those things. I heard no more until the afternoon and evening of 12 January, a Saturday, when I received agitated phone calls from Walter Gordon, Paul Martin, and others. What exactly had Mike said in his lunch-time speech in Toronto? I didn't know but quickly found out. He had substantially followed the earlier part of my notes but had moved to a very different conclusion. Whereas I had proposed that we should *either* succeed in renegotiating our commitments with our allies *or* follow the existing commitments, Mike had said firmly that we should fulfil the existing commitments – that is, equip our forces with nuclear weapons under joint control with the US – and *afterwards* discuss with our allies "a role for Canada in continental and collective defence which would be more realistic and effective."

I was appalled. While I recognized that the practical effects would probably be the same – renegotiation would not give us a different role until the alliance moved to a new generation of aircraft and other equipment – to explore alternatives first was different in principle from doing so after we had accepted nuclear weapons. It was also, in my view, a far sounder position politically for a party that had in the past consistently opposed commitments to nuclear weapons.

The leader of the party, however, had come to his decision and the rest of us had either to accept it or to quit. In the following few weeks I tried to console a good many unhappy Liberals. A few of them left the party, most decided to stay. I made that decision myself almost immediately. While I disagreed with Mike, I understood and respected the motives that had led him to his conclusion. He had always worked so hard for collective decision-making in the international community. He just could not bear the thought of Canada as a renegade, not doing what it had undertaken, by a collective process, to do.

In my view there was no disloyalty to the collective process in a new government seeking first to renegotiate commitments with which it had disagreed, provided we made it clear that, if the renegotiation with our allies did not produce agreement on a changed role, we would fulfil the existing commitments. But international affairs were not my area of expertise. Closely as I worked with Mike – indeed, I had just written a survey of international affairs in 1962, to be published under Mike's name, for the *World Book Encyclopedia* – I did not feel justified in challenging his judgment in this area in the way that I did (some might say all too often) on many political and economic issues.

My feelings were shared by others. Some were critical of Mike's position not only in itself but also because they questioned his right to make so sharp and single-handed a switch in party policy. True, there was a long-established tradition that in the last analysis policy decisions were for the leader alone to make. But Walter, in particular, felt that tradition was not enough; we were in a new political era, for which a more democratic style was appropriate. He thought seriously of resigning. Mike mollified him, by apologizing for the lack of consultation and making a meaningless promise that defence policy would be drastically revised when he was in office. The deed had been done, anyway, and there was nothing useful to do but make the best of it. That was confirmed as we got evidence of the feeling in the party organization across the country. While many people were puzzled by Mike's position, they were elated that at last on one matter he had appeared as a decisive, courageous, "no-nonsense" leader. That outweighed doubts both that the issue he had chosen was the most politically effective and that his new policy was correct.

Because it was followed in early February by the resignation of Douglas Harkness as Minister of Defence and then by the defeat of the government, on a Social Credit sub-amendment referring to defence, Mike's switch of policy on nuclear weapons was soon hailed by some Liberals and regarded by some commentators as a political master stroke.

The interpretation is wrong on two counts. The first and more important is that it completely falsifies the Pearson character. Mike took the position he did because he was utterly dedicated to the co-operation of the Western nations as a group; he could not bear the thought of Canada failing to carry out an agreement with them. Because he saw the world that way, and continuity in external and defence policies was therefore important, he was completely sincere in believing that in these matters there should be as little partisanship as possible. He was no more capable of taking the position he did as a matter of political calculation than he was of murdering his mother. That was why, most unusually, he did not discuss his decision with his closest associates. He knew that we would disagree and that the arguments we would press would be not on the merits of the case, on which we would defer to him, but on the political tactics – on which he would have difficulty in answering us, but which were not to him decisive.

If Mike's motivations are set aside, and the decision to commit a Liberal government to accepting nuclear warheads before a reassessment of defence policy is considered only in terms of political calculation, then in my view it was a very bad calculation. It did not affect the timing of the election significantly, if at all. And it resulted in the Liberal party forming only a minority government when in all probability it could otherwise have won a majority.

First, on timing. Douglas Harkness was an honourable man. He did not need Mike's speech to egg him to resign. It more probably would have deterred him, if anything could. There is no doubt that he would have resigned anyway if the government continued to make no decision on nuclear warheads. The probability, as I noted earlier, is that in fact it would have decided to accept them.

In any event, however, defence was not central to the government's condition of collapse. It had lost the capacity to make decisions and adopt policies on matters far more important to Conservative politicians than international obligations. Much of the Cabinet and more of the Tory establishment were ripe for a movement to depose Diefenbaker. But he was not a man to go. He would have used his best weapon to rally the party behind him, by dissolving Parliament and appealing to his fellow Canadians to save the country from power-hungry lackeys of the United States and Bay Street. His ingenious mind would have had no difficulty in concocting a pretext with enough superficial validity to enable his vast emotional resources to be deployed with some effect in denunciation of the Liberal party, and incidentally of the NDP and Social Credit.

That, of course, was if he needed to take the initiative of dissolution. It is probable that the government would have been defeated at much the same time, whatever Mike had said or not said about defence. The humiliation of keeping alive a clearly derelict government would in any event have been brought home to the smaller parties, and especially to the Créditiste members. They were rapidly becoming aware that, fearful of an election though the Social Credit party in western Canada was, Créditiste prospects were still good and were likely to be worse rather than better with the passage of time.

In short, the election would have taken place very little later – almost certainly, within the period from the end of March to May that in December Walter had told the Liberal organization to plan for – if Mike had never said anything about nuclear warheads. But in that event it would have been a very different campaign. As the analysis of 1962 voting had shown, the difficult problem in a second round would not be to reduce the Conservative vote; that *would* happen, probably to a considerable extent. The problem would be to convince people that voting Liberal was the way to make things different – above all, in employment and other "bread-and-butter" issues. To gain a majority we must do better at the expense of the smaller parties as well as the Conservatives.

In Quebec, that meant at the expense of the Créditistes. To capture any of the protest vote that had gone to them in 1962 we had to offer something different from the "old guard" image of the federal Liberal organization in the province. That required, above all, some new personalities as leading candidates. The principal prospect was Jean Marchand. He was ripe for politics. He was sympathetic. He was a pupil of Father Levesque. He had attended the Kingston conference. Above all, he had risen through the tough school of the trade union movement, and the asbestos strike in particular, and was entirely capable of taking on the Créditistes in their own terms. But he was too wise a man to come to Ottawa alone. He wanted compatible associates like Trudeau and Pelletier, representing other strands in the web of the new Quebec and providing the combination of skills to make the group a powerful force in Ottawa.

At the end of 1962 it seemed probable that the group was willing and that, despite some reluctance in the old guard, suitable good seats could be arranged for them. But they were repelled by Mike's position on nuclear arms. With that went our best hopes of substantial gains in Quebec, and without those the chances of gaining a clear parliamentary majority were not good.

In the event, the 1963 voting extended the trend of the previous year. The Conservative vote in Quebec suffered a substantial further decline. Indeed, it was smaller than it had been in 1953, in the days of St Laurent and Drew. But while the Conservative vote fell by 210,000 from 1962, the Liberal vote rose only by 127,000. The NDP and the Créditistes got the rest of the benefit from Quebec's disillusionment with Diefenbaker. What else could have been expected? If there was one issue calculated not to win votes in Quebec, it was the espousal of nuclear arms. That Mike's decision could ever have been thought to be good politics was an extreme example of the English-Canadian blinkers of most political comment.

In English Canada there was no such specific event as the repulsion of the three Quebec wise men to dramatize the consequences of the switch on defence policy. The effects were none the less clear, in the campaign and in the polling. The NDP had had a miserable role in the 1962-3 Parliament and there was every reason to think that, if we campaigned vigorously on our economic and social policies, we could persuade many more potential NDP voters that support for a Liberal government was the practical way to get genuine improvements in employment and social security. But those were also voters unlikely to be sympathetic to us on the nuclear issue.

The effect was illustrated by the difference between the results in British Columbia and in the rest of English Canada. In that province, we campaigned strongly on economic and social policies and said as little as possible about the nuclear issue. In the event, the Liberal vote in BC increased from 1962 by 30 per cent, a far higher proportion than in any other province. The NDP vote did not decline, but our relative positions were reversed. Whereas in 1962 the total vote for NDP candidates had been 25,000 greater than for Liberals, in 1963 the Liberal vote exceeded the NDP vote by 25,000.

Elsewhere, the effect on the campaign of the nuclear issue was that the Conservative vote held much firmer than anyone had been entitled to expect when the government entered the campaign in such complete disarray. There was not much logic to that, but the campaign was on the hustings and on television, and nuclear weapons were an emotional issue.

That suited Diefenbaker not only because of the issue itself but because it also gave him an opening for what he did best of all: to identify the Liberals with the establishment that he had overcome in 1957 and 1958, with the big interests and the Americans. That was what we had tried so hard to avoid with the development of our progressive policies and the recruitment of new candidates with an activist view of public policy. The nuclear issue went some way to undo it all. On that, paradoxically, Mike's rational virtues made him more inferior to Diefenbaker as a campaigner than he now was on economic and social policies. On those he had public emotion on his side without having to contrive to pull at any heart-strings. For his defence policy he did not.

The outcome was indeed a tribute to Diefenbaker's skill if he was given openings to campaign on issues that suited him. His government was for all practical purposes dead before the campaign began, his party a shambles. Nevertheless the Conservatives' loss of votes in 1963 in English Canada was small – 131,000 or less than 6 per cent from 1962. Their share of the vote for the four parties was still bigger than in the last pre-Diefenbaker election, ten years earlier, by 5 1/2 per centage points. Nationally – that is, even with the revulsion of Quebec taken into account – the Conservatives did somewhat better, relatively to the other parties, than in 1953.

The Liberal share, in contrast, was over 9 per centage points less than in 1953, 42 per cent compared with 51 per cent. The smaller parties had taken up the difference; the NDP was modestly stronger than the CCF had been in 1953 and Social Credit, thanks to the Créditistes of Quebec, had 12 per cent of the total vote for the four parties in 1963, compared with 5 1/2 per cent ten years earlier. The Liberals, were well ahead of the Conservatives, but short of the margin needed to produce a majority of seats in the House of Commons.

"Might-have-beens" are always debatable, but it seems to me beyond serious doubt, on the evidence of the opinion surveys, of people's reactions during the campaign, and of the pattern of the polling results, that if the Liberal party had not changed its defence policy and had instead concentrated the election campaign clearly on economic and social policies it would have won enough additional votes to secure an overall majority in Parliament.

On 21 January 1963, however, when Parliament reassembled, all this was no more than a fear of what might still be avoided. Mike had been persuaded that it made no sense to be expecting an early election and not producing an up-dated version of the basic platform document. I hurriedly finished my drafting, making improvements of the kind referred to earlier but, except on defence, essentially reproducing the 1962 program. It was agreed that the format of the publication would also be the same, but to distinguish it a new title was necessary. In place of "The Liberal Programme" I favoured "What a New Liberal Government Will Do," but what was adopted was, dully, "The Policies of the Liberal Party." The final wording also reflected some minor concessions to the people who wanted to be less definite, but those changes were less significant than the improvements made by polishing the earlier presentation.

A shorter, "popular" version was again produced for wide campaign use and, while it was less forceful in wording and in presentation than the 1962 "concertina," its content was pretty satisfactory. Unfortunately, it appeared too late in the campaign to be used with anything near maximum effect. Otherwise, there was very little new print material at the national level of the campaign. Candidates had to support their local literature chiefly with the same leaflets as in 1962 and with the "What We Stand For" section of *The Canadian Liberal* referred to earlier.

In the House, in late January and early February, there was continual excitement, intensified by each day's rumours of contemplated or attempted palace revolutions against Diefenbaker. I was also busy, along with Keith and others at the Federation, with preparations for a meeting of the National Council of the Federation scheduled for 11–12 February and which we were going to combine, in the providential event that the election had by then been called, with a meeting of the National Campaign Committee. In that event my particular responsibility would be to speak on campaign strategy in a morning-long session at which Walter would talk about organization and Keith Davey, Jack Pickersgill, and Mike would also speak.

More work was involved, however, in organizing and obtaining texts from a considerable number of MPs who were to speak in the "policy panels" making up most of the first day's business. Paul Martin was one, and required no help; the names otherwise were largely a roster of ministers-to-be, but then they were in most cases new MPs wanting to discuss what they would say with each other and with me. They included Herb Gray, Maurice Sauvé, "Ben" Benson, Lucien Cardin, John Munro, Jack Davis, Hazen Argue, and John Stewart. For the most part, they made crisp, positive speeches. The tendency to work with the MPs generally, rather than so much with Mike, was growing. In particular, I found myself preparing notes for Walter and Paul Martin; both in the House and outside, they made more effective use of the material than Mike was doing.

The government had little legislation to bring before Parliament. Its central problem was the authorization of expenditures. Its disorganization was so complete that the estimates for 1962–3 – the basis for Parliament's appropriation of funds – had not yet been brought forward, although ten months of the fiscal year had gone. The normal procedure, to provide funds during the early months of the year before the expenditure estimates are approved by Parliament, is the voting of interim supply by months; each department is thus authorized to spend up to one-twelfth, or three-twelfths, or sometimes more as the year advances, of the amount proposed for it in the estimates.

In normal situations such motions are passed with little or no debate. But in late January the government was in the extraordinary situation that it would need the extension of interim supply to eleven-twelfths of the undiscussed estimates. The beginning of February came and the motion had not been brought forward. The government obviously intended to wait until the last moment and hope to force the opposition to agree with minimum debate because otherwise civil servants and contractors could not be paid and the normal business of government would be brought to a halt because, allegedly, the opposition insisted on pointless debating. At a dinner party at home on 1 February with some public service and journalist friends as guests, the absorbing topic of discussion was for how many days the government could get by before it ran out of money.

Among MPs there was much discussion of what we should do. To let the extraordinary measure of eleven-twelfths supply pass quietly was deeply offensive to most of the parliamentarians. On the other hand, it was agreed that a filibuster in the ordinary sense – with speech after speech on almost any topic – would be vulnerable to criticism. Most MPs therefore favoured a compromise that was labelled "the Kent plan." It was that we should treat interim supply as the one occasion to have the kind of discussion that there should have been months earlier on the estimates proper. Our MPs would be tightly organized, as was possible thanks to the working groups, to ask questions and make short policy speeches about each of the departmental estimates in turn. In that way we could advertise the government's disorganization and indecision to maximum effect, and without the odium of the kind of filibuster that would seem silly to the public.

Preparations of that kind were begun but Mike did not give final authorization to the plan. Indeed on 27 January there had been a news report from Quebec City, where Mike was visiting for the weekend, that he had said that we would not oppose interim supply. I got the usual agitated phone calls and made the usual enquiries, with the eventual result that Mike denied that he had meant any such thing as was reported. He did not, however, say what we would do.

The government would have put the issue to the test promptly, if at that point it had been capable of a decision on the most elementary tactical issue. But it was too preoccupied with its internal divisions to have any longer even any collective wish to survive. For the next week Parliament drifted while the important battles were waged in and around the Cabinet. Diefenbaker got help from an unexpected source on the Wednesday evening, when the US State Department foolishly issued a statement criticizing what he had said on defence. We did the best we could by sharply attacking such a comment on another country, but Mike was not very effective and Douglas and Thompson took the opportunity to join Diefenbaker in condemning us for the alleged subservience of our defence policy to American wishes. Still, the business of the House went nowhere and by 4 and 5 February it was time for one of the regular, so-called supply debates, in which the opposition has the opportunity to choose the topic and, by moving an amendment, express no-confidence in the government.

At first – on the preceding Friday and again in a meeting at Stornoway on Sunday – the general inclination was to make defence the topic for debate. It was recognized, however, that we could not move an amendment on the nuclear policy; there was no possibility of the NDP and Social Credit supporting it. The favourite idea was therefore to propose the setting up of a defence committee, which the smaller parties would have difficulty in opposing. I did not like it. I doubted that the public had much enthusiasm for committees and we would seem to be making a mountain out of a molehill in trying to use such an issue to bring down the government. My underlying motive, of course, was that I wanted defence policy to be given as little prominence as possible in the election campaign, and that would be more difficult if it was the last thing we talked about before the government fell. The argument I used, however, was tactical: the proposed motion gave Diefenbaker an easy opportunity to dish us. He could simply agree to set up a committee, in which by this stage he had little more to lose.

That argument was reinforced on Monday morning with the news that Harkness had resigned. I drafted an alternative amendment which simply criticized the government in general terms for its indecisiveness; the charge applied to defence but to everything else as well. It would be almost impossible for Social Credit and the NDP not to vote with us on such a motion. During Monday morning I used all the persuasive powers I had and finally, just before the House was due to sit, it was decided to go with the general, "indecision" wording.

Thompson, of course, moved a sub-amendment for Social Credit; while it referred to defence, as an example of indecision, it was so generally worded that we could have no difficulty whatever in supporting it. The NDP was on the spot and its spokesman on Monday, David Lewis, was non-committal enough to sustain the excitement. Diefenbaker on Tuesday made one of his fighting speeches against us – foreshadowing what was to be feared in the campaign – but on that occasion somewhat spoiled the effect by abjectly crawling to Social Credit in an attempt to get them to sustain the government. By that time, it was a hopeless endeavour.

When the vote came in the evening of 5 February Social Credit was solid against the government and so were all but two of the NDP members. The government went down to defeat by 142 votes to 111. We had got our election.

In the following few days there were intensive discussions, attempts to get planning completed, and some writing, rather half-heartedly making up for our lack of preparation in campaign literature and advertising. The National Campaign Committee met on 10 February and the National Council delegates assembled; there were three days of extensive talking. On the 12th, at the combined Council and Campaign Committee meeting, I gave the final version of my campaign strategy paper. It was enthusiastically received at the time, perhaps because it was shamefully over-optimistic. That would have been hard to avoid, given the mood of the moment. I was concerned to underplay the nuclear issue as much as I could. Some delegates noted, and privately expressed agreement with, the regret about the change in nuclear policy implied by my insistence that the 1962 program should be stuck to: "we mustn't change our minds and we mustn't waffle."

There was the usual plea to concentrate on our main policy proposals, simply and positively, and there were homilies, required in the circumstances, against overconfidence; against arrogance, especially in criticism of opponents; and against being diverted into arguments, particularly with the NDP, that wouldn't win over the marginal voters. And this time the "team" of candidates should be secondary. Our propaganda should emphasize Mike Pearson, offering (without attacking Diefenbaker personally) a style of leadership different from one that had clearly failed.

The wisdom of hindsight doesn't enable me to think of much different that I could usefully have said at the time, but it had limited relevance to the campaign that actually followed.

16 Victory, of a Sort

I knew that in the strategy speech I was in part singing to keep my courage up. There was little doubt that Diefenbaker would dominate the Conservative campaign. And given the kind of campaign that he would wage, it was inescapable in Mike's nature that he would keep trying to reply; that he would tangle with the man he now so much despised, more than he would clearly proclaim our policies; and that in such a personal tussle, related particularly to nuclear arms, Diefenbaker would gain more points than he lost. I found myself dreading a campaign in which I tried to play the same role as in 1962. There would be constant friction between us.

No doubt, I could, with patience, still exercise enough influence to give the campaign more positive elements than it would have otherwise. But would the compromise be better than Mike campaigning in his own way? We might well get the worst of two worlds and fall to an even lower point of ineffectiveness. I was in a dilemma. On balance I had greatly enjoyed the 1962 campaign, learned a lot, and gained a great deal of satisfaction from it. The assumption of most associates, and even of people who were far from being my fans, was that the same thing was needed again, and until recently I had shared the assumption. Now I doubted whether, in the changed circumstances, I could stand it. I also doubted whether Mike could. For some days planning discussions proceeded on the assumption that I would travel again, and Mike said nothing to me to indicate that he wished otherwise. But I was pretty sure that he did. At that point he was confident of an easy victory, convinced that his switch on defence policy had already done the trick, and wished to campaign accordingly. In that case, I wouldn't be the right help. He knew it as well as I did.

Keith Davey, as before, wanted me to be a candidate. Over the previous months, he had suggested several ridings where there had not yet been a nomination and there were prospects of winning. He still had a few up his sleeve. No longer feeling needed with Mike, and also perhaps because I had become more caught up in the political battle, I began to wonder whether I would have been wiser to identify a suitable constituency some time earlier, nurse it, and now be able to feel natural and reasonably confident as a candidate. But to parachute into a "good" constituency after the election had been called was a different matter. I felt that it was contrary to the proper political process. At heart, I suppose, I was also afraid of losing; Maurice Lamontagne had shown me how devastating that could be.

Even so, I was tempted, particularly because a number of MPs had generously expressed the view that I ought to run and go into the Cabinet. The extremist was Judy LaMarsh, who was more given to extraordinarily generous impulses than anyone I have ever known. She offered to stand down in her very safe Niagara riding and campaign for me if I would be the candidate. Needless to say, I declined with thanks; Judy lived for politics and she had the promise of a successful career in it. But that was not the end of her generosity. During the campaign, she said publicly in Burnaby-Coquitlam that she had made this offer and I had preferred a harder path. For that she got into some trouble in her riding, but not enough to affect her hold on it.

It was the ingenious Keith Davey who came up, seven days after the government's defeat, with a solution to the dilemma. I should run against Tommy Douglas. The issue of parachuting was then irrelevant. Douglas, although the former Premier as well as leader of the NDP, had been defeated in a Saskatchewan riding in 1962 and had in the fall himself been parachuted, though the resignation of the member and a by-election, into Burnaby-Coquitlam. It was about the safest NDP seat in the country. The Liberal candidate in the by-election had lost his deposit.

The point of my running was not that there was any thought, at that stage, that Douglas could be beaten. Keith's argument, quickly supported by Walter – who was influenced, I suspect, by understanding the difficulties in my again campaigning with Mike – was a matter of national strategy. The Conservatives, we then thought, were not the problem. The government had fallen apart. Keith presented the case in the terms of my own strategy paper. Our problem was to convince people that we were an attractive alternative, and in English Canada it was the NDP who would argue otherwise. If we did not gain a great many seats it could only be because the NDP attracted enough of the voters dissatisfied with the Conservatives to have the paradoxical effect of enabling the Conservatives to hold seats with small pluralities over us.

For me to run against Douglas, Keith argued, would be a dramatic move that could transform the campaign at what might otherwise be our weak point; I more than anyone could show that the NDP was irrelevant because the kind of economic and social improvements looked for by people who might be marginal NDP voters could in truth be ensured by voting for a Liberal government. This was especially important in BC, where the NDP was at its strongest, but there were a number of seats that we could take. I might not win in Burnaby-Coquitlam but the kind of campaign I could wage would help to win more marginal seats for us.

Such a campaign would get national attention and, in addition to its value in BC, it would worry Douglas enough to compel him to spend more time in his riding and be less effective in the national campaign. And even my Englishness, Keith pointed out, would not be much of a liability in British Columbia.

I was hooked. This would take me away from the problems I feared and enable me to contribute, in a more effective way than was now otherwise possible, to the kind of national campaign that had become so dear to my heart. A quick telephone call confirmed that the BC organization would be enthusiastic. I accepted. That was on 13 February. There were friends who disagreed. Maurice Sauvé and Paul Martin, for example, said that, despite the problems, I ought to stay with Mike. But my mind was made up. Mike consented, though he did not show enthusiasm. I suspected that he would have been keener if he had felt that he was making a great sacrifice so that I could do what I wanted. I thought that, though he would not say it, he shared my relief that we were going to avoid a situation ridden with tension between us.

A week was needed to contribute what I could to getting the preparations for the campaign into some sort of order. On 20 February – with polling little more than six weeks away – I flew from Ottawa to Vancouver and that evening went to Burnaby for the first time.

My first few days there were grim. Six people constituted the committee of the constituency Liberal Association with which I first met. They were well intentioned but they clearly had no experience of organizing a serious campaign. The constituency had in the past been conceded to the NDP, the Liberal campaign a token effort by a few local people unsupported by a provincial organization that saw less hopeless places to put its resources. I was a more conspicuous candidate but I had no experience; my ideas of campaigning at the constituency level were entirely second-hand. And I had the grave handicap of no local knowledge and little time to learn.

We were saved by two things. One was the enthusiasm of the very able people who made up the federal campaign committee in British Columbia. They were extraordinarily helpful in providing organizational ideas and resources. The other factor was the media. They regarded me as an object of interest; I was asked to appear on numerous TV and radio programs and was well treated in newspaper coverage. Our campaign committee room soon began to be filled with volunteers who had never worked for the Liberal party before.

Still, my inexperience was painful. I seemed to get across quite well on television and, I was assured, very well in small meetings. Certainly, many enthusiastic new workers emerged from the "meet Tom Kent" coffee parties. In the handshaking, small-talk aspect of campaigning I was not good, though not as gauche as I feared I would be. As a platform performer I was, at best, indifferent and "at best" meant when I spoke for other Liberal candidates in more favourable ridings. In Burnaby-Coquitlam meetings were tough. The NDP always sent a large gang of men, apparently prepared for the occasion with plenty of beer, whose function was less to heckle than to drown out the speakers (except, at all-candidate meetings, Tommy Douglas). It would have been rough for an accomplished platform orator; for me it was disconcerting as well as unpleasant. I tried to console myself with the thought that the noise-makers might be helping me, with marginal voters, as much as my indifferent platform oratory would have done. Certainly, on one occasion, they helped my morale. A left-wing BC weekly had asserted that I was a CIA agent (presumably because I had done intelligence work during the war). My Englishness, as I mentioned earlier, was something of an inhibition to my running. I was delighted to make out that what the goon section was chanting, to prevent me from being heard, was "Yankee Go Home".

In Burnaby-Coquitlam I saw a side of the NDP that I had known nothing about. Innocently, I had rather envied what seemed to me a more policy-oriented approach to politics than that of the old party organizations. That was not the reality of the NDP as it then operated in an area like Burnaby-Coquitlam. It might not have patronage as an incentive to party workers but it certainly had massive resources, including organizers loaned by trade unions, and its close association was not with the kind of church-going socialism I had met on the Prairies, and from which Mr Douglas himself came, or with the rather middle-class, intellectual socialism of Ontario; its close association was with the more violent strands in a tough trade unionism dedicated to ensuring that every worker paid his dues and no one got through a picket line. The organizers clearly put all the pressure they could do on union members to vote for Douglas. Their most visible techniques, however, were to tear down opponents' signs and create as much disruptive noise as possible at their meetings. I could not believe that Tommy Douglas relished these proceedings on his behalf, but if he tried to prevent them he failed.

The propaganda on his behalf could play loose with facts in a way matching Mr Diefenbaker's style. Late in the campaign, the BC Federation of Labour – at the prompting, I was told, of an assistant of Mr Douglas – published an attack on me on the grounds that in 1954 I had supported Premier Smallwood's decertification of the woodworkers' union (the IWA) in Newfoundland. The IWA had, of course, many members in Burnaby-Coquitlam. The "evidence" was obtained by selecting, from a long editorial in the *Winnipeg Free Press*, three sentences which regretted that Mr Smallwood had been given his opportunity to attack the union by the violence which had unquestionably disfigured the dispute. Those sentences were used entirely out of the context of an editorial that was mainly devoted to criticism of the Smallwood action against the union. We immediately published a reply but by then it was the last weekend of the campaign, too late for television and radio coverage, and – as the timing was no doubt intended to secure – the correction could not have fully caught up with the misrepresentation.

In fairness and objectivity, however, I must say that Tommy Douglas's greatest advantage over me was as a platform speaker. He was also easier in his contacts with people. And he was more skilled as a debater, though many Liberals were excited because they thought that I matched him in our television confrontation, staged late in the campaign. If they were right, however, it was because the Liberal case was inherently stronger than the NDP's, not because I was a match for Douglas in the technical skills of debate.

We did all we could to offset such factors by use of the medium in which we were strongest. We covered the riding with a series of newsprint handbills each carrying "a message from Tom Kent" – on jobs, medicare, pensions, family allowances, aid to municipalities, and other main parts of the Liberal program. I was also helped by visits to the riding from some of my good friends among leading Liberals – Judy LaMarsh, Paul Martin, and Maurice Sauvé.

It is impossible to go through the excitement of an election campaign without developing the hope, or illusion, necessary to make all the hard work feel worthwhile to the people who are canvassing, stuffing envelopes, putting out signs, distributing leaflets and all the rest: "we have a chance of winning ... we have a good chance ... more work and we're going to win." I had gone to Burnaby-Coquitlam without any thought that it was possible to beat Douglas; the purpose was simply to give him a good run and thereby help the campaign elsewhere. But as the volunteer army swelled, as the aphrodisiac of all the publicity had its effect on them, I could not stay immune. In the last few days I began to half-believe that I might win.

It was nonsense, of course. But we did make a good showing. In both the general election and the by-election of 1962, the Liberal vote had been less than half of the NDP vote. The publicity of the 1963 campaign brought out many more voters: the total poll was 41,128, compared with 32,530 in the by-election. Even so, the NDP's lead over us was cut from 8,284 to 4,919. Instead of one Liberal vote for every two NDP votes, we had three Liberal votes to four for the NDP. Liberals at least thought it was a considerable achievement, and certainly those in Burnaby-Coquitlam, and in BC generally, could not have been warmer in their pleas that I should at once make a commitment to running again and expecting, on the second round, to win.

The results elsewhere in BC were gratifying, too. Compared with 1962, the per centage gain in the Liberal vote was well over three times that in the rest of English Canada. I therefore had no personal sense of disappointment. I thought, though some disagreed, that I had contributed as much to the national campaign as I could have done by travelling with Pearson, probably more. I had learned a great deal about the practicalities of political campaigning. And my status, in the minds of Liberal MPs and, shortly, ministers had changed. I had been, from their viewpoint, a man of ideas and words. By doing pretty well against Douglas – for whom they all had a healthy respect and even awe – I had proved myself as a "practical" politician. If it had not been for that I doubt that I could possibly have been accepted in the role that circumstances unexpectedly required me to play in the government during 1963-5.

For anyone absorbed in BC there was no time to pay close attention to the 1963 national campaign. Walter and Keith and a few others called me occasionally with their woes. Given the advantages with which we started, the campaign did not go well. Diefenbaker, back in the underdog role that suited him best, campaigned brilliantly. He still mixed as well as ever the kinds of emotion and wit that are most effective, for many audiences, from the platform. He poured his scorn on Liberals, touched every emotional concern about nuclear bombs, and pulled effectively on every string of anti-American and anti-establishment feeling. So many of his ministers had resigned or retired that he seemed to be fighting single-handed, and was the more effective on that account.

He was beaten before he began, and no doubt knew it, but he kept the Conservative vote more solid than anyone could have thought likely. In essence, his campaign was that the Liberals were untrustworthy, and he was effective enough to deter many people who might have switched their votes to us; they stayed with the Conservatives or the smaller parties or apparently, in the Atlantic provinces particularly, they stayed home.

The Liberal campaign did not cope well with Diefenbaker's strength. The fact that it was ill prepared should have meant at least that it was flexible, but it was not. It began with Keith Davey's mistakes of overconfidence, such as the notorious "truth squad" and the colouring books, and then the power of tactical decision-making seemed to evaporate. Mike was persuaded not to talk as much about nuclear weapons as I had feared he might, but that was not because he talked clearly about our positive policies.

One of my saddest moments was when I received, in late March, a long and angry letter from a friend who was closely involved in the administration of the campaign. It was not going well. It was marred by indecision, by failure to do things on time, by lack of precision and clarity in what Mike said, and above all by lack of political skill in adapting to what opponents were doing and in creating new opportunities to make our points. All this was different, the letter said, from 1962 and it did not spare my feelings: the fault was mine for not being there. In a sense I was flattered but I was more distressed, though I continued to think that, to a large degree at any rate, my correspondent misjudged the situation; in 1963 I would not have been able to do what I had before. Above all, however, I was saddened by this evidence that the national campaign was going even worse than, from a distance, it had seemed.

Walter, as usual, did what could be done to save the situation. He called me to say that he was going to insist to Mike that the last nine days of campaigning must be devoted to sharp, clear statements on a series of points from our program. These would be stated as the things that a new Liberal government would do in its first hundred days in office. What did I think of his list? I thought it was all right, though it was a measure of desperation that we should commit ourselves to so tight a timetable. It was not at all what I had in mind when I proposed earlier that we divide the program into annual instalments.

I was more sceptical when I learned later that Mike thought people would identify a hundred days with Napoleon's progress to Waterloo, and had therefore shortened the period to "sixty days of decision." Also, some of the policy points became somewhat foggier in Mike's pronouncements than Walter had intended. In essence, however, he accepted the change of tactics, with the result that – in contrast to 1962, when a strong campaign flagged towards the end – in 1963 a weak campaign improved a good deal in the last two weeks. If it had not, I suspect, we would have been appreciably short of a majority. As it was, we came out with 129 seats in a House of 265 – five short of what was needed, after the election of a Speaker, for a bare majority. Our net gain of twenty-nine seats came from declines of twenty-one for the Conservatives, six for Social Credit and two for the NDP.

Mike had spoken in Vancouver at a massive meeting on 1 April. The goons, as I had come to think of them in what I hope was an uncharacteristic partisan feeling, were present in force and tried to do their work not only by shouts but by throwing paper darts and shooting peas at Mike and the rest of us on the platform. He stood his ground and, though only parts of the audience could hear it above the din, made one of his best campaign speeches ever. He stressed the pension plan and medicare (for my sake, I suspect) and listed all the actions promised for the sixty days: to set up the Municipal Development and Loan Fund, the Department of

Industry, the National Economic Council, a National Development Corporation, a federal agency for development of economically backward areas; to provide a capital fund for the Atlantic Development Board; to create a Commission on Biculturalism and an all-party committee on defence; to "establish" a contributory pension plan; and to bring in a June budget "to stimulate production and jobs."

In the end the hooliganism subsided in face of the enthusiasm of most of the audience, and the meeting became a real triumph for Mike. That was the more remarkable because he was at the time not only tired from the campaign but unwell. For that reason he disappointed my supporters, who had hoped that he would come into the riding and, they believed, thereby give us the final push to victory. But I spent some time with him, and absence had made the heart grow fonder. He was insistent in asking that I return to Ottawa immediately after polling day; I would be needed at once. Accordingly, after what was on the whole a celebration by the principal BC campaigners on the night of 8 April, I took the morning plane out of Vancouver on 9 April.

The elation as I returned to Ottawa was stronger than the forebodings. We had remade the Liberal party. There was going to be a government with detailed commitments to what I believed to be the progressive policies for the times. I had no doubt that Mike would want to fulfil those commitments, and I was optimistic that, with Walter's drive and organizing capacity, it could be done. The outcome of all the struggle was going to be a good government.

I would not have been so cheerful if I had had any idea how great the difficulties, many of the government's own creation, were going to be, and, in particular, how constant a preoccupation for me those difficulties would be over the next few years. Nevertheless, I do not, in retrospect, feel any less satisfaction than I did then about what had been achieved by April 1963. The change is that I would now make a different assessment of the reasons for qualified satisfaction.

That the Liberal party had been remade was, in itself, a fairly temporary pleasure. By the elections of 1972 and 1974, I found myself thinking that the country would probably be better for a victory of the Conservatives under Stanfield's leadership. And by 1980, though a majority of Canadians again decided otherwise, I thought that the two old parties deserved about equally to be humbled. The Liberal party had been responsible for some periods of poor government before 1963, and it was again after 1968. I had gone into politics as a somewhat reluctant partisan, and the effect of inside experience was that such ardour as I developed was soon cooled again.

The things that mattered to me in 1963 were the policies for which Walter and I and others had struggled hard, and for which we continued to fight in government. Those I do not in any way regret. Several would have been better if implemented rather differently. Some were inadequate to the needs. There were further policies that should have been developed after 1963, and were not. As it approached exhaustion, the Pearson government fell into serious misjudgments on a few important matters. Yet when all that has been said, it was a government that dealt with the needs of its times far better than most governments do.

However, greatly as I cared about them, the particular policies of the remade Liberal party were not its chief distinction. What mattered most was that in opposition it told people what it would do if they elected it, and in office it did what it had said it would do. Despite all the complexities of party consensus, there was a simply quality of forthrightness, of political honesty translated into determination in government. The reflection from experience that I would emphasize above all others is the importance of that quality. It is the quality most easily submerged by the elaboration of modern government and most easily surrendered to the temptations of image-making by contemporary media techniques.

We have not yet found how the democratic process can cope successfully with those developments. If we do not, a growing public cynicism about politics, inevitably responded to by more cynicism among politicians themselves, will further endanger the quality of government performance in a free society. Against that, the only defence is to find some way of ensuring that political parties are more motivated to put definite policies before the electorate, and in office to do what they have said they would do. That was now our task.

Though the Liberal party had come out of the election a few seats short of a parliamentary majority, it was certain that the NDP and Social Credit would not sustain Mr Diefenbaker. He hesitated for a few days before resigning, but the change of government took place on 22 April.

For Mike himself, the main task in the interval was Cabinet-making. He asked me to go to Stornoway, the official home of the Leader of the Opposition, to talk quietly about it. He wanted my opinion on three particular points. The first was the Department of National Health and Welfare. Its Minister would be responsible for the pension plan and for medicare, two of the most complex as well as important of the programs to which the Liberal party was committed by its election platform. Since I was, as Mike put it, the custodian of the program preparations that we had undertaken while in opposition, it was particularly important that the Minister responsible for two such major programs should be someone with whom I could work closely. What about Judy LaMarsh?

That was easy to answer. There was no possible candidate for the post with whom I would be more confident of working well. That proved to be the case, through many difficulties. I was also excited that a woman should have so major a portfolio, in contrast to the minor ones that Diefenbaker had given to Ellen Fairclough.

There was an opening to express an opinion not asked for. Mike referred to "a" woman in the Cabinet. I commented that there was no necessity to have only one, which smacked of tokenism. While Judy was the only woman with claim to a senior portfolio, Pauline Jewett was more capable of assuming a junior one than were most of the new members. Mike demurred. He had to consider seniority in the party, regional balance, ideological balance. He would be personally delighted to consider Pauline, not now but later. He never did. Mike was not happy in dealing with women as colleagues. He soon came to think of Judy as a problem, and to conclude that it would be multiplied by another woman.

The second question he asked was startling. What would I think of the idea that Walter Gordon should be Minister of Industry, the new department that we planned to create and to which Walter, particularly, attached much importance? I said that there was no way Industry could be as important as Finance. I had some sympathy with people who argued that in contemporary conditions Finance should not remain so much the pre-eminent portfolio for economic policy that it had traditionally been. While I was personally doubtful, there was a respectable case for a new Economics Ministry to which both Finance and Industry would be subordinate. But if that were ever contemplated, it would have to be as a major reorganization of government requiring careful preparation. There could be no question of undertaking it in the near future. Meantime, at any rate, Finance was the senior portfolio. Surely it was where Walter and everyone else expected him to be. I could not see any alternative acceptable to opinion in the party, quite apart from Walter's own expectation.

At the time I wondered whether Mike was simply testing my loyalty to Walter, or whether he was serious in the idea and thought that, if I agreed, I could help to persuade Walter to accept it. The second hypothesis may have been the closer to the truth, since I learned later that he did in fact make the suggestion to Walter himself. It was, of course, rejected and not pressed.

At this distance, it may seem that Mike was prescient in thinking about a portfolio other than Finance for Walter Gordon. That is belied, however, by the fact that in the following two months Mike actively encouraged Walter in what turned out to be the overambitiousness of his first budget. Moreover, if he had really wanted Finance to be in conventionally "safer" hands than Walter's, he would surely have thought of a more appropriate alternative portfolio than Industry. The obvious one would have been President of the Privy Council, enabling Walter to function as the recognized deputy to the Prime Minister. That would have been the best use of his distinctive and outstanding talents.

With the advantage of hindsight, I have little doubt that the Pearson government would then have been both more managerially efficient and more politically effective. It is natural, however, that Mike did not fully recognize the extent to which Walter was regarded, by the most active workers within the Liberal party, as the chief architect of their victory; he had to be visibly the second man in the Cabinet of April 1963. Nor did Mike fully foresee the magnitude of the management task for which he needed help that could best come from a Minister and which Walter was by far the best qualified to give. The mishap of the first budget diminished his power and reduced his effectiveness, but as Minister of Finance his authority within the Ottawa structure was still greater than it would have been if he had been initially appointed to a relatively junior portfolio.

One of the government's early moves was to be the establishment of a parliamentary committee on defence policy. The third question Mike put to me was what I thought of asking Maurice Sauvé to chair the committee. It was an urgent question only because of the implication that Sauvé would not be in the Cabinet. I responded that Maurice would be excellent for the committee chairmanship and I would certainly urge him to take it rather than sulk because he was not in the Cabinet. Mike's relief at that point was patent. But, I went on, he ought to be in the Cabinet. I recognized the difficulties. Mike was, at that time, devoted to Maurice Lamontagne, whose relations with Sauvé were strained. Further, Sauvé was widely regarded as too overtly ambitious for anyone's good, including his own. With rare exceptions, differences in ambition among politicians are of small degree, but for that very reason it is a breach of the unspoken rules to wear the ambition on one's sleeve.

Our liking for Maurice Lamontagne as a friend could not, however, alter the fact that he was now indebted to the "old guard" of Quebec Liberals for his election in the safe Outremont riding. Alone he was no longer a sufficient offset to Chevrier and all the other federal Liberals who were strangers to the Quebec of the "Quiet Revolution." Our relations with the new Quebec would founder unless Sauvé was closely involved. That it would be difficult did not alter the necessity of finding a way to get the two Maurices to work together. To leave Sauvé out of the Cabinet was not a solution.

Mike did not argue otherwise, but offered instead a degree of reassurance. He felt it necessary to construct a Cabinet that initially respected seniority enough to avoid a lot of the disgruntlement that would be more damaging the further the government departed in policy from the inclinations of the old guard. Once they had enjoyed the prestige of privy councillorship for a while, and had "hon." permanently attached to their names, he planned to retire a number of the initial ministers. He recognized that, in the reconstruction, Sauvé would be the obvious first candidate from Quebec.

That gave the opening to clarify my position. It was not my business to make threats, and to do so would be meaningless because I had no idea whether my being in the Pearson office would work out well for any length of time anyway. I offered the prediction, however, that if the government did not evolve in a way that brought Sauvé into the Cabinet within twelve months it would also be a government in which my interest would have ended. It was as much as I could do to emphasize the opinion that, whatever the Prime Minister's feelings about him, Sauvé's talents were greatly needed in a Cabinet that was in danger of being out of touch with the new Quebec.

On that note our discussion of the Cabinet closed, and was not resumed until the fall, by which time the weaknesses of its composition had become too obvious to ignore. The subsequent reconstructions were never radical enough to make the best practicable utilization of the talents available in the Liberal caucus. This was commonly attributed to Mike being too nice a guy to hurt people's feelings in the way that a Prime Minister, or any other leader, must be prepared on occasion to do. The truth was more complicated. Mike had intense difficulty in telling people, face to face, anything unpleasant for them. He would go to almost any length to avoid or minimize personal confrontations. When changes were being made in the Cabinet, he talked to the people who would be pleased but devoted some of his considerable tactical ingenuity to finding other ways, as I shall illustrate later, of breaking the news to those who were going to be disappointed, or worse. The evasion did not make it easier for them.

Mike could in fact be hard with people, sometimes very hard. His perceived "softness" was real but selective, and it was the lesser of the reasons why his Cabinet was never as strong as it could have been. The larger reason was the theory of government that he propounded to me many times. His was, as he liked to put it, a government of reform. Such measures as the pension plan and medicare, however, were seen as radical by people of conservative mind, and particularly by the many people in the business community who were Liberal supporters in the sense that they preferred us to Diefenbaker, but who wanted as little government intervention as possible. Mike was not persuaded by them but he was always sensitive to opinions to which he was much exposed.

The way to bring the conservatives along, as he put it, was to have a good proportion of ministers who would be regarded as conventionally "safe" men. Great reforms were made sooner and more acceptably if they were undertaken by governments that looked ideologically conservative. He could give many historical illustrations. And since the more able MPs who might have been brought into the Cabinet were generally less conservative, the theory served as a rationalization, at least, for holding on to some of its weaker members.

There was, I always replied, a considerable element of truth in the theory. But, like most things in politics, it could not be pushed very far. The nineteenth century had been different, but the contemporary media made government too open a process for there to be much separation of appearance and reality. If the government stuck to its reformist programs, everyone knew that the safe men were not the powerful people. Their value as reassurance for the conservative-minded was very limited.

The even greater weakness of the theory was that it ignored the management problem of government. In the past, when the range of government responsibilities was small, it had been sufficient to have a few men in the Cabinet who made all the big decisions, while most of the thinking and almost all the administration could be left to civil servants. Government, however, had become much more complex, even in the fifteen years since Mike had been a civil servant. The pressures on key people were much greater. The central process had to be much more organized for decision-making. Cabinet had too much to do for its meetings to be leisurely. If it contained a considerable proportion of people who wanted to discuss yet again policy principles that were already settled in Mike's mind, if many Ministers were weak in parliamentary debate or in administration or in both, the effect was greatly to heighten the strain on key officials, on other ministers, and above all on the Prime Minister himself.

As time went on, I found myself arguing with increasing vehemence that one main cause of the government's troubles and errors was this heightening of strain, especially on the Prime Minister, which could be lessened by strengthening the Cabinet and improving the organization of work and decision-making. Mike did not dispute the diagnosis and, as I shall show, there were improvements from time to time. But they never caught up for long with the factors that tended to increase the strain and create new troubles.

Mike Pearson was certainly neither the first nor the last political leader to approach government with a style that has too little regard for its management aspects. Indeed, while the reasons have varied in detail, the upshot has been the same for all our federal governments since 1953: faced with the complexities of public affairs in the modern state, none has succeeded in organizing its central processes in a way that fosters the sense of reasonableness and foresight, of coherence and efficiency, which is at the heart of good management in all collective activities.

The challenge to do better should not, in my view, be pointed to "Ottawa" as such. The problem is not one of public administration. The challenge is to the political parties, equally to all of them. The problem lies in how they prepare themselves for the power that they seek so ardently or strive so desperately to maintain. It would be naïve to suggest that parties should be any less concerned with gaining power, and therefore with propaganda, with presenting the best possible face to as many people as possible, with organization for the conduct of campaigns. But it is realistic to point out that all those efforts are of small value if, when they have succeeded in producing an elected government, the party soon shows that it was poorly prepared to run the nation's business.

In a democracy, prime ministers and their principal associates are not entitled to the luxury of learning on the job. They should come to office on the strength of having told the electorate what they will aim to achieve. They owe it to the people, to their parties, and to themselves to understand the management of government well enough to be capable of achieving what they have said. Whether they have such aims and such understanding depends on the political processes internal to the parties. It depends on how much thought has been given to specific policies understood and agreed within the parties. It depends on how much weight has been given, in the emergence of party leaders, to management capabilities as well as histrionic skills. For his deficiencies in both these respects, Mike Pearson paid a heavy price, privately and publicly. They created strains that, in combination with his tendency to indecision, sometimes dragged even his resilient spirit into frustration and confusion, and hence into further error and temporary despair.

This midway point in my account, with Mike about to become Prime Minister, seems the best place for the emotionally difficult task of attempting to summarize my perception of Pearson the politician. Those who knew him were constantly distressed by the contrast between his personal qualities, which until 1957 were reflected in the easy distinction of his public performance, and the frequent humiliations that he encountered as leader of a party and a government – unable to project his purposes clearly, dogged but somehow suspect as to his sincerity, not in control of his government and frequently changing his mind as he slipped from crisis to crisis and skirted the edge of scandal.

I was often asked whether the explanation was that he really hated politics. There is no simple answer to that, or to any other questions about Mike's complex personality.

One neglected element in understanding him is that he was by academic training a historian, and indeed practised as such before he became a diplomat. He had a historian's sense of public roles as well as a deep moral sense of public service. And while he was too happy-go-lucky a personality to be precise in his ambitions, his desire to leave his mark on history was stronger than that of many men with more overt desires for position. And to leave a large mark meant, for him, being a politician. That politics involved some activities for which he had no particular taste or talent in no way deterred him. On the contrary, by upbringing he had the kind of conscience that accepts doing things you dislike as the regular price of a good life.

What Mike disliked was not, in fact, any of the activities of politics as such. He was not uncomfortable in the personal contacts. He had no inherent dislike of debating. He rather enjoyed making a speech, if he felt he was making it reasonably well. He liked discussion in small groups of almost every kind, and had a very special skill in chairing them. While he was at times impetuously decisive, and rather more frequently indecisive, he always got satisfaction from decisions made, from action undertaken. In that sense, not as self-gratification, he enjoyed power.

His dislike was not of the political process but of the things that he did not do well, which hurt his pride. In style he had a disarming modesty, illuminated by a self-deprecating wit, but underneath the pride was strong. He hated being bested by Diefenbaker, as he often was, and failing, as he often did, to impress an audience or to put his view across on television.

In this book I am bound to refer quite often to weaknesses and mistakes; there is no need to catalogue them now. Devastating as their effects were, they were essentially tactical. Mike's skills were those that he practised so successfully in diplomacy. They helped him greatly, not only inside Cabinet and at gatherings of party adherents, but also in many other meetings. He was almost always at his best with groups of conflictingly minded students and usually coped well with critical delegations, not to mention groups as difficult as ten provincial premiers. The Pearson we saw in all these situations was very much the same man in 1958–67, as party leader and Prime Minister, as the statesman the public had previously known, the worthy winner of the Nobel Peace Prize.

The impression of Mike as a weak Prime Minister derived chiefly from his performance in the House of Commons where, under pressure, he was often uncertain, even obviously confused. But while those and other weaknesses imposed great strains on his colleagues and associates, and above all on L.B. Pearson himself, they had little bearing on his strategic abilities and none at all on his determination.

The Cabinet system requires of a Prime Minister much patience and highly developed skills of persuasion. Even more, it requires clarity of mind and great firmness. Above all, he must ensure the trust without which a Cabinet cannot work effectively. Ministers do not have to like each other greatly, but must have considerable respect for the abilities of most of their principal colleagues. Those who do not earn respect – there is bound to be such a minority – must learn to admit to a junior role and keep their peace. A powerful Minister may occasionally get his own way, even against strong contrary views of almost all the rest, by the threat of resignation. But that is a weapon blunted by any but the rarest use. It cannot be allowed to qualify the overwhwelming presumption that, in the last analysis, every Minister will go along with what emerges as the Cabinet decision. And that must be a decision for which the Prime Minister takes, in the end, personal responsibility.

A Cabinet does not have long to endure if many of its conclusions are ones that would have failed if they had been put to a secret vote around the table. Equally, however, a Cabinet cannot endure if a majority forces significant decisions on an unwilling Prime Minister; it is a lesser evil that he should occasionally insist on the decision that is his, against the opinions of most of his ministers.

Mike's performance in this role deteriorated as he aged, but for much of his prime ministership – and particularly while he had Walter Gordon's invaluable help, to the end of 1965 – he was the master of a Cabinet as talented and argumentative as most. His historian's sense of the movement of influences and events helped him to have, usually, a realistic sense of the competing strengths of the various factors in play in any complex situation. And that is among the most important qualities on which substantial political achievement depends. However many small mistakes he made, on large issues Mike's judgment was generally sound and far-sighted. His purposes were those of a moderate reformer, and he sustained them through all the incidental troubles of his administration. That gave him the stoicism to view the troubles not lightly but in perspective. His depressions and anxieties and humiliations were more than balanced by the feeling of accomplishment.

PART FOUR

Beginning to Govern

"Please, Mr. Kent, may I take a picture of Mr. Pearson?"

17 *Fifty-Two Days*

Why Mike had urgently wanted me in Ottawa, for the early days before his government took office, was not to help in constructing the Cabinet. It was to prepare the actions that the Cabinet would have to take.

The extreme urgency arose from his campaign commitments for the first "sixty days of decision." They were the unfortunate product of the weakness of most of the 1963 campaigning. Walter Gordon had undoubtedly been right to insist that the final stages must be a rescue operation. By then the vagueness in which the Liberal program had been enveloped could be effectively corrected only by concentrating on a limited number of measures on which definite action could be promised within a short period. If that period had been a hundred days, as Walter proposed, it would have been hectic but not unbearable. The unwisdom was in Mike's shortening to sixty days, for what seemed to me a frivolous reason.

A crash effort of this kind was very different from the scheduling I had suggested in preparing the Liberal programs as a whole. I had spread their implementation dates over the four years of a normal government term, and calculated their financing on that basis. I was, I suppose, something of a hen with her own chicks. I disliked the disruption of my careful programming by the sixty-day declaration. However, I had agreed during the campaign that, regrettably, some crash program had become electorally necessary, and it was pointless now to argue about details. The only thing to do was to try to ensure that the show got smartly on the road.

Mike wanted me to put together at once a memorandum on the actions that would be needed to carry out his immediate promises. I pointed out that a realistic plan could not be limited to the things he had said. There were other administrative actions that had to be taken. A useful working document would have to be a check-list of all the priority items. That would not be easy to compile while I was still sitting in the offices of a party in opposition, without access to the civil servants who knew the routine needs better than I did.

We agreed, however, that what I could put together before the government was sworn in, though likely not to be complete, would at least help to get it off to a more planned start. My "check-list for sixty days of action" was prepared in the following four days and delivered to Mike on 15 April, a week before the government took office and the sixty days began. (They ran to 20 June.) It contained thirty items, of greatly vary-ing complexity.

The measures Mike had promised that required legislation included the establishment of the Department of Industry, the Municipal Devel-opment and Loan Fund, the Economic Council, capital funding for the Atlantic Development Board, and the Canada Development Corpora-tion. Except for the Economic Council, my notes were well short of the crucial stage in preparing legislation – "drafting instructions" – but they prepared the way for it in all cases but one: the Canada Development Corporation was a casualty of the June budget mishap, and was only revived much later and then in considerably changed form.

On the most complex legislative item – the pension plan – we could not, whatever Mike had said or implied, present a Bill within sixty days. We needed an interdepartmental task force. It was necessary to produce an "outline draft" before we could ask for the provinces' agreement to the constitutional amendment necessary in order to include "non-aged" benefits. Disability pensions and pensions for widows under sixty-five, dependent children, and orphans were part of a complete plan but not within federal jurisdiction. If the provinces would not quickly consent to the constitutional change, we should still go ahead with our legislation – in the fall – and hope to add the additional features later.

The Pearson commitments included meetings with President Kennedy and with the British government. The memorandum suggested the possi-ble dates and in each case items for the agenda, to be fleshed out by External Affairs. On the meeting with Kennedy I set the sights high – far higher than was achieved – by ending the agenda with "some general initiative on the need for expansionary international economic policies – the reform of IMF to provide greater international liquidity, increased investment in under-developed countries, support for international com-modity agreements." This could "lift us into something truly important and give the sense of a new life" to Canada's place in the world. At that stage I was still capable of great optimism.

I urged that Parliament should open on the earliest possible date, which was 16 May. That would make it psychologically easier to get fast action on the priority legislation, adjourn before the heat of the summer, and get down to other business in the fall. We could be ready enough for 16 May if we were determined, and extra time during the adjournment would be even more valuable, for real program planning, than extra time before Parliament met. The 16 May date was agreed to and announced on 23 April, but of course the row over the budget destroyed the psycholog-ical effect and delayed the adjournment.

One of the recommendations to which I attached most importance was that from the start, and in contrast to the way Diefenbaker had operated, regular committees should be organized to do a great deal of Cabinet's business. This was essential for the competence to which we aspired. But striking the committees would occupy a good deal of valuable time if it was left to be done in Cabinet itself after its formal appointment. The organization and membership of the committees should be settled before Cabinet first met. In practice I was still negotiating memberships a few days after that, but thanks to Mike's full endorsement of the committee style of operation we did get off to quite a smart start.

There was less success for my aim that the "Bi and Bi" Commission, on bilingualism and biculturalism, should be got into existence in May. That required promptness in carefully consulting the provinces, drafting terms of reference, and approaching members. In practice it was late July before the Commission was set up. Even less came of my recommendation that, since the Commission would no doubt sit for a long time, a task force should be set up, under a senior civil servant, to suggest what early administrative action could be taken, even if on a small scale initially, to improve the use of French in Ottawa.

There were other important reforms on which action could promptly be set in motion without early demands on the time of ministers. The tempo of parliamentary proceedings could be quickened by more use of committees for legislation, and a special committee should be charged with a more thorough review of parliamentary procedures. My hope that it could report by the fall was not realized, but some useful reforms did eventually materialize. More urgent was the redistribution of parliamentary constituencies. The Diefenbaker government had done nothing about the redistribution required following the 1961 census. The Chief Electoral Officer should be promptly authorized to start the technical work. The importance of that became apparent two years later, in all the heart-searching about a 1965 election. In 1963 my concern was to achieve a momentum which would make it easier to get on with legislation to provide for redistribution by an independent commission, in place of the traditional gerrymandering. This eventually did become one of the significant Pearson reforms.

The memorandum listed, of course, items to be incorporated in the early writing of a Throne Speech to start the parliamentary session. On financial matters, it was cautious. The Diefenbaker government had never had an Appropriation Act to authorize its spending in the financial year 1962-3, by then ended, but there was no point in recrimination; what had been spent should be approved and done with. In the same spirit, we should not attempt to do much about the spending estimates for 1963-4 prepared under the previous government. They could not be thoroughly revised in time for a June budget, which was one of the commitments of the sixty days, and there was no point in hasty tinkering with them. In that budget, we should go with the estimates substantially as they were, though "with the warning that some fairly extensive changes will probably be presented to Parliament in the fall."

The June budget would have to provide for some program additions, financially quite minor at this stage, and for tax incentives to stimulate employment, particularly in development areas. But, in order that it could be introduced within the promised sixty days, the budget "has to be, in respects other than those mentioned, a fairly stand-pat budget, but with the promise of more thorough reforms to come, and the possibility of a supplementary budget statement in the fall." Rarely has advice, good or bad, been more completely ignored.

On 15 April, however, Mike offered no disagreement with the memorandum. He was pleased enough to make a somewhat daring suggestion. The formal change of government was still a week ahead. In the meantime civil servants who would shortly have a great deal to do were sitting on their hands. We could not have any official contact with them until the change-over. But since many of the senior ones were friends of mine, couldn't I ask them to my home and go through the memorandum with them, privately and confidentially? They might have some useful suggestions about things we had overlooked and about implementation procedures. And anyway it would enable them to use the following days to start thinking about the tasks ahead.

I was somewhat taken aback, not least because of the inferences about my role in the new government that would immediately be drawn within the inner Ottawa circle. As impending Prime Minister, Mike seemed to have shed completely the inhibitions that had, understandably, bothered him in opposition, when Diefenbaker was denigrating him by characterizing me as "the leader of the leader." That unspoken thought aside, there were, I pointed out, practical difficulties. The civil servant who could contribute most to such a meeting, and to whom it would be most helpful immediately after the change of government, was Bob Bryce. But as Secretary to the Cabinet and Clerk of the Privy Council, he would be in close contact with Mr Diefenbaker until the last moment of the old government. Friends though we were, to meet with me at this moment would be too awkward for him; it would be unfair to ask.

There were other senior people who would have to be excluded for various reasons. Even so, given the range of the "sixty-day" programs, the number who should be asked, for a comprehensive discussion, was far beyond the capacity of the Kents' living room. To divide them up for a series of meetings would make the scope for gossip, and therefore the probability of leaks to the press, too great.

Mike's conclusion was that a meeting nevertheless should be held. I could confine it to a dozen or so people I knew well enough for it to be natural to invite them to my house, and yet make the gathering sufficiently representative of the senior public service to be useful.

It turned out to be moderately so. Some five years later, an alleged account of the meeting was given in print, in Peter Newman's book *The Distemper of Our Times*. According to him, at my home I unfolded to the assembled civil servants the government's intentions, "including the broad outlines of Walter Gordon's first budget." If that were so, it would have been a massive indiscretion for which I should have been summarily removed from the government's service. In fact, of course, I had neither knowledge nor expectation of the kind of budget that was to be. I went through the memorandum, as Mike had asked me to do, and thereby unwittingly misled the company by talking about a "fairly stand-pat" budget.

The rest of the Newman account was no more accurate. He asserted that there was a sharp exchange because some of the civil servants objected that the program was not realistic; so much could not be done so quickly. Presumably his informant aspired to look wise after the event. In fact, there was indeed a brief confrontation, but of a different nature. Two of the participants objected to some items in the program, notably the pension plan, on the grounds not of practicality but of desirability. I responded that this government, unlike some, was coming to office with firmly declared policies. That produced a comment that these were mere election promises; they might be politically necessary but they did not have to be taken seriously in Ottawa.

To this point, of course, I reacted strongly. A Pearson government would do, to the best of its ability, what it had told people it would do. I knew that senior public servants were accustomed to a large role in formulating policies for politicians who themselves had no clear ideas of what they wanted to achieve. But that was not going to be the situation for the next few years. No Prime Minister would be more open than Mr Pearson to their advice on how best to implement policies, and on policy proposals for the new situations that would no doubt arise. But it was not the responsibility of the public service to debate policy objectives that had already been settled by the electoral process.

The confrontation ended there. The meeting went on to practical discussion. Some relatively routine matters that needed to be attended to, but I had overlooked, were added to the list. Some good suggestions about details, for example on the agenda for the Kennedy meeting, were made. Some organizational questions, such as which Minister the Wheat Board would report to, were raised. The bottleneck in legislative drafting was lamented as a long-standing problem, and ways of getting round it were canvassed. Certainly the difficulties of completing some of the planned actions within sixty days were brought out. That was neither surprising nor worrying to me. What mattered was to get started vigorously on all the measures Mike had promised, so that they were taken as far in sixty days as could sensibly be done. If the more complex measures were not completed, the opposition could enjoy making jibes but they would not be significant for the public provided the government's decisiveness and competence in pursuing its declared intentions were clear.

In that spirit, the discussion proceeded, at least as far as most of the participants were concerned, amicably and constructively. If it was true, as Newman asserted, that some departed with a "disconsolate" feeling, it must have been because they did not like the government's policy objectives; it was not because any practical wisdom about timing and implementation had been rejected.   Relations between the government and some of the bureaucracy did become strained by the end of the sixty days. As I noted earlier, most senior public servants are concerned to do their professional job but not more. They are not power hungry. Only to the extent that they are dealing with politicians who lack ideas of their own, who do not know what they want to do, do public servants attempt, quite properly, to fill the vacuum by promoting policies of their own conception.

The trouble is that such vacuums are fairly common, and they produce a conditioning from which the less sensitive of the bureaucrats do not readily free themselves. They become bad at recognizing the change when they encounter politicians who do know what they want to do. Even then, their resistance is not prolonged, unless the Minister with ideas lacks the support of his own colleagues, who are happy to use the bureaucracy to shoot him down rather than have to do it themselves.

The Department of Finance can, however, be a special problem. It regards its territory as involving, more than others, matters of policy as well as administration that professionals understand and amateurs, whether politicians or civil servants of lesser departments, do not. The attitude readily develops, among some Finance officials and particularly those who are not good at giving clear explanations, that everyone else should simply accept their word as to what will work and what will not. Walter Gordon was a victim of, in part, this attitude.

None of us, however, foresaw any such problem on 22 April. The Cabinet that took office that day was far from an embodiment of the Liberal talents elected to Parliament. In part, of course, that was for reasons operative in any national organization for a country as diversified as Canada: there have to be balances reflecting geography, culture, origin, and religion. But it was not only to those considerations that Mr Pearson subordinated talent. As he had indicated in our discussion at

Stornoway, his choices also gave great weight to seniority in the party. He believed that the weaker members would be satisfied with status and could be jollied along in activist policies. The rest, he and Walter and others, would do the work.

That was how it was, except that, to an even greater extent than I feared, a Cabinet so constituted proved to demand far too much of the energy and time, patience and tact of the doers, and particularly of Mike himself. As always, he underestimated the managerial considerations. His government was activist enough, but only with strains that quickly diminished its competence. This was the major factor contributing to the confusions, errors and so-called scandals that marked his administration, to a degree that would otherwise be hard to account for.

Hitherto, I have referred to L.B. Pearson mostly as Mike, because up to 1963 and after 1968 that was how I thought of him and talked to him. But between he was "Prime Minister" or "Mr Pearson." I reverted to Mike only when we were not merely alone but talking in particularly intimate terms. The rest of this account will reflect that difference.

I was appointed to the Prime Minister's Office (PMO) as "Co-ordinator of Programming." The title was proposed to me by Mr Pearson but it was Walter Gordon's invention. It expressed as clearly as was tactful his concept of the role needed in PMO. The public announcement said that "Mr Kent will work with committees of Cabinet in the development of legislation and will assist the Prime Minister in liaison with the Ministers and departments of government." At my request, the appointment was for one year, not for the undefined term usual for appointments to Ministerial staffs. I had serious doubts about how the role would work out and wanted to be able to leave without creating an impression of conflict.

The PMO was then utterly different from what it became in the Trudeau era and has since remained. There was no bevy of deputies and assistants and principal this-and-that, with crowds of support staff. There was Annette Perron, the charming and able private secretary Mr Pearson had inherited from Mr St Laurent. There was Mary Macdonald, his long-time executive assistant, who alone dealt with constituency affairs but, more generally, passionately protected her boss in every way she saw to do. There was Jim Coutts, who in those days looked like a baby but efficiently controlled the Prime Minister's door and telephone and supervised the logistics of his life and, when necessary, Mrs Pearson's. Dick O'Hagan was press secretary. He had an assistant, Hal Dornan, who did well most of the writing of speeches and statements that were outside the government process. Dick also had a very competent secretary, and the invaluable Pauline Bothwell moved from the Liberal party office to remain my secretary. There were a few other secretaries, and a small civil service staff to handle correspondence that the Prime Minister did not see himself.

That was the Pearson PMO. It was a little too small, and some of the government's problems were consequential. But more people would have made it worse, not better, unless the increase had been based on a reorganization providing clearer allocations of responsibilities than Mr Pearson was ever prepared to make. He was a generalist who never became fully convinced of the virtues of the division of labour.

The small PMO operated in conjunction with a Privy Council Office (PCO) that was also tiny by subsequent standards. The East Block, as the two together were commonly dubbed, in fact occupied only one corner of that building, then given over mostly to the Department of External Affairs. The PCO/PMO central organization of the Pearson era certainly gave the public a great deal more per dollar than its elaborate successors. I would also argue that, despite the faults that this account will describe, on the whole it made better decisions than its successors do.

On 23 April and a few following days the structuring of Cabinet committees was completed. The most important, at that point, we called the Sessional Committee, which was to be responsible for determining priorities in legislation. Jack Pickersgill was chairman, I was secretary, and there were six other members – Messrs Chevrier, Lamontagne, McIlraith, MacEachen, MacNaught, and Teillet. Over the following few days there was a flurry of list-making, categorization, and discussion, which polished my earlier check-list for the sixty days and extended for the business of a full parliamentary session a fairly detailed program of actions to be taken, by whom.

Judy LaMarsh came to my office on her way out of the first Cabinet meeting, on the afternoon of 22 April. She telephoned her two deputies, for Health and for Welfare, and I was involved in my first administrative action as a public servant. Joe Willard, the able and dedicated Deputy Minister of Welfare, explained that he was scheduled to leave the next day for a meeting of a United Nations agency. Judy, in her good-natured way, was disinclined to change his plans. I had to point out that work on the pension plan should be started at once. Joe cancelled his trip.

The three of us met at Judy's office the next day and quickly set up the Task Force on Pensions, which held its first meeting on 26 April and laboured mightily for, as it turned out, the best part of two years. Joe was its chairman. He was brilliantly informed, endlessly patient, and completely dedicated to practicable improvements in the social welfare of Canadians. The membership varied somewhat from time to time but included, besides other senior staff of Health and Welfare, representatives of the departments of Finance, Insurance, National Revenue, Justice, Labour, the Unemployment Insurance Commission and the Dominion Bureau of Statistics. Few men can ever have worked harder than some of its members.

The Task Force reported to the Cabinet committee on Social Security, which in the circumstances was of special importance. As we established it on 23 April, the committee had Judy in the chair, six other strong ministers – Messrs Gordon, Martin, Pickersgill, Lamontagne, Favreau, and MacEachen – me, Joe Willard, Don Thorson (an Assistant Deputy Minister of Justice and crack legislative draftsman, with whom I was to work closely and pleasurably on many matters), Hart Clark of Finance (also one of the outstanding members of the Task Force), and Frank Milligan of PCO as secretary. Later Bob Bryce, as Deputy Minister of Finance, joined us.

The Cabinet committee on Economic Policy also got off to a prompt start. The Prime Minister was technically the chairman, but in practice he largely left it to Walter, and I represented him in the discussions. Perhaps the greatest ill consequence of the sixty-day rush, however, was that ministers were too pre-occupied to get down to a tough consideration of economic policy related to foreign investment in Canada. That was not Walter's fault. He offered the committee his definition of the new government's basic economic policy as being to further development through a mixed economy, involving some government ownership of industry where it was clearly desirable, but based on diversified ownership by the largest possible number of small Canadian investors. He naturally related the objective not to the immediate measures he was thinking about, for which the tradition of budget secrecy was dominant, but to his proposal for the Canada Development Corporation. That, however, need not have inhibited a thorough discussion. It could have had either of two consequences. Other ministers might have become more consciously committed to the objective in Walter's mind, and he could not then have been so miserably let down by his colleagues as he was after the budget. Alternatively, and I think more probably, it might have become clearer that there was not yet enough support for tax measures such as he planned, in favour of Canadian rather than foreign ownership, to be brought forward so early in the life of the government.

In either event, the government's greatest difficulty might have been avoided or lessened. But it was not so. Meanwhile, there was in effect a division of labour between Walter and me. I took no part in the items of the sixty-day program that were of principal concern to him as Minister of Finance: the budget itself, the Municipal Loan Fund and the Canada Development Corporation. He left his interest in other measures to me.

The rest of the legislation required was, the pension plan apart, fairly simple. Much of the wording required for the Bill to establish the Economic Council of Canada already existed, in the amendments I had prepared for Paul Martin to propose to the feeble and aborted legislation that the Diefenbaker government had introduced in its final days. It was easy, working with Don Thorson, to draft a Bill from that material. It was, I still believe, good legislation, providing what was necessary to initiate the kind of consensus-building about economic policy for lack of which Canada has suffered and suffers so much. The Bill contained, that is to say, what was necessary for its purpose if there had subsequently been the political will to make it work. There was not, for reasons and with consequences to which I will refer later.

The legislation to provide a capital fund for the Atlantic Development Board was simple, and there was little difficulty about the Bill to establish the Department of Industry, though the caution of the intended Minister made the section creating an Area Development Agency more limited than I had hoped. That was corrected later.

In these and other matters there was good speed, without sacrifice of care, in preparing what proved to be satisfactory measures reflecting the priorities that had been declared for the sixty days. The Prime Minister held his promised meetings with the British government and President Kennedy, both of which were diplomatic successes. Above all, twelve days after its first meeting, the Pension Task Force had prepared a set of proposals, presented to the Cabinet committee on 8 May. They fleshed out, in considerable though not complete detail, the plan proposed in the Liberal election platform. There were some modifications and elaborations, reflecting the expertise of the civil servants, but they did not change the nature of the plan and they were readily accepted.

Neither then nor at any subsequent point in the gyrations through which the Canada Pension Plan evolved was there conflict between the public servants on one side and politicians on the other. There were, of course, differences of opinion within the Task Force. Most were disagreements among the experts, resolved among them when they were purely technical. The officials were fully supportive of both the objectives and the nature of the pension plan; and Judy and I quickly came to trust the competence and good sense of the Task Force. We were therefore fully willing to be flexible about the details of the plan in response to their technical and administrative advice.

In almost all respects, the Cabinet committee was equally responsive. The one point on which there was not formal agreement on May 8 was the opinion of the Task Force that the earliest practicable date to make the plan operative was more than twelve months ahead, July 1964, and that might well become 1 January, 1965. Ministers were not then ready to accept such a timetable, and the issue was formally left in abeyance. That did not worry us. The Task Force was plainly right, and I had no doubt that within a little time its realism would be accepted. While some of Mike's words on the hustings could be taken to mean that the plan would be legislated within sixty days, few people had ever taken that seriously. Honour would be fully satisfied if, within the sixty days, we developed the plan to the point where a resolution to introduce the legislation could be placed on the parliamentary order paper and Judy could make a statement describing the plan in all the detail required for credibility.

This was the necessary preliminary to discussion with the provinces, and particularly to finding out whether there would be the necessary agreement to a constitutional amendment making it possible for federal legislation to include survivor and disability pensions. The most doubtful province was Quebec. We did not want a repetition of Lesage's rebuff to Diefenbaker, saying that he would not take a view about a constitutional amendment until he knew what Ottawa intended to legislate. The Prime Minister therefore told Lionel Chevrier and Maurice Lamontagne, as the senior Quebec ministers, to prepare the way by outlining the plan in a confidential meeting with Lesage as early as possible. On 8 May, I provided them with notes on the plan to use in this discussion.

They reported back that, while he had not committed himself, Lesage had raised no objections to the proposals. Jean himself later gave me rather a different account. He claimed that, though Chevrier and Lamontagne had notes in front of them, those had not been shown to him and the two ministers had talked so vaguely that he concluded the plan was not developed very far and there was nothing of substance for him to respond to. I am inclined to think that his attitude was justified. There turned out to be a similar misunderstanding, or whatever it was, about the Municipal Development and Loan Fund. Chevrier and Lamontagne were supposed to have outlined the proposal to Lesage, without getting any adverse reaction, but when the legislation was put forward he criticized it severely.

These incidents resulted in a substantial change in the conduct of relations between the Pearson and Lesage governments. When he was in Ottawa a little later, Lesage informed Pearson that he would not in future deal with any of his ministers. If he could not speak directly with the Prime Minister, as he recognized would not always be possible or appropriate, he would be happy to deal with either Gordon Robertson or Tom Kent. Such willingness to use subordinates, rather than insist on speaking to the Prime Minister directly, was not modesty; that was not a Lesage characteristic. He and Pearson did not communicate easily. Lesage was precise and decisive, and he regarded Pearson as unclear and evasive. He knew well the qualities of Gordon Robertson, who on 1 July succeeded Bob Bryce as Secretary to the Cabinet. Gordon had been his Deputy Minister when Jean was in the federal Cabinet. Lesage and I also had a longstanding relationship. Thereafter the contact on policy between Quebec and Ottawa was almost entirely through Gordon or me. Whether the results were good is for others to judge, but certainly some significant agreements were achieved and disagreements were not compounded by misunderstanding or distrust.

In May, however, this was in the future. We took the reports from Chevrier and Lamontagne at face value; preparations for both the pension plan and the municipal loan legislation proceeded with a confidence that proved to be misplaced.

In the second week of May most of my energies were concentrated on writing the Throne Speech for the opening of Parliament. We early decided on a procedural change. Hitherto Throne Speeches had been read first in English and then repeated in French translation, with considerable boredom for both reader and audience. We decided that the speech would be read only once, in alternating passages of English and French.

Throne Speeches tend to be wearisome for another reason. Every Minister is anxious to have something for his or her department to feel important about. The result, particularly if the government has no strong direction or major policies, is a rag-bag collection of items, often expressed in verbose jargon and loaded with platitudes. I was fully supported by the Prime Minister in the determination that the first Throne Speech of the new government should be different. It should concentrate on major items, and it should express the main direction of government policy in terse, straightforward terms.

My first draft was dated 9 May and a final draft was sent for printing on 14 May. Under the pressure of Ministers it had grown a little in the interval, but I still felt that the Speech, as read on 16 May, clearly expressed the thrust of a firmly progressive government. The emphasis was that "Steady work is the basic need on which men and women depend for the well-being of themselves and their families. Unemployment ... is therefore the most urgent of our domestic problems."

The legislation briefly defined included the Economic Council, the Department of Industry and Area Development Agency, the Municipal Development and Loan Board, a funded Atlantic Development Board, the Canada Development Corporation, and the Canada Pension Plan, "for the purpose of enabling all Canadians to retire in security and with dignity," to be "operative as soon as possible." The fisheries limit was to be extended from three to twelve miles, there was to be an independent commission for the redistribution of electoral districts, and there were to be committees to review parliamentary procedure and defence policy. There was a commitment to "co-operative federalism," and the establishment of the biculturalism commission. Even my favourite themes for international relations were stated more positively than is common among the generalities of Throne Speeches. The government would seek "measures of controlled disarmament, including a treaty to end nuclear tests under reasonable safeguards." There should be "policies that steadily reduce the barriers limiting trade. It is equally important to pursue active policies for the economic development of the newer nations, for the expansion of trade in primary commodities at reasonably stable prices, and for the improvement of international payments."

In the latter part of May and the early part of June, the world felt good. The Prime Minister, no doubt remembering my plea about women in the Cabinet, suggested that I invite Pauline Jewett to have the honour of making the first speech in the new Parliament, moving the formal address that begins the debate on the Throne Speech. She spoke well. On the following Sunday, Pauline drove with the Kents to lunch with the Pearsons at Harrington Lake, the then fairly modest Gatineau retreat that the nation provides for its Prime Minister. Before lunch Mike uncorked champagne for the five of us to toast the Throne Speech: "words by Kent, music by Jewett," as he put it. The day was beautiful and after lunch Mike rowed me around the lake and we explored a beaver dam on the stream flowing into it. Not for five years, until after his retirement, did I again see him as relaxed and confident as he was that day.

When Parliament got down to business it was, thanks to the irrepressible Diefenbaker, more fractious than we had naïvely anticipated. The legislation that we had worked so urgently to have ready proceeded with disappointing slowness. Even so, there were in May and early June no serious difficulties. At the end of that period I was able to prepare for the Prime Minister notes that accurately boasted:

> We called Parliament at the earliest possible date, as we said we would. I told the people, in my television address on April 23, that we would have our legislation ready. We have. It is a legislative programme of wide-ranging action for employment, for the strengthening of our economy, for improving the security of our people. I do not know when in Canadian history, or indeed in the political history of any parliamentary country in peace-time, so extensive and so vigorous a programme was prepared and put forward in so short a time. It is a programme that implements the priorities that we identified when we asked for the confidence of the people in the election campaign. We said what we would do first, and we are doing it.

It quickly became the conventional wisdom that the "sixty days" had been the beginning of the Pearson government's disasters. The reality was different. The commitments had indeed been rashly heavy, but in fact they were reasonably discharged without very great strain. Any fair judgment made on the fifty-second day would have been that the Pearson government had been as decisive and effective as it promised.

It fell into disarray after the fifty-third day, the day of the budget. That, however, was not because there was anything wrong with the sixty-day program as such. It had to include a June budget; in the state of financial disorganization created by the Diefenbaker government, there could not be a delay. The Pearson commitment did not specify what kind of budget it would be. If it had been one that could go through Parliament much as it was proposed, the sixty days would have been seen in history as a fine beginning for a government.

This is not to claim that the government would have long stayed free of trouble. But the sixty-day idea was not the reason why trouble came so early.

18 *Retreat and Reorganization*

The honeymoon period of the Pearson government ended on its fifty-fourth day, the day after the budget of 13 June. The initial attack was not on the content of the budget. It was an irrelevancy, stirred up first by the rambunctious Douglas Fisher, then an NDP member. He asked whether outsiders had been involved in preparation of the budget.

At this point, Walter paid the price of parliamentary inexperience. He should have given a straightforward account of the preparation of the budget. But, according to his explanation to me, he was inhibited by whispered advice from Jack Pickersgill not to answer the question. He fell between stools with a hesitant, evasive reply. It clearly would not do, and there began a rescue operation that turned out to be prolonged and painful. Together Walter and I wrote a fuller statement, which he made in the House later in the day. It was a simple acknowledgment of the role of the three special consultants Walter had brought temporarily from Toronto to his office. There was nothing undercover about their role. Their appointments had been properly made, they had taken the oath of secrecy, and had been in no way hidden. No shred of an indication of any indiscretion or impropriety was ever produced. But that did not prevent the opposition from suggesting it.

If the question had been fully answered immediately it was asked, the opposition could never have made much of it. The delay gave an oppor-

tunity for the kind of innuendo and political game-playing that Walter
did not have the temperament to deal with well, and he got no help from
his colleagues, with the notable exception of Mitchell Sharp. He and I
remembered that, when the Diefenbaker government carried out its
extraordinary loan conversion operations in 1958, it invited no less than
forty-two people from the financial community to advise it. Then it
called some 200 more to Ottawa for a sworn-to-secrecy briefing on what
was to happen, in circumstances where some could have made money by
misusing the information. Walter was now being pilloried for bringing
three advisers from the business world. It was ridiculous. Mitchell made
a fighting and effective speech on those lines. The attack on the consultants, even when conducted with Diefenbaker histrionics and innuendo,
was an artificial storm that would have soon blown itself out if the
budget had taken the normal course.

It did not, and the consultant issue became a disturbance that had
already set nerves on edge when the real storm broke. The Draconian
measure in the budget was a 30 per cent sales tax on takeovers of
Canadian companies by non-residents. The financial community took a
few days to absorb its significance, but by 18 June there was seething
indignation. The tax would badly hurt some pocketbooks. As is unavoidable with any new tax of such a kind, this one involved some technical
difficulties in administration; they could be overcome, but not readily so
unless there was a reasonable measure of cooperation from the financial
community. That was plainly not going to be given. The atmosphere was
one in which there was danger of a sharp break in stock-market prices
and perhaps the kind of financial panic that would produce another run
on the Canadian dollar.

Walter decided himself – not, at this point, under Cabinet pressure –
to withdraw the takeover tax, at least temporarily. He made the announcement in the House on 19 June. Before doing so, he had told the
Prime Minister that he would resign if Pearson wished. The Gordon and
Pearson memoirs are in conflict on this point. According to the latter,
Walter offered his resignation some time later, after the Cabinet meeting
which was held at Harrington Lake on the evening of 4 July, to settle
further budget revisions. Mr Pearson's memoirs, unfortunately, were not
completed before his death, and the posthumous publication of an edited
version of what were no more than rough notes towards the third volume
was an ill service to him.

The Prime Minister told me on the morning of June 19, in considerable
agitation, that Walter had decided to withdraw the takeover tax and had
offered to resign. Did I think he should? That this was then the state of
the Prime Minister's mind was confirmed when Dick O'Hagan canvassed
the Press Gallery for opinions as to whether Walter should resign. It is

inconceivable that Dick would have done this unless the Prime Minister had led him to believe that resignation was an open question, though it was a foolish procedure in any event and certainly added to the strain on Walter.

My response to Mr Pearson's question was that if Walter resigned the government would not long survive. I went at once to talk to Walter, and was relieved to find that, as happened often, the other participant's impression of the conclusion of a conversation with Pearson was more definite than Pearson's. He had said that he would resign if the Prime Minister wished. He had been answered with a question: had he lost confidence in himself? He replied that he had not. That had seemed to settle the matter. He had left without resigning. But now he was beginning to wonder what Mike really wanted.

I said that was not the issue. Nor was his self-confidence. That was bound to be temporarily shaken, but not destroyed; it could be rebuilt. The issue was the future of the government. For him to leave after one mistake might be hailed by some as showing that Pearson could be tough. The reality was different. Because Walter was so personally close to Pearson, his departure would greatly weaken internal confidence in the leadership of the government. Mike could not run it without him. Deep disagreements would surface within the Cabinet and the caucus. Mike would not have the authority, any more than he had the temperament, to control them. The government's sense of purpose, based on the election platform that politically was identified chiefly with Walter, would quickly disappear. In the House the NDP would become less supportive. The government would become insecure and indecisive; it would soon make further mistakes, worse than the takeover tax. It would survive miserably and not for long.

In all this I was merely saying what I was sure Walter thought himself; but in an emotional crisis, sincere confirmation is comforting. The alternative to resignation, we both knew, was grim. For some weeks he would go through hell. But he had the fortitude to live through it, and recover. To a remarkable extent, he did recover. Despite the Pearson memoirs, I do not think that he considered resignation again; by 4 July, certainly, he had steeled himself to the humiliation of the budget retreat.

For a few weeks Walter did indeed go through hell. The tigers were out in full force. After he had retreated on the takeover tax, every interest hurt by any provision of the budget clamoured to have it changed.

In this environment, small technical problems were inflated into major errors. Because of the secrecy in which they have traditionally been prepared, almost all significant changes in our complicated tax laws prove to have side-effects unforeseen by the official experts in their

Ottawa offices. Normally, professional reactions make many of these apparent and they are corrected, almost unnoticed politically, by "technical" amendments and additions as the legislation goes through the parliamentary committee stage. The weakness of the Department of Finance as Walter had inherited it, in addition to the haste in which the budget was prepared, made the 1963 proposals more vulnerable than most – though not worse than some, notably those of November 1981, prepared in more favourable circumstances. In the atmosphere of 1963, however, modifications that would normally have attracted little notice were treated as further examples of the Minister of Finance's alleged ineptitude.

It was clear that there would have to be some revisions as well as the withdrawal of the takeover tax. In my first memorandum on the subject, written on 20 June to the Prime Minister and Walter jointly and discussed with them on the Sunday three days later, I suggested some minor modifications and one major change. The budget provided for accelerated capital cost allowances as a way to stimulate early investment and increased employment, but companies not having a substantial degree of Canadian ownership were excluded from the benefit. The exclusion was in conflict with the budget's short-term aim of economic stimulation, and the discrimination was hard to defend on top of the measure that had more long-term significance for foreign ownership: a differentiation of the rate of withholding taxes as between companies with and without substantial Canadian ownership. We should stick to that, the memorandum argued, but remove the additional short-term discrimination. By doing so we would strengthen the stimulus to employment and improve our answer to those who were objecting that another budget measure, the extension of sales tax to building materials and machinery, would depress the economy. Further, we would take the edge of the greatest technical difficulty in the budget, which was that its definition of "a substantial degree of Canadian ownership" was not one that could be firmly established for some widely held companies. If the discrimination in capital cost allowances was retained, it was essential that the definition should quickly be made precise. If all that was affected was the rate of withholding tax, however, there was much less urgency.

Otherwise, I argued, the budget should stand. We had to steer a careful course between seeming unreasonable and arrogant, in face of all the demands for change, and being an easy push-over, "a weak government that knuckles under to the financial community and political opponents." Walter was happy with my suggestions, but the discussion made it plain that the Prime Minister was inclined to be more yielding to the critics. I was not at the time as disturbed by that as Walter was entitled to be; it was only later that I found out how much he had been encouraged by Mr Pearson in the budget-making. But, that moral issue aside, it would have been better politics to make only the minimally essential changes and otherwise use a stonewalling technique until the critics had exhausted public attention. I have never understood why Mike seemed almost to lead, and certainly not to discourage, the majority of the Cabinet in the revisionist urge that dominated the next three weeks.

Much that was written with the wisdom of hindsight was misleading, and almost all of it was unfair to Walter Gordon. The Prime Minister himself asserted, in a letter to Senator Crerar on 9 July 1963, that the basic mistake "was to have attempted to produce a budget at all in such a short time." In truth, there had been no choice. A budget is the government's financial plan for twelve months ahead. It should be produced before the start of the financial year on 1 April, preferably a month or two before. By 13 June, over 20 per cent of the financial year was already history. Sixty-day promise or no, delay would have been indefensible. Mr Pearson's election promises for sixty days of decision would have deserved to be laughed out of court, they would have been wildly irresponsible, if they had not included the commitment to produce a budget. From election day to 13 June, I never heard one suggestion, from a politician or a public servant, that the budget should be delayed.

The only question was what kind of budget. On 15 April the Prime Minister apparently approved my suggestion that it should be "a fairly stand-pat budget"; more thorough reforms would come, but not earlier than the fall. That was the burden of the budget item in the memorandum that he asked me to reveal to public service friends so that they could get to work.

There was no doubt that reforms, from Walter, would include measures with the objective stated in general terms in the Liberal election platform: "to reverse the trend towards absentee ownership of Canadian industry." Specific measures had not been defined, precisely because they would necessarily involve tax provisions that would have to be delicately adjusted to economic circumstances at the time of their introduction. It did not occur to me that they would be given "sixty-day" priority. Walter took a different view, for reasons which he explained to me later. He judged, rightly, that relevant and effective measures would meet a great deal of opposition in much of the business community. That would considerably deter many of the Cabinet, which was far from solid on the issue, and Mike would be influenced. The problem would grow as the government became established, and presumably comfortable. The interests in favour of the status quo would become better prepared to resist its disturbance and the Pearson will for changes, other than those that were precisely committed, would weaken. Walter therefore felt that his power to make his views prevail was greatest if he moved fast, while the government was new and Mike was in an enthusiastic mood.

The diagnosis was correct. The conclusion, however, depended on whether effective measures were prepared in practical detail. The preparation could hardly have proceeded in more difficult circumstances. Walter started with the best possible idea for improving them. Before the Cabinet was even sworn in, he asked that Bob Bryce be moved from the Privy Council Office to become Deputy Minister of Finance. Mr Pearson agreed, and so did Bob. Ken Taylor – intelligent, charming, but ready for retirement – was, correctly, informed as soon as Walter became Minister, and so were the assistant deputies who might be aspiring to the succession. But the Prime Minister then decided that Bob could not be spared from the PCO until the government had settled in. He would hand over to Gordon Robertson on 1 July – after the "sixty days."

The delay was reasonable in motivation but most unfortunate in effect. Ken Taylor remained technically in place. (He was moved in July to a special assignment before complete retirement.) But since not only he but his close associates had been told of the impending change, he had no authority. The department was disorganized. The assistant deputies were individually able and had grown accustomed to a good deal of authority. They were not able to work effectively as a team for a Minister as strong as Walter, and they resented his special assistants from Toronto. The net result was that the information and advice Walter received were incomplete and less than coherent. After the budget had run into trouble, some of the senior Finance officials turned into its most virulent critics. If Walter had had an effective Deputy Minister during the crucial period, he would have relied less on his untried special consultants and the resources of the department would have been usefully deployed. The budget might not have been different in substance, but it would have had fewer of the weaknesses, marginal in nature, that in the circumstances made it so vulnerable.

As it was, there were only two senior people in a position to have any influence on the budget. One was the Prime Minister. Though his memoirs do not reveal it, I know that during this period he and Walter saw each other frequently. I have no doubt that Walter's account is correct. He would not have got into active politics if Mike had not assured him that he shared his views on foreign investment. And the Prime Minister came back from his meeting with President Kennedy elated by the warmth of the relationship. I can well imagine him saying, as Walter has recorded, that this was a good time to go ahead with measures about foreign investment, that Canadian-American relations were in such a friendly state that some economic nationalism on our side could be absorbed with minimum irritation. That, presumably, was the main reason for his change of mind between mid-April, when he endorsed my "stand-pat" prescription, and May-June, when in their many discussions he clearly encouraged Walter's more ambitious ideas.

The one other man in a position of influence was the Governor of the Bank of Canada, Lou Rasminsky. He objected to the foreign investment measures. His views were voiced not only to Walter but also, by invitation, directly to the Prime Minister. The latter dismissed them. It was Walter who was the more inclined of the two to be given pause by the criticisms. He suggested that, contrary to normal practice, the budget proposals should be discussed in advance with some at least of the ministers on the economic policy committee of Cabinet. Mr Pearson thought it unnecessary; it would risk dilution of a good budget. Walter's request for permission to show the draft budget to me was also refused.

Since I did not know of this until much later, I can only speculate about the reason. It could hardly have been concern about secrecy, given the intimacy of my involvements. It could have been momentary irritation: both Walter and I were sometimes tactless, no doubt, in indicating how much we valued each other's opinions on some matters more than Mike's. More probably it was simply concern, on the part of a generally considerate man, that I was already working too hard and should not be further burdened. In any event, the effect was that I knew nothing of the budget until I listened to it from the Speaker's gallery of the House.

The following two weeks were very different. Walter was almost alone in his trouble. Mitchell Sharp, as was noted earlier, defended him on the special consultant issue. Maurice Lamontagne made a speech on behalf of the budget as a whole. Judy LaMarsh and a few others gave what moral encouragement they could. Most of the ministers were silent, the Prime Minister's defence of the budget no more than the formal minimum that, under questioning, he could not avoid. Many of the Finance officials were chiefly interested in telling everyone that they had had nothing to do with the budget. The three special consultants were paralyzed by the uproar. For lack of anyone else, I for a couple of weeks became something near to a part-time Deputy Minister of Finance.

Walter was punctilious in appearing in the House and at Cabinet and its committees. But even he for a time shrank from more social occasions. At the suggestion of his perceptive secretary, I many days had lunch with him in his office, rather than leave him to eat there alone. That, thanks to Walter's unfailing courage and wit, was a respite for us both. My files for the second half of June were full of drafts and re-drafts, sometimes two the same day, of revisions to the budget proposals. Claude Isbister, the most constructively-minded of the assistant deputy ministers, was heroic in carrying most of the burden of the technical work. Even so, the relief of 1 July, when Bob Bryce immediately provided a strong hand at the helm of the Finance bureaucracy, and I could withdraw, was beyond words.

The revisions to the budget were completed at the Cabinet meeting at Harrington Lake on the evening of 4 July. Before it began I gave the Prime Minister a note that, I suggested, might amuse him in a dull moment during the meeting. Recalling the proud boast of our election literature, "The Liberals Have the Answers," I offered him a quotation from Louis MacNeice's verse:

> I stand here now dumbfounded by the volume
> Of angry sound which pours from every turning
> On those who only so lately knew the answers.

Even Pearson's normal self-deprecating humour was not, however, operative at this point.

Cabinet's revisions to the budget were, in my opinion, more extensive than was either financially necessary or politically wise. Certainly they could have been presented in a way that would have made the impression of surrender less abject, the humiliation of Walter less intensive. But in a crisis of this kind the weaknesses of the new Cabinet were painfully apparent. The ministers were badly rattled, the Prime Minister not least. A herd instinct to run for cover took over, and in the panic the only cover that could be thought of was to get as far as possible from the source of the discomfort. The nastiest part of it was that some ministers could not conceal their pleasure in the crumbling of Walter's pedestal; it seemed to more than console them for the dust that fell on the government as a whole.

Walter accepted it all stoically. As he said, he had to do so or resign and he had made up his mind not to resign. He announced the revisions on 8 July and continued to handle the budget in Parliament with all the equanimity possible in the circumstances. In consequence the affection for him in the Liberal caucus increased. The failure of most ministers, and particularly of the Prime Minister, to help their colleague as they should have done was seen by most backbenchers as a fault. In part perhaps because of caucus sympathy, Walter's spirits rebounded with remarkable speed. But the mark of the budget retreat on the Pearson government was deep and lasting. It could never thereafter be either as harmonious or as confident as it had had the promise of being.

The budget retreat was devastating to the internal dynamics of the government. Its external effects compounded the disruption. The idea that a minority government is necessarily a weak government is a myth created by politicians out of self-interest. Certainly a government has to be more on its toes if it lacks a tame parliamentary majority. There are, for the politicians, fruits of office that cannot be so easily enjoyed and dispensed. But those are trivia that have little to do with the substance of power. A minority government is less comfortable to be in, but it is not necessarily less able to govern.

On the day the Liberals came to office in 1963 they were as well placed to implement their policies as they would have been with twenty more members in the Liberal caucus. As long as the government did what it had promised with reasonable effectiveness, as long as it looked at all competent, there was no conceivable electoral advantage for the smaller parties in defeating it before it had served at least a good part of a normal term. In that sense, the government was secure. Mr Pearson realized this more clearly than most. He rarely had any doubt that the government should proceed with its program just as if it had a majority, and if it did so it would not be defeated. Continuing doggedly to live is, however, one thing; to live with grace and in comfort is quite another. Since what we would do about foreign investment had not been speci- fied, the budget retreat was not in itself a major setback to the govern- ment's program. But in the parliamentary battle it gave the opposition a taste of blood. The supposedly competent government had stumbled and been wounded. It might not be hounded to death but it could be harried into more retreats, made to look blundering and ineffective.

The tactics of parliamentary opposition require a nicely judged bal- ance of two considerations: the government must not be allowed to be comfortable; but on the other hand, an opposition loses public sympathy and credibility if perpetual denunciation has little apparent result. For the Conservatives the point of balance, the acceptable level of denuncia- tion, was shifted a long way by the budget retreat so early in the 1963 Parliament. There could hardly have been men for whom the shift was so temperamentally welcome as it was to Diefenbaker and associates such as Nielsen. They took their opportunity to the full. And in doing so they were able to choose battle ground on which their advantage over Mr Pearson and most of his associates was at its greatest. The Pearson mind often seemed to be paralyzed by the Diefenbaker denunciatory style. He and his ministers had reason enough to feel unfairly treated but their reaction, when it was not one of being stunned, was a mixture of indignation and constant apprehension that merely led them into more misjudgments.

In the end, of course, Diefenbaker went too far; after 1965 he produced a revulsion that eventually enabled wiser heads in the Conservative party to get rid of him. But for what seemed to its victims to be a very long time, the Diefenbaker style of opposition was made profitable by the governmental discomfiture that began so spectacularly with the 1963 budget and continued through many lesser incidents.

The second followed very soon. The Municipal Development and Loan Bill was introduced in Parliament on 17 June. It was tactless, in relation to the provinces. It conformed, of course, to the constitutional necessity of providing that no loan would be made for a municipal project of which the relevant provincial government did not approve. It also provided, however, quite broad discretion to the federal authority to decide whether or not, and on what terms, to make loans for projects that the province did approve. This was a reflection more of the great caution that is characteristic of legal drafting than of any deliberate flouting of our declared intention of "working with the provinces" to promote employment by helping to finance municipal improvements "which provincial governments approve." In previous circumstances the rough edges of the legislation would probably have been smoothed with no more that a little quiet diplomacy, hardly noticed in Parliament.

After the budget retreat, however, the provincial governments – most of them politically unfriendly – were not going to let "the feds" lightly off the hook. The opportunity to help the opposition in Ottawa to enjoy another government retreat was too tempting. It was made easier by Jean Lesage, who understandably saw no harm in distancing himself somewhat from the federal Liberals. In the early part of July he loudly denounced the Bill as an aggression on Quebec's constitutional rights.

Clearly, there had to be a federal-provincial conference and, since we had attached so much importance to the municipal measure as an early step to improve employment, soon. On 20 June we had written letters to the provincial Premiers which, in transmitting to them the parliamentary resolution and statement on the pension plan, suggested that a meeting to discuss it should be held before long. By 8 July I was drafting letters which shifted the focus to an urgent meeting on the municipal issue, together with some preliminary discussion of pensions. The dates for the meeting were arranged as 26–27 July.

The federal government's problem was to get the provinces' approval of the municipal legislation at a minimum cost in changes that would expose Walter, particularly, to more jeering about another retreat. In those days federal-provincial conferences were held behind doors closed to the TV cameras and the press. It was customary, however, for many of the first ministers to issue partial texts, at least, of their opening statements. I prepared two statements for the Prime Minister. One, for the opening, sought to affirm the government's dedication to the purpose of the municipal Bill, to assure the provinces of our open-mindedness about the details of how the purpose was to be achieved, and at the same time to make light of the possible differences over methods. The substance of that statement was released to the press.

The second statement was rather different. Our tactic was that the provinces should have their say for the first day of the conference; we would listen and respond with sympathy, but also in cautious, general terms. At the beginning of the second day the Prime Minister would respond in detail to the previous discussion. Since most of the points could be anticipated, along with the lines of the amendments necessary to meet them, I did a rough draft in advance of the conference and re-worked it during the evening of 26 July. Mike made the statement the next morning and, mercifully, it was well accepted.

The conference was complicated by having two unrelated topics. The pension plan was discussed, simultaneously with the municipal legisla-tion, in what was technically a committee under Judy LaMarsh's chair-manship. There is some account of it in chapter 19. The conference as a whole provided my introduction to the gentle art of drafting concluding communiques that said as much as none of the provinces would strongly object to. Thanks to the skill and charm of the Prime Minister's chair-manship, they all agreed to be generous in their support of the municipal plan. The price, however, was that we offered considerable changes in the wording of the legislation and the procedures under it.

The conference also provided a useful learning experience in the less gentle art of a particular kind of press conference. While federal-provin-cial proceedings were in camera, that did not prevent most of the pre-miers from providing their favourite journalists, particularly those from their home provinces, with their versions of what was happening. It was not considered appropriate for the Prime Minister, as chairman, to join in this sport. In consequence it was often my responsibility to meet with the press, on a "not-for-attribution" basis, to brief them on the federal view before, during and after the conferences. The task required a good deal of concentrated care to put the best face on things that was possible without losing the confidence of the journalists.

It was necessary, after the July conference, to make extensive changes in the municipal Bill before the House. It was essential that the amend-ments be carefully drafted to give full and accurate expression to our undertakings at the conference. It was no less important, we felt, that the Bill should be disposed of before the House adjourned, and that the adjournment should take place very early in the month. Ministers were in no condition to cope with Parliament in the steamy Ottawa August – there was then much less airconditioning than now – and do the work that the rest of the government's program required.

A committee was immediately established and it sat late into the night. It gave me my first experience of working closely with Guy

Favreau. We sat together, working out the final wording simultaneously, he in French and I in English, down to the last dotting of an i for the committee's agreement. Despite the circumstances and our tiredness, it was a joy to do because of the sharpness of Guy's intelligence, the unfailing magnanimity of his good nature, and the vigour of his happy conscientiousness.

I was also given, unhappily, an insight into the cause of his errors as a politician. When we had finished our labour he suggested that we have a nightcap in his office. In those days the parliamentary rooms of junior ministers were small, but even so I was not prepared for what I found. There was nowhere to sit down. The chairs all had files piled on them.

Guy Favreau had been Minister of Citizenship and Immigration for three months. He had inherited a system under which there was little definition of rules to determine who was admissible to Canada and who was not. A great deal was left to the discretion of the individual immigration officer. This meant that, in many of those cases in which someone in Canada made representations, the decisions were pushed up the bureaucratic ladder. Unless the Minister was very firm in delegation, to people he could trust to have good noses for the cases that might be troublesome, many marginal applications were bound to reach his desk. Guy was not a delegater. His great humanitarianism made him acutely conscious that a scribbled decision on a buff file could make a vast difference to the lives of a family. He tried to read each carefully and respond as a merciful judge.

The intent was noble, the activity ridiculous for a man with so much else to do. My immediate reaction, as we talked after moving the files from two of the chairs on to the floor, was to add immigration procedures to the list of reforms I wanted to achieve. (That was done, four years later.) What I could not know was that the characteristics I was observing in this great-hearted man, briefly relaxing over a drink, were those that, in combination with the relentlessness of the political process, would within a few years lead to his being cruelly discredited, heartbroken and, tragically soon, dead.

However, the relentness of the process always had to be coped with as best we could. When the adjournment of Parliament on 2 August had relieved the worst of the day-to-day pressures, the first concern was what could be done to improve the government's organization for future business. Sadly, for me, it was clear that, for the time being at least, we could not look to Walter to carry the major part of the burden of offsetting the Prime Minister's executive weaknesses. Mr Pearson was reputed to have answered a journalist's question during the 1963 campaign by saying that what he wanted to do afterwards was to take a holiday and leave Walter to run the country. It sounded like an off-the-cuff joke typical of Mike Pearson, but it expressed the way that many people expected the new government to operate. I, for one, thought that the government would be likely to succeed only if Walter carried much of the executive responsibility.

After 20 June the joke, if made, would have been macabre. Walter was far too tough to be destroyed by the budget retreat. Until his resignation at the end of 1965 he was by a considerable margin the most powerful of the ministers. That was ensured by his ability as well as by his position as Minister of Finance. And he continued to be personally closer to Pearson than anyone else, despite the element of strain between them that began with what Walter justifiably felt to be Mike's failure to support him in the budget for which they shared responsibility. But while Walter was still the first of the ministers, they would not accord to him the great preeminence that some would have been glad to do and others would, but for the budget, have had to do. He was not able to exercise, in government, anything near the leadership authority that he had established in the later stages of the remaking of the Liberal party.

There was no one else to be what he should have been. There was no one else who could enable Mike to be the chairman, for which his talents were superb, without having to try to be the executive, to which his temperament was unsuited. The concept on which the activists of the Liberal party had based their hopes for an effective Pearson government was shattered when the government had barely begun. Some other way of managing its work had to be found. Circumstances and L.B. Pearson's unusual style combined to fashion a partnership of Gordon Robertson and myself. The partnership was the instrument that Pearson chose to use to offset his indisposition to executive action.

Part of the problem to which the partnership was a kind of solution lay in the Prime Minister's office itself. There were no clear definitions of responsibilities, no procedures that could be relied on and that the Prime Minister, in particular, would consistently follow. The informality did no harm, and was pleasant, when things were quiet. But they rarely were. In crises anyone might do anything that he or she thought would help, or that Mike had asked for, and might not have time to inform those who were doing something different that they thought best. As early as 12 June, I put the problem by means of the analogy that might be most acceptable to Mr Pearson as a lover of sports:

> The essence of effective work in any organization is the same as it is in any team game. That is to say, the people concerned must work together; but they can work together only on the basis of each having a role, a normal function, which his colleagues can rely on him to

perform. There cannot be an effective team if five people try to keep goal, or if one person tries to rush into all positions.

This is elementary. But in the PM's office it is ignored. There is no clear definition of functions, and implied definitions are ignored.

That was the introduction to putting down detailed job descriptions and the procedures necessary for co-ordination. Mr Pearson commented that it was all very sensible, but understandably, given the budget crisis that immediately followed, took no action. In August, with prodding from Gordon Robertson, we tried again. An expert on public service organization was brought in to study the office. He produced job descriptions similar to those in the June memorandum, and this time the Prime Minister issued them. They produced a noticeable improvement for a time, though their influence wore off under the pressure on Mr Pearson that mounted in the second half of 1964, with the flag debate and the Rivard affair.

There was a personal effect for me. The official expert objected to the anomaly that my appointment was for a short term; that debarred me from the fringe benefits of public service employment. After Walter's troubles I had anyway given up serious thought that I could feel free to leave within a year. The change in terms was taken as an opportunity also to bring my title more into line with the general structure. We had initially fought shy of the word "policy," on the grounds that policy was for elected people. The civil servant had no such inhibition. I became, officially "Policy Secretary to the Prime Minister." It made no difference to the actual job. I had hoped that would be to ensure that the implementation of committed policies would be scheduled, co-ordinated, coherent, and that there would be planning, in good time, of the new policy initiatives that circumstances would require. In practice, a large part of the work continued to be inappropriate to the job description: it was to put out fires.

The confusions in the Prime Minister's Office, though an irritation, were a minor part of the problem. In early August I wrote two memoranda directed to the major parts. The first – "State of the Government" – began by refuting the conventional wisdom within the government, the comforting belief that things had gone wrong because we had tried to do too much and would now go right if only we settled down, attempted less, worked at a more normal pace. Certainly we could and should slow down to some extent. However, a case-by-case analysis of the decisions that had proved to be mistaken provided no reason to think that a slower tempo would, in itself, have resulted in better decisions. I pointed out "the inevitability of an unquiet life," listing the pressures that would keep us busy if we were successful, harried if we were not. We could not rely on being more leisurely as the way to avoid errors. The need was to improve our capability: "The true lesson of our experience is that the government needs to be better organized to make good decisions, fast or slow as the case requires."

The Cabinet was more than twice the proper size for deliberative decision-making. In practical politics, not much could be done to reduce it or, quickly, to cut out the dead wood it contained. The only solution to our problem lay in committee operation. The committees set up at the start had been better than nothing, but their value was rapidly diminishing. Many ministers did not take them seriously enough to attend consistently, and that was natural as long as everything discussed, and even supposedly decided, in committee could be reopened in full Cabinet. The committee system could be made effective only if the Prime Minister enforced rules designed to ensure that every government decision would be considered by a number of ministers in circumstances, and with time, to permit genuine deliberation. Any proposal worth going to full Cabinet must be one that the Minister concerned had been able to justify in proper discussion with a group of his colleagues.

The memorandum suggested a revised structure of committees among which all government business could be allocated, and proposed the memberships in detail. The papers for committees should be circulated in advance to all ministers and, with notice to the chairman, a Minister not a member would be entitled to attend for a particular item in which he had a special interest for, say, geographical reasons. The Prime Minister could then enforce two crucial rules. First, no óne except the Prime Minister could bring a proposal to Cabinet that had not been discussed in committee; a plea of urgency could not be made unless the Prime Minister had been satisfied, in advance of the Cabinet meeting, that it was genuine. Second, points on which there had been agreement in committee could be reopened in Cabinet only if the Prime Minister was satisfied that a major issue, not covered by already established policy, was involved.

There would not now seem to be anything remarkable in such proposals, particularly as Cabinet has been so much further inflated in size, but in 1963 they were suggestions for very radical change in the way the government had been operating. I followed them two days later, on 8 August, with a memorandum carefully designated for the Prime Minister only, because its subject was "Role of – and Assistance to – the Prime Minister." It argued that a reorganized committee system would lead to better decision-making only provided that it was accompanied by strong leadership from the Prime Minister.

One of the reasons why Mr Pearson took so much prodding from me in such good part was, I think, that despite the perpetual pressure of time, the memoranda whenever possible examined issues in the historical perspective that appealed to him. On this occasion the memorandum analyzed the reasons why the enhanced role of government had led in most countries to an increasing concentration of initiative and responsibility in the Prime Minister or President, relative to ministers. There were some things we could and should do to return somewhat more policy-making authority to individual ministers, but to attempt to carry this far would replace the chaos of indecision of the Diefenbaker government (if I had been a prophet, I could have referred to the similar future of the Trudeau government) by "a chaos of too many decisions too little co-ordinated." The memorandum went on: "The clear and inescapable conclusion is that you have a heavier responsibility for the initiation and co-ordination of policy than any Prime Minister has ever had before ... And you have this at a time of difficult change both in the internal working of the country – in the relation of Canada to the provinces – and in our economic relationships with the rest of the world."

How to prevent the pressure being intolerable? Given that Walter could not now provide all the support that we had expected, what was the best way to provide adequate help to the PM? The memorandum discussed three possible answers.

The first was to find a politician, junior enough not to be seen as a threat by other ministers, who could be appointed as a Minister without Portfolio. He would not be in effect Deputy Prime Minister, as Walter would have been, but he could relieve the PM by acting as "a sort of deputy-minister" to him. His task would be "to organize the kind of analysis and discussion" needed to provide the PM with the basis for "effective decision-making and co-ordination." This was my preferred solution. I think it would have been the best for everyone, though there was a selfish interest. It would have done most to save me from the excessively executive role, and especially the firefighting, into which the needs of the situation were otherwise propelling me. I could have better concentrated on the less conspicuous work, which seemed to me more appropriate as well as more personally satisfying, of longer-term policy development.

The idea was revived by Walter Gordon, in a slightly different form, when in 1966 he was returning to the Cabinet after his year of resignation. It did not work, I think because by then Mr Pearson did not want it. In August 1963, in the pencilled notes with which he responded to my memoranda, Mr Pearson said that he was "intrigued" with the idea but it could not be done *now* (his emphasis) "in present circumstances and in the present set-up. Since the budget difficulty, there is no minister who would be acceptable to the others or effective for me."

The alternatives were to strengthen, in one of two possible ways, the "East Block" grouping of PCO and PMO. I did not think that strengthening meant any great increase in staff size, and Mr Pearson concurred. However, I did think that there might be one additional, very senior PCO officer and some associated small increase in staff. This would enable the Secretary to the Cabinet to give more time to his central, co-ordinating role by delegating to the new man some functions analogous to those that a Deputy performs for a Minister, and particularly in this case liaison on the Prime Minister's behalf on matters involving a particular Department. For reasons that were not clear in his comments, Mr Pearson did not like this proposal.

That left a final alternative, which he endorsed. It was that there would be no addition to the personnel working directly with the Prime Minister but that the nature of my work would be changed, and it would hopefully be made more effective, by being much more integrated with that of PCO. The Prime Minister's comment described this as "I prefer the present arrangement with you working closely with Gordon R," and he fully endorsed the steps that Gordon and I then took. Essentially, he wanted us to operate jointly as, in effect, a doubleheaded chief operating officer for him.

Gordon Robertson had then been Secretary to the Cabinet for little more than a month, but knew the central operation of government well. The follow-up action to implement the prime ministerial preference was not extensive. I was fully incorporated into the PCO's flow of paper. There was an important staff transfer. A little earlier an able young civil servant, Ed Aquilina, had been recruited through the Public Service Commission to assist me. He moved to PCO, where for some six years he played an important role in federal-provincial relations. (He afterwards rejoined me to become an Assistant Deputy Minister in DREE.) The immediate significance of the move was that it helped to establish two points: we did not want to build up staff in PMO; my responsibilities were almost entirely related to the government process, not to politics in the narrower sense, and therefore could properly be conducted with staff support from PCO rather than an enlarged PMO.

The most important change was a very simple procedure. We had already established a habit that on most days I met with the Prime Minister fairly early in the morning, to discuss the day's business. Henceforth, it became a fixed event that at 9 AM Gordon and I met the Prime Minister together. The three of us came with lists of the things on our minds. Almost all were matters of government decision or process that properly involved Gordon as a public servant. If, as happened occasionally, either the PM's list or mine included an urgent item of a more political nature, we put it at the end of the agenda and, when that point was reached, Gordon excused himself. The proportion of such items was, however, minute.

The Prime Minister at times unburdened himself to me in great detail about political matters, and especially his concerns and grumbles concerning various ministers, but that was usually done later in the day, often over a pre-dinner drink, because it was frequently necessary to meet again on what had happened since the morning. I acted as the intermediary to keep Gordon informed if there were matters relevant to his concerns. In this way he could keep more time available for the heavy burden of meetings and administration that falls on the Secretary to the Cabinet. These roles were reversed for the regular meeting of the PM and Gordon that took place at or around lunch on Tuesdays, when the agenda for the regular Thursday morning Cabinet meeting was decided. I attended very rarely. It was almost always sufficient, if I had any special concerns about items on the agenda, to register them beforehand with Gordon, and he briefed me on the outcome.

Gordon and I knew each other well, initially because, as I mentioned earlier, he was married to the sister of Bill Lawson, of the Bank of Canada, who made his apartment home to me when I first began to spend a good deal of time in Ottawa. Gordon's extensive education was primarily in the law. He became Secretary to the Cabinet after some twenty years of public service, in the East Block and as a Deputy Minister and Commissioner of the Northwest Territories. Though our backgrounds were dissimilar, our thought processes were not. We never had any difficulties of communication. Indeed, I cannot recall one moment of serious tension despite all the stresses under which we worked side by side for thirty months. Our areas of particular interest were highly complementary, not competitive, and there was never any difficulty in deciding which items of the day's business, as they emerged from the morning meeting, which of us would be responsible for. As a partnership we were able, I think, to do what no one person, however well supported by assistants, could have done.

The Prime Minister had, rightly, enormous confidence in Gordon, and he was quickly satisfied that Gordon and I could work as a team. On that basis, he was wholehearted in implementing the new working pattern. The proposal for restructuring Cabinet committees was polished by Gordon and put into effect with some firmness. Mr Pearson even went so far as to spell out to ministers, with his usual tact but also with a clarity that was less usual, the role that he was assigning to the Robertson-Kent team. My notes read in part:

> The Secretary of the Cabinet and the Co-ordinator of Programming, G. Robertson and T. Kent, will be jointly responsible to me for the

smooth and effective operation of the committee system. Between them they will keep in touch with the work of all committees.

Inevitably, there are a good many occasions when ministers wish to discuss matters with me individually, either because they are departmental matters which are not being taken to Cabinet, or because, on broader subjects, it may be helpful to have some discussion at a preliminary stage, before a proposal is prepared for Cabinet. It will be the responsibility of Messrs Robertson and Kent to help to make such discussions as effective as possible, within the limitations of my time. Whenever appropriate, ministers should talk first to these officials with the aim of preparing a memorandum which will enable me to brief myself on the essential points as a preliminary to discussion. While there can be no hard dividing line, and Messrs Robertson and Kent will work closely together, in general this preparatory work should be done with Mr Kent on the more political aspects of policy and on economic subjects, and with Mr Robertson on other policy subjects and on matters of a more administrative nature.

The relationships involved were not altogether easy. Undoubtedly some ministers resented what they sometimes felt to be a barrier to direct discussion with the Prime Minister. Gordon and I were harder to convince than he might have been if approached alone. On the whole, however, I think there was chiefly relief that the PM had constructed an organization capable of producing a smoother, more deliberate and more predictable flow of decision-making. Everyone knew that, if it had not been for the budget stumble, Mike would have conducted the prime ministership by delegating a large measure of authority to Walter. In consequence of that not being so, other ministers felt a little more powerful. At the same time, no one, including Mr Pearson himself, suffered from any great illusion about the limitations to his executive capacity. By and large, therefore, the organizational arrangement was accepted as, at any rate, a lesser evil than any practicable alternative.

Though ministers sometimes felt that the PM was too influenced by Gordon and me, there was not the widespread sense that developed in the Trudeau era, and particularly towards its end, that ministers were being largely cut off from the decision-making process in favour of a group of advisers round the Prime Minister. We were saved from that by the fact, among others, that we kept PCO and PMO so small. Gordon did gradually strengthen PCO, by skilful recruitment of replacements and a little additional staff. But the East Block corner remained minute compared with what became, under Trudeau, the Langevin Block. Except, necessarily, in federal-provincial relations, there were no aspiring experts working in the central agency. The program skills remained where they should be, in the departments, and therefore under the control of the ministers, not of the Prime Minister. Gordon and I worked closely with senior departmental officials, to enlist their skills, but not in a way that cut out the ministers to whom they were responsible.

The differences between the Pearson style of government and the subsequent centralization are worth more thorough assessment than I shall attempt. The Pearson system had both strengths and weaknesses. At this point I will add only that if on the whole it was fairly successful, as I think it was for a time, the credit belongs primarily to Mr Pearson. His government's first three months had been shattering to him. It is true, though he afterwards forgot it, that the cause was as much of his making as of Walter Gordon's. The first budget would not have been so overly ambitious if Mr Pearson had not encouraged its being so. He could easily have restrained it, with Walter's acceptance. But that does not lessen the magnitude of his achievement in coping with the consequences. He responded to his difficulties with extraordinary resilience and great determination. He made, at the age of sixty-six, a massive adaptation of his personal style and methods of work, not only from life as it had been before the prime ministership but, just as much, from the way he had planned the prime ministership to be before the budget retreat. He worked desperately hard to do efficiently what he had not been prepared for. Most decisions were made with due deliberation but without other delay. He was resolute about objectives, practical and flexible about methods. His determination to achieve what he had said his government would do was not weakened but redoubled.

The effort told, as I shall have to record. But the next twelve months, from the summer of 1963 to that of 1964, were the golden period in my relationship with Mike Pearson. Mutual respect and confidence were not marred, as they were before and after, by occasions when we irritated each other, though he, particularly, hardly ever allowed the irritation to show. In opposition I had been greatly distressed by what I saw as evasions, vacillations, failures to carry through decisions to effective action. After he had suddenly aged, as he did during the flag debate, I was guilty of allowing my own overwork to lead me into excessive impatience over spells of indecision. Between, however, Mike was the Prime Minister that some of us had believed he would be. This is the more remarkable because he never had a parliamentary majority. Though, as noted earlier, minority status did not create a risk of prompt defeat, it made the progress of legislation slower and the management of the government's business considerably more difficult. Particularly given the nature of Diefenbaker's opposition, the demands of the House of Commons on ministers' time and attention were much greater than they would have been with a secure majority. There was almost always a tenseness on the Hill that made it hard for even the toughest ministers to maintain their nerve and eqanimity of judgment. That so much was nevertheless done, and for the most part well done, was due to the strength that, despite appearances, L.B. Pearson generally brought to his task.

PART FIVE

Doing What We Said

T.V., radio, magazine writing ... and his new show,
the Sixty Million Dollar Question

19 Pensions: The Phoney Stage

There can be few elaborate social mechanisms that reflect the personality of a man as the Canada Pension Plan reflects that of L.B. Pearson. It is already almost impossible, barely a generation later, to appreciate what strong emotions, interests, and political pressures in 1963–4 clashed around the idea of a comprehensive pension plan. It was denounced as a fraud and as certain to bring the ruin of the nation. It was caught so much in the tensions of changing federal-provincial relations that no sensible man should have been prepared to wager, in late 1963 or early 1964, that it would be achieved in foreseeable time.

Nevertheless, as soon as it was legislated, the pension plan fitted into the fabric of Canadian society as if it had always been there. Few people have disappeared from public notice as quickly as those who, in their words, in 1963 "raised a storm" against the plan. Indeed, it is hard to think of anything of comparable significance to people about which there has been so little subsequent controversy. And, of course, it is the more Canadian for being not a plan but two, one for Quebec and one for the rest of Canada, separate in administration but identical in substance, so that membership in one or other at different times makes no difference to the individual.

The pension plan is very much Pearson's, though he took no active part in fashioning it, somewhat as the Canadian flag is his creation though it is not the flag he proposed. In both cases he was the political leader with the courage to make a contentious proposal and the doggedness to ensure that it was fought through to an outcome close enough to his intention to satisfy a reasonable man, and in the event highly acceptable to almost everyone in the country.

The Pearson commitment to a national pension plan began with the platform for the 1958 general election, "The Pearson Plan." It got no attention in the Diefenbaker wave of the time. By the summer of 1961, however, Mike had made up his mind to campaign again on a precise platform. Pensions appealed to him as a major plank for it. He thought of himself, and on appropriate occasions talked of himself, as a reformer. It was true, but in a rather academic way. L.B. Pearson cannot be understood without recognition that he was, professionally, a historian first. The root of his reformism was the liberal historian's sense of the movement of human affairs, of change generally for the better. He was immune to any "establishment" hope or expectation that society could or should stay much as it is, or even revert in some ways to what it was. At the same time he was, as a diplomat, accustomed to working with society as he found it. His deep humanitarianism was not reflected in any detailed concern for social policies to redistribute incomes, and he could easily be worried by predictions of disaster from government measures encouraging social change.

Against the background, the attraction of the pension plan for Mr. Pearson was not only that it would enable people to retire "in security and with dignity" but also that it was "contributory": people put in money when they earned it and took it out later. I think he did come to understand, and welcome, the fact that a public pension plan with a short maturity period – paying full pensions ten years after its inception – was in fact a considerable redistribution in favour of older workers, in their fifties or so when the plan began, who had not been able to build up retirement savings in the conditions of depression and war. He never, I think, got his mind round the fact that compulsory pension contributions from employers and employees are a payroll tax, and no less taxation for being assigned to a particular purpose rather than taken into general revenue. He always thought of the "contributory" pension plan as more different than it is from social programs avowedly financed from general revenue.

The misconception, however, only strengthened his dedication to the pension plan even at times when he was having doubts about the feasibility of other social reforms. It became the firmest plank in the election platforms of 1962 and 1963. On Walter Gordon's initiative, it was developed, while we were in opposition, in more precise detail than any other measure. Walter assembled a small group of Toronto professionals, with whom he and I met several times to settle the principles of the plan, and who worked hard and well to develop its details: a plan to apply to earnings up to $500 a month (1961 dollars) and to pay, after a ten-year transition period, benefits of one third of earnings at age seventy, with actuarially reduced benefits from earlier ages, down to sixty-five, for those who so preferred. It was to be an unfunded plan, therefore requiring initially only a low contribution rate. And it became the social policy measure featured in Mike's "sixty-day" commitments.

The unfunded character of the proposed plan was, as I shall argue shortly, sound economics from the federal viewpoint. But politically it was unfeasible, in a plan requiring provincial consent. As a result, while there was strong public interest, intense debate, and massive bureaucratic effort, for twelve months the plan had an unreal quality.

We did not realize that in April 1963. As noted earlier, one of the first actions of the Pearson government was to set up a civil service task force to flesh out a pension plan of the proposed kind. By early June, thanks to the dedicated and professional leadership of Joe Willard, as Deputy Minister of Welfare, this had been done to the point that the plan could be described in credible detail to Parliament and to the provinces and we could provide drafting instructions for the complex legal work of producing the actual Bill. The furor over the budget produced something of a hiatus, but on 15 July the detailed plan was approved by Cabinet. Nerves had been shaken by the budget experience, and at the Prime Minister's request on 16 July I recorded to him in writing the formal assurance of Joe Willard that:

a The technical details of the pension plan as approved last night are all drawn from plans in operation in other countries; it puts together what seem to be the best ideas, for Canadian conditions, from those plans; nothing in it is untried; and the package as a whole is simpler than many plans are.

b The plan as approved last night has the endorsement, as being technically sound and workable, of his Department and of the officials from other Departments (including the actuaries of the Insurance Department) who have helped in its preparation.

That was all very well, but it did not help much. In the battle over pensions, our flanks were never in danger. We had ensured, and continued through all the difficulties to ensure, that there were no technical weaknesses in the proposals. The vulnerability was political. It was of two kinds.

One, in English Canada, arose from the shaking of the government's credibility and self-confidence by its retreat on the budget. The insurance industry took heart and raised its storm. The critics could claim pension expertise, about private plans. About a public plan they lacked understanding as thoroughly as they exuded self-interest. But because confidence in the government was at a low ebb, fantastic allegations about errors and unsoundness in the Canada Pension Plan could be made and, though not exactly believed, cause people (including some ministers and Liberal MPs) to be bothered and confused. Judy LaMarsh had a terrible time, with which she coped valiantly.

However, the storm, though unpleasant, would not have been important if we had been standing on firm ground. We were not, because of Quebec. By the end of June both Joe Willard and I had gathered, from our separate sources in Quebec City, an idea of what was afoot: the Lesage government was likely to develop its own contributory pension plan. This intelligence was confirmed at the federal-provincial conference in late July. As noted in an earlier chapter, this meeting was mainly concerned with the municipal development and loan legislation, but at the same time a conference committee discussed pensions. In the main meeting Quebec employed the histrionic tactics that Jean Lesage tended to favour in federal-provincial conferences, denouncing the proposed Ottawa legislation on municipal loans as an invasion of provincial jurisdiction. He spent more of his time, however, in the pension committee, and there he was calm. He did not attack the federal pension proposal. He just said that it was irrelevant to Quebec, because he would have his own plan. There was no disputing the constitutional position: on pensions, it gave precedence to provincial legislation. Lesage was clearly concerned, however, not to appear to give comfort to those who opposed our plan because they were against public pensions as such. His position was therefore gently expressed – with the gentleness of strength. Philosophically, he was in favour of public pensions. How they were provided in the rest of Canada was not his business. For Quebec, he was standing on his jurisdictional rights; he would have his own plan.

The other provinces were cautious. They were well aware that the improvement of pensions had plenty of popular support. The Liberal premiers of New Brunswick and Newfoundland, as well as the Saskatchewan NDP government, were not the only ones ideologically disposed to support a national plan. For Premier Roblin of Manitoba, the same disposition was stronger than the political pressure to help the federal Conservative opposition led by Diefenbaker. Premier Robarts of Ontario was also no lover of Diefenbaker and, despite strong contrary pressures within his party, he was not personally opposed to public pensions. Certainly he had no intention of being put into the campaign position of fighting against pensions in the provincial general election that was close at hand.

Consequently, the first federal-provincial discussion of the Canada Pension Plan could fairly be summed up, in the words that I drafted for the conference communiqué, as having been "conducted in the spirit of the common interest of federal and provincial governments in ensuring satisfactory provision for old age security and other welfare measures in Canada. It was agreed that further discussions between federal and provincial representatives should take place at an early date."

The reality was different. It was clear that the Canada Pension Plan, in the form in which we had put it forward to Parliament, was already dead in the water. At that point, my personal choice would have been to shift to a very different way of improving society's provision for the elderly. It would have been to pay the Old Age Security pension at age sixty-five instead of seventy as it then was; to increase its amount significantly; and to escalate it for the future in line with the general level of earnings. Simple federal legislation, without a constitutional amendment, would then have been sufficient. Earnings-related pensions could have been left to the provinces. An offer of a modest degree of federal cost-sharing would have been enough to ensure that provincial plans provided adequate survivor and disability benefits and that the pensions were portable between the provinces. With some federal administrative assistance to the smaller provinces, the plans probably would have become Canada-wide within a few years and would not have varied much. By this route we could have arrived at virtually the same results, in social security for Canadians, as were in fact achieved through the Canada Pension Plan and the improvements in Old Age Security legislation that were related to it.

Such an alternative would have saved the Pearson government a great deal of stress over the following fifteen months. I was surprised that, as far as I know, no academic commentator pointed this out. But the alternative was entirely academic. It was not politically practicable. It would have required a large and early increase in federal taxes, as taxes are normally understood. For people like Bob Bryce and myself to point out that compulsory pension contributions from employers and employees are effectively taxes was logical but irrelevant. People saw them differently. In 1963, to pay pension contributions was to be an object of envy by many Canadians who did not. It meant that you had a good employer or, more probably, a union strong enough to bargain for a pension plan as a fringe benefit.

The public perception of such contributions, as different from taxes, was even stronger in the minds of the politicians who would have to impose the taxes. Any federal initiative to establish a greatly improved pension system for Canadians therefore had to start from the concept of a contributory plan; it was politically inconceivable to concentrate on the "taxed" part of the structure and leave the popular contributory field to the provinces. It was precisely for this reason that contributory pensions had been given such prominent billing in the Liberal program. There had been no acceptable alternative when the program was written, and there was no going back now. Somehow the Canada Pension Plan had to be pushed forward.

How? Early in August Jean Lesage telephoned to warn me that, in order to avoid any questioning of Quebec's intention to occupy the pension field, as he put it, he would be calling a special session of the Legislative Assembly to adopt a resolution preparatory to the legislation of a provincial contributory pension plan. The resolution was passed unanimously on 23 August.

Meantime I had arranged, over the telephone with Lesage, my annual holiday for 1963. It was to be a four-day weekend, during which my wife and I would take a leisurely drive to and from Quebec City. At the same time Gordon Robertson was ending a short holiday at his family property in Nova Scotia. The Robertsons and Kents, coming from opposite directions, met in Quebec City on Friday evening. On Saturday, 24 August, Jean entertained Gordon and me to what turned out to be an afternoon-long lunch in a small room at the Garrison Club.

We understood each other fully. We agreed on nothing. Lesage was adamant that he was going to have his own pension plan. While he was obviously going to make this, publicly, a matter of nationalist fervour, he made plain to us the motive that was decisive: money. His plan would be "funded" to something near the extent of private pension plans. That is to say, for many years the contribution revenue would greatly exceed the pensions paid. The large reserve of public savings thus accumulating could be used to finance the great requirements of the new Quebec for social infrastructure – schools, roads, and all the rest.

Gordon and I did not waste time trying to argue against this view. It was as sound in economics as it was in constitutional position. If we had been in Lesage's situation we would have had the same view. We recognized that federal legislation of the proposed kind would have to provide that the Canada Pension Plan (CPP) would not be applicable to the residents of any province that chose to have a comprehensive plan of its own. But that did not settle the problems, for us or for Quebec.

The federal government could not withdraw from pension improvements. Indeed, for it to do so would hurt Quebec. Lesage accepted this. He was personally in favour of public pensions for all Canadians. In practical politics, he recognized that Quebecers would not be happy to make compulsory contributions, for pension benefits which under a funded plan would not become substantial for many years, while individuals and companies in other provinces incurred no such costs.

With that recognized, Gordon and I pointed out that both the federal government and Quebec would thus be dependent on Ontario's attitude. If the largest province opted out with Quebec, as would be tempting to a Conservative government, we would be unlikely to legislate a "federal" plan for a minority of the population. In that case it would be a long time before provincial plans became general. Ottawa could not do nothing in the meantime. We would have to increase Old Age Security, substantially. That would cost conventional tax dollars, and therefore prevent us from making available the extra tax room that, as Lesage so strongly insisted, he needed in order to finance his government's current expenditures.

At that point, I introduced the compromise proposal with which I had come prepared, and of which only the Prime Minister was aware. It was that, in the spirit of co-operative federalism, we should agree to share the "tax" field of pension contributions in the same way that we did conventional taxes. The difference would be that, whereas Ottawa had the lion's share of the conventional taxes, provincial primacy in pensions would be recognized by binding Ottawa to a low rate for the contributory levy on earnings. In conjunction with Old Age Security (OAS), this would enable Ottawa to ensure for all Canadians a more adequate, though still minimal, retirement income from age sixty-five. There would be plenty of scope for provinces to establish earnings-related, funded pensions on top of the Canada provisions.

Lesage did not welcome such a proposal. Nor, however, did he finally dismiss it. Both he and we knew that the best next step would not be clear until after the Ontario election campaign that had just begun. We parted, in full friendship, with assurances about keeping each other informed and avoiding actions or statements that unnecessarily hurt either side's position.

Back in Ottawa, I immediately wrote a long memorandum, dated 27 August, on "Pensions after the Quebec Resolution." It was discussed, a day or two later, at 24 Sussex with Mr. Pearson and a few principal ministers. My starting point was that we must acknowledge that the CPP, as proposed, would not operate in Quebec. After the Assembly's unanimous resolution, we would merely make ourselves look silly if we pretended that there was any other possibility. The Lesage plan would have a higher contribution rate than the CPP and the transition period, before full benefits were paid, would be longer; but then they would be considerably bigger. We had to recognize it as provincial occupation, in Quebec, of the contributory pension field. And we could not discriminate. Our legislation must give general recognition to the right of any province to contract out of the CPP.

The memorandum suggested terms that would be reasonable for us and acceptable to Lesage: to be outside the CPP, a province must have its own comprehensive plan and it must provide full portability: that is, anyone entering the province from elsewhere in Canada would be treated as if his previous contributions to the CPP or to another provincial plan had been made in the province being entered. The practical effect, for the individual, would be much the same as if there had been one Canada-wide plan. We would thus achieve the substance of our objective.

There was, however, another implication of contracting out, less happy for federal politicians. Our proposed legislation included a prompt increase in OAS, from $65 to $75 a month, to be financed from the contributory revenues of the CPP. In effect, the CPP included a small flat-rate benefit of $10 a month to be paid universally, irrespective of earnings. Clearly this could not be done, as an OAS benefit for all Canadians, if people in Quebec and perhaps some other provinces were not contributing to CPP. Contracting out meant, I argued, that the extra $10 must be separated from the CPP and paid out of other federal revenue.

This was financially unpleasant, but there was no point in delay. The promised $10 soon was what the public was most aware of. The opposition and the provinces were pressing us to get on with it. It would have to be paid, and the only difference that could be made by delaying the decision would be that we would appear to have yielded reluctantly to pressure and would get no political credit when we did make the increase.

These points were urgent, because the further federal-provincial discussion on pensions, foreshadowed at the July conference, had now been scheduled for 9 September. We would be made to look very foolish if we had not by then made up our minds on contracting out and on the $10 increase in OAS.

Ministers did not dispute this, but were reluctant to bite the bullet. There were more memoranda and discussions over the following ten days. In one memorandum, I tried to sum up the situation. The alternative to a prompt decision "would be to try to act out a farce. We know Quebec won't accept the CPP. We know we aren't going to force it. We know we will have to pay the $10 separately. We can't just keep our mouths shut ... If we try to indicate that we are just going ahead, we look unrealistic and evasive ... If we vaguely indicate that we are considering changes, we look indecisive ... The main decisions that have to be taken are clear ... We have nothing to gain by holding back on them."

In the event, the decisions were taken, just in time to be announced on 9 September. The Prime Minister said that the CPP would not apply in a province that had its own universally available plan providing comparable benefits and portability of coverage between provinces; and, secondly, that the $10 increase in OAS would be separated from the CPP and would be effective the next month.

The rest of the 27 August memorandum, however, was ineffective. It went on to argue that we should also make a prompt decision that our plan should not be the relatively unfunded one that we had proposed. In this, I was asking that purely federal considerations be subordinated to the needs of the provinces. In those days there were no great increases in federal debt to worry about; federal revenue, in relation to expenditures, was as large as sound economic policy required. It was bad economics, from the federal viewpoint, to impose on people the forced saving of a funded pension plan. It was far better to start with low contribution rates, yielding relatively modest surpluses over the pensions paid in the early years, and then gradually increase the contributions as the payments of pensions increased. "Pay-as-you-go" was an entirely sensible prescription, in terms of federal finances.

Federal finances, however, ignored Canada's need for massive improvements in the social infrastructure that lay largely in provincial jurisdiction. In the concern about those needs the Lesage government was simply being quicker off the mark than the governments of other provinces. Across Canada, the requirements were the same: new schools, universities, colleges, housing development, parks, highways, public buildings, municipal projects in all their variety. It was inevitable that, when Lesage had pointed the way, other provinces would see pension funding as the means to help to finance this needed social investment. It seemed to me that the federal initiative on contributory pensions was justified only if we recognized this need. We should do so, and in the course of federal-provincial negotiations we would anyway end up having to do so. I proposed that we take the initiative rather than be driven. We should indicate, at the 9 September meeting, our willingness to make the CPP more funded, if provinces so wished, and to arrange that a substantial proportion of the funds be invested in provincial projects.

The Prime Minister agreed, in principle. But we were caught in the complications of politics in a federal state. For the next seven months, in consequence, we struggled mightily in what was really a phoney war about pensions.

The Ontario Liberals had no good issues on which to campaign against the Robarts government. John Wintermeyer, their leader, decided that his best course was to adopt an issue from the federal Liberals, who had so recently done so well in Ontario. Robarts was being equivocal about the Canada Pension Plan. Wintermeyer would make it a key point in his election campaign that he would accept the plan for Ontario. The federal Liberal ministers and MPs from Ontario could hardly stand aside from such a campaign. Judy LaMarsh, in particular, relished it. They could not contemplate pulling out a main plank from under Wintermeyer by changing the CPP while the campaign was on. Despite Pearson's sympathy with my viewpoint, the proposal to make the plan more funded was turned down flat.

I accepted that as unavoidable in the circumstances. Federal Liberals had to assume, or at least appear to assume, that Wintermeyer had a chance of winning in Ontario. They could not scupper him. And if he did win, the CPP as it stood would be entirely credible; it could be legislated subject only to the minimal changes announced on 9 September.

In the circumstances the federal-provincial meeting that day was a quiet, though strange, affair. It was supposed to be a fairly technical discussion, which meant that the delegates would be mostly officials with, at most, Ministers of Welfare or their equivalents at the political level. In fact, Premier Robarts conspicuously took time out from his election campaigning to attend. He did not want to give any hostages to fortune. He supported the idea of a national contributory plan, provided it was truly national, and sound in financial structure.

The Quebec delegates emphasized that they were attending only as observers, but they were supportive of the principles of public pensions and fully co-operative about ensuring complete portability between the Quebec plan and the CPP. The conference was otherwise occupied with detailed explanations of the CPP and the actuarial report on it, its economic implications, and its relation to existing pension schemes. The provincial delegates asked many questions, the federal civil servants performed magnificently, and it was possible in the communiqué to state the general agreement, Quebec apart, that "a national contributory pension plan is desirable." Arrangements were made for still more detailed consultations at the technical level.

Then came 25 September. The Robarts government had an easy victory in the Ontario provincial election. We had to recognize that, as I put it in an immediate memorandum, Robarts was in the driver's seat. Whether there could be a CPP depended on whether we could work out a compromise acceptable to Ontario. I made two proposals. First, we should clear the air by promptly announcing that we would not proceed with our legislation in the fall, as had been intended. We should make what virtue we could of further consultations with the provinces and say frankly that we would not propose legislation until early 1964 after adequate time for the consultation. Second, we should take full advantage of Robarts's publicly declared support for the principle of national contributory pensions. We should challenge the Ontario government to discuss with us what kind of plan it favoured, instead of simply questioning our proposals.

The Prime Minister announced the delay, which surprised no one, and initiated discussions in a private meeting of Premier Robarts and himself. It did not indicate much hope of a definite Ontario position. There followed months of weary talk, chiefly by Joe Willard and myself on the federal side and a small group of pleasant and intelligent representatives of Ontario. The problem was that they did not agree among themselves and spent almost as much time debating with each other as with us. It was indeed a phoney war. Clearly there were no instructions as to an Ontario government position. Premier Robarts's tactic was to play for time. We could not blame him. He had nothing to lose by waiting at least until Quebec produced its plan, before he showed his hand.

The federal government, however, would look very feeble indeed if it now simply waited for Quebec. We calculated that Lesage's plan would not be produced until nearly spring. We felt it essential that we should get our Bill into the House earlier in the year, in a form that reflected some genuine concessions to provincial viewpoints and would be reasonably received by most, if not by Ontario.

There was a full-scale federal-provincial conference, covering a wide range of topics, in November. Its main features will be discussed in the next chapter. On pensions, there was another long discussion. Jean Lesage, who understood pensions thoroughly, was at his most helpful in explaining and supporting public pensions, disagreeing with us only on funding and a few minor points. Robarts continued to be sharply questioning without being openly hostile. The other eight provinces were mildly questioning but essentially sympathetic. It was clear that, while they were not going to stick their necks out, they would be content, or more, to go along with a slightly modified CPP. It was concluded that the Prime Minister would soon send to the provinces, in confidence, a description of the possible revisions to our proposals which might achieve the greatest possible harmony with provincial views and programs, while retaining the features that the federal government regarded as essential.

By December we concluded that we had got all we were ever going to in the way of definition of Ontario's views. Over the Christmas-New Year period, decisions on the amended plan were made. The most important change was in the level of pension benefits. The original plan provided 30 per cent of earnings at age seventy. Ontario seemed to consider this too high. We reduced it to 20 per cent, but with an important modification. The original plan allowed the individual to choose when, between the ages of sixty-five and seventy, he or she would start to draw the pension, but pensions begun before seventy would be actuarially reduced according to life expectancy. This meant that anyone taking the pension promptly at age sixty-five would get about 20 per cent of earnings. In the revised plan we proposed that the rate would be a constant 20 per cent, irrespective of the age between sixty-five and seventy when it began, but up to age seventy payment would be subject to a retirement test: the pension would be reduced if a person had continuing earnings over $75 a month.

Though we did not much like the retirement test idea, and it would make administration difficult, this seemed the best way to meet one of the Ontario objectives while preserving what mattered most – the level of pension available to people who had to retire at sixty-five.

The plan was also more funded than before, because the extra $10 of OAS was no longer to be financed from it. We proposed that half of the considerable reserves which would accumulate would be available for provincial investments. In other words, we went half-way towards meeting the main motivation for provincial plans. There were some other, lesser changes, but I will not detail them because the whole operation was indeed phoney. We were not going to get, at that stage, Ontario's concurrence in anything like the CPP.

There was only one way we could have called the bluff and ended the delaying tactic. That would have been to adopt what Mr. Robarts's advisers liked to call an "individual equity" plan – that is, one in which contributions and pension rates were related in the same way as in the most conservative kind of private pension plans. To have done so would have been to abandon most of the social purpose of a public plan. In particular, such a plan would have done little for middle-aged and older workers. For them, a short maturity period for pension benefits was essential. There was nothing magical about our proposed ten-year period. Certainly we would have been prepared to extend it to fifteen years if that would have secured agreement. But the Ontario advisers were talking about thirty or forty years, and Premier Robarts was committing himself to nothing. We decided that we might as well stick to ten years.

Premier Robarts wrote a critical letter and our expectations were fully confirmed: trying to find a compromise with Ontario had been wasted effort. However, the somewhat revised plan was the one with which we now had to try to proceed. Thanks to heroic work, particularly by Don Thorson, as legal draftsman, it was embodied in the complex Bill required, and this was introduced into the House of Commons in March. We could do no more than hold our breath for the further reactions from the provinces.

20 *Co-operative Federalism*

The decisive and dramatic point in the achievement of the Canada Pension Plan came in April 1964. Much had happened to, and been done by, the Pearson government during the preceding winter; most of the significant events will be discussed in later chapters. There is, however, one aspect of the winter's affairs that must be dealt with now. The achievement of the pension plan was possible only as part of a larger transformation in the federal government's dealings with the provinces. To tell the pension story it is necessary, therefore, briefly to define the Pearson approach to federal-provincial relations and to explain why that approach conspicuously failed to shape the government's actions, until the

April crisis compelled the Prime Minister to do what he half wanted to do but had shrunk from.

If there were two words that expressed the part of his government's policy that most represented Mr Pearson's temperament, they were "co-operative federalism." I cannot recall how the slogan originated. I was using it in 1961, but whether I coined it, or Mike did, or we got it from someone else, I do not now know.

Though it was a good phrase, there was a considerable difficulty about the idea. We could not frankly state, in advance, its operational significance. A federal system, however co-operative, works through negotiation among politically competitive governments. The nature of the process made it impossible for federal representatives blithely to say, until the deal of April 1964 had been made, what the Prime Minister and I thought: that the federal government ought to have less money to spend, in favour of the provincial governments having more.

It is hard now to appreciate how strongly the Canada of the early 1960s was still marked by the centralization that the second world war had necessitated. We continued to live in a tense world, to which we had not grown accustomed as we since have. And the fears of the depressed thirties still cast dark shadows. The contrasting postwar prosperity was associated, in many people's minds, with the enhanced role of Ottawa. It had the modernized government of the new Canada. Provincial governments, with little money, remained by comparison old-fashioned. Saskatchewan alone excepted, until Lesage's victory in Quebec in 1960, their public services were poor in professional qualifications, their politics largely parochial.

Such factors strengthened normal institutional inertia. They kept power at the centre long after the reasons for its concentration there had faded. One set of figures will serve to illustrate this. Before the war, tax revenues had been divided fairly evenly between the federal government, on the one hand, and the provinces and their municipalities on the other. On average over the years 1926–39, the federal government levied 46 per cent of total Canadian taxation, the provinces 54 per cent. The priority ceded to Ottawa in wartime was only slowly eroded afterwards. For the last five years before the Pearson government, 1957–62, the federal share of tax revenues averaged 63 per cent, against 37 per cent for the provinces and municipalities combined.

This was plainly out of joint with the country's needs in the 1960s. With a rapidly growing population, with rising affluence and the advance of technology, with the move from rural to urban living, the mounting social needs were for education and urban development, for housing and public health facilities, for roads and urban transit, for environmental protection and social security: for services that were, solely or primarily, provincial responsibilities under the constitution. Canada's development required that the provinces, and through them the municipalities, should have more financial resources.

In opposition, Mike and I had often thought together about this, and its implications for a new Liberal government, in the historical context he usually favoured. I particularly remember one conversation because it arose from a friend of mine having indicated his interest in being a candidate in the 1962 election. We talked about this for a time in conventional political terms: in what riding would his candidacy do most to increase the chances of our winning the seat. Mike, however, broke off with words to this effect: "You know, I find this kind of discussion difficult. If I were giving objective advice to a young man who could make a real contribution to public life, I'd have to suggest that he go into provincial politics or a provincial public service. For the next decade or two, that's where there'll be most need for new programs, where the most constructive and interesting action will be."

In our discussions Mike and I had agreed that the classical theory of federalism – that the functions of government can be divided between two layers, each sovereign within its own jurisdiction – was a theory whose time was past. There was nothing very difficult about the division between "national" and "local" affairs when the total role of government in society was small. Then each layer of government could look after its own without often running into conflict with what the other was doing. Federalism was possible on what we called a "live-and-let-live" basis. But with "big" government this was no longer possible. Whatever the theoretical division of powers between federal and provincial jurisdictions, there could be no clear separation in practice. The wide-ranging activities of government were too interdependent. Unless the provinces were to be reduced to insignificant powers, which was unthinkable, policies of national importance could not be hived off as exclusively federal. In many matters, especially those affecting the economy, the effective policies of Canada were bound to be those that emerged from the activities of provincial as well as federal government.

It followed that federal-provincial relations were no longer a matter, even primarily, of ensuring that each layer of government was free and able to be effective in its jurisdiction. Respect for jurisdictions remained essential, but as a base for making possible the consultation and co-operation necessary in order to ensure that what federal and provincial governments did in their respective spheres would meld in a mutually supportive way into policies and programs that could operate beneficially for the country as a whole.

That was the thinking behind the "co-operative federalism" slogan. It now seems trite, but in 1963 it was justifiable to refer to it, as we did in the Prime Minister's opening statement to the major federal-provincial conference on 26 November, as a "new approach."

It means, first, a mutual respect for the jurisdictions and the responsibilities of Canada and of the Provinces. It means, secondly, timely and reliable two-way consultation as the basis for co-ordinating the parallel action which Canada and the Provinces must take on matters of common and overlapping interest. Thirdly, it means that if and when certain tax fields are shared, this should be done in a manner appropriate to the respective responsibilities of federal and provincial authorities. And it means, fourthly, assurance that this sharing not only is equitable between the federal government and the Provinces generally, but also is equitable among the Provinces themselves, so that each separately can discharge its own responsibilities.

Anyone reading between the lines, and believing what he read, could have deduced from this statement the policies the Pearson government would in fact adopt from the spring of 1964. But no actions that might have encouraged such reading were taken in November 1963. The sad fact was that, while there was nothing wrong with the idea of co-operative federalism, we were at that point incapable of overcoming the practical obstacles to its implementation. We had been telling ourselves for weeks how important was the November meeting, the first full-scale federal-provincial conference of the Pearson era. We were, nevertheless, very poorly prepared for it. There had been plenty of preparatory papers and discussions. But, as I commented bitterly to the Prime Minister in a memorandum of 25 November, accompanying the final text for his opening statement the next day, the activity had been "a kind of intellectual masturbation, a way of using up time and energy because we are afraid of the real thing ... We haven't faced the issues that arise as soon as the conference is in motion. We haven't thought through our responses to the proposals that we know will come from the provinces. We haven't developed constructive ideas of our own."

Our preparations had been stultified by the inhibitions, within the Ottawa system, to recognition of the provinces' need for a larger share of taxation. The inhibitions were both political and bureaucratic. No doubt many people were prepared to concede, in an abstract intellectual discussion, the necessity of a trend to greater expenditures on programs within provincial jurisdiction. But one group of politicians does not readily hand over power to other groups. The reluctance was the greater, within the Pearson Cabinet, because seven of the ten provinces had governments of other parties. And of the remaining three, the government of Quebec was little loved by federal Liberals: it ostentatiously kept its distance from Ottawa; it did not conceal a certain contempt, for the federal government as incoherent and for the federal Liberal organization in Quebec as corrupt; and above all, it was the most articulate as well as demanding proponent of provincial rights. Only New Brunswick and Newfoundland had governments that federal ministers regarded as friends to be willingly helped. It was not a political atmosphere conducive to the "surrender" of tax revenues to the provinces.

The resistance of federal officials was differently motivated, but not less strong. The intellectual and administrative hangover from the classical concept of federalism was still almost complete. It was reinforced by the other hangover, of wartime centralization. The subsequent revolution moved so quickly, and has made so much change in Canadian public affairs, that it is now hard to appreciate that until 1964 there was no place in the whole Ottawa structure where federal-provincial relations were seen as an area of policy. Federal departments, Finance particularly, dealt with their provincial counterparts as and when their specific concerns required. In many matters there was reasonable co-ordination, but in the minds of almost everyone in Ottawa, it was a relationship not unlike that of parents and children. It was far from co-operative federalism.

In this environment, the attitude of federal officials was dominated by the consideration that larger provincial programs necessarily meant, in the final analysis, smaller budgets than federal departments might otherwise have. Even those who fully accepted the eventual necessity of allowing more "tax room" for the provinces, as it was commonly put, were none the less inclined to postpone the evil day as long as possible. It was argued that, if the federal government conceded financial resources at all quickly, it would lose its precious power to manage the economy. If we had to accommodate the provinces we should do so only after as much resistance as possible, in the process bargaining for terms that would leave the central control of macro-economic policies unfettered.

Such a strategy seemed to me misguided. It overestimated federal power in the changing situation. The constitutional powers of the provinces were quite sufficient for them to frustrate federal economic policies anyway, if they wished. The imperatives of spending on schools and roads were strong enough to ensure that, if we kept the provinces short of tax revenues, they would borrow to the limit of their capacities. It was notable that, in just the first three years of the "Quiet Revolution," the net funded debt of Quebec had more than doubled. Heavy borrowing by the provinces generally, much of which would no doubt be from outside Canada, could weaken federal economic management quite as much as tax transfers would.

To the Prime Minister, with his instinct for diplomacy, there was no point in fighting the provinces over issues on which we knew we were going to end up agreeing to their demands. I was led to the same strategy by the view that central economic management could be continuingly effective only on the basis of building a wide consensus, kept in sufficiently constant repair for agreement among the major actors in the economy – the larger provincial governments among them – to become almost the habit that everyone expected. From both our viewpoints, the route to federal-provincial collaboration was to be open and willing about the need gradually to adjust tax shares. That was the best way to secure the kind of consultation that would sustain federal leadership, that would enable us to act decisively and effectively in the areas of policy in which national action was required.

Nothing that happened afterwards lessened my conviction that this strategy was correct. But in Ottawa in 1963 it was a heresy. That we shared it was, I think, among the strongest of the forces that, for all our differences, bound Mike Pearson and me, and in a non-political way Gordon Robertson, so closely together.

Except in crises, however, there are tight limits to the extent to which even a Prime Minister can act on a view shared neither by his Cabinet nor by the bureaucratic establishment. Pearson the diplomat was especially conscious of that. The consequence was that, for all the importance attached to federal-provincial relations, the Pearson government had no coherent policy for them until April 1964.

At the November 1963 conference we did not suffer as much as we deserved. The Prime Minister did his best to counter our lack of decisive preparation by constantly emphasizing that this conference was only the first of a series, a mere beginning to a new chapter in Canadian federalism. As always, his skilled chairmanship did much to disarm critics. Thanks to that, the conference was more harmonious than I had dared to hope. But it was so only by putting off until tomorrow, and tomorrow was close.

My notes on the "decisions" of the conference made pathetic reading. We did improve the equalization provided under the federal-provincial tax arrangements, in the sense that we corrected the diminution of it which had occurred under the Diefenbaker regime. We made one small concession to the pressure from the provinces for extra tax room; the federal abatement of estate taxes, in favour of provincial succession duties, was increased from 50 per cent to 75 per cent. It was also agreed that benefits under the shared-cost programs for old-age assistance and for allowances to the blind and disabled would be increased by $10 a month.

Otherwise, all was generalities and postponement. There were to be working groups of officials and ministerial discussions on a host of subjects, and the federal government promised to make, later, "concrete proposals" for close and continuing consultation with the provinces. The shortage of definite decisions on this occasion would not have been serious if it had been followed by good preparations for the next conference. It was not. The predominant attitude in Ottawa was that the November conference had been a successful holding operation in defence of the federal interest against the provinces. The task for the next meeting was to go on resisting concessions.

At the political level, this attitude was strengthened by the Pearson government's sensitivity, after the budget, about any course of action that could be labelled as "another retreat." The lack of any logical connection to federal-provincial relations did not make the association of ideas any less powerful. In so far as Mr Pearson's inclinations to genuinely co-operative federalism were vaguely understood, they were regarded as a threat to Ottawa's management of the country: a disposition to "give away the store," in the phrase that came to be widely used by political friends as well as enemies.

During the winter, therefore, the forces of inertia in Ottawa remained far too strong to be overcome by Pearsonian diplomacy. That could be done only when Jean Lesage had raised his storm. The setting for it was prepared at the November conference. Obviously there had to be another meeting fairly soon; March was favoured. Lesage intervened to say that there was no reason, in the proper spirit of Confederation, why the conferences should always be in Ottawa. They could be in provincial capitals, and he would offer the hospitality of Quebec City for the March meeting. The gesture impressed everyone. We did not realize how much it would add to the drama of the coming storm.

21   *Sixteen Days in April*

The preparations for the federal-provincial conference of 31 March–2 April ended dramatically for me. The Prime Minister had flu during the last week of March and the final pre-conference meeting of the delegation, some two dozen strong, was held in a gloomy, too-small room in the basement of his house at 24 Sussex Dr. The day was 29 March, Easter Sunday, and a cold wind was blowing over the Ottawa river – from Quebec, someone commented. After the meeting, worried by its unsatisfactory nature, I turned out of the Prime Minister's driveway and went a little way along Sussex. There was a loud bang from the engine of my car. The crankshaft had broken. It was an appropriate beginning for perhaps the most miserable week I ever experienced.

On Monday we flew to Quebec City and in the evening I tried to express at a press briefing the reasoned, modest optimism that I did not feel about the federal position. The atmosphere was grim. At that time there had been some FLQ bomb incidents and we had the first experience, for most of us, of tight security arrangements in peacetime. The floor of the Chateau Frontenac reserved for the federal delegation seemed to be frequented by as many police as delegates. When Judy LaMarsh, Maurice Lamontagne, and I went out for a restaurant dinner, our plainclothes RCMP protectors sat at a nearby table. Outside the Legislative Buildings, where the conference was held, demonstrating students shouted loudly. Inside, Lesage was, as always, a gracious host, but the physical arrangements for the meetings themselves seemed designed for confrontation. We met in the Assembly chamber, so that instead of being round the usual oval of tables, we faced each other as opponents. The federal delegates were given the benches on the government side nearest to the Speaker's chair. The Quebec delegation was on the opposition side. With this arrangement, Mr Pearson could not flourish in his usual role as chairman. He hardly had the chance to try. Lesage was not only the master of ceremonies. He was the chief inquisitor. Verbally, he stretched us on the rack. That we largely deserved it, in my view, was not consoling.

This time we were well prepared on one topic of the conference: how to arrange for provinces that wished to "contract out" of shared-cost programs, on financial terms that were neutral between them and provinces that retained cost-sharing. We were committed to this policy by our election platform. It was simple in principle but extremely complicated in detail. Accordingly, it took a good deal of time at the conference. There was not, however, a dispute about principles, and I shall leave the subject for later treatment.

On the other important topics, we went to Quebec City in poor shape. For pensions, we had a perfectly good plan of its kind, and eight provinces would accept it if Ontario did. But no realist could expect that Ontario would. Premier Robarts would be noncommittal until Quebec produced its plan, but after that there would be the death blow. We had lost control of the situation when, in September, we had not accepted the necessity of making the plan substantially more funded.

On two other subjects, our weakness was of a more technical nature. We proposed to provide for loans to university students, free of interest while they were at university; and we proposed to extend family allowances to age eighteen for those who stayed in school. The problem was how these desirable measures should be co-ordinated with existing provincial programs. Quebec, alone, already paid allowances, on somewhat different terms, to students aged sixteen and seventeen; Quebec and some other provinces had loan programs, smaller and less attractive than we proposed. We declared our willingness to find means of co-ordination but did not develop any specific suggestions as to how it should be done. We were therefore vulnerable to the charge of barging into provincial fields like bulls into china shops.

This was deeply regrettable, but would not in itself have been difficult to correct. It was combined, however, with a fundamental weakness: we had no good arguments to defend the position we adopted on taxes. Apart from the small change agreed in November, on estate duties, there were to be no early concessions. We had in reserve a vaguely formulated idea for a joint study of long-term needs and resources at the two levels of government. That was all. On present taxes, we would not budge.

This position was the more difficult because Mr Pearson's attitude at the November conference, though vague, had created expectations that we were becoming ready to give more recognition to provincial tax needs. All the provinces were disappointed. Lesage was desperate, and furious. He had been demanding more tax room since 1960, and had got almost nothing. It seemed to Lesage that, for all his smooth talk about co-operative federalism, Pearson was no better than Diefenbaker. The Quebec budget had been delayed until after the conference, in the expectation of some relief. Without that, Lesage had no choice: the programs of the "Quiet Revolution" could go on only with an immediate increase in the provincial income tax. The dreaded cry of "double taxation" in Quebec would be raised. And this when Ottawa was choosing to spend more on expanded social programs that most people in Quebec regarded as properly their concern.

Lesage denounced our family allowance and student loan plans with a ferocity that would have rung hollow in other circumstances but was all too convincing in its context. Mr Pearson talked, calmly and for other conditions reasonably enough, but he might as well have sat glumly silent.

To top it all, Jean Lesage produced a risky but brilliant stroke. He told the conference, in confidence, what the Quebec Pension Plan would be. It had been decided in outline, though it was far from ready for presentation to the Legislative Assembly. The brain-child chiefly of Claude Castonguay, it was an excellent plan for its purpose. It would provide appreciably larger pensions than we proposed, and with the supplementary survivor and disability benefits that we did not have the constitutional power to include. It would generate, for many years, large investment funds. One could almost see the other provincial premiers licking their lips. There could be no immediate public response, since Lesage was taking a large political risk by telling outsiders about his plan before he presented it to his own legislature. There was no doubt, however, about the effect. With such a plan in Quebec, Ontario would never go along with ours. That was dead.

In a debating sense, Lesage's triumph could not have been more complete. The other premiers were entirely impressed and mostly sympathetic. The federal government was beleaguered. Certainly from inside, and probably from outside, it seemed all but collapsed. Lesage was desperately unhappy, however. He knew what almost no one outside Quebec then understood: that he was riding a tiger. The pro-Quebec feelings of the "Quiet Revolution" were close to becoming anti-Canada feelings. Though federal politicians and officials saw him as an extremist, in his environment he was the man of moderation. He was the federalist, claiming that he could, by hard bargaining, secure the best future for Quebec within Canada. For him the significance of the conference was that he would have to say that he had failed. Ottawa was not understanding Quebec. Even a Liberal government, elected with much support from Quebec, was not giving what Quebec was entitled to. That was why he was having to impose taxes that other Canadians did not pay. He would be politically vulnerable. All his achievements could well turn out to be merely the work of the moderate who prepared the way for the extremists.

Late in the second day of the conference, though flushed with his debating triumphs, Jean Lesage caught my eye across the chamber and signalled that he would like to talk. We met in the classic location for the private conferring of public opponents, behind the Speaker's chair. "Tom, this is awful. Can't you do something about it?" I had to reply: "Not now, not during this conference. Perhaps after we get back to Ottawa ... I'll try, anyway."

I was reflecting the disconsolate discussion in meetings of the federal delegation. Gordon Robertson and I had pleaded for a change of policy, for yielding some ground on taxation. The ministers – Guy Favreau, Maurice Lamontagne, Walter Gordon, Allan MacEachen, Judy LaMarsh, Harry Hays – were adamant: no concessions, no retreat. The Prime Minister was unhappy, but he went along with his ministers.

On the last night of the conference, Bob Bryce, Gordon Robertson and I sat up late, to make all we could of the idea of a joint study. Bob christened it "the tax structure committee." It would consist of one Minister from each province and three from the federal government. It would operate to a specified timetable, and with expert assistance. It would be a comprehensive review of the nature and extent of federal and provincial taxes in relation to the financial responsibilities that now had to be carried by the two levels of government.

There could be little doubt that an inquiry so structured would result, a year or two hence, in some realignment of taxes favourable to the provinces. The provincial premiers so understood it, and nine of them supported the proposal. Jean Lesage regarded it as another delaying tactic and, while he did not finally reject it, he would not commit Quebec to participation. We had difficulty writing a communiqué that papered over this and other cracks. No one was deceived. The agreed outcome of the conference was miniscule. Lesage was ostentatiously absent when the Prime Minister met the press at the conclusion of the meetings. He held his own press conference shortly afterwards, and cleverly contrived to say nothing that could be quoted as a direct attack on the federal government and yet to make his anger and contempt entirely apparent.

It was a dispirited federal delegation that returned to Ottawa on 2 April. I shared a taxi from the airport with the RCMP Inspector who had been assigned to the Prime Minister's protection during the conference. He had not, of course, been in the meetings but sensed our concerns. In reply to his questions, I summed up what seemed to me the significance of the conference: it threatened a chain of events that would probably submerge Lesage and could well make the separation of Quebec from Canada a serious likelihood.

The next day, Friday, I stayed home, for my birthday but not for any rejoicing, and over the weekend gathered up enough spirit to try to do what I had told Lesage I would. Since the ministers' case against a change of policy had been that "another retreat" would be politically devastating to the government, it seemed necessary to cast my case to the Prime Minister in partially political terms. For that reason I did not discuss it with Gordon Robertson, as I would have liked to do. The omission made no difference. Independently, we were engaged in the same weekend task. Gordon's arguments were appropriately different from mine, but the advice our memoranda offered simultaneously to the Prime Minister was virtually identical.

We did not suggest any great change in tax arrangements for the financial year, 1964–5, that had just begun. But the federal government should recognize and announce now what it would otherwise be driven to before long: a committed increase in the abatement of federal taxes, in favour of the provinces, for the two following years, 1965–6 and 1966–7, which would be the remaining two years of the current five-year arrangement.

We both argued that the provinces needed the money more than the federal government did. Gordon concentrated otherwise on the needs of national unity. Having obtained nothing from the conference and being compelled almost immediately to impose extra taxes on Quebecers, Lesage would be viewed in the same way by his own party and by his opponents: he would have been proved wrong in his claim that the province could work with Ottawa to achieve the objectives of the "Quiet Revolution." There would be a breakdown in confidence between the federal government and the provinces that would greatly increase the strain and perils for Canadian unity. Only bold and prompt action could change this outlook.

My argument dealt also with the political prospects of the Pearson government. It was in trouble and showing every sign of getting deeper into trouble. Having gone so unprepared to the Quebec City conference was a prime example, and the resulting row would be deeply damaging. The trend could be reversed only if the government could pull off a major coup. The coup that would count most, in the circumstances, would have to be in federal-provincial relations. This meant: "We must make a deal with Quebec, but it must be one that all the provinces will welcome."

The memorandum outlined in some detail the deal that I thought appropriate. Under the existing arrangement, the provincial share of personal income tax was to be 19 per cent in 1965–6 and 20 per cent in 1966–7. It should be increased by two percentage points a year, to 21 per cent in 1965–6 and 24 per cent in 1966–7. With equalization, this would cost us about $60 millions in the first of those years and $120 millions in the second. We didn't need the money as much as the provinces did. For the current year, we could improve good-will all round by proposing that the provinces should administer student loans with a standard provision for the extent to which we would contribute to the cost of making them interest-free during the years of study. We could also help Quebec's finances to the extent of about $15 millions in the current year, by an arrangement on extended family allowances. In return we could get Quebec to concentrate the arrangements for contracting out of shared-cost programs on an interim period during which Quebec would be committed to maintaining the programs without change after it took over formal responsibility. Above all, we could agree to bring the Canada and Quebec pension plans into line. We could happily accept its plan in many respects, provided they would make the most fundamental change of accepting our shorter, ten-year maturity period over which pensions rose to their full level. The changed plan would generate more funds than our proposal, and these should be under provincial control for investment. On that basis, we would get the agreement of the other provinces to the plan.

"This is a first rough sketch of a complicated arrangement. But the details could be worked out all right if the will was there." We would be attacked for "truckling to Quebec," but the criticism would be of little significance compared with the general public relief that what was clearly a crisis in federal-provincial relations had been resolved. Ministers might worry about another "retreat", but in this case it was a retreat from what? The alternative, to go on as we were, was "unmitigated trouble, a general sense that we don't have a grip on things, deep discontent in our caucus, stalemate in the House, nothing done."

I concluded: "So it's worth a try, I believe." The "first rough sketch" turned out to be almost exactly what was agreed in the following eight days, but that seemed hardly possible to hope for when I gave the memorandum to a very worried Prime Minister on the morning of 7 April.

There had not been any response from him when, in the early afternoon, Maurice Sauvé came to my office. (He was by now a Minister; how that had happened is a story to be told in another chapter.) He had been talking to Claude Morin, the principal official behind the Lesage government. The message was that they did not want to fight with us, they still hoped for a reasonable settlement, they expected me to come up with something. But unless some new word came from Ottawa soon, Lesage would have to go ahead with his budget, increasing taxes, and fight it would have to be.

I hesitated to take Maurice Sauvé into my confidence. His disposition to advance his position by talking to the press was notorious. But he was the one Minister with valid contacts in Quebec City. His tactical judgment could be extremely useful. The hard fact was that the safe paths had ended in the morass of the conference. There was no way out that didn't require willingness to take risks. I let Maurice read a copy of my memorandum.

He was delighted. This was the kind of deal that could be made, provided no time was lost. He and I must get Mike's authorization to go to Quebec City and negotiate it. I was doubtful. We were facing a double negotiation: one with the provincial government, but also an equally difficult one, within the federal government. Maurice Sauvé could help with the first, but his participation would make the second more difficult. The Prime Minister would be better able to sell the deal to his colleagues if, politically, it was his alone, if no inter-ministerial conflicts and jealousies were involved.

For that reason I thought it much less likely that Mr Pearson would agree to my going to Quebec City with Sauvé than with Gordon Robertson and Bob Bryce, the negotiating team I had been planning to suggest. Perhaps I had made a mistake in showing the memorandum to Maurice. He had seized the opportunity, however, and it was too late to turn back. I pointed out the double problem and said that, if he took part in the negotiation with Quebec, he would have to be quiet about it in

Cabinet. Maurice was, in most respects, a realist. He agreed, and loyally kept the agreement – until after the deal was completed.

We therefore marched together into the Prime Minister's office. Mr Pearson was pessimistic but clear. He would be happy with the deal proposed in my memorandum. He doubted its practicality. But if we thought it could be achieved, by all means go to Quebec City and try. We went that evening. The Prime Minister arranged a meeting of some senior Ministers for 8 P.M. the following evening at 24 Sussex. I committed myself to being back from Quebec City to put forward whatever I then could.

For the morning of 8 April, Claude Morin came to the Chateau Frontenac hotel to meet with Maurice Sauvé and me. In the afternoon the three of us went to the Premier's office, where two of his ministers (René Levesque and Paul Gérin-Lajoie) were also present. The mission, I emphasized throughout, was an exploration on behalf of the Prime Minister. I had no negotiating authority from Cabinet. It was obvious from the preceding week's conference that many federal ministers would dislike anything on which those present could agree. The Prime Minister's basic purpose – Canadian unity in a co-operative federalism – would not be served by an arrangement with Quebec at the price of resignation by any significant ministers from other provinces.

With those warnings given, I felt able to be frank about most of the ideas for bridging the gap between Ottawa and Quebec suggested in the memorandum to Mr Pearson. Quebec's immediate financial problem might be eased by providing for "contracting out" of extended family allowances and student loans. This would not be acceptable in Ottawa, however, unless Lesage made it clear that contracting-out as a financial arrangement did not mean contracting-out of Confederation; it would not mean abandoning the principle that substantially similar, basic programs, in these new areas and in established areas such as hospital insurance, would operate for all Canadians. In Quebec, and in other provinces if they wished, "equalized tax points" (in the accepted jargon) would replace conditional grants as the method of financing, but there would be no great changes in the programs. Obviously, this did not mean freezing them indefinitely, but there should be stability for long enough for habits of consultative co-operation to build up, between the provinces and with Ottawa. Lesage fully accepted all this.

On tax-sharing, there was no possibility of any change unless the government of Quebec decided to participate fully in the "tax structure" enquiry that all the other provinces had welcomed. In that case, I thought it possible that the federal government could now be persuaded to give evidence of its good-will. There was no point in beating around the bush on this. What I had in mind was increased abatements of the personal income tax, to the extent of 21 per cent in the next year and 24 per cent in the following one. That was the maximum conceivable. Any negotiation would break down if Lesage insisted on pressing for additional concessions, such as the increase in the abatement of corporate income tax that he had long been demanding.

There was a further condition. The package must include an arrangement on pensions that would save the Canada Pension Plan. I did not go as far as I had in the memorandum to Mr Pearson, by suggesting that the Canada and Quebec plans might be brought into line. That was better left for detailed bargaining. For the time being, I concentrated on the principle that, for contributory pensions as for other major social programs, a way must be found to have a basic level of provision available in all of Canada. That might be achieved by legislating the federal plan in a form in which it could be incorporated into a fuller provincial plan in Quebec or any other province that so wished. This would require modifications to both present plans. We were adamant about our short, ten-year maturity period. If Quebec met us on that, I thought that we could go a long way to meet Quebec on other features.

Lesage was, rightly, sceptical about the practicability of a provincial plan incorporating a federal plan, but he was entirely happy that an effort should be made to harmonize the two. In the discussion he showed as much skill in friendly co-operation as he had shown the week before in argumentative hostility. Speed, however, he insisted was now essential. He would decide there and then to postpone his budget, which had been scheduled for the following week, to 24 April. That would give us ten days or so to see whether a deal could be worked out. If I could let him know by the end of the week – it was then Wednesday – whether something of the nature we had talked about would be acceptable in principle by the federal government, Claude Morin and Claude Castonguay would come to Ottawa on Saturday, to see what could be worked out on the complex details of the pension plans.

We had got further than I had dared to expect. To allow enough time for the discussion, compatibly with my evening commitment in Ottawa, it had been arranged that a Quebec government plane would fly Sauvé and me back to Ottawa. We had sandwiches on the journey, and I went straight to 24 Sussex, with only a few minutes to report the essence of the conclusions to the Prime Minister before the arrival of the ministers. They were Walter Gordon, Guy Favreau, Maurice Lamontagne, Paul Martin, Allan MacEachen, and Mitchell Sharp. Jack Pickersgill would probably have been invited, but he was out of Ottawa – ironically in Quebec City, on transport business, and he knew nothing of my mission.

It was necessary first to emphasize the seriousness of the situation. If we did nothing, there would be a conflict between the Pearson and Lesage governments that would probably be fatal to both, to the Pearson government soon and to the Lesage government not much later. Its consequences would quite possibly place Canadian federalism in jeopardy. I outlined, as earlier to Lesage, the terms on which I now believed that the confrontation could be avoided. This time I could present the proposals not as mine but as what I thought Quebec would accept. They would be attacked by the opposition as a sell-out, but the attack would be demonstrably partisan. It would confirm support for Diefenbaker only among the extremists of English Canada. We must be prepared to face that just as much as Lesage had to do battle with Quebec extremists. He and we were the people who had to find the ground on which most Canadians could stand together. If we did it sensibly, the settlement would be, and would be seen to be, an act not of capitulation but of constructive leadership. Incidentally, it might well save the government from what was otherwise an unpleasant future.

The Prime Minister was fully convinced, and he was at his persuasive best. By the end of the evening, the ministers present were willing to go along with an attempt to make the settlement; and if they were, the Cabinet as a whole could be carried. The outcome was owed to Mr Pearson's skill and, most of all, to the large mind and generous spirit of Walter Gordon. On the budget he had been let down by his colleagues and had had to bear the full brunt of "retreat." The tax concessions to the provinces would be attacked as another retreat, and it would be Walter Gordon that the opposition would try to pillory for it. He was too objective and too courageous to let that affect his judgment. He understood the situation; he wanted it to be saved, and the pension plan to be achieved. After careful but not prolonged consideration, he agreed.

Much had to be done, quickly. The Prime Minister had to convince many doubting colleagues. Gordon Robertson and I had to marshal the work of many civil servants involved in the various programs at issue. In particular I had to prepare, with Joe Willard and Don Thorson, for the pension negotiation. Morin and Castonguay came on Saturday. Maurice Sauvé, though no pension expert, sat in on the meetings, so that the group was six strong. In the morning we examined ways of revising the Canada plan so that it would still be acceptable to us but could be incorporated by Quebec into a somewhat larger and more funded plan satisfactory to them. The difficulties were too great, and over a poor lunch – the location was chosen to be inconspicuous – we were a gloomy party. In the afternoon we turned to the more daring idea: could Parliament and the Quebec Assembly pass identical legislation, creating in law and in administration two plans, but in effect one plan? To do so, both the proposed plans would have to be considerably changed. Could we trade off the changes to make a compromise acceptable to both sides?

It was a tough negotiation, but fundamentally we were, on this issue, like-minded people. What emerged was, I think, a far better pension plan than either of the original proposals. Quebec came all the way to meet us on the point that was most important for all the people aged over forty-five, and still working, who had not had access to adequate private pension plans: the "maturity period" for full pensions would be our ten years, not Quebec's twenty years. We happily accepted a feature of their plan that was helpful to low-income people: contributions would not be charged on the first $600 of annual income, though pensions would be reckoned on all income up to the ceiling. That ceiling had been $4,500 in our plan, $6,000 in Quebec's. We settled on $5,000. The pension rate, in relation to earnings, was to be Quebec's 25 per cent instead of our 20 per cent, and pensions in pay would be adjusted to cost-of-living changes up to 2 per cent a year; this partially corrected one of the greatest weaknesses of our plan, which had not provided for any adjustment, and the protection was later made – and so far has continued to be – complete. There were various other compromises, and from our viewpoint one major extension: Quebec would consent to the constitutional amendment enabling us to include the survivor and disability pensions that could not be provided in our original plan. Financially, the joint plan would be considerably less funded than Quebec's had been intended to be, but considerably more funded than our proposal. In my view, and subsequent events proved it to be a widespread view, we had indeed reconciled the best features of the two plans.

I hope I am being objective in saying that it was a highly satisfactory negotiation. On the Saturday afternoon we agreed on the main principles of what became the Canada and the Quebec Pension Plans. There were, we knew, immense technical complexities ahead, both as to the fine points of the plan and as to the drafting difficulties of producing identical legislation. We trusted each other so well as to be confident that we would find agreed ways through all the problems. We so reported to Prime Minister Pearson and Premier Lesage.

The governmental process is often frustratingly slow and cumbersome but occasionally, when challenged, it can be made to work with speed and precision. On the following Monday and Tuesday, with excellent help from our official colleagues, Claude Morin and I together wrote, over the telephone, a long statement embodying all the elements of the package agreement, on taxation, on contracting-out of shared-cost programs, on family allowances, on university student loans, and on pensions in considerable detail. The document was approved by the Quebec Cabinet on Wednesday, 15 April.

In Ottawa, there was one major alarum on the way. While I worked with officials to complete the negotiations, Mr Pearson worked to persuade his colleagues. Maurice Sauvé loyally stuck to our understanding, and kept a low profile, until the agreement was concluded. He could not resist afterwards telling some of the story of the negotiations to his favourite journalists. Since it was a dramatic story, it got plenty of attention. As a consequence, the process as a whole is in danger of historical distortion. There were, I again emphasize, two negotiations: with Quebec, and within the federal Cabinet. The second remained unknown, and therefore Mr Pearson has not been given the credit he should have.

The only bit of the story of his persuasive work that has become known is the one part of which he made a mess. He was afraid to talk to his female Minister, though she was the one most closely affected. She learned what was going on only on 13 April, and through third parties. I was at fault for not anticipating the problem. While the division of labour was that I was doing the work at the official level, and Mr Pearson was handling the politics, I knew him well enough to have realized that his persuasion would be directed to his male colleagues. I should have talked to Judy LaMarsh myself at an early stage. By the time I did, she was understandably furious. She had endured months of criticism, defending an unfunded pension plan. It had been changed behind her back to a substantially funded one.

Her letter of resignation was written. As we talked, she picked up a photograph of the Prime Minister from her desk. For a moment, I thought she was going to throw it at me. She shattered it on her desk. As calmly as I could, I pointed out that, like it or not, the original plan was going nowhere; explained what had happened; and argued the merits of the new plan. Judy had far too much public spirit to let a personal affront deter her from a cause in which she believed. The letter of resignation, which would have put the whole enterprise into doubt, was not delivered, and Judy went on to champion the new pension plan through Parliament in fine style. But she never forgave Mike Pearson.

That unfortunate exception apart, everything went well. Since rumours that something new was happening were inevitably in the wind, on 15 April we sent a telegram to all the Premiers saying that the Prime Minister hoped before the end of the week to outline "a proposal which I hope you would consider to provide the basis for discussion of a satisfactory nation-wide pension plan." On 16 April Mr Pearson's persuasion had its result in federal Cabinet approval of the whole document to which the Quebec Cabinet had agreed the previous day, and that evening we telegraphed its substance to all the provinces. On Monday, 20 April, the Prime Minister announced the whole set of proposals in the House of Commons.

There was no mistaking the national sense of relief that what had been generally seen as a crisis had been surmounted. Criticism was as minimal as I had dared to hope. In fact, as the next chapter will report, there were more perils ahead before the Canada Pension Plan was finally brought to a happy conclusion. But at the time it seemed that what remained to be done, on pensions, was routine and that the government had at last pulled off a resounding success from which restored confidence and smoother performance would follow.

What had been achieved, with the Cabinet decision of 16 April, was the constructive expression of the idea of co-operative federalism. Though partisans inevitably attacked the changes in the Canada Pension Plan as truckling to Quebec, in fact the integrated plan was clearly a balanced combination of the best of federal and provincial ideas. The extra tax room for the provinces and the arrangements for joint programs were an essential basis for more stable relations and more co-ordinated action by the governments of the federation. Without such measures at that time the country could not have moved on to the further programs – medicare, the Canada Assistance Plan, manpower training allowances, and others – that in the later sixties so greatly improved the opportunities and lives of many Canadians.

Charming though Mike Pearson was in most of his personal relationships, he was not a man to whom the giving of praise to close associates came easily. I therefore cannot resist quoting the generous handwritten note that I received from him on 21 April:

Dear Tom:

Now that the dust of battle has cleared away, and we can appreciate the victory that was snatched from defeat and almost despair, may I send you my thanks for the great results achieved. They are great in their immediate impact and achievement and may become far greater, if we can indeed follow on from this success.

Without you it would not have been possible; even, I think, in initiation; certainly in accomplishment. It was as fine an operation in governmental and policy management and negotiation as I have ever seen. On your part it was almost a superhuman effort of will and wisdom and resolve. I am more grateful than I can say.

as ever

Mike Pearson

The settlement of April 16 had an important internal significance. More than anything else that had happened in the first year, it put the stamp of Mr Pearson's personality on his government. My role as the active agent was possible only because everyone concerned knew that the detail with which I was dealing expressed the spirit of the Prime Minister's view on policy. His support and his persuasive powers were crucial to the outcome. As I saw it, he had at last dominated his Cabinet, and a Pearson government therefore promised to be, after all, what we had hoped for. That happy vision quickly proved to be in accord with reality only erratically.

22 *The CPP Achieved*

The Pearson government celebrated its first anniversary, on 22 April, in better shape than it had been at any time since the first fifty-two days. The settlement with the provinces was received with general relief and approval. Even most opponents felt compelled to cheer, and Premier Robarts was almost enthusiastic in his first comments. Coincidentally, a provincial general election put the Liberal party into office in Saskatchewan; and while the new Premier, Ross Thatcher, was hardly a favourite in Ottawa, the political change strengthened party confidence and made it less likely than ever that the NDP, toppled at last in its provincial stronghold, would take any parliamentary risk of forcing a federal general election. Above all, we now had a long agenda of well-prepared legislation ready for Parliament, and in what promised to be the new mood it was hard to see even Mr Diefenbaker putting up much resistance to what was clearly a popular program.

The mood proved to be short-lived, but it provided a healthy impetus for the intensive work on the details of the pension plan that was necessary in the following few months. The collaboration with Quebec was in the excellent spirit we had expected. We struggled with the complexities as one team. On an occasion when a sizeable delegation of federal officials went to Quebec City, Lesage himself entertained us to dinner and made glowing remarks about this example of co-operative federalism, to which I responded much less eloquently but no less sincerely. The reciprocal hospitality was not so successful. I took the two Claudes, Castonguay and Morin, to 24 Sussex for dinner with the Prime Minister, but it was on a day when their main impression was of how exhausted he was.

The final outcome was a common text for all the elaborate provisions of the pension plan; in effect, the Quebec Bill was the French text of the

Canada Pension Plan and our text, as written in English, was used by Quebec for the English version of their Bill.

In the middle of the process, there was a full conference of officials from all the provinces to review the provisions of the plan before the writing of the Bill was complete. Eight provinces had only minor questions and suggestions, and with Quebec's collaboration we were able to accept the most significant of them. The odd man out, understandably, was Ontario. It was as well placed as Quebec to run its own plan. And, unlike Quebec, it had some financial as well as political motive for doing so. The demography and incomes of Ontario were such that a provincial plan could probably provide the same level of benefits for a slightly lower contribution rate, over the long term, than the Canada plan. Nevertheless, Premier Robarts had made plain his preference for a national plan. In this he was being a good Canadian, as he most genuinely was, but no doubt he had also thought at first that he was speaking from strength: politically, Ontario could play a large part in shaping any plan on which national agreement was possible. The April settlement changed that. Political opponents might say that in revising our plan we had capitulated to Quebec, because there was little else critical that they could say, but the reality was quite different. From the viewpoint of Ontario, as of the insurance industry, we had used Quebec to turn the tables on them. For months the Ontario government had been pressing us to scale down our proposals (and the insurance industry had been demanding that we abandon them), but the new plan went the other way and offered larger benefits. True, it was more funded, which the critics liked. But on the features they most disliked – those most remote from private plans, notably the ten-year maturity period and the indexation of benefit calculations to earnings levels – it was Quebec that had moved to accept the federal view.

The discussions with Ontario officials, which we began a few days after 20 April, were therefore bound to be somewhat strained. For some weeks I had no real concern. There might be huffing and puffing, but the wind of general opinion was so strongly behind the Canada Plan that the Ontario Cabinet would go along with it. Our problem was simply to make that as easy as possible by accepting the views of the Ontario officials on as many technicalities as we could without upsetting any principles of the plan. We had the full collaboration of Quebec officials in this face-saving effort.

Ontario concentrated, however, on one major point: its "agency" proposal. We intended to provide, as constitutionally we were bound to do, that the CPP would apply to residents of a province unless that province legislated and ran, as Quebec would do, a comparable plan. (It would in fact be an identical plan, but the wording of the legislation would not be quite so restrictive.) Ontario argued that the effect was to lock the provinces into a once-and-for-all choice. There should be a third option: if a province legislated a plan that was in fact identical with the CPP, the federal government should then be willing to administer that plan as the province's agent. This would give the province freedom to change its mind if it found the CPP unsatisfactory or if there were changes to the CPP that it did not like.

This seemed an innocent enough proposal, for the short run. We rejected it because of the trouble that it would store up for the future. If the other eight provinces were in the CPP, Ontario was the one that would get a financial advantage from a legislatively separate plan without, under the agency arrangement, the responsibility of administering it. But with Ontario out of the finances of the "national plan", British Columbia and Alberta – the next-richest provinces – would have something to gain by adopting the agency arrangement. With them gone, Saskatchewan and Manitoba could move to the same position. There would thus be danger of a process of peeling-off which would eventually result in the federal government administering a series of plans without maintaining the advantages, for mobility within Canada, of a truly national plan.

We therefore made a counter-proposal: we would incorporate in our legislation safeguards to make it quite practicable for a province to substitute its own plan, with due notice, if it became dissatisfied with the CPP and particularly if the CPP was in future amended in ways that the province did not like. The Ontario officials were not enthusiastic but we eventually agreed on a form of words that both sides undertook to recommend to their cabinets as meeting the substance of Ontario's concerns. The federal government accepted the proposal. The Ontario government left it in abeyance.

This was disturbing, but we pressed on. There was particular urgency about the constitutional amendment required to enable the CPP to provide supplementary benefits, for contributors who became disabled or, in the event of death, for widows or widowers and dependent children. Such an amendment by convention required the consent of all the provinces before legislation in the UK Parliament to change its BNA Act. But the UK Parliament was expected to be in recess from July until it was dissolved for a general election late in the year. If we could not get through all the stages of the amendment process in the summer, there would be a hiatus, compelled by the course of British politics, until after the turn of the year.

The provinces were co-operative, but some were rather slow. The worst was Prince Edward Island, whose government (that of Premier Shaw) attempted to bargain for financial concessions as the price of its agreement. We rejected such conditions, politely but firmly; and when all the other provinces had agreed, Premier Shaw recognized that he could hardly be the one to hold up national agreement on such an issue. The UK Parliament was able to do its duty to Canada before the end of July.

By this time we had completed the White Paper setting out the details of the plan, drafting of the legislation itself was well under way, and my concerns included such mundane details as the design of the social insurance card essential to the administrative preparations for the plan. But as we busily prepared the ingredients we returned to growing uncertainty as to whether the cake would ever be baked. The government's prestige was again deteriorating.

I have no doubt that, if the political situation had not changed, Premier Robarts would have stuck to the warmth with which he first responded to the April settlement with Quebec. It was the kind of pragmatic solution to a national problem that appealed to his Canadianism. But in May Mr Pearson plunged into his proposal for a distinctive national flag. Like many things he did, it came out all right in the end but incurred unnecessary troubles on the way. Mr Diefenbaker seized the opportunity to throw the House of Commons into uproar and a prolonged filibuster. The government, badly rattled, made silly small mistakes. The public perception was again of its ineffectiveness. The insurance industry and other business opponents of public pensions revived their hopes that the plan could be stopped. The Conservatives in Parliament were in a mood in which they saw political profit in strongly attacking any government measure, even one as intrinsically popular as the improvement of pensions.

Mr Robarts must have been under intense pressure from both these sources. He had only to choose some point on which to attach himself to the insurance industry's denunciations of the plan; to say that he would not have it for the people of Ontario; to "do his own Quebec," as we put it in the privacy of our offices, and produce a somewhat different Ontario plan – and, in the again vulnerable state of the government's credibility, the CPP would after all collapse like a house of cards. The Pearson government would be denied what in April had promised to be its most conspicuous achievement. Much the same pension plan, one might guess, would in a few years' time be picked up and legislated by another government with Ontario's agreement and with reasonable provision for integration with the Quebec plan. But the Pearson government would be long gone.

Mr Robarts kept silent. That did not comfort us: the blow would be most damaging if it was delivered after we had started to move the legislation through Parliament. There was, however, nothing we could do but press on as fast as possible, with determination though in apprehension. By the end of September the drafting of the legislation was almost complete. On 5 October we received a letter from Premier Robarts. It arrived on my desk with a pencilled Pearson question at the top: "Is this a bombshell?" It was not quite that. It was a threat to explode the landmine that Joe Willard and I had long feared. It revived the agency proposal, which supposedly had been put to rest in June, and did so in terms that clearly prepared the ground for Ontario to go its own way entirely if we again rejected an agency arrangement.

We prepared our response quickly but carefully, and Mr Pearson signed it on 8 October. Mr Robarts replied on 21 October, reiterating his position, but ending with a warm offer of discussion. Personal diplomacy was clearly the best hope. It was arranged that Mr Robarts would visit with the Prime Minister at 24 Sussex on 5 November.

It would be a momentous meeting and I wrote extensive briefing documents for the Prime Minister, summarizing all the history and deploying all the arguments. But the central issue was much broader than the technicalities of pensions. What we had worked out with Quebec "is a unique and admittedly experimental way of getting nation-wide action in an area of joint jurisdiction. It has large implications for the future: its failure would cause widespread concern in English Canada and would do enormous harm in Quebec, where it would be a severe setback for the moderates who believe that Quebec can work with English Canada and for that purpose considerably modified their own pension proposals."

In that spirit, we could appeal to Robarts to give the experiment a chance. Given the safeguards in the legislation, Ontario could do so without prejudice to its future freedom of action in the light of experience. And given Robarts's sincere and serious concern for national unity, such an appeal "put as the Prime Minister can put it," might succeed. We could hardly expect, much as we would wish, that he would now declare his acceptance of the CPP. But he could agree to what I summarized as a non-aggression pact: he would not attack the legislation while it was under detailed consideration before a parliamentary committee, with extensive hearings of witnesses; he would maintain his non-commitment until he saw how the plan stood up to such scrutiny.

So it turned out. The meeting produced no formal agreement, except that I drafted (and the Prime Minister to an unusual degree edited) two letters to Robarts, one official and one personal, which in effect set out the arguments he would use in resisting pressure to attack the Canada Pension Plan, at any rate while it was in the process of examination by parliamentary committee. The upshot was, in short, the kind of gentlemanly arrangement equally appropriate to the characters of Pearson and Robarts.

We were able to proceed in a more optimistic spirit. The legislation was introduced on 9 November. The only significant change from the proposals as they had been agreed in April and elaborated by early June related to the existing old-age security program. It represented, from my viewpoint, a victory in an argument that had been strongly fought among ministers and officials. The amount of old-age security payments would in future be automatically adjusted to increases in the cost-of-living, within what then seemed the generous ceiling of 2 per cent a year escalation. This merely extended to the flat rate old-age security pension a provision that had already been included for the pensions to be provided under CPP, but its logic had not prevented it from being strongly resisted.

A resolution to establish the joint Senate-House of Commons committee on the pension plan was passed on 16 November. It met for nearly three months, holding fifty-one sittings and hearing well over a hundred witnesses. Judy LaMarsh started it with an excellent outline of the plan and her parliamentary secretary, John Munro, did a fine job of organizing the participation of the Liberal members. I had my first, intensive experience of parliamentary committee work. The heroes were the officials led by Joe Willard. They were far more impressive than any of the outside experts on pensions. The Department of Finance contributed a helpful paper on the economics of public pensions. Criticisms from the insurance industry fell remarkably flat, and were more than offset by the witnesses who spoke in favour of the plan. Ontario was the only province to send its officials as witnesses, and they were clearly under instruction to present only muted criticism.

At first the Conservatives on the committee, led by Senator McCutcheon, seemed disposed to support criticisms on the lines of the insurance industry, but as the hearings proceeded that attitude faded. It disappeared completely when Premier Robarts at last showed his hand. He played fair. He watched how the committee discussion proceeded, and when that was clear he did not wait to the end. In mid-January he made it publicly clear that Ontario would accept the CPP. Mr Robarts never received as much praise as he deserved for his willingness to put the Canadian national interest first. But, large-minded as he was, his course would have been much more difficult, and perhaps would not have been possible, if he had not been helped by Mr Pearson's diplomatic persuasiveness, reflecting as it did the force of a concern for national unity that the two men shared. Without that quality, in them and in Jean Lesage, a national pension plan for Canadians would not have been established.

As it was, the final stages of the consideration of the plan were a strange experience for those of us who had been long involved with it. We were no longer defending it against the storm from the right, the charge that it was a Trojan horse to destroy the Canadian economy. In January and February 1965 we had to shift to a different stance: we had to defend the pension plan not against denunciations of its radicalism but against the complaints, of Conservative MPs among others, that it did not go far enough.

The parliamentary committee reported the Bill with only a few minor, and entirely acceptable, amendments but also one general recommendation: that the government consider further measures to help people who, because they were or soon would be retired, would not benefit from the CPP.

The later stages of the committee proceedings had made it clear that this criticism would be pressed. It united the NDP and Mr Robarts, and with him most of the Conservatives. Liberal backbenchers were in sympathy with them. A week before the committee reported, therefore, I was writing memoranda urging that the government should not wait to be pressed to a change during the parliamentary debate, but should decide in advance on the modest measure that would be a reasonable response to the criticism. The legislation already provided that the age at which the old-age security pension could be taken would be progressively reduced, during the period 1966 to 1970, from seventy to sixty-five; but if it was begun before seventy, the amount of the pension would be not the age-seventy pension (then $75) but its actuarial equivalent from the earlier starting age. The simple, and not very expensive, way to do more for people in their sixties, who would get little or nothing from the CPP, was to drop the actuarial adjustment and make the full $75 (in future escalated to the cost-of-living) payable from age sixty-five.

The Prime Minister and Walter Gordon agreed, and there was little resistance. We had the necessary resolution ready for the Prime Minister to move on 17 February, when the committee's report was presented. The subsequent discussion provided the opportunity for the Prime Minister also to foreshadow the next measure on which we were working to ameliorate poverty – the Canada Assistance Plan, which will be described later.

For the pension plan, it was all over but the shouting. The legislation was smoothly through the House before the end of March. I remained involved in the writing of the pamphlets explaining the plan to its beneficiaries, and in the summer Judy LaMarsh gave a typically magnificent party for the officials of the Task Force who had laboured so hard and well. One of its wits had written the "Task Force Blues," which began:

In the beginning was the Word
And the Word was Kent,

But nobody knew
Quite what it meant.

That had turned out to be all too true, but the "Blues" ended triumphantly:

The CPP is up in the air.
Let others turn to medicare.

We soon did.

23   *The Federal State*

The changed relationship of Ottawa and the provinces was the sharpest transformation in the public business of Canada during the Pearson period. Opinions differed at the time, and historical assessments will no doubt vary also, as to how far the federal government was simply dragged unwillingly along, by forces it could not or would not resist, and how far it was a creative agent of the change. Certainly there were elements of both roles. The first was in part unavoidable. After nearly twenty years of comparative centralization, the established habits and interests of many officials and politicians were too strong to be swept immediately aside by writs from the East Block; even the Prime Minister's wish could be father to only a gradual change in detailed action.

Nevertheless, Mr Pearson's will for change, for adoption of the attitudes of co-operative federalism as I described it earlier, was strong and, for the most part, consistent. In April 1964, he had to use all his power of leadership, as well as his diplomatic skills, to get his Cabinet to anything near wholehearted acceptance of the agreement with Quebec. Thereafter, while it would be an exaggeration to say that the centralist mould was shattered, it was sufficiently weakened to be increasingly pushed aside. This chapter is about some of the results.

One was to foster the image of Pearsonian weakness, of the diplomatic compromiser endangering the nation by surrendering rightful federal power to the demands of Quebec. Critics of the Diefenbaker temperament had no other line to take; to the extent that the fake image stuck, it was a penalty of change that had to be incurred. It was none the less galling, particularly since the new federalism was in fact far from an easy option. A good deal of effort was required, on two fronts. Negotiations with the provinces became more extensive, and they were properly tough-minded on both sides; and much had to be done in Ottawa to get the principles of the new federalism understood, accepted and acted on with some regularity.

The true criticism of the Pearson government's performance in the changing environment of federal-provincial relations is not that it was weak but that it was not far-sighted. The problems of the time were reasonably well dealt with. As I shall argue later, however, the government did not move far towards the more fundamental structural changes that the new federalism required.

In extenuation, it may be said that the immediate preoccupations were intense. The resistance to be overcome was not only bureaucratic inertia. It was rooted also in economic ideology. In Ottawa it was well understood that the proud progress of the postwar Canadian economy reflected the wisdom of its central management, and a key element in that wisdom was the determined devotion of the managers to the general good, measured by the gross *national* product. The criterion of economic efficiency was essentially anti-provincial, in the sense that the object of national policy was seen as maximum development wherever in Canada it occurred. To worry about locations was small-minded interference with beneficent progress. It was up to people not to champion local interests but to respond to the glorious opportunities open to them somewhere in Canada. The necessary mobility was seen in moral terms, as the stern pioneer virtue still proper to Canadians.

This was the conventional wisdom deeply rooted in Ottawa and shared by most of the business community, though with reservations in areas where opportunities were not glorious. It was incompatible with a co-operative federalism embracing provinces with such disparate economies as those of Newfoundland and Prince Edward Island at one extreme, Ontario and British Columbia at the other. The federal government cannot be co-operative with the provinces unless it shares the concern that each must have for its own economy. National policy cannot ignore those concerns any more than it can be dominated by them. The problem is to strike a balance among provincial interests that also serves the general interest. The way in which this is done cannot be allowed to subtract much from the strength of the national economy as a whole, but nor can we expect that it will always coincide perfectly with the maximum economic efficiency that might be achieved if it were the only criterion that mattered to people.

What these generalities mean for the practice of government was first brought home intimately to me in a fight with Air Canada, or TCA as it then was. In its early days the national airline was naturally headquartered at the centre of the country, in Winnipeg. As flight ranges increased, and international traffic developed, there was an equally natural shift eastwards. Of most industrial significance was the establishment in Montreal of facilities for the maintenance and overhaul of new aircraft. Work at Winnipeg was reduced to the Viscounts, the turbo-prop aircraft then used in short-haul services. Employment at "the base," as it was generally known as a hangover from the war, had been at a peak of over 1300 in the late fifties. By the end of 1961 it was down to a little under a thousand, and in 1962 TCA announced that the base would be phased out completely by 1966. In the alleged interests of efficiency, all the work would be centralized in Montreal. In opposition at the time of the announcement, we said that no such decision should be made until government had formulated two national policies – for the aviation industry specifically, and for regional industrial development including manpower policy in face of job displacements. The Diefenbaker government, however, did nothing about the problem; we inherited it.

The removal of a thousand skilled jobs would be a desperately severe weakening of Winnipeg's thin industrial base. There was much agitation in the community; the Conservative government of Manitoba was cautious while Diefenbaker was in office, but assumed leadership of the agitation when there were Liberals in Ottawa to be pressured. The federal reflex, conditioned by long habit, was to resent and dismiss this: TCA was a federal Crown corporation, its management was responsible for running the airline as it thought most efficient, and that was none of Premier Roblin's business. The Pearson attitude was different. My first memo on the subject stated the obvious, but in Ottawa then heretical, principle: "in a matter of such importance to a province, the spirit of cooperative federalism means that we should treat the provincial government as adult and responsible, and be prepared to share the problem with them."

TCA's defence against its critics was that it was taking nothing from Winnipeg that would not soon be lost anyway: it would be shifting to an all-jet fleet; the Viscounts would go, and the new, smaller jets could best be serviced in Montreal in conjunction with the existing ones. There were economies in preparing the way by promptly shifting the diminishing Viscount work there.

Our opportunity to deal with the problem therefore came in the fall of 1963, when TCA brought forward its plans to purchase new aircraft. The Cabinet had no power to issue directives to TCA about its operations, but capital budgets, involving borrowing guaranteed by the government, required approval.

The corporation had considered five possible aircraft. One was the French Caravelle, and there was strong lobbying on its behalf from Quebec. Another candidate was a British aircraft for which some of the component manufacturing would, happily, be done in Winnipeg. TCA, however, had decided that its needs would best be met by the American DC9. Despite the lobbying, there was no disposition in Ottawa to challenge the corporation's view on so crucial an issue of airline management. Nevertheless, I read the documents presenting its case with fascination. The purpose of the DC9s was not to replace the Viscounts. It was partly to accommodate the projected growth in traffic and partly to replace the larger and less satisfactory turbo-props, the Vanguards – which were serviced in Montreal anyway. The Viscount fleet was to be almost unchanged over the ten-year planning period projected in the documentation. There were forty Viscounts in service in 1963 and in 1973 there would still be thirty-four.

The conclusion of the memorandum in which I summarized TCA's documentation for the Prime Minister was "we should make a deal." We should approve the capital budget for the DC9s but not any expenditures on enlarging the Montreal overhaul facilities to accommodate Viscounts. Instead we should require TCA to change its intentions regarding Winnipeg; it should commit itself to maintaining the facilities there for as long as there was a significant Viscount fleet to be serviced. This would not perpetuate the TCA operation in Winnipeg indefinitely, but in face of an unavoidable industrial shift it would provide what a regionally sensitive federal policy reasonably should: a substantial period during which there would be fair opportunity to attract substitute activities. In fact, Boeing took advantage of the availability of experienced workers to establish a plant in Winnipeg.

The Department of Transport, whose officials worked closely with TCA management, did not like the proposed compromise. The Minister, George McIlraith, was for approving exactly what TCA wanted, and apparently had no compunction about telling the corporation where the resistance came from. The tough President of TCA, Gordon McGregor, henceforth regarded me as his sworn enemy. The Prime Minister and Cabinet, however, were happy with the deal and, though McGregor wriggled as hard as he could, it was implemented. In the Cabinet shuffle of early 1964 McIlraith, as noted earlier, was fortunately moved from Transport in favour of Jack Pickersgill.

The Roblin government in Manitoba co-operated with us in clarifying and explaining the arrangement. While it could not formally withdraw from the local demand for an assurance of complete permanence of TCA operation in Winnipeg, for all practical purposes it accepted the compromise.

The TCA incident was an early example of the practical application of co-operative federalism. It was some time before we formalized the underlying principle, by requiring that no proposal could come before Cabinet without discussion, in a section of the document, of its implications for federal-provincial relations. That was a considerable innovation which helped gradually to break the entrenched Ottawa attitudes of centralization.

An easier change to make effective, though more conspicuous because it required legislation, was the provision for provinces to receive financial compensation if they wished to opt out of established shared-cost programs. This had been a commitment of the election platform. Though Quebec alone had a practical interest in it, we regarded the principle as essential to good federal-provincial relations and, therefore, a prerequisite for Ottawa's retention, in the new circumstances, of an effective power of initiative in developing new shared-cost programs.

The practical details, though complex, were worked out harmoniously with the provinces. Quebec agreed to remove what would otherwise have been the political heat of the matter by giving an explicit undertaking, as part of the April 1964 settlement, that it would for a transitional period maintain the programs exactly as they were and had no intention that later changes, if any, would involve dismantling the programs.

"Established programs financing" has since been given a bad name, as a result of the legislation of the Trudeau government. It should therefore be emphasized that what was proposed in 1964, and actually legislated in 1965, was of an entirely different nature. It was in no way a mechanism, as the subsequent legislation has turned out to be, for enabling Ottawa and the provinces to squabble over who is to blame for restrictions on programs for health and post-secondary education. The Pearson legislation was simply and solely a matter of giving the provinces the choice either to take federal grants for part of the cost of certain provincial programs or, alternatively, to levy their own taxes, with federal tax rebated commensurately, and with equalization payments adjusted so that the net financial result was the same as the grants provided. There was no change in the nature or the scale of the programs.

The "option" therefore could be regarded, and by some people was dismissed, as a mere formality. A federation, however, rests on getting its formalities right. Whether it does more than rest, whether it works well, depends on the real intent of co-operation. For that reason generalities, though they can always be sneered at as mere words and sometimes are, nevertheless have at times an essential significance in the relations among governments. There was one sentence of that kind in the detailed memorandum, on the pension plan and the rest, negotiated in April 1964 and approved by both federal and Quebec cabinets. It was: "The government of Quebec has expressed its firm belief that the wishes of all Canadians can best be fulfilled within a federal structure, and its resolute determination that the rights of the provinces should be exercised not to the disruption but to the enhancement of the unity of Canada." The Lesage government was faithful to that intent on, I think, all but one significant issue.

The exception was its change of mind on the amendment of the constitution. In September 1964 there was a federal-provincial conference in Charlottetown, mainly devoted to commemorating the centenary of the meeting there on Confederation. The nostalgia of the occasion produced unanimous agreement that it was urgent to "patriate" the constitution in the sense of providing for its amendment in Canada, thereby avoiding the humiliating anomaly that, although the centenary of Confederation itself was close, the only way to make any change in substantial parts of our constitution, and notably the distribution of powers between the federal and provincial governments, was to go cap-in-hand, in a formal sense, to the Parliament of the United Kingdom to request amendment of its British North America Act.

In 1961 Davie Fulton, Minister of Justice and by far the brightest intellect of the Diefenbaker Cabinet, had negotiated with the provinces a formula for constitutional amendment. It had not been regarded as completely satisfactory, however, and the Diefenbaker government had done nothing more about the matter. At Charlottetown there was unanimous agreement to proceed quickly to develop an amending formula "based on" the 1961 draft. The Minister of Justice and attorneys-general of the provinces were instructed to prepare proposals for the consideration of a full federal-provincial conference to be held only six weeks later.

The principal representatives of the federal government in the ensuing negotiations were Guy Favreau and Gordon Robertson. I was no constitutional lawyer but, because Guy had grown comfortable with me as the English draftsman of thoughts that for him were first formulated in French, I was also a participant in what seemed at the time to be a model exercise in the spirit of co-operative federalism. There was a lot of hard discussion but no deep controversy as the road to unanimous agreement about what came to be known as the Fulton-Favreau formula. In effect, the principles of the 1961 proposal were reaffirmed but some points that had then been left murky were satisfactorily clarified. There was a precise identification of areas of the constitution that could be amended by the federal authority; by a province alone; by the federal authority with the concurrence of at least two-thirds of the provinces having at least 50 per cent of the population of Canada; and – for some of the most fundamental provisions – only by unanimous consent of the federal and all provincial authorities. In order to lessen the rigidity that can be the price of any federal constitution, there was provision that provinces so wishing could delegate the exercise of their authority to legislate on certain matters to the federal Parliament, and conversely that Parliament could delegate its authority, for a specific item of legislation, to a minimum of four provinces.

This Fulton-Favreau formula was approved at the full federal-provincial conference by all the First Ministers. Most of us were greatly elated. It seemed that at last, and before we celebrated a hundred years of Confederation, we would have a fully Canadian, "patriated" constitution. A substantial "white paper," detailing and explaining the proposed constitution, was produced; the government even undertook the unusual step of making some special, hard-cover copies. Mine came with a letter from the Prime Minister expressing appreciation of an invaluable contribution to "this achievement." There proved, however, to be no achievement.

The proposal was criticized in English Canada by a number of constitutional experts, the most notable being the then professor of law Bora Laskin. Their case was that the formula was too restrictive of major amendments and therefore would have the effect of entrenching what the academics regarded as excessive powers in the provinces. The NDP took up this position, but it did not much concern us. It encouraged nine provinces to think that they had got a good deal and to stick to it. We knew that, whatever the professors might wish, the Fulton-Favreau formula provided as much flexibility as the provinces would agree to for the foreseeable future. The amendment procedures were as big an advance as possible from the unanimity requirement, for significant amendments, that had by convention become the effective procedure for changing the BNA Act in Britain.

This view was confirmed by the quite different reaction in Quebec. Lesage was bitterly attacked for conceding too much. Some criticized him for giving away Quebec's traditional "right" to veto virtually everything. Some criticized him for accepting a formula that would give other provinces power to prevent changes that Quebec might want. Understandably, in the mood of the time, Lesage buckled under the pressure. Quebec withdrew its agreement and the Fulton-Favreau formula was dead. The issue of constitutional amendment and patriation was submerged under the mounting wave of separatist sentiment in Quebec.

Whether Jean Lesage had any alternative, whether he could have toughed it out and got the constitutional change through the Assembly without great and permanent damage to the provincial Liberal party, may be doubted. Though at the time I wished he would try, subsequent events make me think that he was caught by pressures too strong for him to overcome. But it was sad. If the Fulton-Favreau formula had been adopted, Canada and Quebec would subsequently have been spared the contortions and confrontations of Mr Trudeau's drive for constitutional change in the early eighties, which played such havoc with the other business of the nation and ended in the isolation of Quebec, as well as an amending formula worse, I think, than the Fulton-Favreau one. Happily, the isolation has been ended if the 1987 "accord" holds, but at the price of a new formula that makes some provisions of the constitution yet more difficult to amend.

We had more success on another major federal-provincial issue. In the exercise of its responsibility for external affairs the federal government often deals with matters of great concern to the provinces. Negotiations on bilateral free trade with the United States have recently provided a conspicuous example. In the early 1960s it was painfully accurate to say that the federal government's attention to the effects of foreign policy on provincial responsibilities had often been brusque or even non-existent. On the other side of the coin, as provincial government policies became more positive, there was a growing tendency to express them in international dealings. Quebec, in particular, began to deal directly with France and other Francophone countries on arrangements related to education and culture. President de Gaulle openly encouraged a direct France-Quebec relationship ignoring Ottawa. With this encouragement, some Quebec ministers and officials began to talk as if Quebec had sovereign power to make international agreements on matters within provincial jurisdiction.

The scope for conflict and confusion was painfully apparent, and on Lesage's initiative we held a meeting at the Queen Elizabeth Hotel in Montreal on the weekend of 8 and 9 May 1965, to try to contain the problem. The federal party consisted of the Prime Minister, Walter Gordon, Guy Favreau, Gordon Robertson, myself, and one or two others. The aim was to reach an understanding on procedures that would minimize the danger of conflict. A province wishing to make an international agreement, on a matter within its jurisdiction, would give advance information to Ottawa and submit the text, for concurrence as to its foreign policy aspects, before signature. Unless the agreement was of the nature of a contract binding under private law, either Canada or the foreign government could require that it be sanctioned by a diplomatic exchange of notes between them.

This was a sensible procedural understanding that preserved the proprieties of international negotiation and proved to be successful in reducing the potential for federal-provincial conflict.

Quebec was, of course, the province most concerned to exercise its jurisdiction to the full and to resist any federal intrusions, real or imagined. By the mid-sixties, however, Ontario was increasingly its companion. There were, I think, two factors. One was the strong concern of

Premier Robarts that Quebec should not be isolated. The other, even more important, was the increasing size and sophistication of the Ontario bureaucracy; its public servants and ministers wanted and felt able to do things their way, to take initiatives that had previously been left to Ottawa.

It was this development, I think, that stimulated Claude Morin several times to broach to me a speculation about the root cause of the problems on which we had to negotiate. Was it that Quebec was inherently different from the other provinces? Or was it, to a greater extent, simply that the ten provinces were so disparate in size? Larger provinces inevitably wanted to do things that smaller provinces were content to leave to Ottawa. Though later, as a Minister in the Levesque government, Morin was one of the strongest, and in the end most bitter, of separatists, in 1964–5 he was still looking for ways in which the kind of Quebec he wanted could implement its social reforms and economic planning within the context of a federal Canada. Would it not be very much easier for federal-provincial relations to operate on a consistent pattern if there were, say, five provinces instead of ten – an Atlantic province, Quebec, Ontario, a Prairie province, and BC (with the Yukon incorporated)?

I had to agree that the division of powers that the Fathers of Confederation and the judicial interpretations of the British Law Lords had provided to us would lend itself far better to an effective system of government if the provinces were more equal. I also had to point out, however, that while the cultural differences between, say, Nova Scotia and New Brunswick seem small beside those between English and French Canada, they are none the less too great for political union in the foreseeable future. Moreover, the fact of geography was that evening up the size of the provinces would not lessen the economic disparity which meant that one Atlantic province, just as much as four, would require Ottawa to do far more for it than for the rest of Canada. Nor would such a change lessen the need to recognize the mingling of responsibilities and concerns which meant that federalism could work only by building new mechanisms of co-operation between federal and provincial governments. Our success in that would be the chief determinant of Confederations's future. Morin lost trust in such co-operation, but not during the Pearson period.

While the political criticism of co-operative federalism, from some friends as well as foes, was that we were surrendering federal "rights" to the provinces, my fear was that we were not moving fast enough to remake the working of Confederation. A sympathetic, but I think fair, assessment was given by Bill Wilson, one of the ablest members of the parliamentary press gallery, in a letter he wrote to me on 28 October, 1964. He was commenting on a speech that Mr Pearson had made the night before to the Association of Universities and Colleges of Canada. I had taken advantage of the nature of the audience to write more analytically than was usually appropriate about the federal concern in education (on which more will be said later) in the context of co-operative federalism. Wilson emphasized the definition of this, in terms of the interplay between areas of constitutional jurisdiction and the legitimate concerns of each level of government with the activities of the other, and commented: "if this concept ... can spread, the functioning of the full system of government will come closer and closer to meeting the true needs of the country. A great deal, of course, has already been achieved towards this, and rather rapidly. We are not today in the Canada of even a year ago. The achievement in fact *is* great." He went on, however, to point to the gravity and danger of the problems and to suggest that more progress depended on a reversal of the government's poor parliamentary performance.

In retrospect it seems to me that there were two major deficiencies in our handling of the great transition in federalism. One was in the building of mechanisms for co-operation. The extent of co-operation increased greatly, but by accretion. Much of the change was at the level of officials, not politicians; it was gradual and largely inconspicuous, often it seemed almost shamefaced. We should have moved openly and dramatically to propose wholly new arrangements for co-operation in such major areas as budgetary and monetary policies and in economic policies involving, particularly, manpower adjustment, education, and training. The short-term results might have been no more, or even less, than was achieved by inconspicuous gradualism, but the psychological advantage of far-reaching and imaginative proposals would, I think, have done more good within a few years and thereby lessened the perils that grew so great in the later seventies.

The second failure was that we did not foresee how greatly the change in federalism would be distorted by Canada's lack of the direct representation of regional interests as such that is provided in other federal constitutions. Our Senate is irrelevant in this respect because it is not elected and appointment to it is almost entirely a political reward that, with few exceptions, marks the neutering of the recipient as a legitimate spokesperson. Members of the House of Commons are elected to support or oppose a government as a whole. Their role in representing local or regional interests is rightly subordinated to party loyalty. The absence of elected senators means that there is no mechanism, within the federal government structure itself, for representing regional interests in national policy. The vacuum has necessarily been filled, but from outside. Provincial premiers have increasingly assumed the role of speaking for their provinces on issues in federal jurisdiction. They are not elected for that purpose. They are elected on provincial issues and live with caucuses that are generally narrow, if not parochial, in their concerns. They lead party organizations that are, in most cases, closely linked to either the government or the opposition in Ottawa. Their emergence as the principal spokesmen of their provinces on national issues, while inevitable in the absence of an elected Senate, has no legitimacy. It accentuated the confrontations of the seventies and early eighties. It has inhibited the growth of genuinely co-operative mechanisms across federal and provincial jurisdictions.

I do not suggest that the Pearson government could realistically have added the constitutional reform of an elected Senate to its long agenda. The problem did not become acute until later. But we could have foreseen its emergence. Our concern for co-operative federalism should have led us to begin to talk about the need for an elected Senate. If we had done so, the consideration given to it in the eightiess, or even the seventies, might have been more serious and productive.

There were, however, extenuating circumstances, and it would be dishonest to end this chapter on an adverse note. The Pearson government had imperfect foresight, but few governments have been more in the van of the opinion of their times than it was in coping with a major change in the nature of federalism.

24 *Cabinet Shuffles*

The Quebec settlement of April 1964 was the main, but not the only, reason why the government at that time regained some confidence, though temporarily so as it turned out. The economy seemed to be in good shape, employment was improving, and Walter Gordon's second budget, in March, was optimistic in tone and non-controversial in character. Also, earlier in the year, the Cabinet had been somewhat strengthened.

This was in accordance with the intention that Mr Pearson had indicated at the beginning. During 1963 it had become increasingly clear that some weaknesses at least must be corrected. As Christmas approached we talked about it at some length and the Prime Minister invited me to set out my suggestions in detail. Shuffling a Cabinet on paper is as complex as any game. Each move opens up several options, which in turn create multiple options. There are soon scores of possible combinations, each one of which must make sense in terms not only of the suitability of people to portfolios, but also of many balances – provincial, ethnic, ideological, religious.

My initial game plan was based on the departure of five ministers. Ross Macdonald, the gentlemanly leader of the government in the Senate, wanted to retire. Azellus Denis, a veteran Montreal member of the old school, was clearly ripe for the Senate. Lionel Chevrier was a man of great charm but the other capacities that had brought him political promotion did not make him either a strong Minister of Justice or an appropriate lieutenant for relations with the Quebec of the 1960s. He seemed happy enough to go to London as High Commissioner. I urged also that Messrs Benidickson and MacNaught should be retired from the Cabinet, but in the end the Prime Minister did not agree and my more radical combinations, which would have produced a net reduction of three in the number of ministers, were ruled out.

I was more successful with some of the other recommendations. Jack Pickersgill had great skills, but he was too abrasive to be the leader of the government in a House of Commons as volatile as we had to deal with. His energies would be better directed to a major administrative portfolio; several possibilities were suggested, Transport chosen. That suited Jack's interests, and it enabled George McIlraith to be moved from a portfolio to which he had proved to be ill-suited. Another talent not being properly used was that of Maurice Lamontagne, in the amorphous role of President of the Council. The Prime Minister had the excellent idea of making him Secretary of State, in place of Jack Pickersgill, and attaching to that portfolio the various agencies of a cultural nature. In that capacity Maurice served the country well for nearly two years.

It would be tiresome after this interval to retrace, even if I could remember, all the permutations that were considered through late December and early January. It was an intriguing experience but I had not anticipated either how long it would take or how awkward would be the concluding tasks. The Prime Minister was committed to a trip to Paris in mid-January, but rumours of Cabinet changes became rife, and he decided that they must be ready to announce on his return. He had time, before he left, to talk to the more senior ministers and especially those who would be pleased with the changes. It became my task to discuss their fates with some of the others.

Jack Nicholson had been appointed to the Cabinet in April as Minister of Forestry, a portfolio that did less than justice to his administrative capabilities. He was legitimately hoping for promotion. I had to tell him that his move would be to Postmaster General, making all I could of the important challenge of clearing up the mess there. Fortunately he was a decent man, and our relations were not soured. I also had to tell René

Tremblay, whose interests were in economic policy, that his portfolio would be Citizenship and Immigration. A more pleasant task was to telephone Maurice Sauvé, who was vacationing, to convey the invitation to join the Cabinet as Minister of Forestry, to which Rural Development was to be added. That meant, however, bearing the initial brunt of negotiating, with the tough-minded Harry Hays, the transfer to the new Minister of some bits of his Agriculture department.

The intention when the government came to office had been to overcome a historic problem by having Ministers for western and for eastern agriculture. That was not a good idea, and certainly it would not work unless the personalities were highly compatible. A little experience of Harry Hays as the incumbent minister had made it plain that there would not be room for another, sharing responsibilities in one department. My suggested solution was a Department of Land Development, with responsibility for ARDA, PFRA (prairie farm rehabilitation), farm credit and other programs that needed extension. What emerged, as Forestry and Rural Development, was somewhat less.

The most important of the changes was the promotion of Guy Favreau to Minister of Justice. He then enjoyed the respect and regard that he merited. Administratively, the portfolio was less demanding than Citizenship and Immigration had proved to be for a man of his temperament. He undoubtedly had the talent to be a great Minister of Justice. Unfortunately, he was also appointed government leader in the Commons, in succession to Pickersgill. My first choice for that role had been Allan MacEachen, second Mitchell Sharp. The Prime Minister said that he did propose it to Allan, who rejected the double workload. Guy, less worldly wise, accepted.

John Connolly's was the inevitable appointment as government leader in the Senate. I was fully in agreement with it, but argued that ideologically it was a sufficiently right-wing move to balance the Sauvé appointment. Mr Pearson did not agree. He felt that the departure of Chevrier and Denis required an appointment to please the older school of federal politicians from Quebec. Yvon Dupuis, though young in years, fitted the bill in political style. He was appointed a Minister without Portfolio – briefly, as it turned out. Even that was not considered enough to offset Sauvé. Guy Rouleau was appointed a parliamentary secretary to the Prime Minister, which also proved to be unfortunate.

The reorganization of January 1964 involved, however, a more lasting error. I say this with hindsight wisdom. At the time, I was a strong advocate of the appointment of George McIlraith as President of the Privy Council, with the intention that he would "if Parliament approves the necessary legislation, become President of the Treasury Board." The error was not in the person. Greatly as I had quarrelled with him as

Minister of Transport – notably, as I mentioned earlier, about what was then TCA – he had talents that suited him to Treasury Board. Our mistake was in the structure.

The Glassco Royal Commission had in 1962 recommended major changes in the management of the public service. The Diefenbaker government, in this as in so many matters, had not got around to taking any action on the report. There were strong reasons to do so. The central recommendation concerned the Treasury Board. Technically a committee of the Cabinet, this had hitherto been presided over by the Minister of Finance and its staff was a small division within his department. Glassco recommended that Treasury Board should have a separate Minister, with a staff located in the Privy Council Office instead of the Finance department, and that in addition to its supervision of departmental budgets and control of major expenditures it should be given broad responsibilities for the management of the public service. A preliminary proposal to implement this was brought forward as early as August 1963. Its incompleteness bothered me. In a memorandum to the Prime Minister I urged that the organizational decision not be made until ministers had reviewed, understood, and favoured the considerable changes in departmental management without which the structural change would be ineffective.

The review was made, over a period of some months, and another issue was injected. Glassco by implication proposed greatly to strengthen Privy Council Office as a central agency. Some of us feared that the accretion of management responsibilities would weaken it in its crucial role as the co-ordinating agency on the Prime Minister's behalf. Walter Gordon, as Minister of Finance, fully agreed with Glassco that his direct responsibility for Treasury Board should be transferred to a separate Minister. But he and his department argued that – as in Britain – the connection with Finance should not be broken. The enlarged Treasury Board organization should remain associated with the Finance department, not transferred to PCO.

In retrospect, I have no doubt that this would have been the best course. The Minister of Finance's broad responsibility for economic policy should carry with it a general oversight not merely of the total of expenditures but of their distribution among the principal programs of government. But a good many ministers preferred to stick with Glassco, in some cases no doubt from a wish to contain Walter's influence. The solution eventually adopted was a "neither one thing nor the other" compromise: the new Treasury Board would be connected neither with PCO nor with Finance, but would instead be an additional, separate central agency within the governmental structure. To my subsequent regret, I at the time supported this course, a compromise between the forces in play but organizationally a move to something very different both from what had been and from the proposed reform.

At first, with the urbane George Davidson as Secretary of the Board, the new organization promised quite well. He soon moved, however, to the presidency of the CBC and was succeeded by Simon Reisman: a man of strong talents but, as the perceptive Pearson had commented to me earlier, the most dedicated and aggressive empire-builder of all the bureaucrats of the time. The separate Treasury Board accumulated a massive staff. Ministers and their departmental officials, faced with such a development, are never supine. They devised new divisions to deal with Treasury Board's aggression against their programming and managerial functions. Treasury Board, intent on its objectives, added more staff to deal with the departments. What had been intended by Glassco as a great improvement in the effectiveness of public management became a major cause of a vast increase in work-making work, in the unconstructive pushing to and fro of ever thicker piles of paper, reviewed in ever larger and more numerous meetings. This was a significant factor in the atrophy of government decision-making that marked the Trudeau era.

No doubt these side-effects would not have been entirely avoided if Treasury Board had been associated with either PCO or Finance. I still think, despite Glassco's recommendation, that association with PCO would have been an error. PCO subsequently became overly powerful anyway, and the Treasury Board connection would have made it worse. But association with Finance would have been logical and workable, and might have avoided the worst of the ill effects that resulted from the Board as an additional central agency. That set the pattern for the 1970s inflation of the Ottawa bureaucracy. In the Pearson period, however, the beginnings of this development were no more than the cloud no bigger than a man's hand that presaged the cumulus to come.

The Prime Minister's announcement of the January 1964 reorganization included a statement about Cabinet committees:

> In addition to the changes in departmental organization and Ministerial responsibilities, there will be a continuing reorganization of the internal work of the Cabinet. Since September, the use of Cabinet committees has been developed to a greater extent than in the past. This development will now be carried farther in order ... to obtain, under the Prime Minister's leadership, thorough consideration of policies, co-ordination of government action, and timely decisions, in a manner consistent with ministerial and cabinet responsibility.

The nine standing committees were listed, together with the establishment in PCO of a small unit responsible for general liaison arrangements with the provinces. This would report to the Prime Minister, who would also oversee the operation of the Cabinet committee system. The announcement concluded by noting that I was "responsible for assisting the Prime Minister in this co-ordination and in the direction of federal-provincial liaison arrangements."

With the January 1964 operation, the Prime Minister had understandably had his fill of large Cabinet shuffles. They are time-consuming and emotionally exhausting to a degree that I, at least, would not have imagined without experiencing them. Until December 1965, when virtually a new administration was created in the aftermath of the failed general election, the further changes in the Pearson Cabinet were only those that circumstances necessitated. In March 1964 the wise and good-natured Jack Garland died. He was succeeded as Minister of National Revenue by Ben Benson. In October 1964 – too late, unfortunately – Guy Favreau was relieved from the House leadership by George McIlraith. On 22 January, 1965, Dupuis left the Cabinet. He was under threat of prosecution, but reluctant to resign. It was one of our most dramatic days, particularly for Maurice Lamontagne, who was in this case the intermediary, and for the PCO officer who had to drive over icy Laurentian roads to collect the resignation letter that had been dictated over the telephone.

By this time I was urging another major reconstruction. The Prime Minister rejected it. In February, however, Jean-Paul Deschatelets resigned, by his own wish, and in the summer came the changes consequent on the Dorion report's criticism of Guy Favreau's handling of the Rivard affair (on which more must be said later). At that time Benidickson was called to the Senate and the unfortunate René Tremblay – a victim, as later parts of the story will show, of circumstances – was shuffled down to the Post Office. The net results included promotions for Lucien Cardin and, to my great relief, Jack Nicholson. Léo Cadieux, Larry Pennell, and Jean-Luc Pepin (as a Minister without Portfolio) were brought into the Cabinet.

None of this made much difference. I went on urging more thorough changes in organization and personnel. The Prime Minister preferred to soldier on with what he had, as far as possible.

25 The World Outside

Almost everyone, I suppose, leaves public service with regrets about the things he or she hoped to do and did not. My disappointments were greatest in the field of external affairs and particularly of development in the Third World. I had expected that, working with Mike Pearson, I would have such involvements. In practice the difficulties of domestic politics compelled him to leave external affairs almost entirely in the safe hands of Paul Martin. They were safe in two senses: competent and cautious.

Paul as a Minister in the Pearson government was very different from the hard-fighting reformer that he had been as Minister of National Health and Welfare in the St Laurent government. While entirely loyal to Pearson, he hoped to succeed him. And since the perception in Ottawa was that Pearson got into trouble through rashness, it was natural to think that the party would be looking for a safer man next time. What was thereby illustrated, of course, was the frequent difference between the way Ottawa sees Ottawa and the way it looks from outside. What the public perceived was the greyness of the Pearson period; what the Liberal party, and subsequently the electorate, turned to was the greater adventurousness that Trudeau seemed to embody.

Paul, however, in 1963-8 chose the role of man of caution. Our external policy was therefore sensible but undistinguished. We took part in some useful endeavours, we got on well with our friends and were civil to others. Canada's role in the world was raised from what it had been in the Diefenbaker years. But one cannot say much more. We took few constructive initiatives, either for lessening current tensions or for long-term economic improvement.

As always for Canada, our bilateral relationships with the United States took most attention. They began with the friendly meeting of President Kennedy and the new Prime Minister of Canada at Hyannis Port on 10-11 May. Appropriately for the two men, one of the first generalizations in their communiqué set the bilateral relationship in the context of relations within the Atlantic community as a whole. And, while much was naturally made of the points of agreement, it was equally appropriate that the communiqué recognized matters, such as the extension of Canada's fishing zone from three to twelve miles, on which the two countries could disagree without quarrelling.

In a speech a few weeks later, at Notre Dame University, Mr Pearson discussed Canada's relationship with the United States in the same spirit as that of the Hyannis Port communiqué. Materially, it involves the greatest trade exchange between any two countries, but its importance is far wider than the mutual economic advantage. It is of the utmost importance to the world that the Canada-US relationship should be an example of how two free and independent countries can work together without the smaller having to sacrifice anything of its true identify or its real sovereignty. I am not sure how precisely Mr Pearson followed my notes for the speech, but I am sure that they coincided with his viewpoint. I argued that "Canada is the world's hostage of American good intentions." The world sees Canada as a country very like the United States; if the Americans could not get on well with Canada, with whom could they get on well? Good relations are a primary interest of Canada, because of economic interdependence, but they are also a primary interest of the United States in its international role. Mike saw that as our bargaining weapon, powerful provided we use it with discretion. It remains so, but its effectiveness varies with the degree of understanding and concern of both countries for broader international relationships.

Nevertheless, the first crisis in external affairs that the Pearson government had to face underlined the peculiar closeness of Canada-US entanglements and the consequent risk that US policy may do unintended economic damage to Canada. On 18 July 1963, President Kennedy announced an "interest equalization tax" on foreign borrowing in the United States, designed to stem the amount of such borrowing by increasing its cost. Canadian provinces and municipalities, as well as companies, were among such borrowers. The tax threatened to be highly disruptive of the Canadian capital market, closely integrated with that of the United States. Since the borrowings in effect financed a deficit with the United States in Canadian current transactions, the tax threatened another forced devaluation of the Canadian dollar. Walter Gordon moved quickly. Officials of the Bank of Canada and the Finance Department went immediately to Washington, and by 21 July (a Sunday) the US government had agreed virtually to exempt Canada from the tax. A panic was smartly averted.

The real irony of the incident was little noted. The June budget expressed Canadian concern about the extent of US equity investment in Canada. The July tax expressed US concern about US loan investments in other countries, including Canada. If the budget proposals had been put forward five or six weeks later than they were, they could fairly have been presented as complementary with US policy; the US administration had acted to stem an outflow of capital on loan account, which it could most readily influence; the budget sought to lessen the outflow on equity account, which the Canadian government could influence.

I do not suggest that the outcry from Canadian financial interests, hurt by the budget, would have been any less vehement. But it would have been much harder for such critics to represent Walter as spitting at the Americans to the detriment of Canadians generally. The political impact of the budget would have been very different. This did not mean that, if it had been introduced in the different context following the US interest equalization tax, a budget exactly as it was on 13 June could have gone through unscathed. But the purposes of something like it would have been much better understood, there would not have had to be anything near the same retreat, and the whole subsequent course of the Pearson government might have been significantly different. Such accidents of timing do more to shape political outcomes than most of us like to recognize.

The sense of crisis about the interest equalization tax resulted in considerable importance being attached to an early meeting of the Canadian-American cabinet committee on trade and economic affairs. Our delegation was led by Paul Martin, with Walter Gordon, Mitchell Sharp and some other Ministers and senior officials. We were in Washington for 19–21 September. The United States side was led by Dean Rusk, the Secretary of State, and Douglas Dillon, Secretary of the Treasury, with other members of the Kennedy Cabinet and senior officials. The one with whom I got on particularly well was Walter Heller, Chairman of the President's Council of Economic Advisors. It was an occasion of the kind whose value lay less in the formal meetings than in the frank discussion over dinner at the State Department. The meeting probably did improve mutual understanding and, along with a subsequent session in Ottawa, helped to prepare the way for the Pearson government's important achievement in bilateral economic relations, the Auto Pact.

Meanwhile, however, there was a different kind of visit to Washington. After President Kennedy's assassination it was considered important that there be an early, get-acquainted meeting with the new President. This was arranged for 21–22 January, 1964. We were royally treated. It would be a dull soul indeed who did not get a certain pleasure in being whisked by helicopter from Andrews Air Force Base to land on the lawn of the White House and be received by the President of the United States with "ruffles and flourishes," as well as the two national anthems, from a military band. The small party contained Paul Martin, Gordon Robertson, and Edgar Ritchie. We were put up at Blair House, entertained the President to dinner at the Canadian Embassy residence, met with him and his Cabinet in the White House, had lunch there, and so on. The dinner was somewhat marred by the discourteous scorn with which the

President received Mr Pearson's gift of an RCMP saddle. He clearly did not think it fit for a Texan, and Mike was put out by such lack of social grace. My keenest recollection, however, is of the visit to Arlington National Cemetery, where Mr Pearson put a wreath on President Kennedy's grave.

There was not the easy communication with the new President that there had been between Pearson and Kennedy. The formal business was an exchange of notes, signed by Paul Martin and Dean Rusk, on the Columbia River Agreement, and the signature of the Campobello Agreement, in memory of Franklin Roosevelt, by the President and Prime Minister. The item of more general significance, which came from the discussion in the Oval Room, was the agreement to appoint a "working group" to draft a statement of "principles which would make it easier to avoid divergences in economic and other policies of interest to each other."

The "group" consisted of Arnold Heeney for Canada and Livingstone Merchant, a highly understanding and able former US Ambassador to Canada. The resulting report was an illustration of the sad truth that in public affairs it is often unprofitable to be intelligently terse. The Heeney-Merchant report was widely condemned as a facile statement of the kind of quiet diplomacy that in practice makes Canada a mere satellite of the United States. In fact it stands up, in my view, as a clear statement of the way in which two close but disparate neighbours can best conduct their relations, on most issues in most circumstances. This qualification is crucial to an independent Canadian foreign policy, but it does not remove the good sense of the general statement.

By far the most important achievement of the Pearson government, in its bilateral dealings with the United States, was the Auto Pact. In concept this originated with Walter Gordon, though the responsibility for negotiating it lay with Bud Drury, as Minister of Industry. The detail required a tough style, which Simon Reisman provided. Because it abolished tariffs on the internal business of the automobile corporations, the pact has been held up by some people as an example of the benefits to Canada of economic integration with the United States on free trade principles. That is far from the truth.

The Auto Pact has no relation to free trade as it is advocated by those who see it as the transfer of economic decision-making to "market forces," free from government intervention. That requires the removal of tariffs and other government barriers affecting people's decisions as to what and where they buy. The Auto Pact did not remove tariffs for the individual buying an automobile. It has been, in fact, a successful experiment in managed trade. The automobile manufacturers were freed from tariffs on their trans-border transactions. The special status thus given to them was conditional on specific performance criteria. In effect, they were subjected to new government-imposed rules of the game, under which it was in their interest to increase production and employment in Canada.

They did so, to an extent that they would not have contemplated, at the exchange rate then prevailing, if their headquarters had been making unfettered corporate decisions for an integrated North American market, free from tariffs on their end products, as is desired by the proponents of bilateral free trade. As oligopolists, in the economists' sense, the automobile companies accepted the new rules of the game because they anticipated that Ottawa might otherwise take more drastic measures to "Canadianize" the industry here. Far from abandoning the role of government intervention in the market, the Auto Pact used it to induce the industry to structure its production in a way more beneficial to Canada both than it had under the old tariff regime and than it would have done in an integrated "free" market.

For a short period, my closest involvement in external affairs related not to trade and development but to defence. In February 1964 the energetic Minister, Paul Hellyer, produced a draft White Paper on defence policy. Mr Pearson was appalled by it. He passed it on to me with a worried question as to whether I could suggest what we do about it. Paul looked ten years ahead. While the draft paper made a nod to the need for flexibility, it proceeded to set out quite specifically the role, equipment, and manpower of the Canadian forces for the ten-year period on the assumption that nothing in the international situation would change meantime. The main danger would continue to be Russian aggression in Europe; the Canadian air force should maintain its strike role there and we should engage on quite a massive scale in stock-piling equipment in Europe. The White Paper policy would have modernized our naval forces for the possibility of another war of attrition in the Atlantic. It paid no attention to the possibility that upheavals in Viet Nam, or elsewhere in Asia, the Middle East, Africa or Latin America, might become the main tension points. In particular, it took little account of the Pearson concern that Canadian forces should be able to contribute quickly and significantly to UN peace-keeping operations. It had the additional disadvantage of being an extremely expensive set of proposals.

In the latter part of the paper, a good case was made for unification of the three services. It could increase efficiency and effect some savings. At that point, I saw a glimmer of light. My response to the Prime Minister was to suggest that the draft paper could be made palatable by revising it in two main ways. Unification of the services should become the centre-piece of the policy. It was a sensible measure, but difficult and creative enough to absorb a lot of even Paul Hellyer's energies. If his interest could be concentrated on it, many of the specifics could be removed from the other proposals. It would be no use arguing with Paul, who was a stubborn man, that his specifics were inferior to others. My memorandum commented: "Paul ... wants to give the country a nice, new shining defence policy all neatly put together and packaged for the next ten years. The best counter-argument is not that other people have a better idea of what the package should be. The argument is that, while his package may well turn out to be the right one to develop, it will have to be *developed*; we can't unveil it now with sufficient sureness to carry conviction with people less far-sighted than the Minister."

The White Paper should therefore be restructured, to shift the emphasis from equipment of the forces to their organization. Integration of the services should become the major point. The rest of the paper could then be less detailed, without Paul feeling that he had laboured to produce only a mouse.

The Prime Minister was delighted with this solution. Privy Council officers and I did a thorough editing of the paper. The Prime Minister took great trouble. He personally transcribed the editing on to a clean copy: Paul would be more receptive to his handwriting than to others. Even so, much discussion was necessary. Walter Gordon was even more critical of the original White Paper than the Prime Minister. He questioned the value of our contribution to European defence and thought that defence expenditures should be reduced; that would be the best way for the federal government to free more resources for the provinces without increasing total taxation. In the end, however, Walter agreed that the revision of the paper met his strongest objections and Paul Hellyer accepted a ceiling on defence expenditures. He flung himself with great determination into the task of service integration, stoutly withstanding much interested and prejudiced criticism.

My closer personal interest was in the international economic system and particularly the economic and social progress of the Third World, which seemed and seems to me the truly basic requirement for reasonable stability and security within the global village. That I had any involvement with these issues during the Pearson period was due less to the Prime Minister directly than to Barbara Ward (Lady Jackson), my friend and former colleague on the London *Economist*. Barbara combined great intelligence and perception with extraordinary eloquence and tireless energy in the cause of international understanding and development. She knew almost everyone who mattered and almost everyone was charmed by her. She seized on my association with Mike to weave another strand in her web of international connections. He shared the general admiration and welcomed the unofficial link with the liberally-minded international community that friendship with Barbara provided.

That influence was at work on 2 April 1965, when Mr Pearson made his famous speech in the United States suggesting a stop to the bombing of North Viet Nam. It was perhaps because this was the view of some members of his own Administration, as we knew through Barbara, that President Johnson was so cross with Pearson about the speech.

The connection did not, however, produce as much involvement in international development as I would have liked or indeed, during his prime ministership, Mr Pearson wished for himself. The demands of domestic politics were always too strong. Nevertheless, the Pearson government's performance in international development was creditable. It had cautious but steady support from Paul Martin, and willing financial backing from Walter Gordon. Funding for external aid was increased and what had been an office within External Affairs was converted to the more prestigious and effective instrument of a separate corporation, the Canadian International Development Agency (CIDA).

Maurice Strong became the brilliant first President of CIDA. In everything he does he combines a first-rate intellectual grasp with an equal practical capacity to get an organization to work. I had the intense satisfaction of introducing him to Barbara Ward on one of the occasions when she was visiting with us. The collaboration that followed, particularly when Maurice had moved to the United Nations, was of profound value in raising international consciousness about the environment and development. In Canada, Barbara was the initial moving spirit, and Maurice was the active agent, in the creation of the Centre for International Development Research. While it has never become all that we, including of course Mr Pearson, dreamed of – the grand first idea was to establish it on a large scale on the Expo site in Montreal – the Centre has made a very substantial contribution to the development of appropriate technologies for economic improvements in the Third World.

Barbara's fine hand was also at work in the establishment by her friend Robert McNamara, as President of the World Bank, of the Commission on International Development that Mike chaired after his retirement. Its *Partners in Development* report of 1969 still stands as one of the important documents on the road to a more equal and stable human community.

During that period Mike expressed to me, as no doubt to others, his anger about the review of foreign policy that Trudeau initiated after he became Prime Minister, in the apparent spirit that the old policy was bankrupt. In fact little change came from the review, because its premise was invalid. It is true that during the Pearson government Canada made no distinctive contributions to world affairs comparable to its role at Bretton Woods, in the creation of the United Nations and of NATO, in the Colombo Plan and the early stages of aid to the developing countries, in the evolution of the Commonwealth as a genuine association of independent countries, and of course above all in the Suez affair and the subsequent development of the UN's peace-keeping role. Mr Pearson's status in the world rests on what he did before and after his prime ministership. During it, Canada's role as the helpful fixer was muted and our stance on the critical issue of Viet Nam and on the recognition of China less than glorious.

On the whole, however, our foreign policy was sensible and our involvements were, as far as they went, constructive. The main change from the early postwar years was simply that our relative importance had diminished. In Pearson's heyday at External Affairs, we had been a big frog compared with countries recovering from the war. We were bound to have less weight in the world of the 1960s. It was not that our policy no longer had the right directions. In trying to be different, the best that the Trudeau review could do was to state the objectives of foreign policy in terms of a narrower self-interest, which for a country in Canada's situation is naïve or worse. The practical result was some further retraction of Canada's international involvements, to no advantage.

26 Publications

No issue created more uncertainty within the Pearson government than how to encourage Canadian publications for Canadian readers. That was not, however, because of particular difficulties within the government. It was because the issue focuses some of the basic dilemmas by which the process of government in federal Canada is hedged around. The story of the Pearson government's struggle with the publications problem is one that illuminates the inner dynamics of much Canadian decision-making. It illustrates the tension between national concerns and external realities. And it is also a story that demonstrates the political courage of the Pearson government in facing down perhaps the most powerful of the country's pressure groups, its newspaper publishers.

There was no dispute, within the Cabinet, about the objective of encouraging Canadian publications. The difficulties were about the means, if any, to do it. They had three sources.

One was the American connection. Concern for Canadian identity does not have to be anti-American, but the simple fact is that the alternative to reading Canadian viewpoints in Canadian publications is to read American viewpoints in American publications. In particular, in the fifties and sixties the main competition to Canadian publications dealing with national affairs was the Canadian edition of *Time* magazine.

In editorial content, as opposed to advertising, it was Canadian only to the extent of a few pages, and they were put together by US staff. The rest of the content, identical with that of the parent magazine, was the product of resources far beyond the command of any Canadian publication. The technical quality and attractiveness of the journal were indisputable.

Yet, if *Time* merited its wide readership, that made it all the more important that Canadians should have other views of Canada and the world to read, of a better quality than it seemed possible to produce in Canada in competition with the circulation, and consequent advertising revenue, of the Canadian edition of *Time*. Any action to counter its role in the Canadian market was bound, however, to be a major irritant to relations with the US government; the influence of *Time* in Washington was quite sufficient to ensure that.

The second major difficulty about the publication issue was and is constitutional in origin. It did not occur to the Fathers of Confederation that publications were as important to nationhood as, say, banking. There is no specific provision for Parliament to legislate directly about the ownership of publications as it does about banks. An ingenious lawyer can make a case that such jurisdiction derives from the general responsibility for good government in a free society, but the action would be, to say the least, highly contentious.

This consideration interacted with the American connection. If Canada had been a unitary state, with power in the national legislature to enact simple prohibitory legislation against foreign ownership of the media (as, for example in France), the publications issue could more easily have been treated as a special case, quite divorced from general policy towards foreign businesses. But if we had to use indirect means – in effect, the power to tax or subsidize – there was bound to be more fear of a precedent that could readily be extended to other kinds of business. The *Time* lobby, as we called it, could more easily arouse sympathetic fears among other American interests and thereby use the US administration more effectively to protest against damage to its Canadian edition.

The third complication arises from the special character of the business economics of the media, both print and electronic. Because it is so familiar, we often forget how remarkable it is that an industry should draw very little of its revenue from the sale of its product or service as such. The purchaser of a daily newspaper, for example, pays directly only about a fifth of the cost of the information and entertainment that the paper provides. The rest of the cost he pays indirectly, because it is included in the prices of the groceries and other goods that are advertised in the paper. Any tax measure affecting the media has to be related to this fact of the business. But a "tax on advertising" is bound to rouse fears and opposition from interests far wider than the publications directly affected.

For a government to take any action on behalf of Canadianism in publications was, in short, to stir up several nests of hornets of great ferocity. The St Laurent government, in its last budget in 1957, had bravely tried. It instituted a small tax on advertising in "non-Canadian" publications such as the Canadian edition of *Time*. The criticism was vehement, and the opposition Conservatives allied themselves with it – not, as subsequent events proved, from conviction, but on the common principle that any government measure that is not universally approved should be opposed. In office, they promptly abolished the tax. They then discovered how strong was the feeling on behalf of Canadian publications, and particularly of the magazines that were in danger of disappearing before the competition of *Time* for Canadian advertising – most notably, *Maclean's* and *Saturday Night*. The government responded by appointing a Royal Commission, headed by Senator Grattan O'Leary, an eminent Conservative as well as journalist. A bright young future Senator, Michael Pitfield, was on its staff.

The O'Leary report, in May 1961, went much beyond the measure that the Diefenbaker government had abolished. It recommended the ultimate tax on advertising directed by Canadian businesses to Canadian buyers through foreign publications, including so-called Canadian editions of them: such advertising should not be deductible at all as a cost in computing company income for tax. This would, of course, have killed the Canadian edition of *Time*. The Diefenbaker government, in its remaining two years of life, characteristically did not get around to doing anything about the recommendation, while sometimes making noises as if it would.

The resulting uncertainty was the worst possible environment for magazines; it influenced advertisers towards preferring other media. By the time we inherited the problem, it was becoming more desperate. *Maclean's* was operating at a heavy loss. There was little doubt that, if nothing was done, it and other commercial magazines would disappear before long. If the Canadian edition of *Time* faced competition in future, it was most likely to be because other US publications would imitate it, to the extent at least of producing special runs containing Canadian-oriented advertising. There would be no Canadian publications on a national scale.

A Pearson government battered by its first budget was not eager to face the problem. It seemed to me, however, that simply to let it drift, as Diefenbaker had done, would be unforgivable. Rather than that, we should make a public decision that we saw no satisfactory way to help Canadian publications, and put them out of their misery. The Prime Minister, Walter Gordon, and some other ministers agreed that we should not drift, but a negative decision was highly unpalatable. I was challenged to produce a proposal.

The first effort, in a memorandum dated 5 September 1963, was a failure. I searched for an alternative to the advertising tax as an instrument. The only possibility I could see turned on the fact that the economics of the periodical press were based on the privilege of second-class mailing. The Canadian edition of *Time* was carried through the mails for just over one cent a copy. I calculated that mailing the same weight of paper would cost the ordinary Canadian (in those days) 20 cents. This privilege – in effect, a subsidy – could be justified by the public interest in the easy flow of materials of information and opinion on public affairs. It would be entirely defensible to limit such a subsidy from the Canadian public to Canadian publications.

Though the effects would be the same, US interests could not object to not getting the subsidy with anything near the effectiveness that they could to the imposition of a new tax on them. *Time*, of course, would object that we were changing the rules of the game after its operation in Canada had become well established. We could take some of the wind out of that by offering to treat the Canadian edition as a Canadian publication provided that over a reasonable transition period, say three years, the Canadian-edited proportion of its content was increased to, say, 75 per cent. If the exemption was taken on such terms, we would have achieved our basic purpose. In fact the offer would almost certainly be spurned, *Time* would go, and genuinely Canadian magazines would survive.

That was, I still think, a reasonable proposal. It came to nothing because it involved poking into another nest of special interests. The structure of postal rates reflected a horde of concessions and cross-subsidizations, granted at various times, no doubt often with political pressure of one kind or another. There was a vague general justification to the effect that the Post Office should maximize its business at marginal costs, with the taxpayer bridging the difference between average cost and revenue. The political consideration was that the concessionary rates entrenched all kinds of special interests. One change could not in practice be looked at in isolation. It would rouse a great variety of concerns, protests and alliances of those who feared that they might be the next to be hurt by any rationalization of postal charges.

In some circumstances this would not have deterred the government, but in 1963 the Pearson Cabinet was too rattled willingly to take on a fresh controversy. If anything had to be done about magazines, at least it should be by the method that the O'Leary Report had made familiar and with which all three opposition parties had said they agreed. I gave up hope of the postal rate alternative and the Cabinet continued to hope that the whole issue could be treated as a sleeping dog.

It was nothing of the kind, as I kept on pointing out to the Prime Minister. The certain consequence of inaction was that *Maclean's*, *Saturday Night*, and the few other national magazines would die, probably sooner rather than later, and there would be more foreign control of the Canadian printed word. The government would then be reduced to wringing its hands while it was treated with contempt for having failed to do anything at all to lock the stable door while there were still some horses at home.

The Prime Minister and Walter Gordon, at least, agreed. With the turn of the year and the reconstruction of the Cabinet, the government's spirits were reviving, and in February 1964 a decision was made and announced: the O'Leary recommendations would be implemented, but with recognition of "squatters' rights" for existing Canadian editions (*Time* and also *Reader's Digest*). The exemption avoided great trouble with the United States but it meant that, while the danger of further Americanization was removed, there was nothing to improve the profitability of Canadian publications in the short run. The concession of squatters' rights was widely denounced.

All three opposition parties were, naturally, critical. There could be no clearer example of the "in" and "out" cynicism of politics: what we were proposing was at least as much as any Conservative government might have got around to doing. But a good many Liberal backbenchers were deeply unhappy about the exemption, to the point that some defections were likely when the issue came to a vote. Walter Gordon became troubled about the proposal, and he was greatly concerned that his second budget be non-controversial. The appropriate tax resolutions were written, but Walter ignored them in his budget speech. There was again uncertainty as to when, if ever, anything would be done.

It was therefore in some distress that I wrote a memorandum of 11 May 1964. Despite the danger of defeat we should not, I argued, remove the exemption for *Time* and *Reader's Digest*. The political argument was that the government would once again be vulnerable to the charge of not knowing its own mind, of retreating, but the main point was one of principle. Squatters' rights should be recognized, and therefore we should not now throw *Time* and *Digest* headlong out of the country. The memorandum continued in broader terms about the US–Canada relationship:

We have a chance of getting on reasonably well with the United States, while doing the things that are indispensable to Canadian identity, if we concentrate on measures to preserve existing Canadian ownership and control and to assist the development of this control for new enterprises. We are bound to be in a running war with the United States if we hit at existing US enterprises in any sudden way; that is, in so far as we have to alter the rules as they apply to existing enterprises, we must at least arrange that the change takes effect gradually.

This was not, admittedly, a view in which I had been entirely consistent, but experience had strengthened it.

However, we could not put through the proposal exactly as it was. We should, the memorandum continued, stay with the squatters' exemption but do something else to strengthen the measure. The best solution was to broaden it to cover not only periodicals but all the media. There was nothing to prevent Canadian daily newspapers being taken over by foreign owners. Already, as I had pointed out in an earlier memorandum, "a lot of daily newspapers are controlled by a man (Thomson) whose residence and main interests are outside Canada". (That was the first Lord Thomson, who was living in Britain and flouted Canada by acquiring an English peerage.) The point was strengthened by subsequent rumours that *La Presse* might be acquired by interests in France, and that some prominent English-language papers could soon be up for sale to the highest bidder, who would probably be American.

Canadian ownership of newspapers was, I argued, important to our national identity, and in this case we had no excuse for failing to lock the stable door before the horses bolted. We should therefore generalize the tax measure, to provide that advertising would be disallowed, as a business expense, if it was directed to Canadians but placed in any non-Canadian media – newspapers, TV and radio as well as magazines. There should be the same exemption for all existing foreign-owned media (the small Red Deer paper had British owners) as for *Time* and *Reader's Digest*.

I again suggested, as in the earlier postal rate proposal, that a conditional exemption would be reasonable, and this time made the condition less onerous: 55 per cent, instead of 75 per cent, Canadianization of content within three years. There was no enthusiasm for that in Cabinet, however, on the grounds that it invited *Time* to conduct a running battle against the government for the next three years. My suggested compromise was a modest content requirement (15 to 25 per cent) within one year; if *Time* objected to that, it would not get much sympathy anywhere. Walter Gordon, however, felt that the government would thereby be appearing to confer a certain legitimacy on *Time*, without significantly helping Canadian magazines to compete with it. If there had to be an exemption, he preferred that it be simple and unconditional.

Government and Parliament continued, however, to be preoccupied with other business. There was now no doubt about the Cabinet's intention to act eventually, but the delay was hurting. I therefore tried, in September, for another minor addition to the proposal, to give a little help to genuinely Canadian publications in their competition with the squatters. It was that the latter should pay the postal rates applicable to foreign magazines brought into Canada in bulk for mailing to subscribers here. This could be justified reasonably enough; it was fair as between *Time* and its American competitors, such as *Newsweek*. But the extra cost to *Time* would have been small, and the effect of the suggestion was therefore to rekindle consideration of more drastic differentiation in postal rates. There was even last-minute thought of applying higher rates to all magazines but offsetting them, for genuinely Canadian publications, by a rebate or subsidy. Fortunately, in my view, that idea did not get far.

In the end, therefore, the action taken, in the budget of April 1965, was confined to the main proposals of the memorandum of the previous May – the advertising measure applied to newspapers as well as magazines but with exemption for publications already foreign-owned. Walter Gordon remained unhappy about the exemption but reconciled himself and the Liberal caucus to it by the argument that otherwise the opposition of *Time* and its friends would be so strong as to imperil American approval of the Auto Pact. The exemption was, of course, later withdrawn by the Trudeau government.

In 1965, as it turned out, the main controversy was not about the exemption, as the government had feared, but about the application of the advertising provision to newspaper ownership. The newspapers' lobby group, the Canadian Daily Newspaper Publishers Association, vehemently declared that the government's action was a "fundamental violation" of press freedom. Not all newspapers agreed with this nonsense, but that did not lessen the fury of the critics. It could be explained only by unstated motives. In truth the tax treatment of advertising in no way restricted anyone's right to publish anything. It was hard to think that many newspaper proprietors were so muddleheaded as to think that it did. But no one would sympathize if they said they did not like the one effect that the measure had: to reduce the potential value of their properties in the sense that if they wanted to sell, foreigners would be unable to bid up the price over offers from Canadian purchasers. The critics wrapped themselves in the flag of press freedom because they had no genuine argument with which to appeal to the public interest.

It was, however, an abrasive controversy, in which Walter and I were cast as the villains and Mike, as so often, treated as a well-meaning dupe. This was not good for internal harmony, but the government faced out the storm bravely enough; it was too spurious to blow for long, and there was no indication that it did the government any harm at all in public opinion.

That experience was, however, misleading. The ease with which the supposedly weak Pearson government faced down the newspaper industry caused me to misjudge, sixteen years later when I was Chairman of the Royal Commission on Newspapers, the capacity of the supposedly strong Trudeau government to do likewise.

One other reflection is required before leaving this subject. Because Walter Gordon was more reluctant than Mike Pearson to grant the exemption to *Time*, the affair has often been treated as a prime illustration of the incompatibility of the economic nationalist and the diplomatic internationalist. That is a misreading both of the complex character of Pearson and the straightforward character of Gordon. There was nothing narrow about Walter's nationalism. He was quite as much an internationalist, in the sense of an unprejudiced citizen of the world, concerned that the growing interdependence of nations be recognized in co-operative action, as was Mike. If that had not been so, they would not have been such close friends as they were for many years and Walter would not have been a Liberal politician.

The difference was that, while Mike shared the Gordon recognition of the limitations on Canadian economic development imposed by a very high degree of external ownership of business, the complexities of his make-up produced a less steady sense of the significance of this economic factor. In other respects, it was just as clear to both that, in the bilateral relationship with the United States, Canada must walk a very fine line. We could not run our heads against the facts of close interdependence, but on the other hand we could not play an effective part in the world as a whole unless we kept a clear distance from the United States in some matters. The distance was as important to Mike as to any practical internationalist. The importance of internationalism was as clear to Walter as to anyone who, while particularly concerned about the policies of his own country, recognizes the inevitably diminishing scope for autonomous action in a world of instant communication. Where they differed, as men who are like-minded but of very different characters frequently do, it was on tactics, not on the fundamentals of Canadian policy. That was as true of *Time* as of other issues.

27 *The Flag and the Death Wish*

The Pearson government was committed to a Canadian flag. In the words of the 1963 election program: "Within two years of taking office, a new Liberal government will submit to Parliament a design for a flag which cannot be mistaken for the emblem of any other country. When adopted, this will be the flag of Canada." There were three reasons why the timing was more precise than for other policies. One was to overcome scepticism about a proposal long talked of and not acted on. A second was that no significant expenditure was involved. The third, and most important, was the strength of Mr Pearson's personal feeling. It reflected his experience in the Department of External Affairs. Concerned as he was about Canada's role in the world, he had often felt humiliated, as he described it to me, and no doubt to others, because the flag flown at our embassies was identified in other countries as British.

In May 1964 the government had been in office not for two years but for thirteen months. It had been battered. Though some optimism and confidence had returned, particularly with the April settlement on the pension plan and federal-provincial tax-sharing, it was still a minority government, in Parliament very unsure of itself in face of the venom of opposition in the Diefenbaker style. Parliamentary business was slow, and there was a long agenda of already declared items. Activist though I was by temperament, it seemed to me that we needed a couple of months of comparative calm, working through that agenda; then during the summer we could regroup and prepare, and by September be able to return, with more credibility, to further major measures in the ambitious program that we had set for a four-year term of government.

Mr Pearson listened to this assessment but did not share it. On 17 May he announced his intention to proceed immediately with the flag. He chose the most critical audience possible, a Legion convention, and the project was therefore launched with booes. As far as I know, none of Mr Pearson's normally close associates was consulted. No doubt he knew that we would counsel delay, and he did not want to have to argue.

After the Winnipeg speech, there could be no retreat. Cabinet approved the flag design that Mr Pearson had chosen on the recommendation of heraldic experts – three red maple leaves on a white background flanked by vertical blue bars – and the proposal was introduced to Parliament on 27 May.

In the circumstances it was an obvious invitation to the opposition to filibuster. On 25 May I had written a memorandum about the effect on the timetable for the rest of the program, urging that we must nevertheless make every effort to get it through and pointing out that, at best, we would have to forgo the usual summer recess of Parliament. I did not anticipate either the length or the ferocity of the filibuster. It was the middle of December, and even then only after the use of closure, before the House of Commons eventually approved a distinctive flag, of the much better design produced by a committee.

As was usually the case, Mike Pearson had in the end got what he wanted, but in this case it was at a cost that he had not foreseen and never calculated afterwards. The message on the Pearsons' 1964 Christmas card was no doubt influenced by the approval of the flag: "What a year – and it could not have ended so happily if it had not been for the Kents ..." The reality, however, was that the government had been greatly harmed.

If there had been no flag debate in 1964, if the issue had been left to 1965 as it well could have been, the Pearson government would not have been distracted, confused, and all but destroyed by the so-called scandals that dominated politics through the winter of 1964–5. The events from which the scandals originated would still, of course, have occurred. Some, indeed, had happened before the flag was introduced. But the opposition was able to inflate them to a condemnation of the government as a whole, and particularly to a demonstration of the Prime Minister's weakness, because they were superimposed on the parliamentary turmoil that the government invited by introducing the flag proposal too soon and ill-prepared.

A government not distracted by that turmoil, a government that was getting on with its business in an orderly way instead of being so clearly unable to cope with Parliament, could not possibly have handled the Rivard affair and the rest so badly. And it was the general sense of the government's incompetence that made disasters out of incidents involving only a few people, and most of those not of great importance. Above all, it was the flag debate that gave Mr Pearson his rationalization for the worst item in the whole sad business: his own moral cowardice in not promptly telling the House of Commons that he had misled it.

This arose from the most spectacular of the scandals, the Rivard affair. Lucien Rivard was a character in the Montreal underworld, wanted in the United States on a major charge of drug smuggling. The lawyer handling the extradition proceedings for the US government, Pierre Lamontagne, naturally opposed bail for Rivard. He informed the RCMP that he had been offered $20,000 to drop his opposition. The offerer of the alleged bribe was Raymond Denis, a lawyer who had been brought to

Ottawa by Lionel Chevrier and afterwards became executive assistant to
the Minister of Citizenship and Immigration, René Tremblay.

The RCMP started to investigate and as soon as Tremblay heard of it, on
31 August 1964, he sent Denis off on leave and afterwards secured his
resignation. The RCMP investigation was subsequently shown to have been
less than efficient, but the Commissioner advised Guy Favreau, as Minister of Justice, that there was insufficient evidence to lay charges against
Denis. Favreau read the file and decided that was so. He remained
entirely confident of the correctness of his decision even when rumours
began to circulate and it was apparent that he would be attacked in
Parliament on it.

The attack, chiefly by Erik Nielsen, began on Monday 23 November
1964. Favreau was unprepared and, under the ferocity of the questioning,
unsure and unconvincing. Asked whether "anyone else higher up in the
government" was involved, he could do no better than "my recollection
is not" and he confused the situation further by asserting that the RCMP
investigation was continuing, which was not – at the time – true. The
crucial point was brought out not by the showman inquisitor, Nielsen,
but by the most gentlemanly and able of Conservative MPs, Gordon
Fairweather. He asked if the case had ever been referred to the law
officers of the Justice Department for an opinion on whether or not
charges should be laid. Told that it had not, he that day summed up the
destruction of Guy Favreau in three words: "Well, it's tragic."

That evening and night Ottawa was agog with rumours about the
reference to someone "higher up in the government." Long after I knew
the Prime Minister would be in bed, I got the answer to my enquiries. It
was Guy Rouleau, Parliamentary Secretary to Mr Pearson himself. At 9
A.M. the next day, I reported so. Mr Pearson sent at once for Favreau and
the Commissioner of the RCMP. We examined the file. The story was
correct. Rouleau had also telephoned Pierre Lamontagne about Rivard.
He had expressed his interest in the case and implied that the favours of
legal business to Lamontagne would be better if he went easy about the
bail application.

Rouleau was asked, and agreed, to announce his resignation from his
parliamentary secretaryship that afternoon. (Subsequently, after the
Dorion report had criticized him, he retired from politics altogether.)
With this, there was no doubt that there had to be a judicial inquiry into
the affair. The question was what its terms of reference would be. Terms
acceptable to the Conservatives would be humiliating to Favreau to a
degree that the government could not accept. The only way the government could escape defeat was to find compromise wording acceptable to
it and to the smaller parties, particularly the NDP. To find such a solution
became the responsibility of Paul Martin, aided by the drafting skills of

Favreau himself. The Prime Minister went off on the Tuesday afternoon for a long-scheduled series of political engagements on the Prairies. Before he left, however, he answered a question from Douglas Harkness. When had he first been informed about this Rivard affair? Mr Pearson at first evaded a direct answer but, pressed, said he thought that it was the previous Sunday.

There followed three days of comic opera, with Mr Pearson vacillating as to whether he should continue with his prairie engagements or return to lead his embattled forces in Ottawa. The situation was complicated by Guy Favreau telling his colleagues that he had in fact informed the Prime Minister of the affair at an early stage, on 2 September. It had been only a brief conversation in an aircraft, and he had confined himself to the main point: an allegation of bribery against an executive assistant; he had not mentioned Rouleau's involvement in making representations. The Prime Minister asked no questions, but Favreau said that he would be informed of the results of the RCMP investigation. Faced with Favreau's recollection, the Prime Minister agreed that it was correct.

It is hard to think of two politicians except Pearson and Favreau who could in any circumstances have let such a matter drop after one such brief conversation. But Favreau was desperately overworked, his inability to delegate reflecting a boundless wish to spare other people from trouble: why add to all the Prime Minister's worries by telling him more about a sordid little matter which, he believed, was satisfactorily dealt with by Denis's departure from government service? That Mr Pearson thought no more about it, that when he answered Harkness's question he truly had forgotten all about the conversation of September 2, would be inconceivable if one did not know how strained and distracted he was by the flag controversy on top of all the other problems of office.

The fact remained that, however unintentionally, he had misled the House of Commons. And while he was on the prairies the price was being paid by Guy Favreau. He would have been much criticized in any event, but at that stage, with many of the facts of the Rivard affair still unknown, his stated failure to inform the Prime Minister was a principal item in the indictment. Both the opposition and the press treated it as clear evidence of his incompetence to be a Minister. Favreau, utterly loyal to Pearson, said nothing to defend himself.

When the Prime Minister returned to Ottawa on the afternoon of Sunday, 29 November, Gordon Robertson and I were anxiously waiting. Jack Pickersgill also turned up at 24 Sussex, in a state of great distress. Jack could be overly clever and narrowly partisan, but he was also a man of warm sentiments and he liked Guy Favreau. He and I were equally concerned that the agony of Favreau should be relieved by immediate correction of the misinformation that Mike had given five days earlier.

Gordon Robertson, as Clerk of the Privy Council, was particularly concerned also that there be immediate action to underline the moral responsibility of ministers, extending fully to their staffs: they must all act in ways that would bear the fullest public scrutiny, favouring no one with treatment that would not be accorded to other citizens; they must have no pecuniary interest that would even remotely conflict with their public duty; they must not place themselves in any position that could give even the appearance of obliging them to give special consideration or favour to anyone.

On that Sunday afternoon Mr Pearson appeared fully to agree with us on both points. The broader one was implemented at once. Gordon Robertson completed the draft of a letter which set out the rules of disinterest, for ministers and their staffs, at least as clearly and comprehensively as has been done in any of the conflict-of-interest guidelines promulgated since. The letter was sent to all ministers, over the Prime Minister's signature, on 30 November.

On the Monday morning also, the Prime Minister told his colleagues that when the House sat that afternoon he would correct his error about when he was first informed of the bribery allegation. He did not. The excuse was that, because of the flag debate, the normal "orders of the day" – the usual occasion for a Ministerial statement – were in abeyance. That was no excuse at all. The Prime Minister could readily have caught Mr Speaker's eye and made a statement as a matter of privilege. Other members were being allowed to do that constantly, even as a way of getting trivial matters of constituency interest on to the record. But Mr Pearson said nothing. Every day when the House assembled his colleagues were expecting him to speak. Day after day Jack Pickersgill and I, separately and together, pleaded with him to get it over. Almost every day I redrafted and redrafted the prepared statement, in the hope of somehow making it more palatable to Mr Pearson. I failed. Every day, indeed, it became more difficult, because the statement had not only to correct the misinformation but also to gloss over the unexplainable delay in making it.

The delay was excruciating not only because of its cruelty to Favreau. It was also so pointless. Favreau could go on enduring the unfair criticism until the Dorion Commission of Inquiry began its hearings. Then, however, he would have to testify under oath. Cross-examined as he was bound to be about his communications with the Prime Minister, he could not conceal the 2 September conversation. The Prime Minister would be revealed by his own Minister of Justice as a liar. It would be too late then to plead forgetfulness or to explain his failure to correct himself. The Prime Minister was drifting to destruction. Apparently he had advisers, notably Mrs Pearson and Mary Macdonald, who thought Favreau entirely to blame for the casualness of the information given on the aircraft, and considered that Mike need not regard it as having taken place. That Mike could for a moment think so remains, after all allowance for the stress he was under, incomprehensible.

Yet the miserable two weeks dragged on. The Dorion Commission was to begin its hearings on 15 December. On 14 December the Prime Minister escaped from the noose of Favreau's testimony by the extraordinary device of writing a letter to Dorion, confessing to the 2 September conversation and giving a contorted explanation of his misleading answer in the House and the absence of correction there. Dorion had the letter read into the record on 16 December. The newspaper stories concentrated on the essential point: the Prime Minister now admitted to having known of the bribery charge ten weeks earlier than the date he had given to Parliament.

There, the next day, the response was inevitable. Mr Pearson was attacked not for his original forgetfulness – even Mr Diefenbaker graciously acknowledged that Prime Ministers could forget – but for his failure promptly to correct the misinformation to the House, a failure for which he could give no coherent justification. Indeed, in doing his best, he misled the House again, though no one outside the Cabinet realized so at the time. Questioned as to when he learned of his original mistake, he said that when he returned from the Prairies the Minister of Justice had informed him of it. In fact the Minister had told Cabinet, and Paul Martin had told the Prime Minister by telephone, on 26 November – only two days after the error. It was now twenty-three days after.

The opposition moved to have the Prime Minister's statements referred to the House's disciplinary body, the Committee on Privileges and Elections. The Speaker ruled the motion out of order, and was sustained by some Social Credit as well as the Liberal votes. The crisis was over, though not without nearly half the members of the House of Commons having voted, in effect, to question the integrity of the Prime Minister. Though I don't think he ever admitted it to himself, it was the lowest point in L.B. Pearson's political career.

His resiliency, however, was remarkable. When the Rivard affair was out of the House of Commons and in the hands of the Dorion Commission, it was as if a great weight had already been lifted. This was a mark of the respect and affection for Guy Favreau of all his associates. He was hopeless as an administrator and inept in parliamentary debate, but he was the soul of honour. He could not have done anything wrong. It was his humanitarianism, not any intent in any way selfish or sinister, that had made him feel that Denis had suffered enough by losing his job and there would be no point in pushing a prosecution that probably would not succeed but would nevertheless damage him deeply. It seemed to

Favreau's friends that, much as he had been hurt by the kind of partisan political debate with which he could not cope, it was impossible that an impartial inquiry would find serious fault. Dorion might condemn Denis, and criticize Rouleau, but they were now long gone from government. The Commission report would not hurt Favreau or the government more. That was the expectation, it must be said, not of the government only but of almost all politicians and observers.

We misjudged. Dorion took his time. It was 28 June 1965, when his report arrived. It was strongly critical of Favreau. The Prime Minister had been away and was returning to Ottawa that evening. I almost always avoided formalities, but on that occasion I drove out to the airport with Paul Martin to meet him. It seemed unfair to delegate to anyone else the painful necessity of handing over the report and the summary of it that had been prepared in PCO. Mr Pearson arrived relaxed. "How is it?", he asked cheerily as I gave him the package. I could only say: "It'll hurt, but you must read it tonight."

Guy Favreau resigned as Minister of Justice the next day. Though he was persuaded to stay in Cabinet, as President of the Council and without departmental duties, he was broken. The harshness of politics has destroyed no better man.

He had been hurt in a different way by another of the scandals. The only federal significance of the Dupuis affair was to illustrate how poor was the political process that resulted in Mr Pearson ever appointing him to the federal Cabinet. During his year there he contributed nothing. He had barely been appointed before there were suspicions within the Quebec government that Dupuis had been paid $10,000 in order to use his supposed influence to obtain a licence for a racetrack. It was a provincial matter and, if it had happened, had preceded Dupuis's elevation to the Cabinet. That however, did not lessen the alleged offence. Premier Lesage warned Mr Pearson of the possibility of scandal, but no action was taken. By early December 1964, Lesage added urgency to his warning – rumours were beginning to spread – and Eric Kierans, the Quebec Minister departmentally concerned, telephoned me to say that it was certain that the affair would come up in the Quebec Assembly early in the New Year and almost as certain that it would go to court.

There had to be an RCMP investigation, and Mr Pearson delegated to Favreau the task of telling Dupuis that he should resign. Dupuis was adamant: to resign would be interpreted as admitting guilt, and he claimed to be innocent. Hours and hours of Favreau's overburdened time were taken in vain efforts at persuasion. Eric Kierans wrote a toughly specific letter to Favreau about the affair and eventually Mr Pearson confronted Dupuis himself. Favreau pressed again while the Prime Minister was taking an early January vacation. In mid-January they returned to the attack together. It all took an inordinate amount of their time and energy, but eventually, as noted earlier, Dupuis yielded to an ultimatum and on 22 January 1965, resigned.

The worst of all the scandals, because it was one in which administrative discretion had clearly resulted in favoured treatment, was that involving Onofrio Minaudo. He was an immigrant with a clear criminal background. As a result, a deportation order had been made in February 1961. But it was not executed during more than two subsequent years of Diefenbaker government. He was deported in March 1964. Late in 1964, at the same time as the Rivard affair was before the House, questions were asked about Minaudo. It appeared that representations on his behalf had been made from both Conservative and Liberal sources. Mutual embarrassment meant that little was made of the affair in the House of Commons. There clearly had been actual discrimination in administration; but because it was a past government that was chiefly at fault, the case attracted far less political attention than one where only the possibility of such favouritism was insinuated.

This was the furniture affair. Of all the scandals, it was the one that probably did most damage to the government. It came close to home with the public, since most of us buy furniture. Many finance the purchase with an appreciable down payment, and for the rest make instalment payments that include a substantial interest charge. Maurice Lamontagne escaped both requirements. In 1962 and 1963 he acquired lots of furniture from an expensive Montreal store owned by the brothers Sefkind. They were apparently successful businessmen, Maurice knew them, and he accepted the loosest of terms for his two transactions: he should pay for his furniture when he could.

Unfortunately for Maurice, the Sefkinds in January 1964 left the country, with the furniture store and other businesses bankrupt. Only then, when the Bank of Montreal, which was the main creditor, demanded settlement of the account, had Maurice begun to pay for the furniture in monthly instalments.

The name of a second Minister, René Tremblay, was associated with the furniture affair, most unfairly. He simply had the misfortune to patronize the same store. He bought a considerable amount of furniture, but not all of it was delivered. Perfectly reasonably, he had delayed payment until it was. When he was billed, he had promptly paid for all he had received. In the atmosphere of the scandals, however, the propriety of his dealings counted for nothing. He was involved by association.

Maurice Lamontagne was the kind of honourable and able man who has the unrealism about his own financial affairs born of an innocent lack of care. It was entirely in this character that he bought expensive furniture which he could not promptly pay for. Apparently the Sefkinds, whatever their business morality or judgment, were cultivated people whom he regarded as friends. He would have been as shocked as anyone, and as resistant, if asked to secure some favour for them because he owed them money.

Naïveté is not, however, a defence acceptable in public life. Neither as a member of the staff of the leader of the opposition, which he was when he "bought" the first batch of furniture, nor subsequently as a Cabinet Minister, should he have put himself in the position of apparent obligation that his furniture created. The irony is that this became public knowledge only because Maurice, in his innocence, himself told two reporters all about it. There were rumours about the Sefkind bankruptcies and the involvement of Cabinet ministers as debtors, but it is doubtful whether hard evidence, of the kind necessary for the publication of such a story, could have been obtained. Nevertheless Maurice, disturbed about any innuendo that could affect the integrity in which he felt impregnable, innocently believed that the truth was his protection, and told all.

I have known few men wiser in large matters than Maurice Lamontagne, but he was no tactician. His story of his furniture destroyed him as a politician, more by its pathos than because anyone seriously thought that he had succumbed, or ever would succumb, to any improper influence. The agony was prolonged. The Prime Minister, much as he owed to Maurice, thought that he and Tremblay should resign from the Cabinet. By the hard test of political utility, this was correct. But they did not see why they should seem to admit to wrongdoing when they thought themselves entirely innocent. The Prime Minister did not insist, until the 1965 election completely changed his political landscape. But his view was known, to the two Ministers and to many others. It was hardly the way to run an effective government. For a year, it made the brilliant but emotional Lamontagne embittered and far less effective than his talents warranted. It completely destroyed such effectiveness as the innocent, decent, and intelligent, but unforceful Tremblay might otherwise have had.

Tremblay's career, like Favreau's, ended in an early death. There were other medical reasons, but both had broken hearts.

Maurice Lamontagne, thank heavens, recovered. He proved to be one of the few brilliant exceptions to the generalization that an unelected Senate contributes nothing to the political process. For him, Senatorship served like a tenured professorship to a man of active mind, rather than the inordinately early and large pension that it is for some. Few Canadians had contributed more to political and economic ideas in the 1950s. His aspirations to the leadership of Quebec in federal politics were so intellectually valid that he was far from alone in failing to see his temperamental incapacity for the role. In the 1960s those hopes were dashed. In the 1970s he again made important contributions to ideas about economic policy, political institutions, the constitution, and science policy. His achievement helped to put the scandals into perspective.

Perspective does not condone the incidents that made the Pearson government seem scandal-wracked. But they involved very few of its members and assistants, and for the most part they were not sins of corruption but errors of judgment, compounded by further errors into political disasters. The setting for the compounding was the extraordinary pressure of the flag debate. Without that, the Prime Minister would not have been so distracted and confused as to put himself at the centre of the errors in the Favreau affair. And without that, it would be impossible to understand how a Cabinet of mostly able people came to be harried into so much disrepute.

Ironically, since it was in the House of Commons that the government's weaknesses were paraded, there is another side to the picture. Despite its tactical ineptness, despite the lack of imagination which caused it to fail time and again to anticipate how Mr Diefenbaker and his henchmen would conduct their opposition, the Pearson government got an unusually heavy volume of legislation through a Parliament that it did not control by a majority. I think that was because most of the Ministers were masters of their individual briefs; and the briefs were well-prepared. Mr Pearson's flag proposal, unfortunately, was a conspicuous exception. For the most part, however, the legislation was sound enough and popular enough for the opposition to see no political advantage in more than a brief exercise in sound and fury.

Those measures included two important reforms regarding the House of Commons itself. One was provision for the redrawing of constituency boundaries, after each census, to be performed by independent commissions rather than by the political gerrymandering of the past. The second was reform of some of the archaic and time-wasting procedures of the House of Commons itself.

A special committee for this purpose was established early in the government's life, in the summer of 1963. For a long time it made no progress because, while some Conservative members were willing enough, Mr Diefenbaker had no wish to allow the government's business to proceed more efficiently and persisted in treating any suggestions for reform as an attack on the prerogatives of the opposition. Appropriately, he himself destroyed such credibility as his case might have had. The length and irrationality of the Conservative filibuster made the NDP as convinced as the government that reform of the rules of Parliament was necessary to save it from sterility. From late 1964 the NDP worked closely with the Liberal members in the procedure committee. Eventually, on the basis of the committee's work and with some expert help that we got from outside, the government in May 1965 introduced proposals for extensive changes in parliamentary procedure. The threat of an election, then very much in the air, helped to get them accepted. They were a significant step in enabling Parliament thereafter to handle the public business more efficiently, with somewhat more relevance in debate and a little more scope for private members to make themselves effective.

In the meantime, however, the government's troubles in Parliament over the flag and the scandals had destroyed the returning confidence of the spring of 1964. The ministers understandably felt that the fates were against them. Most were running their departments well. They were introducing soundly constructive and popular measures on a scale few governments could rival. The economy was growing strongly. Unemployment was being rapidly reduced. Yet increasingly, as 1964 wore on, it was not these achievements but mishaps and scandals that dominated media attention. The government's virtues seemed to do it little good in the country and to count for nothing in the House of Commons.

There the government members were frequently the underlings, harried and outmanoeuvred. The reason was not in the stars. It was in the personalities of L.B. Pearson and John Diefenbaker. The Conservative Minister who in 1957 had warned me that Pearson would not be able to cope with Diefenbaker was proving to be increasingly correct.

In history Pearson will be seen as a fairly successful Prime Minister and Diefenbaker as a highly ineffective one. But it was Diefenbaker who was given widespread credit for good intentions. The side of his personality that in 1964 was still best known was expressed in his avuncular stance with his fellow Canadians: in the speaking style of sentences without logical beginning or end, words without clear meaning, but words replete with a good man's emotions. The cloud of obscurities often made it hard to appreciate the sharpness of Diefenbaker's mind in debate. He was a matador in a contest where Pearson often seemed to be his victim, hurt, slow and blundering. Diefenbaker was entirely unscrupulous; he could set aside facts or invent whatever alleged facts suited his purpose at the moment. And he was cruel, a master of innuendo with an unerring instinct for what would most hurt his opponent.

Debate with Diefenbaker was, therefore, a game that Pearson was utterly incapable of playing. For Diefenbaker, a politician was a platform orator and a parliamentary debater. He therefore despised Pearson, who was little good in either role. Nevertheless Pearson had taken the prime ministership from him. That this was so inappropriate, in Diefenbaker's terms, meant that the despising was mingled with hating. Pearson on his part, hurt as he was by Diefenbaker's attacks, came to hate too. And he despised, because of Diefenbaker's intellectual dishonesty and his evasiveness and indecision when he was the leader of a government. But above all, Pearson was afraid of Diefenbaker in the House of Commons. That mixture of feelings seemed to numb the normally agile Pearson brain. In anything but a set speech, his parliamentary performance was increasingly evasive and indecisive.

It was this, above all, that fostered the public impression of Mr Pearson as a weak Prime Minister. In most respects, he was not. He got his own way within a talented and diverse Cabinet. The leadership was not less real for being achieved by reason and diplomacy, rather than a high hand. He resolutely withstood attacks on his program from powerful interests, often with friends at court – from the insurance industry, from the doctors, from the newspaper publishers; in 1965 he even resisted the genteel pressure of the presidents of his beloved universities.

The Prime Minister's inner strength was not, however, apparent, and he was acutely sensitive to the charge of weakness that Diefenbaker cultivated with such skill and venom in the House of Commons. The plunge into the flag issue, without consultation or preparation, was an attempt at compensation. The manner of it, I am sure, was determined by Mr Pearson's wish to convince himself and others that he could be strong and decisive. Driven by that desire, he seemed not to think at all what he was doing: he was throwing the rest of the government's carefully prepared program into chaos; and, worse, he was exposing himself to further hurt where he looked weakest, in the House of Commons. When he reaped the whirlwind of the filibuster, he was surprised and demoralized. He was not going to back down on the flag, but the price of the uncalculated strain was that he became more confused and indecisive than before.

Two incidents, in particular, made June 1964 a month of emotional hell. The first arose from the Pearson film. Some months earlier, bright people in and around the CBC had conceived the idea that a film showing people what it was like to be Prime Minister, giving an intimate picture of him at work and at home, would be spectacular television. It was a good theory, if you did not know Mr Pearson. How he came to agree to it I never understood. For some days he, a man who valued privacy, was followed almost everywhere by a television crew. I was horrified one morning to find them there when I went into his office and was told by Mr Pearson to behave as if they weren't there. Nor had many, if any, ministers been consulted.

A good deal of film was shot. The producer selected and melded bits of it to make his program. He did a clever job. Since much of the material was notable only for its dullness, he seized on the one device available to give the finished product some dramatic quality. That was the contrast between the Prime Minister and the staff member who was frequently in attendance on him: the so-called appointments secretary, or personal aide, Jim Coutts. He was young enough anyway, and in those days he had a baby face that exaggerated the contrast with the Prime Minister's sixty-seven years. Moreover, where Mr Pearson on film seemed gentle, unaggressive, tentative at best and at times waffling and uncertain, Coutts was bright, eager, confident. If Mr Pearson or anyone else had hoped that the film could correct the public image of him as a weak man, they could not have been more wrong. As he bitterly explained to me, the film made it look as though he was leaving the running of his life, if not the country, to someone young enough to be his grandson.

The arrangement with the CBC provided for review of the film before showing. The Prime Minister was entitled to ensure that it contained nothing that was properly confidential. There were few problems of that kind. The reasons for disliking the film were not grounds for requiring the CBC to make substantial changes in it. Dick O'Hagan, as press secretary, pressed for as many changes as he could make an argument for. Mr Pearson assured me that neither he personally nor O'Hagan suggested that it be suppressed. However, after much discussion and delay, CBC management decided to scrap the program. Presumably they decided that its portrayal of the Prime Minister was unfair. Certainly it was, but not more so than could have been foreseen by anyone who knew Mr Pearson's inability to be anywhere near his best on television.

Those who had been involved in making the film were, naturally, angry about its cancellation, and inevitably the story got around. Mr Pearson had to face questions, then debate, in the House. He was, to put it kindly, confused. At one point he drafted a long statement that included an evasive description of the kinds of changes in the first version of the film that had been asked for. One item was that the prominence given to one member of his staff should be reduced "in the interest of inter-office harmony." For that, I had to point out, he would deserve to be laughed out of the House of Commons chamber, and probably would be. And it had the additional demerit of being false. His objection to the prominence of Jim Coutts was that it hurt L.B. Pearson, not other people in his office.

That passage was removed from the speech before it was made, but the final version was still weak and evasive. Worse, Mr Pearson was provoked in the debate to say that he thought the CBC should show the film. This was, of course, a latter-day wish. Blown by the winds of criticism, he wanted to get the whole affair behind him as soon as possible; and, with public interest aroused, this meant showing the film. However, Mr Pearson's self-defence was that he had not earlier suggested that the film should be suppressed, and the same principle made it equally inappropriate to ask the CBC to do what would now be beneficial for the government.

A worse error soon followed. On the last Friday of June, in the question period, the Prime Minister was asked whether the government was studying the effects that separation by Quebec would have on the rest of Canada. There was no reason to be surprised; the question had come up before, and was obviously designed to trick the government into some indiscreet statement. But Mr Pearson was not prepared for it and, unaccountably, he said that "that kind of investigation" was being made. Whether the answer was an attempt at a sort of one-upmanship in the heat of the question period, or was given from a wish to stop the questioning by being accommodating, or just plain confusion, never became clear. In any event, the answer was a lie. No such study was under way or had even been contemplated.

The opposition and the media, however, naturally took the reply as a revelation, extracted under questioning, that the government regarded separation as a serious possibility. It was enough to set the Press Gallery seething, even on a summer Friday afternoon, and the wires out of Ottawa humming.

The afternoon business of the House did not require the Prime Minister's presence. He fled to Harrington Lake. The few ministers who were around were distraught. A Privy Council officer and I had to reassure them that there was no sinister plot of which they were unaware. The Prime Minister's statement was simply untrue. We quickly agreed that it could not be left to fester over the weekend; unless some correction was made promptly, the opposition could have a field day, exploiting this evidence, from the Prime Minister's own mouth, that the Pearson government was knowingly involved in the break-up of Canada. I had to write an immediate "clarification."

I was late for a dinner engagement that evening. The "clarification" was the most distasteful, and therefore slowest, job of draftsmanship I ever undertook. We decided that it could be made at all convincing only if the PCO officer and I interpreted the Prime Minister's remarks in the House as a request to us that a study be made, and we were now promptly engaged in the first, exploratory stage of what it would be. It could not be a study of separation. That was a misunderstanding. It must be a study of the economic unity of Canada, a unity too important to all Canadians to be violated by any separation.

Like everyone who writes, I have made many unintended errors. Like most controversialists, I have occasionally used arguments that I later realized to be flawed but did not go out of my way to say so. This was the only occasion when I wrote anything that was deliberately dishonest. The gist of it was:

My answers to a series of questions in the House of Commons this afternoon seem to have been misunderstood...

What I have asked for is not a study based on the possibility of the separation of Quebec from the rest of Canada...

What I have asked for, and is now in the exploratory stage in my office and the Privy Council Office, is a study of the economic inter-relations between the parts of our country.

I believe that this study will show how essential all parts of the country are to each other. I believe that it will show, to the satisfaction of all Canadians, that any separation within Canada is unthinkable...

To interpret what I said in Parliament today in any other sense would be a complete reversal of the purpose of the examination which I have asked for.

Canadian unity is far too important to permit of any such distortion. My own dedication to that unity must stand on the record of my life and on my determination since I have been Prime Minister to make co-operative federalism the foundation of national unity.

When eventually it was done – I don't think any other few hundred words took me so long – I read it over the telephone to Mike. He approved it readily enough. And, though I did not say so, I think he realized that it had been difficult to write. In thanking me, he broke down and sobbed over the telephone. I said what I could in comfort, but could not help reflecting to myself that this was not the man of six years before, who had begun his career as party leader with as bad a mistake as anyone could make. He had not sobbed then. He had bounced back with extraordinary determination. This time there was no such resiliency. He seemed to be a broken man.

In fact, while it would be an exaggeration to say that he was any longer capable of bouncing back, Mr Pearson was still toughly resilient. The prompt statement was successful in deflating the immediate issue, and he recovered from it, as he did from many other near disasters. The causes that produced those remained, however, and all of us close to him feared that, sooner rather than later, there would be one too many. We were not, I fear, as helpful to him as we might have been. Most of us – Gordon Robertson, Walter Gordon and I conspicuously – were people who liked to work systematically. To us it seemed obvious that Mike would make fewer mistakes if only he were more organized in the way he worked and used assistance. Simple changes would relieve him from giving so much attention to comparative trivia, would free time for wider consultation and more orderly consideration of major decisions, would enable him to go into the House better prepared, and therefore more confident and less likely to be driven to evasions, indecisions, and errors.

After the shock of the first budget he had tried hard to work to a more orderly and organized pattern, for his own and the government's business, than came naturally to him. Through the fall of 1963 and the winter of 1963–4 the results had not been too bad. There were no great fumbles, no scandals were apparent, legislation was well prepared, most decisions were sensible. By the spring of 1964 the government had significant achievements and seemed set for many more. But the flag debate did not only disrupt the government's program. Its tensions destroyed such order and organization as there had been in the Prime Minister's work. His office was again chaos and confusion, with everyone falling over everyone else in frantic efforts to cope with one of the crises of the moment.

The experiences of June underlined the perils, and Mr Pearson responded to pleas from Gordon Robertson and me by saying that he accepted the need for reorganization. No doubt he meant it when he said it, but he didn't stick to it.

Gordon responded with a memorandum that put the main point tactfully but very firmly. Reorganization was imperative because "Not only can the efficiency of the office and the handling of things in relation to Parliament, especially, be very greatly improved, but I am sure that the strain on you can be very substantially reduced by effective changes." The crucial change was that there should be one person clearly responsible to Mr Pearson for the operation of the office as a whole, with other staff reporting through him. That was fundamental to good administration, and Gordon bolstered the argument by appeals to precedent and experience. The change should be made at once, and I was the only person who could take on the broad responsibility.

For once, I disagreed with Gordon. In administrative principle, he was correct. But there were three reasons for not applying the principle. One was perhaps selfish on my part. I had become involved out of interest in policies and programs. I had no difficulty, in this job or in others, in combining that interest with a good deal of administrative work, which I also enjoyed. But in the circumstances of the Prime Minister's Office, broader administrative responsibility was likely to require so much dedication to the fighting of fires, discouraging because many of them need not have happened, that longer-term activities would be crowded out even more thoroughly than they already were. I could not muster much enthusiasm for helping to keep the Pearson government going if it was a sterile government, too absorbed in the crises of the moment to do any fresh thinking about emerging needs.

My second concern was that I doubted whether a more centralized organization would work, given the Pearson personality. He might intend it to do so, but under pressure the old habit of assigning a task to whomever was at hand would reassert itself. I would have responsibility but not control.

The third, and most important consideration, was the relationship with the Cabinet. Ministers already felt, I knew, that Mike was growing too dependent on the Robertson-Kent team, and they were right. I don't think they blamed us, but certainly the political dimensions of my role could not be free from difficulties. They had been accentuated by Mike's use of me as his emissary in unpleasant Cabinet changes. I had had to cross some ministers, on issues as varied as the TCA Winnipeg base and the priorities of business in the House of Commons. The stronger ministers, in particular, were bound to resent my role when Mike at times used me in effect as a barrier between him and them. So far the problem had been, I thought, manageable; but I did not want to risk increasing it, as an enlargement of my responsibilities might do.

Therefore, while I told the Prime Minister that I would undertake the change if there was no other way to get the essential better order into the business of the office, I suggested an alternative. Its central feature was the creation of a parliamentary strategy group, consisting of half a dozen senior ministers plus Mary Macdonald and me. When the House was in session, this group would meet with the Prime Minister at 9:30 each morning, immediately after his meeting with Gordon and me on administrative matters. Its job would be to foresee questions, problems and opposition moves, and to plan the government's strategy and tactics in the House. It would be Mary Macdonald's responsibility to see that decisions were implemented in the sense that Mr Pearson went into the House adequately prepared with the appropriate papers and reminders, and that any necessary information had been passed to other Liberal parliamentarians. In order that this could be better done than in the past, she would be relieved of her general responsibility for the flow of paper in the office. Jim Coutts would be promoted to that role, and I defined the task and procedures in detail. The consequential effect, I said bluntly, would be to give me more control of the operation of the office as a whole, which Gordon recommended, but it would not be overt.

The Prime Minister and I discussed all this while sitting on the lawn of 24 Sussex on a hot afternoon. He was not very happy about it, wondering whether the committee would be seen as in effect putting the prime ministership into commission and worrying about the promotion of Jim Coutts relative to Mary Macdonald. He agreed, however, that it would lessen many of his difficulties. There was another problem on his mind, much smaller but about which he was obviously embarrassed. He was due to leave within a few days for a Commonwealth Prime Ministers' meeting in London. I was scheduled to be in the delegation, and was looking forward to it, both as a break from the normal work routine and also, as Mr Pearson knew, because I planned afterwards to meet my family for a transatlantic holiday. But, with the House still in session because of the flag and so many other problems on hand, he had become worried about my being away while he was. I readily offered to stay in Ottawa for that period; I could join my family later. But this, I argued, reinforced the urgency of the reorganization. That should be made known to all concerned before he left, because it would put me in a better position to cope while he was away. Gordon Robertson, who of course had to go to London, made the same point.

So it was quite explicitly settled; I was to draft a memorandum for circulation. But the days went by and it was not circulated. Mr Pearson was about to leave, and nothing had happened. I felt that the last straw had come, and told him that, since he was leaving me in an impossible situation, I was resigning.

In retrospect, I fear that I and others were wrong to press Mike to be better organized. For us, that would mean better decisions, fewer errors. But he was a different person, an exception to many rules. Perhaps, more realistic than the rest of us, he knew that more time for the big decisions, better preparation for parliamentary questions and debate, would not make much difference. When he got into the House, facing Diefenbaker, he would still be numbed or panicked into errors. In that case, all the fuss about organization was beside the point. He might as well go on working the way he was accustomed to do.

Though he often said it, I am not sure that he in truth recognized how far the troubles he was in so constantly were of his own making. But certainly he had come philosophically to take frequent crises for granted, and for coping with those his haphazard methods and organization were as good as any. They might offend the rest of us, and make life more difficult for us most of the time, but he was the Prime Minister. I suspect he felt that the haphazard way and informal style enabled him to get us to rally round, to help him in trouble, more effectively than would have been possible with an organization approved by the textbooks. The Pearson charm, which he used so well to disarm critical colleagues, boisterous provincial premiers, indignant businessmen – indeed, almost everyone provided he met them a few at a time – concealed a strongly developed instinct for self-preservation. A number of people – Walter Gordon, Guy Favreau above all, Lucien Cardin later, and others – suffered acutely from events in which L.B. Pearson was quite as involved as they were. Yet somehow he always emerged, a little tarnished perhaps, but not deeply scathed.

The charm was indeed strong. One could become frustrated and angry, but he was so reasonably willing to listen, to join in criticism of himself or at least in half-recognition of a regrettable error, that it was difficult to be angry for long. Time and again I left such confrontations feeling, against my better judgment, that things would improve and anyway it was worthwhile to go on trying. Working with Mike Pearson was rather like the kind of love affair in which affection seems to be maintained, for a time, by quarrelling and making up.

In July 1964, separation wasn't really possible. But, while I should not have pressed him so hard to reorganize, he was wrong – then, and on other occasions with me and with other people – to say that he would do something and then, without explanation, do nothing. At the time, I felt too let down for us to go on exactly as before. The only people who knew of the quarrel were Walter Gordon and Gordon Robertson. Since Mike was going to Alberta and then directly to London, he left with a request that we find a solution. Gordon Robertson thought of the "unity study," as we had christened the investigation I had invented after Mike had told the House that we were studying separatism. I should take charge of that. It could be broadened – this was Walter's idea – to be in effect the vehicle for policy development, leading to a new election platform. A major project with which to be particularly concerned, as the pension plan had been earlier, would make it more possible than it had lately been for me to stand aside from some of the day-to-day preoccupations of the Prime Minister. That, we agreed, would be healthier for everyone.

Mr Pearson was apparently delighted with the idea, but it didn't work out. It would only have done so, given the volume and urgency of the day-to-day preoccupations, if someone had been recruited to do part of my previous work. No one was. After I returned from holiday it quickly became apparent that the Prime Minister expected me, refreshed, to do as I had before, with the unity study as an extra. It therefore came to very little. There wasn't time for it. It did serve, to a small degree, the purpose that Walter had suggested: by providing a little opportunity for reflection, it acted as an impetus to the policy developments adopted in early 1965. We then wound up the study with an "interim" report which was tabled in Parliament on 7 May 1965. It got no attention, perhaps because it ended with a recommendation that the studying should be continued under the aegis of the federal-provincial Tax Structure Committee.

Perhaps I should have avoided this disappointment, for me at least, by refusing some of the other responsibilities. But by now I was beginning better to understand the inclination of Mr Pearson, aging visibly and under strain, to go on in the way to which he was accustomed with the people who had grown familiar to him. In any event, I did not think it likely to be for very much longer. After the summer of 1964, the government's death wish was growing strong.

Those whom the gods treat badly may become bewildered enough to confuse the location of their troubles with the cause. The government's troubles, as ministers perceived them, were chiefly in the House of Commons. Their cause was not incompetence. Most of the ministers were capable enough in the House. Occasional difficulties and embarrassments would have been unimportant if the Prime Minister had been a confident parliamentarian and better able to deal with Mr Diefenbaker.

However, while weak political parties can be quick to blame their leaders for their troubles, the Liberal party then was made of sterner stuff. Mike had a great capital of respect on which to draw. In Cabinet discussion he was still, generally speaking, both strong and diplomatic. His charm continued to be disarming. His problems made the affection for him protective. Above all, in practical politics, there was no one to whom ministers were disposed to turn as an alternative leader. Judy LaMarsh was the only one who, while still in the Cabinet, became resentful and avowedly critical of the Prime Minister, less because of his treatment of her – though that was not good – than because her impulsively generous nature recoiled from all the unfairness to the greathearted Favreau. Otherwise, while there was some disillusionment and frustration, in the eyes of the Cabinet as a whole Mr Pearson's virtues continued far to outweigh his defects. There was grumbling, but not disloyalty.

Yet ministers had to look for some relief to their troubles. And since it was in the House of Commons that they felt their troubles, there was a tempting answer. They had come rather bitterly to expect that everything the government undertook would be spoiled by parliamentary fumbles. Since they had little reason to blame themselves, and were not prepared to blame the Prime Minister, something else had to be corrected. As 1964 wore on, many ministers became increasingly convinced that the root problem was the lack of a parliamentary majority. If only they could dissolve this Parliament, call an election, gain a majority, cut Mr Diefenbaker down to size, everything would be different. And – despair showed at this point in such discussion – it should be soon because otherwise there would be more fumbles further to weaken the government's position and its chances of gaining the magic majority.

I labelled all this the death wish. I doubted that a parliamentary majority would improve the government's performance, and I doubted even more that an election, deliberately called for the purpose, would produce a majority. This was confirmed by an opinion survey late in 1964

– or rather, by my interpretation of it; others detected more grounds for optimism. The survey certainly showed that people did not think much of the Liberals, and even less of the Conservatives. Many were noncommittal. The mood seemed to me to be that the country would indeed be relieved to be able to give the government a majority *when* it had improved. But they would be sceptical if the government's case was that it needed a majority in order to improve. The improvement had to be demonstrated first, and to see an early election as the means to a majority and hence improvement was simply escapism. It was a myopic reaction to the government's troubles, unrelated to the realities of how people would make up their minds to vote.

This argument, however, made no difference. Many of the politicians continued to look to an election as their relief. To my surprise, even Mr Pearson was infected. I was surprised because, much as he dreaded facing Mr Diefenbaker across the floor of the House, he was even more worried by the prospect of electioneering at the level of vituperation to be expected in what we thought of, with partisanship, as the old chief's last agonies.

But the infection was there. I saw it on 28 December 1964, when I gave the Prime Minister a memorandum on the program for 1965. He was to be away for a short New Year holiday, and I wanted a basis for planning work meantime. He therefore revised the memorandum the same day. I was taken aback to find that, at a point where I had referred to "this year's circumstances" (that is, 1965) he had inserted "which may well require an election."

The writing was on the wall in larger letters at a meeting of the Liberal campaign committee on 5 January 1965. The committee had been kept in existence as an obvious precaution, given the government's minority position, but that was not the spirit of the discussion now. I reported to Mr Pearson that it had made sense only if it was presumed that he had already decided to dissolve Parliament in April. I tried to counteract such thinking in a 15 January memorandum under the heading "Strategy for Government: NOT Election Strategy." It deployed all the arguments against regarding an election as the way out of the government's troubles. Unless it was defeated in Parliament the government's duty was to govern, and the primary question of the moment was what was it going to try to do, as a government with a program for the people of Canada, in 1965. It had to show that we meant business, that we could get things done, smoothly and efficiently. In that case, there was a good chance that the House would be a different place, and we would have a much improved record behind us when an election campaign was necessary. A successful election must grow naturally out of a chain of events arising from our effort to govern well. Opposition to that effort *might* make a 1965 election appropriate, but the decision must be derivative, flowing from what we were trying to do, not primary.

The danger was that it would become primary because talking made it so. If the expectation of an early election continued to be built up in the press, as it was being, the opposition had a strengthened incentive to obstruct enough to contain the record on which the government could campaign. We probably would get ourselves into an election, but from weakness not strength. The danger could be removed only if the Prime Minister made it crystal clear that he rejected the early-electioneering position and insisted to ministers and the party organization that their talk of it must stop.

Mr Pearson wrote at the top of this memorandum: "I agree with the ideas and tactics of this memo and will make the position *clear...*" He never did. The election talk continued and was increasingly reflected in press speculation. The government drifted, as I feared, into a "damned if we do, damned if we don't" situation. If, after all the build-up of expectations, there wasn't an election, it would be taken to mean that the government had lost its nerve, did not think it could win, and the opposition in Parliament would be more difficult than ever. If there was an election, it could easily be presented to marginal voters as the planned contrivance of power-obsessed men demanding a parliamentary majority in their own interests rather than for any good they would do for Canada.

The election talk became the cause of an entirely unnecessary movement to failure. Mr Pearson, despite his expressed agreement with my view, did nothing to stop the drift.

28 *Success, but Short Vision*

In fairness to the ministers and other Liberals who went into 1965 intent on an election soon, it should be said that, despite its troubles, the government now had solid reasons for thinking that it would be able to campaign strongly on the record of its two years in office. Above all, during the Pearson years the economy performed well, far better than it had done in the Diefenbaker years. The unemployment of the five wasted years, as we had called them, was virtually eliminated. Real economic growth was strong, prices were comparatively stable.

In this, we had to count ourselves lucky. But that was not all. While it is true that economic circumstances were favourable, it is also true that the quality of the government's economic management was better both than it had been and than it was to be.

Walter Gordon, who had suffered so much for his first budget, had every reason to glow with satisfaction when he introduced his third one (and, as it turned out, his last) in April 1965. The gross national product had increased by almost 16 per cent in two years. Half a million additional jobs had been created. Real income per person – the most meaningful statistic of economic performance – had been stagnant during the 1957 to 1962 period. In one year, from 1963 to 1964, it had risen by 4.4 per cent. Unemployment had been halved, to under 4 per cent. This economic buoyancy was barely affecting prices. The cost of living was rising at only the same structural rate, under 2 per cent a year, that it had done during the 1957–62 years. Externally, we were competitive. Exports of goods and services in the first quarter of 1965 were 22 per cent greater than in the same period of 1963.

And the public finances had been brought into order. Whereas the last Diefenbaker fiscal year, 1962–3, had produced what then seemed the enormous budgetary deficit of $692 millions, the 1964–5 deficit was a mere $39 millions. Those were the figures on the conventional accounting. In economic terms, the federal finances had moved into substantial surplus, and Walter was therefore able in the 1965 budget to make a substantial cut in tax rates, on a pattern that made taxation more progressive. Properly, given a growing population and the scope for further economic expansion, he budgeted for a small deficit, on conventional accounting, of $300 millions. Since growth did in fact continue vigorously, the actual result for 1965–6 was again a virtually balanced budget. Walter Gordon, in his short term as Minister of Finance, put the national finances back into as good shape as they had been under Doug Abbott. Unfairly, he has never been given the same credit for it.

Broadly, it seems fair to say that there was little wrong with federal economic policy during the years 1963–5. Walter's judgments, supported by a strengthened Finance Department under Bob Bryce, proved to be sound. It is true that not everything was done that needed to be – there is never time – but the priorities were about right. The valid criticism of economic policy over the whole life of the Pearson government is that it coasted on its early success. The buoyant state of the economy induced complacency. The vision was short. Some of the longer-term measures needed to meet emerging needs were not put in place during the government's second phase, in 1966–8.

Part of the reason was that the new institutions which were important to the government's program disappointed the expectations we had of them. That was equally true of Walter's pet projects – the Department of Industry and the Canada Development Corporation – and of mine, which was the Economic Council of Canada.

The Department of Industry, in its original form and its subsequent incarnations, spent plenty of money to subsidize a great variety of industrial activities and projects. In the process, it created a large, well-meaning and fussy bureaucracy. What it failed to do was to develop any coherent industrial strategy to guide its interventions. Except for the Auto Pact – the child of Walter's original concept of the role of the department – it has not done much to assist the major structural adaptations in Canadian industry required for success in a rapidly changing world economy.

The Canada Development Corporation has been an equal disappointment. Walter's concept of it was developed early, but action was inhibited in 1964 by the government's induced caution about anything that smacked of economic nationalism. The resolution preliminary to the legislation was eventually presented to Parliament on 3 May 1965. The corporation then envisaged would have been able to contribute in a major way to financing the initiation and expansion of Canadian enterprises. It could have become a large shareholder in companies that might otherwise pass into foreign ownership, and also in the subsidiaries of foreign companies willing to embrace substantial Canadian participation in their activities here.

Walter's proposal died, however, with the election of 1965. His attempts to revive it, late in the life of the Pearson government, failed. The institution of the same name that was established in 1971 was very different from the original concept in form, and even more different in the management objectives it pursued. It was one of several creations of the Trudeau era that, in terms of positive impact on Canada's economic development, might as well not have been.

The story of the Economic Council of Canada is less unhappy, but not much less disappointing in actual results. It was the subject of resolution number one on the order paper of the twenty-sixth Parliament, in May 1963. The legislation encountered little difficulty in the House, and was assented to on 2 August. The twenty-five members of the Council were appointed before the end of the year, and the Council met for the first time on 14 January 1964. Welcoming the members on the government's behalf, Maurice Lamontagne eloquently expressed the high hopes that we then entertained:

> I have waited a long time to address just such a group in my country. With anxiety, I have watched other industrial countries of the western world making significant strides which we have failed to match.

The secret of their success did not lie so much in the application of sophisticated economic techniques, although these were not absent, but rather in the consensus they were able to generate as to what their economies could look like five to ten years in the future. Until today, Canada has lacked an institutional framework within which to build this consensus, this long view. You collectively are such an institution.

Since the Economic Council has existed for a generation with the purpose for which it was created long ignored and forgotten, I shall enlarge on that quotation. The reason is not only to illustrate the frequently sad contrast between the intent of one government and the reality that bureaucrats create when subsequent politicians are indifferent to that intent. The stronger reason is that now, more than ever, Canada greatly needs a way of doing what the Economic Council was supposed to do.

Its purpose had been set out, in somewhat more detail, in notes that I prepared for the Prime Minister when the resolution was introduced in Parliament. The objective was to achieve

by consultation between government and the public in its many manifestations, a broad consensus about the objectives and methods of economic policy. The government's hope is that we can establish an Economic Council of Canada which will be an effective instrument for creating in Canada the kind of economic consensus we need if we are to make the most of our resources, achieve and maintain high levels of employment, make our economic growth rapid and consistent, and compete successfully, as we must, in the new trading world...

The great value of an Economic Council will lie in bringing together the thinking of government and the thinking of our great industries, our trade unions, our farm organizations, so that they can together take an understanding and far-sighted view of the policy needs that exist in the private sphere, just as much as in the public sphere of our national life. This cannot be done in vague generalities. It means that the Council and the representatives of the major sectors of our economy should sit down together and freely discuss how they see the prospects and the needs of each sector of the economy and what the needs of one sector imply for the needs of others...

The legislation gave the Council the terms of reference required for this major purpose. The original membership was strong and the Council began, under John Deutsch's chairmanship, well enough. But careful nursing was required if the fledgling institution was to grow to its intended role, with its purpose understood and established. Unfortunately, John Deutsch did not stay long. I expostulated to him about the sad loss to the public interest, but his preference, understandably, was the major role in academic administration offered at the university, Queen's, that meant so much in his life.

John's successor, Arthur Smith, was able enough but did not have the status, in Ottawa and outside, to overcome the inertia and resistance that stood in the Council's way, unless there was strong government backing. That disappeared with the departure of Walter Gordon and Maurice Lamontagne from the Cabinet at the end of 1965. The bureaucracy had no use for consensus-building, particularly by an "outside" agency. It regarded the Council as an infringement of the bureaucracy's rightful monopoly of policy-making, or at least of advice to ministers. There was resentment of economists paid by the government but enjoying independence of it. Such attitudes would have been submerged quickly enough if the politicians had sustained their interest in the role they had given to the Council. Preoccupied with short-run problems, they did not.

Subsequently, neglect of the Council was replaced by something close to contempt. The Trudeau system provided little place for consultation and consensus, and certainly none for an agency that was located in Ottawa yet partially independent. The effect on the Council was magnified by an accident of personality. The officialdom of the Finance Department was no longer headed by the wise Bob Bryce. It would entertain no challenge to its professed monopoly of economic wisdom, and the Prime Minister was its disciple. The Economic Council was pushed to the sidelines. It became no more than a competent research organization. It was given neither the personalities nor the resources to pursue its major purpose of consultation and consensus-building. Even when, as the Trudeau government approached deathbed repentance, it recognized the need for new approaches to long-term economic policy, the Council was not re-called to its function. Instead, the elephantine Macdonald Royal Commission was created.

This is the story of a sadly missed opportunity. The assumption of easy postwar prosperity had been broken in the late 1950s. In the mid-sixties the economy was again strong, there was no sense of crisis, but there was growing recognition of long-term problems. The public mood, extending to both business and labour, was one in which broadly based understandings about socio-economic objectives and basic policy directions were possible. I do not suggest that the building of consensus and confidence in a coherent set of policies is ever easy. But in the 1960s the opportunity existed, if the government had given understanding leadership and had encouraged the Economic Council to act as the appropriate instrument.

It seems to me even clearer now than I thought it in 1963 that an economy such as Canada's can operate successfully in contemporary social conditions only if government is a much more open process than is provided by existing structures and procedures. Increasingly complex technologies are constantly intensifying our interdependence and public awareness, but also the disruptive power available to special interests. In these circumstances government policies cannot be realistic and effective unless they rest on broad understanding and agreement in the society. And that cannot be made definite enough without the focus of a representative body, allied to government but not of it, under whose aegis trends are analyzed, possible future scenarios examined, issues raised and frankly discussed, viewpoints deployed, alternatives for long-term policies discussed on a continuing basis. Without such a focus it is hardly possible that there can be the substratum of common concern that would enable the myriad decision-makers of a pluralistic society, governmental and non-governmental, to act with understanding of each other, and without such understanding we cannot achieve the degree of harmony and coherence now essential to a free society.

The Pearson government, however, lulled by prosperity but demoralized by the 1965 election, did not in its second phase do much about things that were not immediate. There was one other institutional initiative of potential importance. We owed it partly to the Glassco Commission but chiefly to the perceptiveness of C.J. Mackenzie, then already some years retired from the National Research Council but as lively as ever. He wrote to me as early as 1963, urging the importance of a science policy and the need to develop a new way of creating it. This was the kind of initiative that Mr Pearson at that time encouraged, and by January 1964 we had a report from C.J. that was the genesis of the Science Council of Canada. It has proved to be at times a constructive influence, or at least a useful prod, but has increasingly been shackled by the same political indifference and bureaucratic hostility to which the Economic Council fell victim.

Walter Gordon returned to the Cabinet in January 1967, in a second attempt to get something done about the extent of foreign ownership in the Canadian economy. The only result was the report of the Watkins task force, which Mr Pearson liked but the majority of the Cabinet dismissed as an academic exercise that the government could not endorse in any part. My own view has remained that, while we should be cautious about measures that affect the outcome of ventures already undertaken, it is certainly the responsibility of government to say when enough is enough. We are long past that point in foreign control of

Canadian industries. A considerable element of external enterprise is likely to be good for most economies, and certainly it is unavoidable in Canadian circumstances. But its vast extent has narrowed the base for our own entrepreneurship. With so much industry directed from abroad, we lack the critical mass of enterprise, experience, technology, capital and innovative skill in the hands of people whose primary interest is in enlarging the scope of Canadian operations both for our relatively small home market and for export. If that were not so, we surely would not have lagged as badly as we have since the 1960s in adjusting our production and our employment to the changing conditions of comparative advantage in world trade.

The opportunity to take corrective action existed in the 1960s and all of us associated with the Pearson government must bear some responsibility for failing to take it. We could have developed coherent policies to enlarge the scope for Canadian enterprise by limiting foreign acquisitions and new foreign ventures, particularly in the manufacturing and service sectors, unless they were undertaken with substantial Canadian participation. We did not, and subsequently the Trudeau government's fits of economic nationalism did more harm than good. The occasional aggressions against established American interests were counter-productive. FIRA, which could have been a good idea, was unfortunately an institution without a policy. As so often happens in the process of political compromise among ministers with different viewpoints, it was set up without clear guidelines for its decisions, for which foreign investments to accept and which to reject. As a result it was a bureaucratic agency that caused a maximum of irritation for a minimum of effectiveness. Understandably but regrettably, the consequence was to give a bad name to all serious ideas for corrective action. The reaction has been to embrace the American connection as if being like the United States was the solution, instead of part of the problem.

In other policy areas the Pearson government can be given credit for more foresight. The need for active manpower measures, in order to facilitate adjustments to economic change and to raise educational and skill levels, was understood and, as will be discussed later, major improvements in policy and organization were made. Thanks to Judy LaMarsh, one of the most fundamental of emerging social changes was recognized through the Royal Commission on the Status of Women.

Unfortunately, another Royal Commission closed off the other most important area in which major reforms were needed to encourage the enterprise, innovative power and flexibility of the economy, as well as to improve social equity and the environment for labour-management cooperation. That area was, of course, taxation. The Carter Commission, established by the Diefenbaker government, dragged on and on, and eventually reported in February 1967. Such value as Royal Commissions enquiries may occasionally have is nullified when they act for so long as a stop to policy development by other means.

In fairness, it should be said that most ministers were probably relieved to have so good an excuse not to come to grips with fundamental issues in tax policy. Nerves had been shattered by the failure of the attempt in the 1963 budget to use taxation as a weapon against foreign takeovers. The 1964 budget would therefore have been a stand-pat one in any event. By 1965, however, two important issues had to be faced. One, discussed in an earlier chapter, was the use of advertising taxation to prevent further foreign ownership of newspapers and periodicals. The other, as noted at the beginning of this chapter, was that the state of the economy and the national finances now called for a tax cut.

Mr Pearson had not maintained the hyper-secrecy which led him in 1963 to tell Walter not to discuss his budget proposals with me. Subsequently, the Prime Minister sought my involvement. In 1965 there was no difficulty in agreeing that a simple cut in personal income tax was the best measure in the circumstances, and that 10 per cent was about the right size for the cut. I emphasized the importance of presenting this popular but crude measure as an interim one; more thoroughgoing reforms in the tax system would be considered when the Carter Commission had reported. However, in studying the draft budget early in April 1965, I was appalled to find that there was, in effect, a structural change. The 10 per cent cut was to be applied across the board, to the amount of everyone's basic federal tax, subject only to a ceiling of $1,000.

In those days $1,000 was a lot of money. It meant that the full 10 per cent rate of reduction in tax would apply to people with annual incomes of $30,000, which in 1965 was riches, or more if they employed a few tax dodges. The man with a wife and two children earning $5,000 a year – then very much a taxable income – would benefit from the tax cut by only $30 a year in take-home pay, as opposed to the rich person's extra $1,000.

This was too regressive for my liking. I argued vehemently that, if the government didn't want to be progressive, it would be better not to raise the issue of a maximum at all: let a few very rich people get thousands of dollars of tax relief by applying the 10 per cent fully across the board. My case, of course, was that we should be progressive. While the tax change had to be simple, and it was desirable to give a substantial benefit to middle and upper-middle income earners, to small businesspeople and managers and professionals, those results could be reconciled with greater social equity if the full 10 per cent cut applied only up to incomes of around $20,000 a year (1965 dollars!). This would be achieved if the ceiling was not $1,000 but $500.

Some argument followed, and in the end a compromise. The ceiling was lowered, but not quite as much as I argued for. It was settled at $600. That made it, for the circumstances, a reasonably progressive budget.

Major developments in tax policy, however, were stayed while the Carter Commission took its time, and unfortunately the delay extended over the whole term of one of the few ministers with the moral courage and intellectual capacity to make fundamental tax reforms, as Walter Gordon might have done. Mitchell Sharp cannot be criticized for failing to act on the report during the last, centennial-dominated year of the Pearson government. The same defence cannot be entered for the next Minister, Edgar Benson, who took until November 1969 to produce a White Paper embracing only a greatly diluted version of the admirable Carter proposals. Worse, it was not until 1971 that the Trudeau government, harassed by the vehement objections of vested interests, legislated minor tax reforms that were a massive retreat even from its own White Paper and meant that Carter's work had come almost to nothing. The uncertainty, extending over the first three years of the Trudeau government, was a significant inhibition to investment decisions, and thereby helped to establish the economic stagnation of the 1970s.

It was then that the country paid a high price for the tensions of its labour-management relations. In this area, the Pearson government's record was mixed. In its reformist phase, it introduced the federal labour code, legislated in 1965. Allan MacEachen, as Minister of Labour, was dedicated to it. During his many years as a Minister, from 1963 to 1984, Allan J. contributed greatly to the tactics of the government and his party, and few politicians can have secured more benefits for their own constituencies. He was not, however, a man for the details of policy. The labour code was his great legislative achievement.

Conventional economists, of course, object to a minimum wage as creating a rigidity that hampers economic adjustments. It is true that, unless the minimum is set well below prevailing rates in union-organized, semi-skilled occupations, it can eliminate some jobs and push some activities into an underground economy where productivity may be low. It is also true, however, that a minimum wage set at a realistically moderate rate, and with its associated provisions regarding hours, overtime and other working conditions, is still a significant protection against exploitation of the weaker sections of the labour force. Moreover, even people whose only concern is efficiency should recognize that legislation on minimum conditions is an essential underpinning for any confidence that organized labour may have in the economic structure, and therefore necessary to the social consensus without which so-called efficiency policies will not work. The 1965 federal measure was realistically moderate and ranks among the important Pearson reforms.

There have to be more questions about the government's other innovation in industrial relations, collective bargaining in the public service. This was planned by 1965 and legislated in 1967, but with a difference. The plan had been to provide for collective bargaining with binding arbitration. There was, however, strong pressure for the right to strike, and the Cabinet in the end agreed on it. Doubting ministers comforted themselves with an unrealistic expectation that in practice public servants would not be so militant as to strike. Reluctantly, I have to say that, in the broad terms in which the right was provided, it was a mistake.

In fairness, the Cabinet in 1967 could not have foreseen the vast burgeoning of the public service that occurred under the next government, and that combined with collective bargaining to transform public service salaries into the leading force of the cost-push inflation of the 1970s. There was, however, an ominous precedent in the Pearson years. In 1966 a strike of seaway workers was averted by government acceptance of a mediation award of a 30 per cent pay increase.

The cause of subsequent trouble lay, not in public service collective bargaining, which was inevitable, but in the broadness of the right to strike and in the carelessness of bureaucratic expansionism that followed. Before the end, the Pearson government was beginning to take fright at the prospects, and in that fright there were already beginnings, in the minds of both ministers and senior civil servants, of the error that dominated the 1970s: the confusion of cost-push inflation and monetarism, which led to the abandonment of demand-management for full employment and cramped the Canadian economy into rigidity, into a loss of innovation and efficiency, as well as into an inability, unknown since the 1930s, to meet the major requirements of a healthy society.

Until 1969, this was no more than a cloud on the horizon, though in fairness to those who came after, it must be said that the government of 1963–8 did not have the foresight to take some measures it could have done to strengthen the economy in the longer term.

29 *At War*

Canada's "war on poverty" was at the time interpreted by some people as a political gimmick: launched to meet a political need, winning much attention for a few months, and abandoned when the Liberals' main objective, to win a majority in the 1965 election, was not achieved. That perception became entrenched, naturally enough, with the abandonment. The reality, however, is rather different and more significant, both for the policies of the 1960s and for our problems today.

There was indeed a political motivation, but it was to provide an alternative to planning for an election in 1965. My hope was that I was proposing a line of government action that would, incidentally, stop ministers and party officials creating the expectation of an election.

The program with which the government had started in 1963 was larger than is usually contemplated for a full four-year term. By 1965 a good deal of it had been implemented, but a good deal also remained. From a managerial viewpoint, there was no reason to add to it. The psychological need, however, was rather different. The government felt and looked tired and worn by all the battering it had undergone. To stick to its program was not enough. If the death wish was to be overcome, if public confidence was to be restored, there had to be a sense of getting a second wind. There might not be, there should not be, significantly more new measures than were already on the agenda. But there needed to be a way of giving them some new coherence as a program: not a change in what the government was doing but the injection of some new spirit into the doing.

My answer to this need was influenced by the "unity study." In the words of the brief report of that study: "The advantages of national economic unity become fully manifest only in circumstances of strong and dynamic growth in all parts of Canada ... the regional inequalities consequent on failure to realize the potential of the various regions have been one of the main divisive forces in our society." It was the same thought that was most eloquently expounded by Mr Trudeau in his 1968 election campaign.

Regional inequalities were, however, simply the most politically significant aspect of a broader feature of the society that in the 1950s and 1960s we saw as affluent. In its excellent first report the Economic Council of Canada, fulfilling the instruction to assess the potential of the economy, estimated that the real income of the average Canadian could increase by over 20 per cent in the seven years from 1963 to 1970. The realization of such potential posed, however, a new kind of problem. While the great majority of people could be much better off, there would tend to be a widening gap between them and a substantial minority who could not adapt to, or were not in a position to benefit from, the increasing sophistication of the economy.

This line of thought paralleled the inspiration for President Johnson's "war on poverty" in the United States. What I proposed was far from a copy of that model. Our economic and political circumstances were very different, and I struggled hard for the use of a different label: the Canada Opportunity Plan. The struggle was in vain. In this as in so many matters, a distinctive Canadian culture could not stand up to the pervasive influence, through the media, of American examples. The program was almost universally identified as the Canadian war on poverty.

It was first suggested in a memorandum I wrote to the Prime Minister on 28 December 1964. He responded enthusiastically. In late January, after he returned from holiday, and when he had agreed, he said, with my anti-election memorandum previously referred to, I presented him with "Canada Opportunity Plan: A Proposal."

While this memorandum made a specific proposal, essentially it was a statement of the thinking that lay behind the main thrust of the policies followed by the government of Canada from 1963 to 1970. After that, concern about inflation led our government, in common with many others, unwisely to set aside the policies required for economic growth and full employment. Great harm has thereby been done to the fabric of Western society and of the world economy. They will not be repaired unless ways are belatedly found to reconcile the containment of inflation with updated versions of the themes of the 1960s. For that reason, those are worth briefly recalling here. The memorandum defined two objectives: "The Canadian Opportunity Plan ... will improve the opportunities of people who are not earning adequate incomes; and for those who cannot take advantage even of improved opportunities, it will furnish improved assistance to raise them and their families above the line of abject poverty."

The plan was not a rigid set of measures, but an approach within which a variety of existing and new measures could be developed according to circumstances. The basics were stated:

> For Canadians as a whole, prospects are good. The Economic Council has shown how much our economy is able to grow ... The federal government has the central responsibility, which it fully accepts, for helping to ensure that this economic progress is in fact achieved.
>
> The federal government has a further responsibility: to help to ensure that such progress benefits all Canadians...
>
> The poor are in many cases poor because things once went wrong for them – they were ill, or in the wrong place, or got little schooling – and they have never had a good second chance; they have been trapped on the outside, unable to push open a door into the affluent society. The purpose of the Canada Opportunity Plan is to create second chances, to open doors, to ensure that people are not needlessly shut out of the affluent society.
>
> Such a program is not, however, a program for the poor alone. It

is a program for all Canadians, because there is no more effective
way to encourage economic expansion than to turn an unemployed
slum-dweller or a sub-marginal farmer into a normal worker, a normal spender; to open up opportunities for people is to put new driving force into the engines of economic expansion...

In doing this, we are recognizing one of the important ways in
which a relatively affluent, expanding economy calls for ideas different from our traditional ones. "Economic" policies and "social" policies are conventionally regarded as different territories; often, indeed, there is an underlying assumption that their requirements
conflict. Today, that assumption can be the enemy equally of good
economics and of sound social policy. The best policies in both fields
will often develop from an understanding and realistic marriage of
the two sets of considerations. That is why a war on poverty is not
to be fought by hand-outs. It involves, certainly, some assistance
measures; but basically, it is a series of programs to improve opportunities.

There were, the memorandum pointed out, many existing federal and
provincial programs that contributed to improving opportunities and
reducing poverty. Some were shared programs, and almost all of the
relevant federal activities required consultation and co-operation with
the provinces. The Canadian way was not to copy the Americans by
setting up a new agency to mount and administer programs. That should
continue to be the responsibility of the appropriate departments. The
requirement was a focal point within government to develop a general
approach to increasing opportunities and removing poverty, to stimulate
and co-ordinate programs and to settle priorities.

For this purpose, a small secretariat within the Privy Council Office
should report to a Cabinet committee under the Prime Minister's chairmanship. The addition to the machinery of government was simply "a
new planning point at which economic considerations and social considerations are brought together as a basis for clarifying and co-ordinating
policy decisions."

The broad result should be to build a "shelf" of programs and projects
ready for implementation as circumstances made them appropriate. But
the Canada Opportunity Plan must be inaugurated with a few specific
measures suitable for action in 1965. The memorandum ended by suggesting that the strongest candidates for such action were:

1 Some new measures of encouragement, additional to tax incentives,
  for the expansion of industries in the "slow-growth" areas.

2 Improved assistance measures for the older people, already retired, who will not benefit from the Canada Pension Plan.

3 The new general assistance program, based on needs, which is being developed as an alternative to unemployment assistance and the categorical welfare programs.

4 Some limited first steps towards the implementation of a medical insurance program, directed to meeting the cases of greatest need.

5 The early development of programs which will facilitate the retraining and, where necessary, the relocation of workers displaced by automation or other industrial changes.

The Prime Minister responded at once and the next day I drafted a short memorandum which he sent to all ministers. It asked for prompt suggestions of items to be included in the 1965 program, emphasizing that this must be at once "simple, clear-cut, realistic" and "attractive and constructive." The program must make an imaginative and important contribution to economic expansion and also continue the government's work in social policy. These requirements "might best be approached by developing a Canadian version of the war on poverty, though it might better be thought of as a campaign to improve the opportunities of all Canadians to participate in economic progress."

This memorandum, dated 27 January gained prompt acceptance. The immediate measures to be included under the heading of the Canada Opportunity Plan were considered and quite soon settled; by 5 March I had written the first draft of the throne speech to open the new session of Parliament. As delivered on 5 April, the speech declared, after noting the country's high rate of economic growth:

> All the great potentialities of our economy are not, however, being realized. The talents of some of our people are wasted because of poverty, illness, inadequate education and training, inequality in opportunities for work. To combat these problems, to improve the opportunities of people who are now at a disadvantage, is to put new power into economic expansion and to enhance the unity of our country.
>
> My Government therefore is developing a programme for the full utilization of our human resources and the elimination of poverty among our people.

The speech went on to list specific measures for the 1965 session. The area development program would be expanded, to improve employment opportunities and help people to take full advantage of them. Manpower measures would include the provision of grants and loans for workers moving to new jobs, as well as improved training in industry and extended vocational services. The ARDA legislation would be amended to create a fund for rural economic development, and a number of measures were promised to "enable farmers generally to achieve larger and more reliable incomes so that their living and working standards will be comparable to those enjoyed in other sectors of our economy." There was also to be an expanded fisheries development program. The Canada Assistance Plan would provide for federal sharing in the cost of comprehensive social assistance on the basis of need. The government would propose "the establishment of a Company of Young Canadians, through which the energies and talents of youth can be enlisted in projects for economic and social development."

On medicare there was, at that stage, necessary caution: for 1965, the commitment was only to discuss it with the provinces, in the declared belief "that public policy should be directed to improving the quality of health services and to ensuring that all Canadians can obtain needed health care, irrespective of their ability to pay."

On the timing of some other measures, the Throne Speech was far too optimistic. It undertook, for example, revision of unemployment insurance, which was not achieved for several years. The instruction to make the program simple had not withstood the activist zeal, at that point, of the Cabinet. The other measures that were listed included establishment of the Canada Development Corporation, the Science Council of Canada, and the Indian Claims Commission. The Fulton-Favreau formula for constitutional amendment was to be enacted. Collective bargaining "and arbitration" were to be provided for the public service. There was to be the advertising tax measure for Canadian publications; a retirement age for Senators; limitation and payment of election expenses; comprehensive reforms of railway regulations. The many areas in which legislation was to be amended included banking, broadcasting, citizenship and immigration.

Most of all this was done by the Pearson government, but much of it after 1965. The immediate measures in the "war on poverty" were, however, promptly pressed forward. The "focal point," in the form of what we called the "special planning secretariat" in the Privy Council Office, was established at once. Mr Pearson held a press conference on 15 April to announce this. The secretariat would report to a special Cabinet committee under his chairmanship. As his policy secretary, I would be secretary of the committee and would direct the special planning secretariat. The occasion was a high point for me. After referring to my "special interest ... in those areas of public policy in which economic and social considerations have to be brought into harmony" and my particular involvement in co-operative federalism, the other essential feature of the program, the Prime Minister said "I have never worked with anybody in all my years of public service who has had greater devotion and ability. I am very happy, indeed, that he will be taking on this job..."

Bob Phillips – imaginative and energetic, as well as an experienced official – was appointed Deputy Director, and the Departments of Health and Welfare, Labour and Industry promptly seconded an able official each to the Secretariat. In the course of a few months, three other people were added to the staff. Information, advice and research were solicited, and gladly provided, from a variety of agencies – federal, provincial and private – and from a considerable number of individuals. The work done between the spring and the end of 1965 was prodigious. Because in organization it was so short-lived, and regarded in hindsight with natural political cynicism, the significance of the "war on poverty" has been generally underrated. At the time it tapped strong currents of enthusiasm. It enabled several major measures to be implemented with unusual promptness. And it stimulated policy-thinking in directions that remained influential for some years afterwards.

Of the immediate measures, the easiest to set up was the fund for rural economic development (FRED). It was in the competently energetic hands of Maurice Sauvé. The fund was $50 millions, at the time a significant sum to be available as seed money. The aim was to carry out some large-scale pilot projects in the development of rural areas with significant problems. The interlake region of Manitoba, eastern Quebec, northeastern New Brunswick and the Maqtaquac area of that province, together with Prince Edward Island as a whole, quickly emerged as appropriate areas. Much of what was done was simply a more intensive application of normal federal and provincial programs to the problems of such areas. FRED financed additional action. It provided at once the incentive and the means to round out the normal programs into a comprehensive development plan for each area.

The legislation was not in practice passed until 1966, but planning went ahead in anticipation and the plans for the Manitoba interlake and the two New Brunswick areas were soon in operation. The more elaborate eastern Quebec plan was begun in 1968. The smallness of PEI – equivalent in population to one federal constituency in growing metropolitan areas – did not alter the fact that the development plan involved a whole province and its government, with consequent delicacies in federal-provincial relations and tensions in provincial politics. The plan was inaugurated only after FRED had been absorbed in 1968 into the new Department of Regional Economic Expansion. It proved to be a long-term plan that made considerable improvements in the island's economy. The FRED plans as a whole were worthwhile, though they disappointed some of the most optimistic expectations and their lessons were not applied to parallel efforts for other regions with weak economies.

The most important of the 1965 programs was the Canada Assistance Plan (CAP). It has become conventional to object to the Canadian welfare state as a confusing mishmash of programs with major inefficiencies. The characterization is correct. What is hard to comprehend is that anyone should be so naïve as to suppose that hard-fought social changes could be achieved, in our confederation and with our cultural and political diversities, by any means except piecemeal programs. Certainly consolidation and reform should follow, but they will not be achieved by a passion for model-building and number-crunching. Computer programs are not a substitute for the observation of people and hard thought about social objectives and causal relations.

CAP was, in part, a considerable rationalization of what had been the separate categorical assistance programs for the blind and the disabled and for elderly people not qualified for the old-age security pension. The assistance per person was limited to a maximum equal to that pension. Since 1956 the federal government had also shared the costs of unemployment assistance for those without both a job and an unemployment insurance benefit. CAP created instead one general social assistance program. It brought in needy people hitherto excluded, notably mothers with dependent children, and removed the arbitrary maximum. The amount of assistance that the federal government would share was henceforth the need in the individual case, as assessed by provincial and municipal authorities. Previously separate programs were consolidated under one administration and, most importantly, the federal government shared the cost of improving the administration. It thereby made possible the great improvement in the quality of social work services that there has been in the past twenty years.

All this was the work, primarily, of Joe Willard, as Deputy Minister of Welfare, and of his able departmental colleagues. They had consulted carefully with their provincial colleagues. No program involved less federal-provincial controversy. The battles had to be fought within Ottawa. They were of two kinds. The important ones were with those who disliked so large an extension of the federal role. The annoying ones were with the Department of Labour which, though it had itself done little that was constructive, belatedly claimed part of the ground covered by CAP as its territory. To dispose quickly of that bureaucratic nonsense provided a useful test of the value of the special planning secretariat within the machinery of government.

The federal-provincial conference at which CAP was accepted, at the

First Minister level, was held in July 1965, and drafting of the legislation followed quickly. It was not as complex as the CPP, but it was bad enough. The Act was passed in 1966. For over two decades now, CAP has served well in its purpose of relieving much of the worst poverty across Canada. This is not, of course, to claim that it goes far enough, or that it lacks inefficiencies. In particular, the needs test, though far preferable to a means test, has some of the same effect as an income test in creating a "welfare trap"; that is to say, it results in some situations in which a person is on balance worse rather than better off if he or she takes low-paid work. A satisfactory cure for that, however, can be found only through thorough integration of assistance with a progressive tax system, including tax credits.

One other important reform in social security was also brought to legislative fruition in 1966, though Joe Willard and I had been talking about it from the early days of the work on the Canada Pension Plan. It was the "Guaranteed Income Supplement" to old age security; we saw it as the means of playing fair, in direct federal action, with the people who did not benefit from the CPP, because of age or lack of paid employment.

The main concern of the Canada Opportunity Plan, however, was not with assistance to relieve poverty. It was to prevent poverty. The Beveridge definition of social security – "a job when you can work, and a benefit when you can't" – is a useful approximation, but it does not express, among other things, the importance of work in giving a person a place in society. We assumed, accurately enough at the time, that the economy could be managed to offer enough jobs in total. The concerns were, first, that more of the jobs should be in areas where opportunities were poor; and, second and most important, to improve people's employability by training, by assistance to mobility, and by environmental measures for health, housing, and other social infrastructure.

The FRED program was designed to improve opportunities in some of the areas where they were most needed. The broader program was the Area Development Incentives Act, to which we gave high priority. Parliament passed the legislation in June 1965, and the details of its implementation were announced in early August. They reflected a lot of struggle and hard work, particularly by one member of the secretariat, Stan Goodman. There was no difficulty in agreeing on the basic point. The area development incentives initiated in 1963, in the form of tax concessions, had stimulated investment by established firms, but they were of little value to new enterprises and to smaller and riskier businesses. They were to be replaced by direct grants of a portion of the capital costs of new plants and expansions of plants. Nor was there much difficulty in agreeing on a reasonable scale for the grants, up to a maximum of $5 millions for a plant costing about $25 millions or more. The problems were in selecting the areas where the incentives would be available.

It was considered essential that there be "objective" criteria; otherwise, local political pressures would cause endless trouble and, unless heroically resisted, quickly make nonsense of the program. But reasonably adequate criteria had to be a complex mix, and a great deal of ingenuity went into their formulation. The final result was the designation of areas in which about 16 per cent of the country's labour force lived. This more than doubled the extent of the previous, tax-concession program, which had applied to areas with about 7 1/2 per cent of the labour force. The new plan applied to all of the Atlantic provinces except the areas of Halifax, Saint John and Fredericton; to most of eastern and northern Quebec; to substantial parts of Manitoba and Saskatchewan; and to small areas in Ontario, Alberta and British Columbia.

All of this was discussed with the provinces before final decisions were made, notably at a large meeting of officials on 31 May 1965. As I reported to the Prime Minister the next day, seven provinces gave general approval to the program and were satisfied with the amount of consultation. The three that had objections, and therefore also regarded the consultation as inadequate, were, naturally, Ontario, British Columbia and Alberta. The proposals had as much acceptability as could be achieved, given all of the differences of provincial interests, and the government decided to proceed. But it was still a far from satisfactory program, and I shall later refer to the great improvements on which we worked in 1968–9.

One of the weaknesses, in performance as well as in planning, related to the role of the National Employment Service. There was, on paper, provision for the liaison of the NES with firms receiving development grants, so that there could be advance identification of local workers suitable for training in the new jobs. The NES showed itself to be incapable of such a task. The special planning secretariat, while working smoothly enough with other federal departments and with many provincial agencies, found itself increasingly in a state of frustration with the NES and with the training branch of the Department of Labour. They were crucial to the purpose of helping people to become more employable, but they seemed to be wrapped in their own worlds of professional and organizational concerns, to which the needs of the people they were supposed to serve hardly penetrated.

The federal government was by this time spending heavily in support of training provided by the provinces, but the curricula and teaching methods seemed to be largely those designed for non-academic school programs. They took little account of the needs and attitudes of the adult trainee. Certainly they were doing little to meet the adjustment needs of people in particularly difficult circumstances or remote locations. We co-operated with the research branch of the Department of Labour to develop the concept of pilot projects to provide less conventional training and something closer to work experience, but the training branch contributed little to the ideas, perhaps because the concept was that the pilot training centres would be staffed on a multidisciplinary basis rather than solely from the educational establishment. The project progressed slowly.

The worst delay, however, was in helping people to move to employment. I set great store by this manpower mobility program, because it seemed particularly tragic that people who were perfectly capable and willing to take jobs in the expanding sectors of the economy and prosperous areas of the country should be trapped in low-employment locations because they could not afford even modest costs to move. The program, readily approved by Cabinet and included in the Throne Speech, was to provide loans to cover actual transportation and moving costs plus a resettlement allowance of up to $1,000 per family. These loans were to be available to anyone who was unemployed or had received a lay-off notice, provided that his or her prospects of permanent employment would be substantially improved by the move. Grants could be substituted for loans if the worker had been unemployed for four or more of the previous six months or if he had been unable to obtain a job after completing a training course.

The principles of the program were clear but the NES made extraordinarily heavy weather of expressing them in precise regulations. The people with the authority to push the NES were the Deputy Minister of Labour and his senior colleagues. They did not do so. I concluded that they were preoccupied with talk rather than action. It seemed that at critical moments they were always away at a conference in Geneva or somewhere. I was irritated, perhaps to an irrational extent, but I found it shocking that a measure approved by Cabinet in March was not fleshed out until November and not made operational until after the start of the following year. Because of that, as well as the weaknesses of the training branch, I began to think that a substantial reorganization of administrative structures would be necessary if the "war on poverty" was to deserve its popular name.

Eventually the most disappointing of the measures in the 1965 program was the Company of Young Canadians (CYC). The idea was appealing: to provide a channel by which the idealism and energy of many young people could be expressed in community service. The imaginative name originated, if I remember correctly, in the fertile mind of Judy LaMarsh. An organizing committee was promptly appointed and included some strong members, but its chairmanship was weak. Its report, in November, was disappointingly vague about the work the Company would undertake and the organizational structure that would be both viable for government and acceptable to the militant youth of the 1960s. The project was proceeded with in 1966, but the purposes remained too vague and the organization was too diffuse. The Company rendered some useful services but it also made enough mistakes to become quickly vulnerable to the people who were disturbed by its militant elements.

The special planning secretariat, meanwhile, was moving on to its longer-term tasks: to analyze poverty problems more thoroughly; to propose a policy framework for improving opportunities; and to identify priorities for specific further programs. What was done, and what was cut off, will be examined in a later chapter. There were more immediate issues that required attention in the summer and fall of 1965.

30 *Medicare*

Medicare is the most important of all the social reforms introduced by the Pearson government. My feelings about the achievement are mixed: satisfaction, but also a sense that, for lack of resolution, I failed in a part of my job.

As soon as people had got used to hospital insurance, in the late 1950s, the expectation of a public plan for medical care became strong. The CCF government in Saskatchewan responded first to what was clearly a popular idea; and after it had overcome the doctors' strike even politicians as ideologically conservative as the Saskatchewan Liberal party accepted the inevitability of medicare. The obstacles to a national plan were still formidable, however, and the Diefenbaker government, true to character, did not face them; it appointed a Royal Commission, under the chairmanship of Chief Justice Emmett Hall.

The Commission reported in June 1964. That it would recommend some national plan, to ensure the availability of medical service without payment at the time of illness, was all but inevitable. What was surprising, however, was the comprehensiveness of its proposals, the vehemence of its insistence on universality, and the great strength of its argument. The Commission report took much of the wind out of the opponents of medicare.

It did not, however, help to solve the main problem faced by a Pearson government already committed to medicare. The Commission assumed that the hospital insurance model was still politically feasible. That is to say, the federal Parliament could legislate in detail the plan for which, if it was instituted by a majority of provinces (in number, or by population, or both), half or thereabouts of the cost would be contributed from federal revenues; the provinces could take it or leave it but, given the bribe and the popularity of the promised benefits, had no real choice but to take – even though it meant submitting to a federal audit to establish that their program expenditures were in accord with the federal legislation.

Such paternalism had been possible in federal-provincial relations in the 1950s. It was out of the question in 1964. While it was as true of medicare as of other major social reforms that it would not be instituted, on a national scale, without federal leadership and financial participation, they would have to be in a form more subtle than the old kind of "joint", cost-shared program. That did not seem to me to constitute an immovable obstacle. But it meant that we must proceed with circumspection, political skill, and ingenuity.

That did not bother me. I was a fervent believer in medicare. That access to health service should depend in any way on ability to pay, or in the case of a child on the parents' ability to pay, was in my view an entirely unacceptable inequality. During the opposition years I had tried to ensure that medicare was always front centre in the program for a new Liberal government. But I had seen it as a difficult and expensive program and therefore put it, in my scheduling, late in a four-year government term. Politically, I saw it as the jewel in the record of achievement on which the government might go to the people in the following election.

Accordingly in January 1965, when the government had been in office for less than two years, my draft of a memorandum about the year's program, to go from the Prime Minister to all ministers, said of medicare: "I do not think that we can plan to take that on, in a comprehensive way, in 1965." Mr Pearson modified the words in parenthesis: they became "at least in any comprehensive way." I interpreted the change as reflecting no more than his disposition to express himself less definitely than I did.

I misjudged the political situation. I thought that the Prime Minister was firm, as he had told me, in his acceptance of the view that our plan for 1965 should be to run an effective and constructive government, not to hold an election. That was not, however, the attitude of most ministers; and whatever he might say privately in agreement with me, Mr Pearson was in practice indecisive on the issue.

If the government was going to call an election in 1965, it had first to take a firm initiative on a definite medicare program. Theoretically, the Liberal party had been committed to public health insurance since 1919.

In 1962 and 1963 it had at last been convincingly specific in the style and substance of its commitment. If it had then done nothing, Liberal claims in a 1965 election would have had a hollow ring. The form of the Canadian medicare system is the consequence of this electoral imperative.

That a workable form of nation-wide medicare was arrived at so quickly is remarkable. The credit belongs chiefly to a then Assistant Deputy Minister of Finance, Al Johnson. The department theoretically responsible, the health part of Health and Welfare, was little help. There could hardly have been a sharper contrast between the two parts. The welfare section of the department was informed, administratively competent, alert to the political climate, constructive in policy formulation. Its capacities were evident in the Canada Pension Plan, the Canada Assistance Plan, and other measures. The health section, however, was narrow in vision and remote from political reality. It was enthusiastic about the Hall report. We asked for consultation with the provinces, and were told that detailed discussions showed a favourable response to the Hall recommendations. As far as the federal health department was concerned, medicare could and should be established in much the same way as hospital insurance. It was apparent, however, that this was the finding of health administrators talking with health administrators. It was quite out of touch with provincial views at the points of policy decision. Accordingly, the responsibility for developing a realistic federal position was put in the hands of a special committee in which the dominant actors were officials of the Privy Council and Prime Minister's Offices and the Department of Finance.

Finance, under the leadership of Walter Gordon and Bob Bryce, was by now a very different department from the one they had taken over in 1963. Al Johnson, who had been the deputy provincial treasurer of Saskatchewan when medicare was introduced there, now took a special interest in the subject from the federal viewpoint. Walter's enthusiasm for the cause was a driving force, and Al was the ablest of all the Saskatchewan mafia: the good public servants for whom the anti-intellectualism of the Thatcher regime made Regina a less happy home than it had been under the CCF government. They found better uses for their talents in Ottawa and, to a lesser extent, in the Robichaud government of New Brunswick.

Al Johnson originated the kind of solution that, once you have heard it, you kick yourself for having failed to think of. It was so simple in concept but so effective. The federal government did not need to legislate the details of a shared-cost program. It needed only to define, clearly, the principles of what it meant by medicare. Then it would contribute to the costs of any provincial program that satisfied those principles. The contribution would not, however, be based on the particular provincial program. There would be periodic estimates of the average per capita cost, nationally, of programs conforming to the principles. The federal contribution to each participating province would be half of this amount. The consequence would be not only to avoid the need for federal audit of provincial expenditures. A province that ran a program more expensive than the average would thus get a lesser share of its cost from Ottawa. The incentive to extravagance, inherent in any program in which the province got back 50 cents of each dollar it actually spent, would be avoided.

The committee had no difficulty in agreeing on this approach, or on a proposition that came from the Health and Welfare Department. Since medicare would obviously increase the need for skilled personnel and facilities, there should be a Health Resources Fund from which the federal government would contribute to the capital costs of improving medical schools, teaching hospitals and research facilities. The controversial issues were the size of that fund and the principles that would constitute a sufficient definition of medicare. The first, as officials, we could set aside for the present. It was not in fact settled until September, after hard battles in Cabinet. There Judy LaMarsh was a redoubtable fighter, and in the end she won agreement to $500 millions. Even with allowance for the softening in other ministers' attitudes when they had entered into an election campaign, the size of the fund was a notable achievement in a good cause, and Judy was justifiably proud of it.

The definition of medicare principles, however, had to come from officials if it was to be clear and realistic. The committee struggled hard with drafts and revisions and refinements; the acceptability of the scheme depended on somehow combining precision with barebone simplicity. In the end, we decided that four principles were sufficient:

First, the plan must be comprehensive in the provision of physicians' services. Some of us would have liked to add drugs and dental care, but we agreed that this would be going too far too fast. The precise definition of physicians' services involved some technical problems, but they were not overwhelming.

Second, the plan must be universal, covering everyone on the same terms and conditions. This, of course, is the issue on which there are both the sharpest differences of philosophy and the greatest difficulties in administrative detail. Involved are issues such as deterrent fees, extra billing, and whether doctors practising outside the plan should be reimbursed to the extent of the fees it provides. While we did not like such practices, we did not feel able to impose an absolute prohibition as part of the definition of universality. Whether they seriously frustrate the essential purpose of medicare – to ensure that health service is accessible irrespective of ability to pay – depends on their extent. We therefore felt that discretion had to be left to the provinces, subject to a pragmatic test: a plan could be accepted as universal if it ensured that 95 per cent of the population had the effective right to the services of a physician without significant payment.

Third, benefits must be transferable between provinces without break in coverage. This involved only minor technical problems.

Fourth, the plan must be publicly administered. We tried to provide for as much flexibility as possible. It did not have to be run directly by the government through civil servants. There could be a special agency, or delegation to a non-government organization provided it was non-profit and subject to public audit. The essential principle was that the provincial governments must take full responsibility for the plan. Otherwise, the federal government could not transfer funds to it.

These conclusions of the committee were eminently satisfactory, as far as they went, and I expected them to be approved by Cabinet as a basis for consultation with the provinces, after which a firm federal position would be determined. That was the procedure to which the Prime Minister had seemed committed by his previous comments at federal-provincial conferences, quite apart from his general position on co-operative federalism. I was therefore taken aback when he in fact submitted the committee's recommendations to Cabinet as the definite federal plan to be proposed to the provinces at the federal-provincial conference arranged for 19–23 July 1965. This meant that it would be made public as soon as the provinces heard it. Cabinet agreed.

The expectation of an early election was now strong, and timetables were accelerated. My first draft of the Prime Minister's main statement to the conference had to be written only five days before it was delivered. It was a long document dealing with subjects as varied as the "poverty and opportunity" program as a whole, regional development, training, the Canada Assistance Plan, the state of the economy, the principles of federalism, the tax structure committee, off-shore mineral rights, and co-operation against organized crime, as well as the main item – medicare. The advance notice to the provincial delegations was therefore minimal. The most we could do was to invite a few of the principal officials to a meeting in my office when they arrived, the evening before the conference began, and give them a quick briefing on the federal medicare policy.

There was justified resentment, but politically the federal government had the initiative. Most provinces did not want to put themselves in the position of opposing medicare, and some warmly welcomed the federal proposal. The exception was Alberta. Premier Manning regarded the plan as of doubtful constitutional validity and, because of the insistence on universality, a heinous assault on the freedom of the individual. His root-and-branch attack had little logic but much vehemence. At one point he protested that the federal government would be proposing grocery-care next. Jim Coutts circulated among federal delegates an impish note asking who had leaked the next item on Tom Kent's agenda!

The serious objections came from Ontario. Premier Robarts was free from the crude ideology of Manning, but he was concerned about the quality of health care and afraid that it would be prejudiced by the stampede into provincial medicare schemes that, as he saw it, the federal government was engineering for electoral advantage. I had some sympathy with his position, but he could not effectively resist the forces now operating. At the subsequent conference of ministers of health, held in September, the provinces generally were more concerned to argue about their shares of the Health Resources Fund than to question the federal plan for medicare. Some adaptations to their suggestions were made, but essentially it was the measure as first proposed that was legislated in 1966. Mitchell Sharp, by then Finance Minister and concerned about what he saw as the fiscal probity of his budget, tried several times to put off its implementation but succeeded in securing only one year's delay. Even Alberta soon conformed to the federal "principles", and by the end of the 1960s Canadians had an effectively national system of medicare.

That the country is greatly the better for it seems to be impossible of serious dispute. The four principles have stood the test of experience; they are as acceptable to most people now as they were twenty years ago. Nevertheless, I cannot help wishing that Mitchell Sharp had got his year's delay not by simple postponement of a scheme that he had rushed into with the rest of the Cabinet, but when it might have made a real difference: that is to say, in 1965–6 when further refinement would have been possible before the plan was cast in legislation.

The doubt that still troubles me is whether, if I had tried harder, I could have secured some improvement. My position as a proponent of medicare was too well established for reservations to be dismissed as opposition. My reservations were that, while I regarded it as morally wrong that money in the bank, rather than severity of need, should determine who got what health services, I thought we had to deal realistically with the obvious difficulties in providing "free" services of such complexity. They depend, in part, on the customer's own perception of factors of which he or she is often not well informed. They depend even more on the judgment of a doctor who is remunerated by fees scaled to the service performed.

Such a system is in obvious danger that priorities will be distorted and that its finances will get out of control, with consequent further distortion of priorities. This would be true even if medical practice had remained relatively simple. The inherent tendency is enormously strengthened when scientific and technological advances are so much increasing the range, choice, sophistication and expensiveness of medical treatments.

The restraint that some governments have favoured is the imposition of user fees. That is inequitable. Such fees are a significant restraint only for the poor, and therefore conflict with the basic purpose of medicare. Extra-billing, favoured by some doctors' organizations, has the same effect, and is even more obnoxious because it vitiates what is most valuable in the vaunted doctor-patient relationship. The fundamental effect of both devices is that poorer people are denied some higher-quality services which richer people receive in return for part only of their cost, the remainder being paid by the community at large. That is an entirely unjustifiable kind of subsidization.

The only solution of which I have been able to think is the one we had discussed in opposition years: that the imputed cost of medical services received "free" should be added to the individual's taxable income. That is fair if the tax system is fair. It would not prevent people with low incomes getting needed service, but it would have an important psychological effect through the whole medicare system. It would make the public at large, and the providers of medical services in particular, far more conscious of the costs of treatments. With richer people in effect paying 30 or 40 per cent of the cost of personal treatments through their tax returns, the climate of opinion would be one in which there was far more incentive to avoid wasteful practices and to establish priorities in service.

In the absence of the kind of financial conditioning that income tax would impose, medicare may serve well – as in Canada it has done, on the whole – but it is exposed to mounting difficulties over time. As services become more sophisticated and elaborate, governments try to set limits to increasing costs. Unless they are wiser than either the Trudeau or Mulroney governments, they set arbitrary expenditure ceilings tighter than were originally envisaged. The system is poorly equipped to adjust in a planned way, setting intelligent priorities. The natural tendency to concentrate on curing illness, rather than on preventive and other measures for health, is reinforced. Inadequate facilities result in an inefficient rationing of some services. Research and the quality of care suffer. Doctors become frustrated and some react with cynicism. Concentration on maximizing their earnings, even to the point of striking on the issue of extra-billing, may be the consequence less of greed than of poorly articulated concern about the inefficiencies of the system.

Much of the crying of alarm is exaggerated and self-interested, but undoubtedly the medicare system created by the Pearson government is showing signs of serious wear. It might have stood up better if there had been more effective consultation with the provinces and, in particular, a fifth principle: the income tax provision. That had been the recommendation of the Liberal party at large, in the policy resolution approved at the 1961 National Rally. In 1962–3 I failed to make this stick with the professional political leaders. They did not think it could be put across to the electorate. In 1965 they were the same politicians, but they had been Ministers for more than two years; and even when their eyes are on an election, politicians are somewhat more conscious of financial factors when they are in office than they are in opposition. It is just possible that a harder effort in 1965 would have succeeded either in getting acceptance of the income tax provision or in stirring thought to some alternative way of achieving the same purpose.

For good or ill, my effort was in fact perfunctory. Excuses are easy. I had many other tasks. At that stage I was so much involved in the problems of federal-provincial relations that I had drifted dangerously close to the attitude that what could be sold to the provinces was good enough, and in this respect the plan as it was adopted was an elegant triumph. Perhaps the most important factor, however, was a tired disillusionment, at that moment, with the government: it was moving to an unnecessary election simply because the Prime Minister had unaccountably failed to arrest the building of expectations that created an artificial necessity for it.

A somewhat better medicare plan could have been achieved only through the building of alliances, in Ottawa and with the provinces. It was thanks to the alliance with Lesage that we had ended with a better pension plan than the original federal proposal. For medicare, Premier Robarts would have been critical. But in this case there was no time to build alliances. I had misjudged the election-induced speed of the government's decision-making. All I did was to reopen the income tax idea with the Prime Minister and a few others. Mr Pearson was sympathetic, of course, but clearly not in a mood to direct any energy into rocking, at that moment, a boat that seemed capable of floating nicely as it was. By that time, as the story of university financing will illustrate, Mr Pearson's role in decisions was not what it had been.

PART SIX

Unfinished Business

"Don't forget to write"

31 *Failures, and Turnabout*

The medicare proposal was hastened by the 1965 election. Two other programs, however, were buried in the aftermath of that election. One was the "opportunity plan," in the broad form in which it had been initiated. The other was university scholarships.

Some of the most important of the policies to which its election platform committed the Pearson government had been summarized in a leaflet under the heading *Canada Needs Trained Minds*. The most basic of these measures, at a time when many people still started work at age sixteen, was the extension of family allowances to age eighteen for those who stayed at school. This was acted on in 1964. It was an important measure for social equality, making it more possible for the children of poorer and larger families to get the level of general education increasingly necessary for most kinds of employment.

In the same spirit, there were improvements to the legislation under which the federal government assisted the provinces to provide vocational training.

Prompt action was also taken to provide a nation-wide program of loans to help students to finance university education. Since some provinces already had small loan schemes, the federal plan provided financing, proportional to provincial populations, greatly to enlarge the programs and to cover the costs of guaranteeing the loans at the banks and making them interest-free during the years of study. In 1963 students were only 8 per cent of the population in the age group eighteen to twenty-four. The loan scheme helped significantly to make possible the subsequent large increase in the reach of post-secondary education. By 1975 the proportion had doubled, to 16 per cent.

We did not proceed, however, with the more important part of the plan to improve the equality of opportunity for education: an extensive scholarship program. Delay was at first unavoidable, for external reasons. The need for rapid expansion in Canadian universities had become widely recognized. The Gordon Royal Commission on Canada's economic prospects in 1956 made the first authoritatively strong statement of the need to raise the quality of universities and secure more equal access to them, as well as greatly to expand university facilities. By 1964 the universities had become very much concerned that their financing would not match the rapid growth of requirements. The Association of Universities and Colleges of Canada (AUCC) set up its own commission, headed by Vincent Bladen, to examine the financing of higher education in Canada.

The rest of this account is the story of how the hard bed on which the universities now lie was made by a combination of the short-sightedness of the presidents of the universities in the mid-1960s and the political miscalculations of the Pearson government. It is told, however, not solely as a sad story but in the belief that the alternative which was then rejected could still provide a way to develop and utilize the human resources of our society more effectively.

Universities, like municipalities, are legally the creatures of the provinces. It would have been tactless, to say the least, to bring out major federal proposals while the Bladen enquiry was in process. The government had, however, to be ready to formulate its approach to university policy and thus to the discussions with the provinces that any policy, whether active or passive, would require in the context of the universities' requests.

The issue was not whether the universities should have a good deal more money. That was bound to be; and however it was done, the net effect would be equivalent to the federal government conceding more tax room for provincial purposes. The question, given provincial jurisdiction, was whether the method of financing could and should give the federal government any role in ensuring that the university system as a whole developed in ways that most effectively served national purposes. There was obvious danger that, with a rapid increase in funding in response to immediate needs, a lot of money could be spent without achieving this result.

During 1964 I developed some ideas about the form of financing that might be most effective. They were unconventional, but Mr Pearson was sympathetic. He even went so far as to express them, tentatively, by signing in December 1964 a letter to Alex Corry, the Principal of Queen's and then President of the AUCC. We suggested that, if it were possible to start with a clean slate, the ideal way to finance universities might be for governments to make no operating grants at all. Fees would have to cover the full cost of the universities' teaching activities. The role of government would then be to ensure equality of opportunity by scholarships on a sufficient scale to enable all adequately qualified students to attend university.

The letter did not go into much detail, but I had in mind a mixture of pure scholarships and loans that would be equitable as between parents at different income levels and secure substantial repayments from students who afterwards earned substantial incomes.

There were three reasons for this unconventional view. The first was one of equity. The system which was developing, and which has since become worse, is that taxpayers as a whole spend a great deal of money on the universities but the costs that remain are still a formidable barrier for poorer people. There is no clearer example of the fault that pervades many government subsidy programs: they assist people in moderate need, but they do not significantly benefit those who most need help. The effect is progressive in the middle income ranges, but at the low end it is regressive. We were avoiding this in health care, to the greatest practicable extent, thanks to the principles of universality and comprehensive coverage. We were avoiding it pretty thoroughly in provision for retirement. (This was before the introduction of tax-exempt RSPs). But we would not be avoiding inequity in university education if we went along with AUCC requests for increased federal financing paid directly to the universities. Students would still face appreciable fees. Those from middle-income families would pay them with the help of the loan program, but many of those from really poor families would not feel able to assume loan obligations. The only equitable financing was by scholarships.

My second reason for the full-fee, scholarship system related to the internal efficiency of the university system. Universities are, properly, self-governing academic bodies. That is essential to intellectual freedom. But the inevitable consequence, if their funding comes to them directly rather than through the fees of students, is that they are imperfectly sensitive to student needs. The community of scholars tends to be the community of professors, each with his or her own interests. The consequence, in a country with so much space in relation to population as Canada, is that resources are spread too thin. It becomes very difficult for any university to assemble a truly first-class faculty in any discipline. Moreover, this academic tendency to dispersion is likely to be reinforced by the political dispositions of the providers of funds, whose natural inclination is to spread the money around, including the creation of new universities which then aspire also to have departments of everything.

The most reliable countervail to these tendencies seemed to me to be students voting with their feet. If they were financing the university by paying its fees (whether from their parents' funds or from scholarships would make no difference), universities would have to be more sensitive to their "market" demand. If a particular university had, say, a biology faculty of high repute, the best biology students would tend to go there and the university would have a direct incentive, and the means, further to improve that faculty. Strength would be reinforced instead of being dissipated. There would be more likelihood of developing the "centres of excellence" required if Canadian research and innovation were to be strengthened as they needed to be.

Finally, there was a third, obvious reason for the full-fee, full-cost scholarship approach to university financing. As we put it in the letter to Corry, "There would be less danger of pressures on the independence of universities." To be financed almost entirely by direct grants from governments might not create serious difficulties when the mood was one of rapid expansion. Certainly professors, in their understandable enthusiasm for leaving lean times behind, showed little apprehension. But the bonanza would undoubtedly end some day. And when it did, governments tugging on the financial reins would develop views about how the universities should be run.

I did not suggest that in 1965 the federal government should plunge into proposing so radical a scheme as full-cost fees. We did, however, tentatively suggest in the Prime Minister's letter to Corry that *additional* federal funding of the universities' operating costs might be linked to scholarships. In recognition that the fees that the scholar was enabled to pay covered only a part of the university's cost of teaching him or her, the federal government might provide a grant of, say, $1,000 a year times the number of scholarship-holders who chose to attend that university. This was obviously too small for the universities' needs, but was a low figure to start what I hoped would be the bargaining.

My concept was that the number of scholarships and the value of the "voucher" for the university in effect attached to the scholarship should be sufficient to provide all the additional funding of university operations that was appropriate from the federal government. The package had, however, two other components: there should be substantial enlargements of the federal programs financing research at the universities; and the federal government should be willing to help the provinces substantially with the capital costs of university expansion. The condition attached to this last component should be that the provinces and the universities agreed on sufficient specialization and co-ordination of university programs for the university structure to develop in a way that effectively served the national interest in economic growth and equality of opportunity.

In the summer of 1965, with the Bladen report impending, the question was how far we should go in stating a position in advance of the federal-provincial discussions that would obviously follow. The Prime Minister agreed that, as a first step, we should reaffirm our scholarship proposal as such. If we took that initiative before the report was released, emphasizing that we regarded the improvement of opportunity as essential to university expansion, we could delay our response to other financial demands until we had talked to the provinces.

This conclusion was facilitated by the start of the election campaign, and the Prime Minister made his public announcement on 5 October 1965.

We polished up the earlier policy statement. That had been to provide 10,000 "Canada scholarships" a year – that is, up to 40,000 would be outstanding at any one time – with a fixed value of $1,000 a year. We decided that somewhat more flexibility would be more appealing. The amount available would be $10 millions for the first year's batch of scholarships, and the maximum would be $1,000 a year per scholar. But it would be up to the provinces to decide on what scale the $1,000 might be reduced, for scholars with lesser financial needs, and the total number of scholarships thus increased in relation to their lower average value. Also, the $10 million for each year's scholarships would be increased in ratio to what was then the 4 per cent a year rate of growth in the population aged eighteen to twenty-four. It would be divided among the residents of provinces in proportion to their population of that age.

Mr Pearson's statement emphasized that the federal concern was "to assure a basic measure of equal opportunity for outstanding young Canadians throughout Canada." The principles essential to this purpose were that the scholarships should be awarded on merit, though the method of assessing it could be determined by each province; that they should be tenable at any Canadian university, not necessarily in the scholar's own province; and that the full $1,000 a year should be provided to students whose parents could not afford any contribution. Within those principles, the operation of the plan would be worked out in accordance with provincial views.

We would have had such a scholarship system if the Pearson government had won its parliamentary majority. But it was not to be. After the election a psychologically weakened government faced intense lobbying from the university administrations. They were determined that federal funds should come directly to them, not via students. The relationships between the academic community and the Ottawa bureaucracy were close. Walter Gordon had gone. Otherwise, no member of the Cabinet except the Prime Minister had thought the student-oriented approach worth asserting against academic opinion; and in 1966 the Prime Minister was dispirited.

Discussion therefore concentrated on federal funding directly for the universities. The universities increasingly used the argument that it was necessary to save them from being entirely dependent on provincial governments. No one in Ottawa seemed willing to tell them, bluntly enough for them to recognize, the obvious fact that such a countervail was out of the question. There was no possibility of the provinces agreeing to substantial direct funding of post-secondary education in a form that would buy for Ottawa any influence at all on university affairs. Through the spring and summer of 1966 we moved slowly but inexorably to an arrangement under which the federal government would make no operating payments directly to the universities but would passively compensate the provinces for a large part of their expenditures.

The scheme was put forward at the federal-provincial conference that began on 24 October 1966. The formula was complicated by the nature of the fiscal arrangements, but in essence it was that Ottawa would provide 50 per cent of the operating costs of post-secondary education in each province, subject to a minimum (which would be escalated) of $14 per capita of provincial population.

In presenting this scheme the Prime Minister reaffirmed his government's "commitment" to establishing a scholarship system, but the "first priority" was now to enable the provinces to meet "their obligations for the construction and operation of post-secondary institutions." Scholarships were not proceeded with, initially perhaps because the government was running out of steam but soon understandably because the program as proposed in 1966 produced a phenomenal rate of increase in the fiscal transfers to the provinces. With the number of students rapidly increasing, the cost of the federal government's contribution to post-secondary educational expenditures by the provinces increased, for the first five years of the program, by an average of over 20 per cent a year – far more than had been projected.

The rate of increase in the fiscal transfers flattened out somewhat after the early seventies, but in 1977 the Trudeau government took the extraordinary step, through the "established programs financing" legislation, of severing the connection between federal transfers for health and post-secondary education and the provinces' expenditures for those purposes. This was a response to the criticism of federal "intrusions" into provincial jurisdiction which was a rising tide in the West and in Ontario, as well as the constant cry of the now PQ government in Quebec. The consequence was inevitable. Most provinces reduced their expenditures relative to the federal transfers, particularly on education. And when the Trudeau government and its successor imposed tighter restrictions on the transfers, the affluence which had come to the universities in the later sixties disappeared with some drama. The bed that the universities helped to make for themselves in 1965–6 became hard indeed.

By 1980 it was ironical to hear some of the talk in the universities turning to the case for the kind of scholarship-voucher system of financing that had been so strongly opposed fifteen years earlier. The idea did again receive some consideration in Ottawa, but to have pressed on with it would have required a differently innovative temperament than that of the late Trudeau period. We therefore end where we were in the early 1960s: the quality and the equality of Canada's educational structures are inadequate to the requirements of a dynamic society able to adapt the utilization of its human resources to the changing technologies of the world economy. The need is so obvious that new methods of meeting it will certainly have to be attempted again.

This story, however, returns to the summer of 1965, when my chief interest was the second phase of the Canada Opportunity Plan. The special planning secretariat had, after the first-phase programs, three tasks: to analyze poverty problems more thoroughly; to propose a policy framework for further programs to improve opportunities; to identify priorities among such programs and to initiate work on the preparation of the most urgent.

Two priorities were strikingly obvious. One related to unemployment insurance, the other to Indian people.

The inadequacy of the existing UI system, both in its benefits and in its financing, had become apparent during the relatively heavy unemployment of the Diefenbaker years. The Gill committee, appointed by the previous government, recommended improvements but of a superficial kind. The Pearson government was slow to get down to a more thorough review, but in August 1965 we began work through an interdepartmental committee. My contribution was limited to four suggestions, of varying effect. One was a compromise between those who saw the scheme as genuinely "insurance" and those who more accurately identified it as a welfare measure. Insurance, I argued, was appropriate when unemployment did not exceed what could be regarded as a "normal" or frictional rate – the 3 per cent suggested by the Economic Council, or perhaps more conservatively 4 per cent. (Such was the range of serious debate in 1965!) Premiums should be designed to cover benefits at that level of unemployment. When there was more unemployment – when the economy was not offering enough jobs for the workers seeking them – the additional cost of benefits was properly a charge to general government revenues.

If the "normal" scheme was insurance, there was no reason to exclude classes of people who had a low risk of unemployment. The contributory requirement should be universal, for employees and their employers, up to a ceiling of insured earnings. By the same token, benefits should not be paid for the normal off-season from work that was regularly seasonal. Certainly there had to be income support for low-income seasonal workers, such as inshore fishermen, but it should be provided by a specific program, not masquerade as unemployment insurance.

Finally, I revived a proposal that I had made at the Kingston conference. For short-term unemployment – for, say, two months within a year – benefit rates should be low. If unemployment was prolonged, however, the benefits should be at a much more generous level, though conditional on the person taking training or relocating (with the help of the mobility program) if a job was thereby available. This was too radical for the politicians, though it might have done a good deal both to lessen abuse and to direct more help to the cases of greatest hardship.

In any case, the consideration of unemployment insurance reform proved to be lengthy. The scheme that eventually emerged, under the Trudeau government, had many merits. Criticism of the generosity of the benefit scale was in my view misplaced, except for short-term unemployment. Where the scheme did go badly wrong was in the shortness of the period of attachment to the labour force required to quality for the benefit. This was related, of course, to the failure to establish a separate program for seasonal employment.

We did not get far in considering what to do about Indian poverty. In August 1965 I accompanied the Minister responsible, Jack Nicholson, and his senior officials on visits to more than twenty Indian communities. In some the poverty was more appalling than my expectations. I reported to the Prime Minister that, if one allowed for the severity of the climate and the scarcity of fresh food resources, the living conditions were as bad as anything I had seen in Latin America.

The Indian Affairs Branch had launched a program of providing new housing. The obvious problem was that these relatively grand houses certainly would not be built on a scale to meet more than a minute fraction of the need in the early future. It seemed to me that, rather than speed up this program to any practicable extent, more good might be done by supplying the bands with materials for an extensive program of repairs and modifications to existing dwellings. This would be a crash program on all reserves. For those with any reasonable economic base, there should be a development program aimed first at providing electric power, reasonable sanitation and pure drinking water. There was a desperate need for different school curricula, teaching methods and teaching skills. I also suggested that Indians who moved from the reserves should receive special housing assistance equivalent to (not greater than) the cost of the programs on the reserves. Whether these were sensible priorities I do not know; to my regret, I never followed through to further involvement in a problem for which new starts were desperately needed.

The "anti-poverty" program was one of the topics of the major federal-provincial conference in July 1965. Apart from the review of specific measures, on which there was little controversy, the Prime Minister invited the provinces to join in the planning and organization of a national conference on poverty and opportunity to be held in 1966. It would be broadly representative.

From such a conference we can obtain, I believe, a number of benefits that are important to us all. First, I think we could get a better understanding and a wider consensus on many of the problems which concern both federal and provincial governments. Secondly, from the point of view of both our programs and yours, I think we would receive some interesting and valuable suggestions. And, thirdly, I am sure that the organization and holding of such a conference would assist us in achieving closer consultation and better working arrangements in future ... [A] public conference in which we are associated is another rather new device which seems to me to hold great promise.

It would have been the best way to proceed with longer-term policy development. But it came to nothing. The provincial premiers did not oppose it, but they were cautious. Ontario and the western provinces probably suspected that it was a design to upstage them politically. All were afraid, no doubt, that a public conference would generate new pressures for programs that would strain their budgets. I was commissioned to discuss the suggestion in more detail with provincial officials. The discussion made it apparent that it would be unwise to push the provinces into committing themselves to a public conference at this stage. We arrived at a typically bureaucratic compromise. As I reported it to the Prime Minister: "without pre-judging the usefulness of holding such a conference at a later date, it was agreed that the early need for consultation on federal and provincial programs could best be met by a federal-provincial conference of officials and consultants. It would be practicable to organize such a meeting for late this year."

The premiers accepted this proposal with relief, and in the following months the special planning secretariat was busy organizing the conference and preparing studies for it, and many federal and provincial departments were enthusiastic in contributing papers on a vast range of problems.

The conference was held in Ottawa 7–10 December 1965, attended by some 170 officials and advisers. Useful analyses were put forward, good ideas exchanged. But, by comparison with the hopes and the work that had gone into its preparation, the meeting was an anticlimax. That was because the intervening federal general election had sharply changed the political climate in which officials operate.

I do not mean that the conference was useless. Such discussions have a long-term influence. By improving the communication of ideas among officials they stimulate the development of compatible programs across the country. While no formal consensus was attempted, there clearly was wide agreement on two main propositions. First, from the viewpoint of professional administrators, it was time for a pause in innovation in the conventional "welfare" field. There was enough to do in digesting the measures already underway or pending. Equally clearly, however, there was a strongly felt need to improve the effectiveness of "opportunity" programs – employment services, training, regional and community development. In setting those directions, we were on the right track.

But how were we to move along that track? The Pearson government, having failed to obtain the parliamentary majority that was the only purpose of the election, would now be in a running-down phase. Everyone assumed that Mr Pearson would retire before long. His government had a good deal on its plate with programs already committed. Its appetite for bold new directions was likely to be small. In particular, the proposal for a great national conference on poverty and opportunity, to which the meeting of officials had been designed by the federal delegates as a preliminary, was obviously now in limbo. Good discussion could not conceal a sense of pointlessness. The December meeting became, in the changed political situation, a passing rite for the opportunity plan as an organized, central activity of government. It was necessary to devise other means by which some at least of the thrust of its policies could survive in the turnabout of the Pearson government.

The turnabout came because the "death wish" of the 1963 government had prevailed. The election decision of the summer of 1965 was made by indecision. The Prime Minister did not stop the election talk among ministers and party officials, as at the beginning of the year he had told me he would. On the contrary, in the spring and summer his own words and actions encouraged the idea rather more than they discouraged it. On this issue more than others, he seemed inclined to the opinion of the last person he had talked to. He rationalized the uncertainty as keeping his options open, ignoring what in January he had said he recognized: that a build-up of expectations would effectively close off the no-election choice.

It must be said that the arguments for an election were tempting to any politician. The evidence of opinion surveys was that, while marginal voters did not think much of the Pearson government, they thought even less of the Conservatives under Diefenbaker. My hunch is that, if the Conservatives had been able in 1964 to replace Diefenbaker by a Roblin or a Stanfield, there would have been no election in 1965 because the Liberals would have been rightly afraid of defeat. But with Diefenbaker still the opponent, the only question was whether the government could gain the relatively few seats needed for a comfortable majority. The temptation to go before the going got rougher was obvious.

It was reinforced by a second factor that seemed to weigh heavily with the Prime Minister. The redistribution of constituency boundaries in light of the 1961 census had started late. Mr Diefenbaker had done nothing about it. The Pearson government had moved as quickly as the opposition allowed it to do. The independent commissions did the redrawing of boundaries promptly, but this meant that during most of 1966 the slow work of establishing the polling divisions for the new constituencies would be in process. For a period, it would be difficult to conduct an election on either the old or the new boundaries. The transition would not be complete until October or November, which the government somewhat cavalierly treated as meaning that a 1966 election was out of the question. And an election campaign shortly before the centennial celebrations of the summer of 1967 was considered inappropriate. So, the argument went, either the government called an election in 1965, on the old constituency boundaries, or it was effectively locked into waiting until the fall of 1967. By then the Conservatives might well have got rid of Diefenbaker, the economy might not be so buoyant, the government might have suffered from all kinds of risks. Again, the temptation was strong to go before the going got more uncertain.

These arguments did not persuade some, including me, but they powerfully reinforced ministers' desperate dislike of coping with the House of Commons without a majority. In the absence of a firm prime ministerial decision to the contrary, Keith Davey's election talk inevitably became dominant. By the summer most politicians and journalists took a fall election virtually for granted. The only question, in many assessments, was how soon the pressure from within his party would overcome Mike Pearson's dithering. We had indeed drifted to the situation I had feared, where we were damned if we did and damned if we didn't. An election might or might not give the government its longed-for majority, but certainly without an election it would face Parliament in a worse state than before. Almost everyone would think that the only reason why there had been no election was that the government had lost its nerve. It had backed off because it did not itself believe that it would win. Mr Diefenbaker would be more blood-thirsty than ever; Mr Pearson would be more worried and distraught than before; ministers' cohesion and confidence, in themselves and the Prime Minister, would be lower than ever.

Reluctantly, I felt forced to change my view. What needn't have happened had. An election had become the lesser evil.

The climactic moment for me was a lunch with Walter Gordon on 29 July 1965. He had pressed for an election in June – which, if there was to be one in 1965, would have been better – and was now most concerned that it not be delayed beyond the beginning, or at latest the middle, of October. We did not argue about which of our views had been correct earlier in the year. Walter's point, fairly enough, was that for good or ill Mike had not acted on my advice to suppress consideration of an election. The resultant expectancy meant that the government would now be most hurt by continued indecision. Given the weight of opinion in the party, it was unlikely that my opposition would prevent an election. What it might have was the bad influence of encouraging Mike to continue to put off an inevitable decision.

I was moved by the logic of this argument and also by being heartily fed up with indecision and by sympathy with Walter. We agreed that I would immediately write a memorandum to the Prime Minister stating the case for an October election as the joint view of Walter and myself.

With the hindsight of what happened in the November election, as it turned out to be, I was wrong to write that memorandum. I cannot say, however, that if I were back in the situation as it was that July day, I would do differently. It was a situation in which the government *could* win its desired majority, if it conducted at all an appropriate campaign. Where I was wrong was to let my weariness of uncertainty lead me to the wishful thinking that Mr Pearson *would* be able to conduct such a campaign.

The memorandum of 29 July made two main points about the campaign. One was that the calling of the election should be keyed not to generalities about the need for majority government but to a specific example of Mr Diefenbaker's irresponsible style of opposition and therefore the need to clear the air, to let the people decide whether they wanted that sort of opposition or wished the government to be able to get on with its program, to continue the things that it had done and to implement the other measures that it had proposed, such as medicare. Except at the opening, in explaining the occasion for the election, the campaign should not be a battle with Mr Diefenbaker, but a positive statement of what the government would do in an extended term; it should not be a defence of the government's record except to demonstrate, from what had been achieved despite the nature of the opposition, that a continuing Pearson government could and would do more, more efficiently. Those points were fleshed out in subsequent strategy papers.

The 29 July memorandum did not have its intended prompt effect. Some ten days later Mr Pearson put to me a series of questions about the case for an election and how it should be conducted. I responded in a memorandum headed "Strategy," dated 10 August. It emphasized that, while the kind of opposition we had had to deal with must first be attacked, the argument had to be devastating but terse. "After a week or two, the public should almost be able to see us wiping our hands, saying that's that, now we get on to more important things ... The essential is to be clear and strong as to what the government wants a mandate for ... We should put it squarely to people: The issue is what sort of Canada you want." The sort of Canada that voting Liberal offered could be summed up, I suggested, in co-operative federalism, economic expansion with full employment, medicare, pensions, and an enlarged opportunity program including university scholarships and rural development.

Mr Pearson responded with notes on "the reason for an election now" and "the kind of campaign." Their weakness provoked me to a memorandum on "The Issues" which ended with a bitter note. Issue one, I argued, "is the job we are doing," despite the delaying tactics of the opposition, and "the job we are trying to do ... more economic expansion, medicare, the war on poverty, election expense reform, university financing, etc." But if the opposition parties meant what they said, we couldn't get on with this business until after an election. They were going to hold us up and try to defeat us in the House. "It is better to clear the air, to have the people decide now whether they want us to get on with the job."

While this memorandum was being written Mr Pearson was in Vancouver, where he not only talked as if an election was probable though not decided but also made promises about local projects in the traditional style of pork-barrel electioneering. The memorandum concluded:

> This first issue would be more convincing if the Prime Minister had not given two million of taxpayers' money to hockey night in Vancouver and however many millions it is to pleasure cruising. No doubt we can digest that. Just as a country can stand a lot of ruining, a government can stand a lot of inconsistent foolishness. But there is a point at which the image gets too blurred to hold even those who want to be devoted adherents. All that we have worked for – a new politics in a new Canada – has been imperilled enough by the embracing of Dupuis, Rouleau et al. of the old politics. With that thick cloud already on us, not much new politics is going to show if we now campaign with the old pork-barrel techniques. If even now we haven't the guts to resist that sort of thing, it's time for people who write strategy papers to occupy themselves more usefully.

I might have followed my own advice for all the impact that the writing of the following two months was to have. But people once immersed in politics do not give up easily. There were still waverings to be dealt with. Mr Pearson, returning from Vancouver tired and dispirited, indicated that he had after all decided against an election. The reversal appalled even Paul Martin, who was not much inclined to an election. (As Secretary of State for External Affairs, he was somewhat above the parliamentary tensions, and easily able to deal with such criticism as he encountered.)

On 1 September there was a special Cabinet meeting at which the

Prime Minister asked each Minister to give his opinion of an election. Only Watson McNaught, who had every reason to expect to lose his seat, was strongly opposed. Two or three were inclined against or non-commital. The rest were definitely for an election. Mr Pearson said that he would make his decision within a few days.

He summoned Walter, Keith Davey, Mary Macdonald, Dick O'Hagan and me to a meeting at Harrington Lake on 3 September. It was a warm afternoon and we sat on the verandah with Mr and Mrs Pearson. The decision was made at last. On 7 September the Prime Minister announced the dissolution of Parliament for an election on 8 November. Happily, campaigning was no longer my business. I still wrote some policy papers but, apart from the announcement of what proved to be the unfulfilled scholarship policy, they had little effect on the words used. Mr Pearson was simply too tired, too uncertain, and at heart too unsure whether he should be campaigning at all, to enhance the public opinion of him and his government or to make what it would do at all clear and convincing. He was stung by Mr Diefenbaker's campaign but his attempts to reply to it were never better than confusing.

Mr Diefenbaker campaigned with gusto, mostly about the scandals, which enabled him also to appeal to anti-French prejudices. By the end, his denunciations had almost reached the point of suggesting that the whole government of Canada had been taken over by big-time criminals. He could not implicate me in that, but he could not leave me out of his attacks. From platform after platform he linked my being in charge of the anti-poverty campaign to a salary increase to $25,000 (then, for most people, large). "He's won his war on poverty" was the slur. In fact, of course, my salary throughout the time in Ottawa was that of a Deputy Minister, changed only as and when there were general adjustments in those salaries. This meant that, in reversal of the usual pattern, I was appreciably less well off during my forties, in public service, than I had been from the age of thirty in the private sector. My feeling that the attack was unfair was heightened by the fact that, throughout my time in government, I deliberately held no financial assets except government bonds. It was a poor investment policy, but removed any risk that my judgment could be affected, or even seem to be affected, by personal interest in the fortunes of any entreprise. But Mr Diefenbaker never allowed facts or fairness to hamper his oratorical flights.

It may be doubted whether Mr Diefenbaker in 1965 won any converts, but the Conservative campaign as a whole, conducted largely in isolation from the titular leader, was better than the Liberals'. Most of the Conservatives who had sat on their hands in 1963 rallied to the party this time. It was not that they wanted Mr Diefenbaker to return as Prime Minister. Many would have been as appalled by that as any Liberal. But it was not a conceivable result. Their concern was the future of their party. They had to do their part now if they were to be influential afterwards in getting rid of Diefenbaker and choosing his successor. They campaigned well.

The one bright spot in the Liberal campaign was that Marchand, with Trudeau and Pelletier, reversed his 1963 decision. The three became candidates, though arm-twisting was required to get a safe nomination for Trudeau, and strengthened the Liberal showing in Quebec. The polling on 8 November proved, however, that the Canadian people as a whole had experienced little to move them politically since 1963. The Liberal share of the poll was slightly reduced, but, thanks to Quebec, the number of Liberal seats increased by 2, to 131; that was still just short of a majority and, the net losses having been those of the Créditistes, both the Conservatives and the NDP were a few seats stronger. The Liberal caucus was more unbalanced than ever, and the effective opposition parties were stronger.

Governments, unlike people, can survive for a while without the equivalent of some of their vital organs. The Pearson government was not destroyed by the 1965 election. It was disembowelled.

Very properly, Walter Gordon offered his resignation immediately after the election. Very improperly, the Prime Minister accepted it. Walter had indeed been the strongest proponent of an election. But he had been articulating a view shared by many, indeed in the end almost all, of the ministers. His advocacy had been of an earlier election – which, if one was to be held at all in 1965, would have been more likely to produce a majority. It was Mr Pearson who had delayed the decision without discouraging the party preparations for an election that made it hardly avoidable. Ultimately, he made the decision that he had made inevitable. If anyone should have resigned because it turned out badly, that was Mr Pearson first. He could not in conscience accept Walter's resignation for the reason for which it was offered. He accepted the resignation because it provided him with a way out of a trap he had made for himself.

The financial community disliked – hated would be hardly too strong a word – Walter Gordon. Taking the opportunity of the election and the call for campaign funds, some of its leading members put their feelings to the Prime Minister in no uncertain terms. What exactly he said I do not know, but it is highly probable that, with his usual desire to please the people to whom he was talking, he was sympathetic enough to lead them to feel that they had been promised that Walter would not remain Minister of Finance after the election. That, at least, was the story that in October was circulating in "informed" circles. When I heard it I put it bluntly to the Prime Minister: if the story was true, I was resigning on the spot. He assured me that it was not true. I believed him. I was and am sure that, for all his convenient obscurities, Mr Pearson was incapable of a direct lie face-to-face to a friend. Equally, I am sure that he had held out enough hope to his other audiences to make them think, equally sincerely, that their wishes would be fulfilled and Walter's days were numbered. Perhaps Mr Pearson's conscience bothered him. On 26 October on a public platform, he declared that Walter would be Minister of Finance in his post-election government.

No doubt he was thinking of a majority government that would give him the strength to face down critics. For the actual situation, he was in a mess. After the election setback he wanted, for the remainder of his prime ministership, a quieter life, a conventionally "safer" government, than he would have with Walter still at Finance. It did not matter that the gentlemanly offer of resignation was for reasons that could not properly be recognized if Mr Pearson was not resigning himself. The offer provided him with a way out. He took it.

I am sorry to say that the enormity of this did not immediately occur to me. I was preoccupied with other problems. By now I had perhaps become imbued with the civil service philosophy that in a difficult political situation one's first concern must be that the government of the country should be carried on. It was clear almost at once that it would still be a Pearson government. He was too proud to retire, if he could help it, at a moment when he would be acknowledging failure. The problem was therefore that the government should be restructured in a way that saved as much as possible from the wreck. My feeling at the time, as a friend of Walter's, was that he was well out of it.

With this short vision, I failed for a while to realize how unfair to Walter the consequences of his resignation would be. The myth was created, and certainly was not discouraged by Mr Pearson, that he was the main architect of the government's greatest troubles, of the first budget and the ill-conceived election. Having taken a different view from his about both of these – at the time; not, like so many, with hindsight – I can perhaps say all the more forcefully that Walter Gordon was in fact the government's main strength. While he contributed to mistakes, as did I and others, the Prime Minister not least, no one else could have done so much to give the government such coherence and direction as it had, to push through its principal measures of economic improvement and social reform.

The one major fault that I have to find with Walter is that he did not learn the lesson of the way he was treated in 1965. He entertained, on the basis of vague promises from Mr Pearson, vast illusions about what he could achieve by returning to the Cabinet in 1967. He soon recognized the mistake, but the sad result was that his active political career trickled off into the sands in a way inappropriate to the man. Any of us might be relieved if he could think of no more serious criticism of himself.

In December 1965, however, the immediate task was to remake the government. Gordon Robertson had prepared the way. During the campaign, realizing that there would in any event be a considerable post-election reconstruction of the Cabinet, he developed ways of using the opportunity to make some important improvements in Ottawa's departmental structures. Two related changes were the most significant and far-sighted. One was to create the Department of Energy, Mines and Resources by combining the rather strange Department of Mines and Technical Surveys with the energy responsibilities of Trade and Commerce, and the natural resource functions of the Department of Northern Affairs and National Resources. The other part of that department could be given a more coherent role by pulling Indian affairs out of their obscurity in the Department of Citizenship and Immigration, to create the Department of Indian Affairs and Northern Development.

I became involved in the discussion of these and other possibilities and thereby hit on what I thought was a solution to the administration problems that had become apparent in examining poverty and opportunity. We could put together the National Employment Service, the training responsibilities so poorly lodged in the Department of Labour, ARDA, with its new FRED, and the Area Development Agency of the Department of Industry. Such units would provide the basis for a new Department of Manpower and Community Development, which could concentrate the federal responsibilities for precisely those matters that had been identified, in the poverty and opportunity studies and conference, as most needing development and better organization for service delivery.

It was an exciting idea, while it briefly lasted. An experienced public servant, George Davidson, pointed out the difficulty to me. Federal concern with most manpower programs rested only on broad responsibility for the economy and the use of the spending power. There was just one manpower matter for which responsibility was specifically assigned to the federal government under the constitution. That was immigration. The federal government could not establish a manpower department without including immigration in its responsibilities.

I had to accept this. But in the course of my firefighting activities during the previous two years I had seen enough of immigration problems to be well aware of the political delicacy and administrative burden involved for any Minister and Deputy. Manpower and Immigration would be quite enough for one department. Sadly, I had to decide that we would have to rely on other structures for the co-ordination of manpower programs with regional and community development.

The Prime Minister was in no mood, immediately after the election, to come to close grips with such issues. He talked to some ministers about their future roles and then went to a remote Caribbean island to relax. He was due to go on to an official visit to Jamaica, accompanied by Ed Ritchie. For that purpose a government Jet-Star aircraft, with Ed aboard, would pick up the Prime Minister at the airport nearest to his retreat. He was concerned, however, to have the Cabinet reconstruction ready to announce shortly after his return, only a little before Christmas. It was therefore arranged that the plane would go a day early. Gordon and I would fly down on it, so that we would have a day and a half of discussion before Mr Pearson went to Jamaica.

The first day was Sunday, 12 December. We landed, thanks to the pilot's skill, on the short runway of St Maarten, in a sudden, fierce tropical storm. Jim Coutts, who had been with the Pearsons on their vacation, drove me in a rented Volkswagen beetle over a cliff road through blinding rain to the hotel where we were to meet. We found the Prime Minister of Canada in his beachside cabin, luxurious enough in normal circumstances, but where the sewer had backed up in the downpour. He was in bare feet, his trousers rolled up to his knees, trying to sweep the results out of the door.

Gordon and I put forward our proposals, his about structures and mine about Cabinet appointments. Over the two previous weeks we had spent a good deal of time working out combinations and permutations and could now present the choices in an organized way. The Prime Minister agreed to our preferred departmental structure and made most of the key decisions about ministerial appointments. A limited range of alternatives for the others was drawn up.

There was one non-ministerial proposal. I said that I would like to leave the Prime Minister's Office to become Deputy Minister of Manpower and Immigration. There were two motives. Negatively, it was clear that the work of the PMO would now be almost entirely firefighting; in the post-election government there would be little policy development to be undertaken in the name of the Prime Minister. Positively, the new department now provided the best opportunity to get on with the things to which I had put my hand; it was the means by which the priority measures identified under the opportunity plan could be implemented.

The Prime Minister was enthusiastic on the second point. He said the right things about losing me, but I am sure he was relieved. He wanted a quieter life, with less criticism from his more conservative associates, and with the new Cabinet my activism would have been an embarrassment to him. After eight years we had come to a point where it was best that our ways should part, but he would have had difficulty in initiating a fair method of bringing it about. Ironically it was Mrs Pearson, with whom my relations had often been strained, who said, after the Prime

Minister had gone to bed and she and Jim Coutts and I were taking a brief fling in the casino, "but what will he do without you?" I said, sincerely, that he would do better, but did not put into words the more immodest part of the thought: "for the kind of government he is now going to run."

Gordon and I flew back to Ottawa on 14 December with a package of assignments. The Prime Minister was to return on the 16th and the new Cabinet was to be announced on the 17th. It was a timetable that necessitated desperate work but it minimized the Prime Minister's exposure to objections and pressures.

The most unpleasant of my assignments was to tell Judy LaMarsh that she could not remain at Health and Welfare and to offer her some choice of alternatives. She was again furious with Mike for not doing his own dirty work, as she put it, and properly refused to give an answer without speaking to him herself. The most pleasant task was to persuade Jean Marchand to take the Manpower portfolio. He was always worried about his imperfect command of English. That was unnecessary. Jean's sharp mind enabled him to state the essence of a problem or a solution more effectively in his second language than most politicians do in their first. But he was realistic about his lack of interest and talent for administration. His idea was that he would be best able to influence general policy, which was his concern, if he could concentrate on it as a Minister without Portfolio. Gordon Robertson joined in convincing him that this was not how Ottawa worked. Policy could not be isolated from detail and a Minister who was going to argue it out effectively, in Cabinet and in its committees, needed the support of a strong departmental organization. He agreed, specifically on the condition that I would indeed be the Deputy Minister and prepared to ensure that he got help on policies generally.

For the swearing in ceremony of the new Cabinet I drove Jean to Rideau hall in my MGB. It was less luxurious and powerful than the sports car in which P.E. Trudeau came to Ottawa, but I hoped it symbolized that there was still a new wave within the government. However much it turned about, to more conservative policies in most areas, in manpower measures at least it would be dynamic.

32 Changing Structures

Nineteen hundred and sixty-six was only just into its second week when the new manpower department's first proposal to Cabinet was written. It acted on one of the most important points that had come out of the enquiries into poverty and opportunity. Adults on training courses should not be regarded as unemployed but should be paid, in effect, a wage. It was not a new idea. Indeed, the election platform of 1962 had included a commitment that a new Liberal government would pay allowances "equivalent to a moderate wage, to those who work satisfactorily in retraining courses."

The subsequent enquiries, however, had reinforced the case for this crucial reform. Accordingly, I had in October 1965 written a memorandum to the Prime Minister that discussed why the federal government's substantial expenditures, in support of provincial training facilities and programs, were doing so little good. There was need for better counselling services and more effective training techniques. These would produce markedly better results, however, only if we dealt realistically with the central problem of motivation. Many adults anyway had hang-ups about "going back to school." We could not expect those to be overcome when they were reinforced by poverty: people taking training courses were often somewhat worse off than they would be if they were simply unemployed. It should therefore be no surprise that trainees were difficult to recruit and drop-out rates were high. A moralist might say that people being provided with "free" training should accept short-term pain for long-term gain, but many of the people most in need of training did not have the resources to act on such middle-class philosophy.

The memorandum therefore urged that we not delay any longer. We should announce that in future all trainees would receive allowances greater than unemployment benefits. But Mr Pearson was then preoccupied with the election campaign, and the proposal was returned without comment. Three months later, however, with the enthusiasm and political clout that Jean Marchand at first brought to such projects, I thought we could do better. We did.

The January memorandum asked for Cabinet approval to negotiate a new arrangement with the provinces. Although the federal government reimbursed the provinces for 90 per cent of their cost, the allowances then being paid to trainees were as little as $10 a week in New Brunswick. Even where they were somewhat bigger (to an Ontario maximum of $55 a week if a trainee had dependants and had to live away from home to take the training course), any available unemployment insurance benefit was deducted from the allowance. This meant that trainees often exhausted their benefit entitlement while they were in training; if they did not get a job immediately after training, they were worse off than they might have been if they had sought other employment from the start.

A new system was not difficult to negotiate. The fundamental point, about which Jean Marchand felt as strongly as I did, was to break away from regarding training as equivalent to unemployment. Instead it should be seen, in a world of rapid technological change, as a natural episode in a normal working life. Therefore people in training courses would not draw unemployment insurance benefits. Such entitlements would remain intact in case of future unemployment.

Jean and I would have liked to institute a training "salary." We faced the difficulty, however, that the federal government traditionally paid its employees on the same wage scales across the country, whereas the provinces rightly felt that training wages adequate in Ontario would be out of line with other incomes in the poorer provinces. We therefore stayed with "allowances" and devised a mixed system. There would be a basic allowance of $35 a week. Since the normal training week was 35 hours, this meant $1 an hour, which was then 80 per cent of the minimum wage under federal jurisdiction. This the federal government would pay in full. There would be additional allowances according to family size, and these would vary from province to province, in ratio to per capita income in the province. The maximum, payable in Ontario, would be $20 per week for a trainee with one dependant, $30 with two dependants, and $40 with three or more. An additional allowance of $15 a week would be paid to anyone who had to live away from home while training. The maximum additional allowance would thus be $55 in Ontario, less in other provinces in ratio to average income levels, and the federal government would reimburse each province for 90 per cent of its scale.

The final result, with the $35 basic allowance, was that a trainee with a spouse and two children would get $60 a week in Newfoundland and $75 a week in Ontario, with amounts in between in other provinces, plus the $15 if away from home. This was well above unemployment benefits at the time and, indeed, not desperately low in relation to wage levels. The plan proceeded smoothly; by June 1966 the legislation was through Parliament.

The other reform that was easy to accomplish was in helping people to move to employment. In early 1965 the idea of the manpower mobility program had seemed to me one of the important components of the plan to improve opportunities. In practice, as I noted earlier, it emerged painfully slowly through the bureaucratic processes of the Department of Labour and the National Employment Service. It proved to be as crabbed in life as it had been in birth. After ten months of operation only 1,900 people had been helped to move.

Accordingly we proposed, in November 1966, radical changes. The basic criterion for eligibility under the original program was that you had been unemployed for at least four months. We proposed that the criterion should be the likelihood of obtaining employment by moving to a place where the demand for the individual's skills was stronger. In such cases, the mobility assistance should be entirely a grant, not a loan, to cover transportation and removal costs and a re-establishment allowance of up to $1,000 for a family. Also, in recognition that the obstacle to movement often was delay in selling one's house in an area of poor employment, there could be an additional grant of $500 to help a home-owner to establish himself or herself in new accommodations.

In addition to these relocation grants proper, there were to be "exploratory" grants to help a person to look for work in an area of greater opportunity, and travel grants to enable a worker to pursue training not available in his or her present area.

This program was approved with effect from April 1967. In the following twelve months, 5,700 people were helped to make permanent moves, and 4,400 used the exploratory grants. The program was then further broadened to cover people who were not unemployed but underemployed, in the sense of having, in their present location, only part-time or casual work, or work that did not utilize their proven skills.

The effectiveness of such a mobility program depended on the judgmental powers of the manpower officers required to assess whether an individual would substantially improve his or her employment opportunities by relocation. The National Employment Service (NES) that we inherited was not staffed for tasks of that kind. It had been created as an arm of the Unemployment Insurance Commission. Its interest was in ensuring that people drawing benefits did so as briefly as possible. As a manpower agency it was, to put it kindly, unsophisticated.

Our purpose was to implement very different ideas and practices of manpower service. Our problem was that this required substantial changes in large administrative structures. It meant disturbing entrenched bureaucracies. That involved difficulties enough where they were federal bureaucracies. Where they were provincial, as was the case in manpower training, it was rather as though one had, while naked, stuck a stick into a wasps' nest.

The establishment of a new federal department requires legislation, but the functions of an existing department can be changed by orders-in-council under the Public Service Rearrangement and Transfer of Duties Act. The creation of the new department therefore took place in two stages. Jean Marchand and I were initially appointed Minister and Deputy Minister of Citizenship and Immigration. The Indian Affairs Branch was transferred out of that department. The National Employment Service and parts of the Department of Labour – technical and vocational training, manpower consultative services, vocational rehabilitation, and much of its research and economics branch – were transferred into Citizenship and Immigration. Under the subsequent legislation, which came into effect on 1 October 1966, responsibility for citizenship moved to the Secretary of State and the new department was renamed Manpower and Immigration.

The basic change in structure was to create across the country some 350 Canada Manpower Centres, as we readily agreed to call them. The NES had operated mostly in corners of UIC offices chiefly concerned with paying or refusing unemployment benefits. The greater part of the NES staff had neither the facilities nor the training to do much more than a clerical job of assigning people on unemployment benefit to the low-skilled jobs for which employers informed them of vacancies. The new centres (CMCs) were to have much broader purposes.

Those were embodied in a decision to designate the operating staff of the CMCs as "manpower counsellors." Their task was to help people, whether unemployed or unsatisfactorily employed, to obtain the employment that was likely to maximize their lifetime earnings. This required much more than information about the existing employment opportunities in the area. It required counselling skills. It required understanding of the abilities and experience needed for various occupations. It required awareness of changing trends in the nature of jobs and the emerging balance of demand and supply in the myriad sub-sectors of the labour market. It required an understanding of what training could and could not do, as well as detailed knowledge of available training facilities and courses. It required the judgment to use training and mobility assistance as effective and efficient instruments to enhance the employability of individuals.

As much as possible of this collection of skills had to be assembled in each CMC. Obviously, what was practicable could be adequate for the job only with the help of a good information system for the service as a whole and, particularly for the smaller offices, with specialist services and guidance supplied from some more central location. Moreover, while the intent was that the managers of CMCs should truly manage them, it would be some time before most of the staff we had inherited would have the confidence to operate in the new way without a good deal of reference to higher authority.

Our most important organizational decision was that the necessary support and direction should be concentrated at points closer to the CMCs than Ottawa. One or two highly specialized functions, notably economic analysis of labour market trends and forecasts, had to be centralized. Otherwise, the departmental headquarters would be concerned only with policy guidelines; operational responsibility would lie with five regional offices, located in Vancouver, Winnipeg, Toronto, Montreal, and Halifax.

Though it now seems routine, in 1966 this was an innovation in the federal public service. Some departments had officers entitled regional directors, but they served as little more than post offices for passing on instructions and reporting information back to Ottawa. The delegation of management responsibility that we proposed was different. It required that the directors be more senior officers than the federal service had previously appointed outside Ottawa. We had to contend with considerable bureaucratic resistance in order to get close to the classification levels appropriate for each regional director and immediate colleagues. In my first discussion paper on the subject, in February 1966, I remarked that "it might almost be taken as a mark of soundness in the organization that the number of senior officers outside Ottawa should exceed the number in Ottawa," but there was not much agreement with such thinking. The outcome was less satisfactory than I had hoped, though certainly much better than a traditionally centralized structure would have been.

In setting up the organization, we had massive help from the Public Service Commission and especially from the strong personal involvement of its able and enthusiastic chairman, John Carson. Most of the fifteen main positions, three in each region, were filled from outside the public service. They included one woman, Jean Edmonds, at what was then an unusually high level; later, she became an Assistant Deputy Minister at a time when women in such positions were still very few.

The new structure was in place, though not complete, by late summer – which was, by the standards of such processes in the public service, fast. In order to limit as far as possible the amount of organizational change that had to be digested quickly, it was initially limited to manpower services. These included, however, one component from the Immigration Branch, which had its own unit for helping new immigrants to settle into Canada. It was considerably more effective than the NES, with the anomalous result that immigrants had, when they needed it, better help in finding suitable jobs than was available to unemployed citizens. This part of the immigration service was absorbed into the manpower centres. The intent was not, of course, to dilute the service to immigrants but to help in raising the quality of information and counselling available to all who needed help with employment.

Later, after immigration policy and practices had been reformed, the administrative reorganization was completed. In April 1968 the admission and enforcement functions of immigration were added to the responsibilities of the regional directors, so that the whole field operation of the department in Canada could use common support services. The regional directors' reporting line to Ottawa led to a small office headed by a departmental Director-General of Operations, with the rank of an Assistant Deputy Minister. The manpower and immigration divisions at headquarters thus became, as far as Canada was concerned, functional support units responsible for program guidelines and information. The only direct management not decentralized from Ottawa was that of the immigration offices overseas, which had to work in the parallel with Canadian embassies and the management structure of the External Affairs Department in Ottawa.

The manpower structure was the first major experiment in decentralization within the federal bureaucracy. Though not free from problems, it worked reasonably well. It was more attuned to the needs of the people it existed to serve than a more centralized structure would have been, and I think it was also less costly. Certainly it later received the flattery of imitation, in the shape of more decentralization in other federal activities.

In 1966 and 1967, however, the nature of the structure was less significant than the task of putting muscle into it. The need was manpower counsellors – more of them, better informed, better equipped, better able to make judgments, better trained to provide sensible advice. The Public Service Commission undertook a substantial recruitment program for us, and we mounted intensive programs for retraining existing staff and training recruits. The first "orientation and induction" course, in early May 1966, was distinguished by an address from John Deutsch, who as Chairman of the Economic Council had done so much to articulate the importance of manpower policy. That summer we also had courses for senior staff, conducted at the Royal Military College in Kingston, which provided adequate facilities at remarkably low cost. For that we got good professionals as seminar leaders, and a person as prominent as Bill Davis, then the Ontario Minister of Education, gave up a Sunday to talk with us. Neither he nor I foresaw the conflict that lay a little ahead of us.

The conflict arose from the need to find, in a federation in which education is the most jealously treasured of provincial responsibilities, effective ways to upgrade the skills of the work force, so that new technologies could be readily adopted and so that older workers, who left school early and relied for their livings on muscular strengths now redundant, could obtain places in the new economy.

The provinces had done little to respond to such needs. Understandably, their resources had been concentrated on providing more schools for more children staying longer. Not until 1960 had the training need become so generally recognized as to lead to a major financial effort – by the federal government. The Technical and Vocational Training Assistance Act of that year empowered Ottawa to share the costs of a wide range of programs that provinces might mount. The largest provided 75 per cent of the capital costs of building vocational high schools, trade schools and technological institutes. Between 1961 and 1967, federal financing under this program was about $600 millions. Under the other programs, the federal government provided 50 to 75 per cent of the operating costs of a great variety of training programs in vocational high schools and technological institutes; of apprenticeship training; of training for vocational and technical teachers; of both basic education and trades training for unemployed people; and so on.

The consequences of such programs were, or should have been, entirely predictable. They were chiefly used by provincial departments of education to subsidize their schools. From 1961 to 1967, two-thirds of the total federal expenditures under TVT (technical and vocational training) were directed to young people within the school system. Even the program specifically intended for retraining of the unemployed – the then famous "program five" – in practice operated mostly for young people. In 1966 the average age of people looking for work was thirty-six; the average age of trainees in program five was only twenty-three.

The ineffectiveness of the program became even more striking if one looked at the people who found it most difficult to get jobs. In the 1960s they were those in the classification "male, aged over 34, less than grade nine education." In 1966, 20 per cent of the people looking for work were in this category. But only a little more than 2 per cent of the trainees in program five were people in this group most needing help to find a place in the world of work.

That the provinces exploited the TVT system to subsidize their schools did not prevent them from voicing their standard, and legitimate, criticisms of shared-cost programs. The federal government had to specify "standards" for the costs it would share. In practice, this involved tiresomely detailed audits of provincial expenditures. The effect of the TVT programs was that the federal government even controlled the salaries paid to some school janitors.

It should not be thought that this fussy control was a guarantee of purity in the use of federal funds. The government of Newfoundland had a private dining room for Cabinet Ministers. On one occasion when I was being entertained there to lunch, I commented politely to the Premier on the quality of the cooking. "Well," said Joey Smallwood with the disarming honesty that was in some circumstances characteristic, "I'm glad you appreciate it. You pay for it." The chef was listed, for salary purposes, as an instructor in the vocational training institute.

Even Premier Smallwood's ingenuity, however, could not alter the inherent characteristic of shared-cost financing of discretionary programs: the wealthier provinces get a disproportionate share of the federal funds because they can better afford to put in their money along with the federal share. In the fiscal year 1965–6, federal expenditures under program five, for training the unemployed, were $34 per unemployed person in the Atlantic provinces, $177 per unemployed person in Ontario. Least was done where most was needed.

The federal-provincial agreements under which the TVT programs operated ran to March 31, 1967. We were determined to replace them by more effective federal action to help people to improve their capability for employment. The needs of provincial school systems were real enough, but they were reasons, as was now widely recognized, for ceding more tax room to the provinces and improving the equalization of their revenues. They were not grounds for shared-cost programs involving the federal government in secondary education under the guise of manpower training. We must get out of what had hitherto been, in practice, the main part of the TVT program.

But how could we ensure that manpower training was readily available to those who needed it, and was more effective and efficient than the courses being provided under the shared-cost arrangements? We had no doubts about the federal responsibility, in the interests of economic progress and employment. But it was impossible, constitutionally, for the federal government itself to mount training courses; good training could not be clearly differentiated from education. We had to find a better way to get it provided.

We pondered the problem for several months. The technical and vocational training branch of the Department of Labour was no help at all: its staff were comfortable with the program to which they were accustomed. They could not see why anyone would want to change it in more than minor ways. If one person deserves principal credit for the solution at which we arrived it is Duncan Campbell, one of the ablest of the people who had come to the new department from the economics branch of the Department of Labour. The solution was, in a sense, a market approach. The need for training was great, but it was not an effective demand because few of the people who most needed training were in a position to pay for it. The federal government's role was to make the demand effective, by paying for the training. We had already moved partially to that role, with our new policy for training allowances. It was a logical completion that we should buy training on behalf of those who needed it.

This was an elegant idea and, unlike some of its kind, it stood up well to consideration of how we would apply it in practice. We would have to be firm in asserting our right to buy training from industry in cases where it was the best supplier, but predominantly we would buy training from the provinces. We would have to pay the full costs, including an allowance for capital charges, of particular courses providing for a spec-ified number of trainees. But we would be in control. The courses would no longer be what it suited provincial departments of education to make available. They would be courses of the kind that our manpower counsel-lors found most effective in improving the employability of the people who needed them. To help the manpower counsellors, we could set up consultative committees on training needs, embracing the relevant pro-vincial departments and also representatives of principal industries in the area. Essentially, training would become the instrument of manpower policy, of matching people and jobs, that it should be. As I put it in a 1967 paper:

> The public provision of manpower training should be based on prac-tical judgments of what it will do to improve the employability of the individual, to enable him at a particular time to take advantage of employment opportunities, to increase his earnings by fitting him for a better occupation that is in demand. Therefore the efficient way for the federal government to respond to adult training needs is to get down into the market, so to speak, and finance the needs of the individual as such. In that way, training can operate effectively for economic growth and full employment in our kind of economy. This means that the federal role is to buy training for the individual who needs it. We make his demand effective.

This new training policy was announced at the federal-provincial conference in October 1966. The federal government would not renew the TVT agreements when they expired on 31 March 1967. It made gener-ous phase-out arrangements for the capital programs in support of school and other construction. But from 1 April, the federal government's role in training would be to buy the courses that would best help the match-ing of jobs and people, that would minimize friction in the relationship of demand and supply in the labour market.

The provinces were stunned. The premiers and provincial treasurers, who had so often criticized shared-cost programs so strongly, could not muster any respectably consistent objection to the demise of this one.

The treasurers of the provinces with relatively high unemployment were quick enough to see that the new policy would do more in their provinces than they had been able to afford under the old policy. But the delegations included education ministers and officials. They were appalled.

There is rarely internal consistency in the attitudes of the provinces to federal programs. The general stance is that the federal government is taking too much on itself. But particular departments often welcome federal action that helps to deal with the problems about which they are concerned. They particularly like shared-cost programs, which enable them to go to their cabinets for approval of, say, $10 millions of activity for which there is the seductive argument that it will cost the provincial treasury only $5 millions or $2 millions or whatever, according to the federal sharing ratio that will reimburse the rest of the expenditure.

On that basis provincial departments of education, especially in the richer provinces, had made a great thing of the TVT program. They were hooked on it. Enforced withdrawal involved unpleasant symptoms.

In fairness to the provinces, it should be said that they had some encouragement. The federal officials with whom departments of education were accustomed to deal were those of the TVT branch. Most of them made no secret of the fact that the new policy was not of their making, that they violently disliked it, indeed – perhaps the most decisive point – that the structure of the new department made some of their positions redundant.

The result was that for six months we lived in two worlds. One was the real world, in which people knew that the new policy took effect on 1 April. The other was the accustomed world that many education officials would not believe could be changed. They acted as if it was impossible that the new policy would actually come into effect.

We breezily initiated discussions on its implementation. Before drafting the legislation for the program, we sent out to the provinces what was probably the most comprehensive paper ever prepared confidentially by one level of government for another, inviting comment and criticism before our proposals were put before Parliament. All this fell almost flat. Only two specific objections were raised. One was entirely legitimate. It was that, in order to supply the courses we wanted to buy, the provinces would have to make capital and staff commitments, but could they trust us? We might cut off the program and leave them holding the bag. Nothing, of course, was further from our minds: it was basic to our thinking that more, not less, training would be needed for the foreseeable future. We therefore had no difficulty in meeting the concern with specific commitments. Our purchases of training would not be less, in any province, than the amount in which we had been involved in 1966 under the old program; and if, after the expansion we anticipated, there were cutbacks in some distant future, the reduction from one year to the next would never be by more than 10 per cent.

The other objection, however, went to the root of the policy change. We wished to make the distinction between schooling and manpower training as definite as possible. Our original idea was therefore that people whose training we paid for would have to have been out of school for at least three years. But exceptions were necessary. The most important was for the academic part of formal apprenticeship programs, but there were other cases where the exclusion would be hard to justify. Rather than have a rule with a lot of exceptions, we readily agreed to reduce the period to one year out of school. The provinces, however, wanted us to provide the same eligibility for training allowances. We refused. If we not only provided training but also paid allowances to people who had been out of school for only one year, we would be creating an incentive to drop out for that period and then take, with the allowance, training that could otherwise have been provided as a vocational course at school.

We recognized one exception. We paid a training allowance to a young person only one year out of school if he or she had a dependant. Otherwise we stuck to the "three-year rule," as it was known, and it became the central point of a quite intense controversy. This was, obviously, phoney. The provincial educational establishments were not really so exercised about the recent school-leavers to whom a hard hearted federal government was denying allowances. But it was the "popular" point that they could make. The real reasons why the program change disturbed them carried no public weight.

Our legislation for the purchase of training – the Occupational Training Act of 1967 – also took the small final step to complete the reform of training allowances made in 1966. We undertook to pay the allowances in full, and to pay them directly to the trainees. Hitherto they had been provincial cheques, though the federal government bore 97 per cent of the total cost. The allowance scales were exactly the same, varying with average provincial income, as had been previously agreed in negotiation. We provided further flexibility, in that we offered to vary them as between high-wage and low-wage areas within a province, if the provincial government so wished. Only Quebec took advantage of this.

There were no grounds for objection that could be made into a public campaign. Provincial officials, however, resented what they felt as a loss of control over "their" trainees. And provincial politicians did not like losing the pleasure of paying out provincial cheques from money that came to them almost entirely from Ottawa.

Control was, of course, the real issue. The direction and administration of TVT programs had been provincial, even though there were some fussy controls by the federal paymaster. The trainees were seen as being much like pupils in provincial schools. Now they were to be our "clients," for whom we purchased training and to most of whom we paid allowances. Assessments of employment opportunities, matched to the manpower counsellors' assessments of individual capabilities, would largely shape the content of the training provided.

Though education officials everywhere naturally disliked the change, the criticism from provinces with relatively high unemployment, including Quebec, was largely ritualistic. The new policy was avowedly designed to do more where needs were greatest. Ontario, which had made such a good thing out of the shared-cost TVT programs, was a different case. Premier Robarts and Bill Davis, as Minister of Education, said little. They would have been uncomfortable, I think, in raising strong public objections. They gave licence, however, to their infuriated education officials. We heard the most dire predictions of how the public's real interests would be perverted by crass federal officials who understood nothing about education. I felt that Congreve, if he could have observed the scene, might have revised his famous line: the fury of a woman scorned can rarely be greater than that of a bureaucrat whose pet program is upset. And a few of those bureaucrats, the TVT staff from the Department of Labour, were theoretically in our own camp, apparently encouraging their provincial counterparts to believe that somehow the change would not happen.

Planning the transitional arrangements was therefore, in some provinces, very difficult. Briefly, indeed, there was enough confusion to create some fears that the dire prophecies would be self-fulfilling. All we could do was to tough it out in the belief that facts would soon be accepted and good sense prevail. It did. Within a short time we were able to be confident that training was serving the public need considerably more effectively than it had done under the old program.

By early 1968, indeed, the Minister and the Department were able to feel that the new manpower service and programs had been effectively established. Most of the Canada Manpower Centres were at least beginning to work as we intended. The new training and mobility programs were proving to be effective tools. We had defined clear goals for the department and, in light of those goals, developed techniques of benefit-cost analysis to guide detailed decisions. We had pioneered, within Ottawa, in establishing a planning, programming and budgeting system – then just becoming the new management orthodoxy. There are many things that I would do differently if I had them to do again, but fewer of them relate to the Department of Manpower and Immigration than to other undertakings.

Certainly the policy, programs, and organization initiated in 1966–7 have, despite the controversies surrounding innovation, stood the test of time in the sense that they have been continued with little change in essentials. Indeed, the problem with the Department is perhaps that there has been too little adaptation and development. There has been one major improvement. In order to establish an effective manpower organization in 1966, it was essential to separate it from the Unemployment Insurance Commission. We had to scotch the idea that manpower services were only for people already unemployed. The UIC had been so much the dominant organization, with the NES as its subservient tool, that the only way quickly to implement a broader concept was to take the NES away from the UIC. But once the new manpower organization had been firmly established, and the unemployment insurance process itself had been made more sophisticated and humane, there were obvious advantages in reintegrating the two. Eventually, in 1976, this was done.

Unfortunately, the benefits of reintegration, which carried with it the change of name to Employment and Immigration, were marred by the larger problems of economic policy. In 1966 we assumed, reasonably enough at the time, that the economy would continue to be capable of providing plentiful employment. Our concern was to help people to be employable, to have the right skills at the right time in the right place. Our concern, to put it in more abstract terms, was to remove obstacles that hampered both the efficiency and the equity of an expanding economy. In the event, the economy did not continue to expand, and in that changed environment no manpower service could contribute as much as we had hoped, either to efficiency or to equity. Inevitably, therefore, the organization has become, in common with much of the public service, somewhat dispirited. The failures of economic policy do not, however, make it any less important that a manpower organization of high quality should be in place, to help both workers and employers to make the most of reviving opportunities.

While new manpower and training structures were being put into place, it was also necessary to reform – I tought of it as civilizing – the immigration process. An earlier chapter mentioned the burden that the administration of immigration placed on a Minister of Guy Favreau's temperament. There was no possibility that Jean Marchand would occupy his time in the weekly consideration of scores of individual cases. I was equally determined that the burden should not be transferred to me. If the Deputy Minister's job was to make many individual operational decisions, there were a lot of redundant officials lower down the ladder. If the Deputy was to discharge the responsibilities he was properly paid for, the individual files, except for a few very specially difficult cases, must be stopped short of his desk.

The basic reason why the administration of immigration was overcentralized was that the policy was obscure. This is a common situation in public administration. The faults of bureaucracy are often taken to mean that policies are too rigid, too little adaptable to particular problems and needs. That is sometimes that case. More often, however, the "rules" that junior officials apply too mechanically are not, in any real sense, policies expressing the purpose of the program being administered. They are procedures, made necessary by the lack of definite policies.

The trouble starts at the top. The policies on which politicians make up their minds are often vague in purpose. Agreement is easier that way. Unless the Minister responsible and his senior officials are resolute, the vagueness of the political decision carries over into the instructions provided to the officials who must administer the policy in detail. The ideal, of course, is to provide them with policy guidelines clear enough to enable all, or almost all, individual decisions to be firmly made within the guidelines. But if the policy itself is woolly, it is easier to lay down procedural rules that can be applied mechanically to a good proportion of the situations that the implementing officials have to deal with. The penalty is that the policy will not give a reasonable level of satisfaction to those affected, and the lives of the implementing officials will not be tolerable, unless a good many decisions, not determined by the rules, are referred back to higher levels of the bureaucratic structure. The price paid is that senior officials, even up to the Deputy Minister and the Minister, then become embroiled in making detailed decisions. Often they are in truth less equipped for that task than officers closer to the action would be, if they had good guidelines, and are thus inefficiently distracted from their proper roles in program formulation and general management.

This, in my observation, is the most important cause of the administrative faults so often alleged against bureaucracies. The administration of immigration was an extreme example.

Politicians were understandably chary of defining immigration policy at all precisely. On one hand, there was a broad public sentiment in favour of easy immigration; so many Canadians, if not immigrants themselves, had known parents or grandparents who were. There were also strong humanitarian sentiments on behalf of the oppressed and the deprived. And behind these general attitudes were powerful special interests: businesses wanting both skilled professionals and cheaper labour; expanding universities wanting professors with doctorates not available in Canada; richer people wanting domestic servants. And, of course, recent immigrants wanted their relatives and friends to join them, and ethnic organizations had strong interests in the growth of their particular communities.

On the other side, there were deep concerns about immigrants taking jobs from Canadians and undercutting union wages. There were even deeper concerns about people with strange languages, customs and appearances upsetting Anglo-Saxon communities or, in Montreal, shifting the linguistic balance by sending their children to English-language schools. The opposition to immigration was far less articulate than the support for it, but there were few constituencies in which a sensitive politician could ignore its existence.

What, then, was our immigration policy? It was a rate of immigration in line with the "absorptive capacity" of the country. It was to facilitate the reunion of families of people already here. It was to accept immigrants who could readily adapt to Canadian life. It was to be open to refugees, in numbers that did not greatly conflict with the other criteria.

That was about as definite as the political statement of purpose could be. How was such vagueness to be translated into the actual conduct of immigration policy?

To 1966, it was done by a strange mixture of devices. The acceptance of refugees was mostly a series of ad hoc responses to dramatic situations, most notably the flight from Hungary in 1956. Otherwise, the immigration movement was divided into two categories: "selected" immigrants, admitted in virtue of their assessed ability to establish themselves in Canada; and "sponsored" immigrants, admitted in virtue of having close relatives in Canada ready and able to assist them in becoming established.

The only precise criterion of the ability of selected immigrants to establish themselves was that they should have eleven years of schooling. It was a normally necessary condition, but not a sufficient one: beyond that, the decision lay entirely with the unfettered judgment of the interviewing immigration officer, based on the applicant's personality and his or her work experience in relation to occupational demands in the area of intended settlement. Indeed, the immigration officer could set aside the eleven-year rule if there was good reason to think that the immigrant could settle successfully despite having less education.

The purpose of family reunion in immigration policy was expressed in the sponsorship system, though here there was an element of avowed discrimination. The full arrangements did not apply to immigrants from countries outside Europe and the Americas. For the favoured origins, they were generous. Any citizen or already landed immigrant had the right to sponsor a wide range of relatives. As long as they passed the medical examination and there were no bars on such grounds as criminality and security, and provided that the sponsor met pretty minimal income requirements, sponsored immigrants were admitted without regard to educational levels or work experience.

This system had the potential for explosive growth in the unskilled labour force. One immigrant who quickly established himself could soon sponsor his brothers and sisters and his wife's brothers and sisters. They in turn could soon sponsor the brothers and sisters of their wives or husbands. And so on. Immigration officials did not like this. Indeed, while they were naturally defensive in response to frequent criticism on particular cases, most of them were far from happy about their operations. Though they did not see how they could do better, given the policy and the resources available to them, no one who observed the process closely could fail to see that it produced only a very crude relation between the avowed main purpose – immigration according to the country's absorptive capacity – and the actual extent and composition of the flow.

Indeed, the selection procedures, for all their elaboration, were by no means the determinant of how many people came to Canada and who they were. The equally important control was, simply, administrative delay. For the United States, the British Isles, and the northern and western countries of continental Europe, our immigration services were reasonably adequate for the normal volume of applicants. In those countries we even did some limited promotion by advertising, if their governments would permit it. (France, notably, would not.) Elsewhere, in southern Europe and in all the rest of the world, our facilities were far from matched to the interest in coming to Canada, then so widely seen as the land of opportunity.

I learned the significance of administrative delay when I visited India. This was done at the request of Roland Michener, then our High Commissioner in New Delhi, who had told his friend the Prime Minister of his concern that our handling of immigration was giving us a bad name. I understood his concern when I went into a file room stacked to the ceiling with letters that had not even been opened.

Under the impact of several controversial cases, the Pearson government had earlier undertaken to produce a White Paper on immigration policy. This was already in draft when Jean Marchand and I arrived. It was largely a defence of existing policy. More was needed, to clarify policy and improve its implementation, but at that stage I did not know what it should be. I removed some of the defensiveness and tried to make the statement of policy more definite and more related to general economic policy, but the White Paper as published, in October 1966, still did little more than propose some tightening of the sponsorship system. Early in 1967, it was considered by a parliamentary committee.

This was very different from the other parliamentary committee with which I had been closely involved, on the Canada Pension Plan. That reflected partisanship as it operates in the House of Commons. The immigration committee did not. Its active members were closely interested in the subject and fully aware that the differences about it did not run on party lines.

The committee had a considerable influence on policy. Its proceedings soon made it clear that the White Paper did not stand up well to informed criticism. We would have to do better. Under the impetus provided by the committee, we at last developed a solution to the problem. Who, if anyone, gave me the basic idea, I cannot now remember. It was the kind of idea that, once had, was so obvious that one wondered how it could have been missed for so long.

The need was for selection procedures that would result, to the greatest possible extent, in immigrants being those who could best settle down as useful and satisfied citizens. The problem was not unlike, in principle, that involved in the comparative evaluation of jobs. Why not try similar methods? If we could identify and define the various factors affecting a person's ability to settle successfully in Canada, and attach relative weights to them, then immigration officers would have a consistent basis on which to assess potential immigrants.

Boris Celovsky undertook the heavy task of examining how our tentative criteria and weights might have been applied to a sample, drawn from the files, of both accepted and rejected applicants. (Dr Celovsky, brilliant if erratic, was one of the able public servants who came to the new department from the economics and research branch of the Department of Labour, led by Jack Francis.) We satisfied ourselves that the evaluation process would work a good deal better than the rule of thumb of eleven years' schooling plus highly arbitrary other judgments.

Education was still given significant weight: one unit of assessment (out of a hundred total) for each year of successfully completed education and training (professional, vocational, or trades), to a maximum weight of twenty. Thus eleven years of schooling, instead of being a *sine qua non*, counted for eleven per cent in the total evaluation. From zero to fifteen units were assigned according to employment opportunities in the occupation that the applicant was likely to follow in Canada; his or her present occupation – not necessarily the same – was given a weight between one (for the unskilled) to ten (for the professional). Youth and early middle age were favoured by giving ten units of assessment to applicants between eighteen and thirty-five, with one unit less for each year of age over thirty-five. Finally, among the major factors, a maximum weight of fifteen was assigned for the immigration officer's assessment of the applicant's relevant personal qualities of adaptability, motivation, initiative, and resourcefulness.

The minor weights were: ten if the applicant had arranged employment in Canada with reasonable prospects of continuity; up to ten for his or her competence in English and French; up to five according to the general level of employment in the area of Canada to which the applicant wanted to go; and up to five if he or she had a relative (not, formally, a sponsor) in Canada.

An independent immigrant would be admissible if he or she scored at least fifty out of the maximum hundred units of assessment on all the above factors. If the applicant was already in Canada as a visitor, the fifty score would have to be achieved without taking account of arranged employment.

Dependants would continue, of course, to be admissible of right, without application of the criteria. One of the advantages of the proposal, however, was that it provided a way of integrating the consideration of other relatives into the assessment system. We renamed them "nominated" immigrants. For them only the "major" factors listed above were to be taken into account, to a maximum score of seventy. The others were regarded as being replaced by the nomination from someone already in Canada. Out of the maximum seventy thus available, the minimum score required, to make a nominated applicant admissible, depended on the closeness of the relationship, whether the nominator was a Canadian citizen or not and whether the applicant was abroad or already in Canada as a visitor.

This approach was tried out in general terms with the parliamentary committee in April, and well received. It was approved in detail by Cabinet in August, and made effective on 1 October 1967. In the interval there was an intensive effort to prepare the department's officers for it. I was afraid that the initial reaction of rather conservative men (there were few women) would be to regard "the points system," as it was inevitably labelled, as a substitution of mechanical counting for the personal judgment of immigration officers. In fact there was, for the most part, remarkably ready recognition that the new system provided a policy framework within which officials could make more consistent decisions more confidently. It was smoothly implemented and proved to be a reform that stood the test of time.

Not the least important aspect of the reform was that the details of the immigration process were for the first time set out in law, as regulations under the statute, instead of being mere administrative directions within the department. We did other things to civilize the process. In particular, we secured legislation, also effective in 1967, which established for the first time an independent board to hear appeals against deportation orders made by the department, and to which also a sponsor could appeal against refusal of admission to a relative.

The new system also removed all traces of discrimination because of an intended immigrant's country of origin and therefore, in effect, race. That was a reform particularly dear to Jean Marchand. It must be admitted that perfect equality was not achieved; there was no practicable way to make it equally easy for people in all countries to be interviewed by a Canadian immigration officer. But we did increase our staffs in the most overburdened posts; establish immigration offices in several new countries; and arrange for touring teams to visit other countries. By these means we substantially lessened the inequalities among countries tolerant of emigration and from which there were any appreciable numbers of applicants.

The 1970s would in any event have seen considerable shifts from the composition of immigration in the earlier postwar years. The end of the Viet Nam war reduced an unusual influx from the United States. The strength of the European economies, and the greatly reduced progress of Canada's, closed the gap in living standards that had been so strong an impetus to movement across the Atlantic. The belated expansion of Canada's universities and technical training facilities lessened the shortages that had induced so large a "brain drain" from older societies to Canada. For all these reasons, the proportion of immigrants from what had been the conventionally accepted sources would have declined. That this trend was offset, by increased immigration from unconventional sources, was the effect of the new selection system.

Since "unconventional" meant, for the most part, non-white, there was some open criticism and a good deal of shamefaced voicing of concern, particularly as unemployment increased during the 1970s. It is not racial prejudice to recognize, realistically, that there are limits to the speed at which the composition of a community can change, bringing new people and unfamiliar life-styles, without creating tensions that are damaging to the immigrants more than to the original inhabitants.

In the late sixties and early seventies, however, I had different reasons to remain concerned about immigration. Pleased as I was with it, the civilization of the selection system was in itself a means rather than an end. It meant that any given immigration policy could be implemented both more efficiently and with more humanity. It was an adaptable mechanism: a changed policy could be accommodated by altering the weights given to the various factors in the assessments.

We had created, in short, a satisfactory instrument. But we had not given thought to how, in the longer term, it should be used. The existing policy was reasonable enough for the circumstances of the late 1960s. But would those circumstances last? I doubted it, and was afraid that the politics of immigration would make policy changes too little and too late.

These concerns were strengthened by a demographic study undertaken in 1969. In the 1950s, Canadians had been producing babies at a markedly higher rate than in the depression years. But from 1961 there had been a dramatic change. In seven years, the fertility rate had plunged from 3.86 to 2.45 in 1968. There were people who regarded this as a temporary change. My hunch was that it was not; far from climbing back, it seemed to me more likely that fertility would continue to decline – the average Canadian woman would have fewer children – to the point where our population would not be replacing itself. This expectation has proved to be correct.

It also was, and is, my view that the Canadian economy still needs the impetus of a growing population for the development that will give us competitive levels of efficiency and high employment. If there is no natural increase, we need more rather than less immigration. Our comparative attractiveness is unlikely, however, to return to the point at which we again draw significant numbers of skilled people from developed countries. They cannot be replaced by skilled immigrants from less developed countries. Even if we are tolerant enough to welcome such people in large numbers, we have no right to take from poor countries the precious minority of their citizens in whose education and training desperately scarce resources have been invested. It would not be bad international behaviour to take unskilled, poor adults from the Third World, but they would be hard put to it to adopt Canada. In large numbers, and if given the help they would initially need at the expense of Canadian taxpayers, they would create greater tensions than our society could reasonably be expected to cope with.

This line of thought led me to suggest, in a report on the demographic study put to Cabinet in 1970, that for the future the ideal immigrant to Canada might be a young orphan. The next best would be young adults who had, or could be expected shortly to have, children brought up entirely or mainly in Canada. It would be relatively easy for Canadian communities to deal with the adjustment problems of such immigrants from a variety of races. In effect, we would be calling on the babies of the Third World to reduce the imbalance of our own fertility. The weights of the selection system could, of course, be altered to implement such a policy.

Apart from Jean Marchand, the only senior person whom I remember as expressing agreement with this thinking was Bob Bryce. From Cabinet as such there was no response. The demographic study had been made on Mr Trudeau's initiative. He was always interested in talking about ideas, but there were only a few that sustained his interest to be carried through into action. And in the centralized style of the Trudeau government, little got done without the Prime Minister's active involvement.

My connection with immigration ended, therefore, with the considerable satisfaction of having civilized the process but with only partial reform of the policy.

33 *Baby on the Doorstep*

One day in December 1967, I was in a Vancouver Manpower office, talking with the staff and with people looking for employment, when an agitated secretary came running to say that I must take a phone call from the Prime Minister. In fact, it was his private secretary calling with a message from him: he wanted me to know, before it became public, that he was about to announce his retirement.

There were plenty of aspiring successors in the wings but, in the tradition of the Liberal party, a candidate from Quebec would have some advantage. That would be Jean Marchand, if he wished. He did not. He expressed the reason, with his usual pithy realism about people, one evening when we were talking in the small bachelor apartment that was his Ottawa home. He put a question: "If I were Prime Minister, could I go on living here rather than move to 24 Sussex?" I said no. "That's it. If I could live here, I would run [for the leadership] Obviously I couldn't. So I won't." His was simply not the temperament required of a Prime Minister, and he was too sensible to be seduced by the power of a position.

The alternative Quebec candidate was Trudeau. He was nationally recognized in that role thanks, mainly, to the January 1968 federal-provincial conference. It was the first of its kind to be televised. Before the cameras, the Premier of Quebec, then Daniel Johnson, gratuitously baited Trudeau, whom he presumably resented as the long-time powerful critic of the Union Nationale. He may thereby have changed the course of Canadian politics. In an angry confrontation, Trudeau mopped the floor with him. The changing of the times could hardly have been more clearly illustrated. Mr Pearson was, of course, chairing the conference. As Trudeau's words became sharper and more vehement, Mike looked away in discomfort; and, seeing in the row behind someone to whom he was accustomed to relieving his feelings confidentially, he leaned over to me and whispered – though not very quietly – "Tom, Pierre shouldn't be doing this."

I think it can now be said to be proven that the country is better served by Pearson-style diplomacy in federal-provincial relations than by Trudeau-style confrontation. But in 1968 the Trudeau style in general struck a chord that suited public attitudes. I think that Mr Pearson himself on balance preferred Trudeau as his successor; he did not think too much of the other leading candidates and admired, as most of us did, many of Trudeau's qualities. He found the arrogance, however, rather hard to take. It was with evident relish that, when we were having lunch together some months after the changeover, he said: "I think Pierre's learning that his 'look, no hands' style won't do. He's finding that being Prime Minister isn't so easy as he thought."

The 1968 election could hardly have been more different from those of the previous ten years. On the Liberal side, it was all style and eloquence, with practically no substance. Mr Stanfield was at something of the same disadvantage, in dealing with Trudeau, that Mr Pearson had in facing Diefenbaker. A Pearson versus Stanfield election would have been a genuine debate about policies. Diefenbaker versus Trudeau would have been a matched contest of a different kind. Both were so much better on the hustings than they were in performance as prime ministers. Superficially so different, as politicians they nevertheless had enough in common to have deserved each other as opponents.

In 1968 Mr Trudeau's most precise commitment was to combat regional disparities. That was hardly a new idea. The Diefenbaker government, indeed, had instituted a few special programs to help the Atlantic provinces. The Pearson policy had attached considerable importance to regional development, and had done quite a bit about it. But in the Trudeau campaign it was given a new dimension, if only because it stood out from what was otherwise a vacuum of policy.

There was little doubt that Pierre Trudeau would win the election, and even greater certainty that, if he did, his great friend Jean Marchand would be the minister responsible for regional development. That April and May, therefore, I was considering what the main lines of regional development policy should be and how we should organize it. There seemed to be a second chance to do as I had first suggested for the restructuring of departments at the end of 1965: to establish what I had called a Department of Manpower and Community Development.

The deterrent then had been that manpower must include immigration. That was no longer decisive. We had got the administration of immigration into a shape in which it fitted comfortably with manpower programs and no longer imposed particularly exacting demands on the attention of the Minister and senior officials. It was therefore now possible to consummate the marriage that was most likely to be productive of the economic and social improvements for which the 1965 "opportunity plan" had been conceived: manpower services, helping people to take employment opportunities, could be closely co-ordinated with the improvement of opportunities where they were particularly deficient.

I wrote a series of memoranda, which Jean Marchand passed on to the Prime Minister, on regional policies to improve employment and their linkage with manpower programs. They culminated in early July, when Mr Trudeau was constructing his new Cabinet, in a fairly detailed plan for the structure of what I called a Department of Development; in my thinking, this was an appropriate name for a department that would have Canada Manpower Centres as its operational units serving individual needs.

That it would be a large department did not worry me. It had long been my view, and still is my view, that the structure of government would be more effective if responsibilities were divided among only ten to twelve major departments. Their ministers would constitute a cabinet of the right size to be an effective decision-making body, which our large Cabinets are not. In addition, there would be junior ministers, responsible for satellite departments or particular functions, but on policy issues subordinate to one of the senior ministers. I proposed, for example, that in addition to the Minister for Development there would be a second Minister with specific responsibilities for relations with the Atlantic provinces, and that some agencies with related functions – most notably, Central Mortgage and Housing Corporation – should also come under the senior Minister's supervision.

I thought that this kind of rationalization of government would appeal to Pierre Trudeau. I did not know him well enough and was surprised, at the time, when Jean Marchand warned me: "you'll find that on many things Pierre is really very conservative."

While I was writing my memoranda, the rest of the senior bureaucracy was also busy. It is difficult now to appreciate how thoroughly the Ottawa of 1968 was still devoted to the policy views that had ruled in the days of the great postwar economic expansion, the period of C.D. Howe. They were centralist views. The concern of national policy was the overall good, measured by the growth of the gross *national* product. Where in the nation development took place was the business of the market. Ottawa might intervene to help the "natural" economic forces, but not to counter them. That would be a distortion which would hamper the total national progress.

From this viewpoint, regional policies were local politics, to be resisted by the wise managers in Ottawa. If some parts of the country lagged in economic growth, people could and should move to take advantage of the glorious opportunities open to them elsewhere in Canada. Such mobility was the contemporary equivalent of the stern pioneer virtues that had built our society.

This viewpoint had not been seriously shaken by the mild measures for regional development adopted during the Pearson years. Ottawa men were practical. They knew that Victorian family virtues could not have flourished without some occasional discreet prostitution. But to have regional development put front centre on the 1968 election stage, otherwise empty, was rather different. The effect, as Mr Trudeau organized his new government, was of an illegitimate baby that otherwise quite proper politicians had brought from the hustings and dumped on the Ottawa doorstep.

The child could not be ignored. The existing regional programs – ARDA and FRED, the area development incentives of the Department of Industry, the Atlantic Development Board – would have to be put together in a new department. No doubt there would have to be some expansion, but it would still be small enough to be absorbed into the Ottawa system without too much disturbance. The empire-building idea of Marchand and Kent, that they should combine regional development with the manpower department for which they had already grabbed so much money, was quite another matter. That must be scotched. It would create a concentration of power the likes of which had not been seen since C.D. Howe's Trade and Commerce and Defence Production. It would entirely upset the balance of the present Ottawa system. That was the unanimous view of the leading bureaucrats, and it was no doubt shared by the politicians: Trudeau as their boss was one thing, but also to have Marchand wielding so much power would be to make the Quebec takeover too complete.

The issue was settled, a few days after Trudeau's electoral triumph, over a lunch at 24 Sussex of the Prime Minister, Jean Marchand and myself. Mr Trudeau had clearly been listening to the civil service. He gave, with skill, all the arguments against our proposed big department. It was clear that he agreed with them, with particular concern about the magnitude of the work we would be undertaking. He ended, nevertheless, by saying that it was up to us: if we wanted to do it, he would agree.

Jean was as frank as usual: in that case, I should decide, because I would have to do most of the work. He knew me well enough to say this without, I imagine, much doubt as to what, in the circumstances, I would decide. It was clear that there was not going to be any general restructuring of government into larger departments. Therefore a Department of Development, with the manpower organization, would stand out too much. With the bureaucracy and many politicians resenting it, it would encounter dogged resistance from the central agencies and some other departments; it would be the favourite target for blame when mistakes were made; other departments would be able to make it the scapegoat for weaknesses in many of their own programs. We would have overcome this if the Prime Minister had been in favour of the big department. But clearly his support of it would be reluctant. Even if in the end we could make a success of it, life would be hell meantime. For a period, we would be so occupied in fighting bureaucratic battles that public programs would be slow to start. The government would be vulnerable to the charge of not getting on with one of the few things it had firmly proposed.

It did not take long to go through this line of thought. Before we left 24 Sussex the decision had been made: Marchand and I would leave Manpower and set up a new department for regional development.

Perhaps this was a coward's decision. Within two years, I was wondering whether I would have made the same decision if I had foreseen the economic policy of the Trudeau government, with its indifference to unemployment. The big department would have been able to put up more resistance. But, while I would have felt better for the battle, I do not think it would have made too much difference; the weight of conventional economic thinking in the macho style of Simon Reisman, fitting as it did with the Prime Minister's attitudes, was too great.

In July 1968 the main decision did not dispose of the organizational problem. There were those who thought that a regional development department should be purely a planning, negotiating and co-ordinating agency. The actual programs would remain with "line" departments: industrial incentives for regional development would continue to be administered by the Department of Industry, and so on. The role of the new department would be to inject the purpose of lessening regional disparities into the whole structure of federal action and into arrangements with the provinces.

In my view, this was a prescription for not allowing the baby on the doorstep to grow up. The inertia of established programs is very great. To get the line departments to adjust their priorities for regional purposes would be a slow process indeed. It would be particularly slow at a time when the departments were already struggling against the growth of central agency power in the Treasury Board. This was not the time when an additional central agency could be effective.

I should say that I would not take this view in all circumstances. A decade later, when regionalization had become more accepted in federal policies and structures, when the Department of Regional Economic Expansion (DREE) had itself run down in innovative capacity, and when there was some reaction against so much centralization in the Treasury Board, I could observe a case for switching to concentration on planning and co-ordination. It might have given DREE a new lease on life which would have produced better results than its run-down to absorption into the Department of Industry.

That, however, is another story. In 1968 it was essential to moving at all quickly that the new department should have the responsibility and the budget to improve the main regional programs itself. That we called it Regional Economic Expansion, rather than Regional Development, was Jean Marchand's idea. He was worried about the range of meanings of "development," particularly in French. My concern was that the functions of the department should be spelled out as firmly and clearly as possible. The statutes creating departments are often worded very vaguely; both ministers and officials like the "flexibility" this allows to them. My fear was that, given the prevailing Ottawa attitudes towards regionalism, vagueness about its role would work against the new department; flexibility would be in the direction of compressing it.

The attempt at precision produced a great deal of resistance, particularly from Treasury Board, with the Department of Justice as, in this, its ally. The most general opposition, however, was to the "sunset" clause that I proposed: Parliament should give the department a fixed life of fifteen years. The intent was to drive home the thoughts that, on the one hand, we were not offering quick, band-aid remedies for stubborn problems; but nor, on the other hand, were we going to fob people off with measures for the "long term" in which we are all dead. But to arrange for a department to self-destruct was an innovation greeted in the bureaucracy with an opposition no less vehement for being legalistic: it conflicted with the principle of security in civil service employment, and so on. I dropped the point, and concentrated on the definition of the department's functions. Though watered down from the early drafts, the final version was not bad. In essence, it gave the department extensive powers "to facilitate economic expansion and social adjustment" in "areas requiring special measures to improve opportunities for productive employment and access to those opportunities" because of the "exceptional inadequacy" of such opportunities either in the area or in "the region of which that area is a part."

Plans for this purpose could be formulated and implemented, with "provisions for appropriate co-operation with the provinces in which special areas are located and for the participation of persons, voluntary groups, agencies and bodies in those special areas." In particular, a federal-provincial agreement on a plan for a special area could "provide that Canada and a province may procure the incorporation of one or more agencies or other bodies, to be jointly controlled by Canada and the province," for the purpose of "undertaking or implementing programs or projects to which the agreement relates."

The main battle had been over the provisions summarized in the previous paragraph. Stripped of their legal language, they meant that the department had the power to assist genuine community development. What was clear to me, from the experience of the previous few years, was that, however helpful some federal services – manpower counselling, training and mobility, industrial incentives, and so on – might be, substantial development in the areas of worst opportunities depended on local involvement and local organization. In the long run, the success of the department would depend, not on general programs but on what it could help to get done, case by case, place by place, on the spot.

Some other parts of the government organization Bill, which was to incorporate various items of departmental restructuring, were developed even more slowly than ours. It was not until April 1969 that the new department was formally constituted. Meantime we proceeded, as we had at Manpower, under the Public Service Rearrangement and Transfer of Duties Act. Marchand and I were Minister and Deputy Minister of Forestry and Rural Development, but forestry had been transferred out of it. The small branch dealing with rural development (the ARDA and FRED programs) had transferred into it the Area Development Agency (ADA) from the Department of Industry, the Atlantic Development Board (ADB) and the Prairie Farm Rehabilitation Administration (PFRA). We also brought with us the pilot projects branch of the Manpower department.

It would be hard to imagine a more mixed bag of relatively small units. They varied greatly in their histories, purposes, structures, attitudes and management styles. To meld them into a department was a painful process. Each unit tended to hang together as much as possible while, contradictorily, its senior people aspired to be the ones who became bigger frogs in the bigger pool. The internal problem was made more difficult by the external factor: Treasury Board's prejudice against the new department was expressed in reluctance to grant the classifications of positions required for a new organization. It was at this point that I first learned about Mr Trudeau's lack of follow-through. A word from him would have quickly subdued Treasury Board. Despite the importance he had publicly attached to regional development, the word was not given. He seemed to think that, with the creation of the department, his work was done. Making it effective was up to Marchand and Kent.

In the end we got some, though not all, of the classifications needed for senior people in the new department, and moved to the next difficulty. By no means all of the people we had inherited were the most qualified candidates for the positions to which they aspired. This kind of reorganization is not recommended work for anyone whose concern in life is to be liked. I earned some long-time enemies among those whose expectations were disappointed. There were enough disaffected people grumbling enough, and willing to talk about it outside, for the press and the opposition to get hold of stories of alleged administrative confusion in the department. We had further trouble because some of the disappointed people got jobs with provincial governments, which created personality clashes in some of our negotiations, notably with Nova Scotia.

Such teething troubles were tiresome, but they did not prevent us from instituting, in 1969 and 1970, a considerable range of program innovations. We negotiated agreements on special areas with the Atlantic provinces, Quebec and the prairie provinces (where the emphasis was on developments that would improve employment for Indian and Métis people in northern areas of the provinces). The initial development plans for these areas were hardly sophisticated, but we were concerned, for the sake of long-term relations with the provinces as well as the early improvement of employment opportunities, to move ahead smartly with projects on which there could be ready agreement with the provinces and municipalities. The results were needed improvements in the infrastructures – serviced land for industry and housing, schools, roads, water and sewer systems, and so on – in communities where new jobs were developing or, with the help of the improved services, in prospect.

The ADA program, which had proved to be too rigid to be either efficient or very effective, was replaced by new legislation. This provided industrial incentives that could be much better matched to particular opportunities to establish new enterprises or to expand or modernize existing operations. We rationalized the principles for defining, in consultation with the provinces, the areas in which the incentives were available. We also soon added the power to provide loan guarantees, in addition to grants towards capital costs and, in some cases, start-up costs. The guarantees, unlike the grants, were available for some kinds of service industries as well as manufacturing and processing. For a time at least, the new program was effective in stimulating, at a gratifyingly low public cost per continuing job, a good deal of development in communities which would otherwise have been passed by or would have declined.

The special development plan for Prince Edward Island had been largely drafted under the FRED legislation, before the department was created, but had some features that were unacceptable in Ottawa and others that the provincial government would settle for only under duress. While that government was naturally impatient to get the federal funding which it had been led to expect earlier, the considerable pain in redrafting the plan arose less from difficulties in federal-provincial relations than from the sensitivities of some of the original draftsmen. A more realistic plan was put into operation early in 1969.

New ARDA agreements were made with all the other provinces. Most of them considerably broadened the scope of previous programs. There were also special agreements with the western provinces, to assist in improving employment for Indian and Métis communities. Substantial contributions to some of those communities in the northern parts of the prairie provinces were also made by the pilot projects, or New Start Corporations as we called them, which DREE took over from the Manpower department. The engineering resources of PFRA, which had done so much for farming and conservation on the prairies, were brought into play to provide improved water supplies for some small towns and Indian reserves. We put funds into a development corporation for small businesses in Newfoundland. Substantial contributions were made to highway construction in the Atlantic provinces. As a fallback, a special development loan fund was established; from this all the provinces were entitled to borrow, in proportions reflecting the number of their unemployed, for development projects not covered by any of our particular programs.

And so on. All of this involved continual negotiations in Ottawa and extensive travel across the country, to talk to people on the spot about their problems and opportunities, as well as to negotiate with provincial governments. The result could fairly be criticized as a hodgepodge of measures, too little co-ordinated.

That did not worry me in the early stages. There were plenty of urgent needs, and it seemed to me essential that, in order to win the co-operation of people and of provincial authorities, we should demonstrate that we were not a remote, bureaucratic agency; we were concerned for prompt action on the spot. For that purpose, we had to use the tools that were on hand or could be fairly quickly made. Improvisation was not at this stage bad, on two conditions.

One was that the projects were fully within the department's purposes; they were in fact so, except perhaps for a few marginal cases that may have slipped by. The other condition was that we should move to more thorough planning as soon as was practicable. On that point I was confident. By 1970 we had built up a strong departmental staff. We had been joined by public servants of proven ability, such as Jack Francis, Ed Aquilina, and Duncan Campbell; and we had secured good recruits from the private sector and from provincial government services. How good the planning was, how soon, would necessarily vary with the differing capacities of provinces to participate, but we were equipped to do our part.

Nevertheless there were, in early 1971, reasons for concern. One was that too much of our staff strengthening was at headquarters. It was more difficult to get people with the required talents outside Ottawa. The staffing and classification policies of Treasury Board increased the difficulties. In the fairly near future, however, our success would depend on a great deal more decentralization to the offices in each provincial capital (not in my view, to "regional" offices, for the Atlantic provinces and the western provinces collectively, as was done at a later stage of DREE). Down the road, if policies were developed as I intended, it would be equally important to have field staff able to work well with community organizations and the local agencies that, under the provisions of the legislation, could be set up jointly with the provinces and were, I believed, the best way to carry out development plans in special areas.

This was an important but not immediate concern. In 1971 I was more worried as to whether our capacity for industrial intelligence and promotion, in order realistically to identify industrial ventures that were viable, was adequate to the scale and flexibility of the new industrial incentives program. This was a delicate issue, because the provinces were very much in the business of industrial promotion. In the 1960s and 1970s, regional industrial development earned a bad name because of some conspicuous failures that wasted much public money – Clairtone and Deuterium in Nova Scotia, Come-By-Chance in Newfoundland, The Pas forest industries in Manitoba, Bricklin in New Brunswick, and others. Critics have too rarely noted a common feature of these major disasters: all were projects in which the government involvement was solely, or at any rate primarily, that of the province. The success rate of federally supported ventures was and is a good deal better. Nevertheless, we had to be very much on guard, lest our enthusiasm for development lead us into supporting projects that, if they were similar disasters, could quickly destroy the credibility of the new department.

One safeguard was to establish a small but strong advisory committee from the private sector, with which to review major incentive decisions. The second was to attempt to persuade the Maritime provinces to establish a joint industrial intelligence agency. We offered to contribute half of its costs. Apart from the direct gain in more sophisticated intelligence work, I hoped thereby to lessen the pathetic competition of the smaller provinces for the favour of foreign investors. I had already encountered one example of this: a large American corporation unashamedly provoking two provinces to outbid each other in their subsidies for a project which, though spectacular in its construction phase, would have produced in operation comparatively small benefits of continuing employment and income for Canadians. The project was set aside only because the subsidy scale was appallingly large for either province and we refused any federal involvement – which did not earn us any thanks from the provinces.

In the summer of 1971, when the Deutsch report on maritime union led to the tentative step of setting up the Council of Maritime Premiers, we seemed close to the creation of the joint industrial intelligence agency. But the vested interests of the provincial industrial promotion agencies were too strong.

A deeper concern about the whole regional development policy arose from the October 1970 "emergency" in Quebec. Ottawa then seemed to be turned temporarily into an armed camp. Three incidents recall for me the disturbing atmosphere of the period. One morning I came down to the lobby of my apartment building just after an eighteen-year-old member of a military escort, jumping out of his truck in front of the building, had somehow fired his weapon and killed himself. Late one night I was wakened by a worried building superintendent and an army officer. They thought perhaps that this was the most likely place for the Honourable Mr So-and-so, who had an apartment in the building, to be visiting for a nightcap. He was lost. His military escort, they explained, had accompanied him from the House of Commons to the elevator in the lobby, but the soldier on guard outside his apartment had not seen him. I did not volunteer a guess as to the lady's apartment in which they might find their quarry.

The third incident provided a breath of comparative normalcy. During this sorry period Barbara Ward visited us, with the result that the Pearsons, the Maurice Strongs, and we spent an evening talking about international development. As a former Prime Minister, Mike was supposed to be attended with great security, but he resolutely refused to have the army around him. It had to be an RCMP officer who kept watch on our apartment while Mike was there.

Strange as that brief period of feared insurrection in Canada now seems, it had more than short-term repercussions on government policy. The depressed economy of Montreal was considered to be a breeding ground for separatist sentiment. Measures to create more employment there were called for. But what? People who had been strongly opposed to our industrial development incentives suddenly saw them as the means to salvation: they could be applied in Montreal. I did not like that, but saw the opportunity for a trade-off that would give us some of the improvements in our programs that were needed.

The compromise was that there would be a special, short-term industrial incentive program for the Montreal area and eastern Ontario. I insisted that this should also be available in the Atlantic provinces, as an addition to the ceilings for the regular incentive program. On paper, their relative advantage would be maintained. But in practice it was not so. By early 1971 I was noting that, while ventures in the Montreal area were being offered close to the maximum incentive for the area, offers in the Atlantic region were far below the theoretical maximum. I could not fault the handling of the particular cases, given the program criteria. But the general effect was devastating to the original purposes. If companies could get sizeable subsidies for projects close to the country's industrial heartland, they were not going to be induced to go to more remote locations for the sake of marginally bigger subsidies. The inclusion of Montreal took much of the force out of the regional development program.

It was, in fact, the beginning of a trend towards generalizing regional policy which, inevitably, depreciated it; relatively, the benefit to areas with specially difficult problems was diminished. In the atmosphere of the 1970 "emergency," it would have been very difficult to stand aside from one of the few measures that could be quickly taken to show that the rest of Canada's concern about Quebec was positive, not merely repressive. It would have been particularly difficult for a department whose Minister was strongly convinced of the danger to confederation. Nevertheless, I should have resisted the dilution of regional development programs and somehow found other ways in which federal goodwill to Quebec could be demonstrated.

It might be said, in partial excuse, that in the winter of 1970-1 there was an even more direct threat to regional development policy. Activity in the Canadian economy as a whole was slowing; nationally, unemployment was increasing. If this were to continue, it would knock away the very foundations of regional development policy. If most of the country was prosperous, as it had been and we had assumed it would be, then it was both sensible economics and practical politics to spend federal tax money to help the less favoured parts of the country to catch up in employment and production. But if there were unemployed workers even in Ontario, there was far less reason for a company to choose to locate in the Maritimes; and there was even less political attraction in spending money to influence the choice.

These were my worries, the last by far the greatest, but as I reviewed the situation in the summer of 1971, when I had decided to leave, there were also solid grounds for satisfaction about what had been achieved. It was too soon for any sophisticated benefit-cost evaluation of programs in operation for only two years or less. But one simple index was available. The most critical disparity was in unemployment; the broad region where job opportunities were poorest was that of the Atlantic provinces. From 1953 (the first year from which comparable statistics were available) to 1970, the unemployment rate in the Atlantic provinces during the months of January to May had been on average 80 per cent greater than the national rate. For the first five months of 1971, the Atlantic regional rate was only 36 per cent greater than the national rate.

By this crucial measure – the extent to which Canada's poorest region had particularly severe unemployment – the disparity had, in two years of our programs, been halved. It could not be proved that the programs merited all the credit for the improvement, but the statistic was certainly encouraging. The baby on the doorstep had so far been fairly well nurtured. Regional development policy had accomplished all that, as yet, anyone could reasonably expect of it.

The lessening of disparity was small comfort, however, if absolute levels of unemployment were rising across the country. The purpose of regional development was to achieve a broader distribution of employment opportunities, not a more even deprivation of opportunities. Indeed, if the recession continued, even the relative improvement could not be sustained.

The problem of the market economy, of course, is that market forces are exaggerated by the herd instinct. Because of that, the equilibrium position of economic theory is often approached not by rational adjustments but through wild swings. In the process, some enterprises are damaged beyond repair; some areas are depressed beyond recovery; some people are deprived for the rest of their lives. That is the source of much of the economic waste and social inequity of the system, and the government interventions that are sensible are often those that simply moderate the operation of the herd instinct. But they cannot turn the herd around. If most of the economy is buoyant, if a good deal of investment in new undertakings is being considered, it is practicable to fight the herd instinct by inducing more of the investment to go to regions where activity is relatively slack and workers are more plentiful. But in periods when most companies are standing still, or contracting, no practicable inducements will produce much development in peripheral regions.

That regional policy could succeed to a significant extent, in favourable circumstances, seemed to me to have been demonstrated by 1971. But the good that it could do would be submerged, realization of its effectiveness would be lost, the political will for it would evaporate, if the economy continued on the course on which the government seemed to be setting it. That the fault lay in national policy, not in regional policy, might be some consolation to me, but not to the unemployed. And all those who had never liked the baby would be able to claim that not only was it expensive to keep; it would never be anything but a weakling anyway.

34   Battle Lost, War to Win

I left Ottawa in 1971 because I could not live with a government whose economic policies were inducing unemployment. It was not, at the time, severe unemployment by the standards to which we have since become accustomed. I was convinced, however, that the policies on which the government was set, and which I had despaired of changing, would stultify the Canadian economy and result in heavy, long-term unemployment. That was not, in fairness, the government's intent. But I thought that, given the policies, it was the way the future would unfold as, to vary Mr Trudeau's phrase, it should not. It did, and I was glad to have decided to stand aside from it. But the lost battle may be worth briefly recounting, because I think that the policies then rejected are still revelant to the policies we could follow now.

The Trudeau government's poor management of the Canadian economy has been referred to at earlier points in this book. Criticism should not be made, however, without noting the other side of the political reckoning. Trudeau performed an essential service to Canada. He demonstrated, for the first time and at a critical time, that Québecois could have their turn as masters in Ottawa. If he had not done so, the continuation of Canada as an effectively united country would have been challenged even more strongly than it was; probably the issue would still be seriously in question today.

Wilfrid Laurier and Louis St Laurent were largely absorbed into the political culture and governmental system of British Ottawa. It was British because, though even the Highlanders had largely abandoned a language of their own, Scots did as much or more to fashion it than did men of English origin. Until the 1970s, the Québecois who came to Ottawa as legislators, and the relatively few who worked there as administrators, were influential to the extent that they fitted with the Anglo-Scottish mandarins.

Pierre Trudeau was a man of the world and diverse culture, but he was intensely French in politics and in style, in the methodology of logical confrontation rather than incremental compromise. He and the Quebec federalists who came with him and behind did not move into the old Ottawa. They quickly changed it. The increasing use of the French language had begun under Pearson and, while its momentum was important, it was secondary. The fundamental change was in the political culture, expressed in either language. Its Anglo-Scottish characteristics were mingled with new French strands. Whether it was thereby more Canadian could be questioned. I sometimes felt that the strongest new influence, irrespective of the language of those through whom it was expressed, was the Harvard Business School. But undoubtedly Ottawa was changed, and the driving force operated from Quebec.

Credit for the initial impetus belongs to Jean Marchand who, when the Liberal party wanted him, insisted that it would have to take Trudeau and Pelletier too. He knew better than to be isolated in new territory. Thanks to that, the Liberal party was in large measure taken over by people who were as new to it as they were unseasoned in government.

There was, of course, resentment, but the just grounds for it were not special to English Canada. Mr Trudeau became dominant over all. Marchand and Pelletier soon faded into the background as surely as did the former strong men of English-Canadian cabinets. At the official level, new people were brought from Quebec, as was the need, but they were additions. English-speaking Canadians were not pushed out. On the contrary, the new people came from everywhere. The centralization of power that in fact resulted was Trudeau's particular style, not inherent in the realignment of Ottawa. That did no more than give Quebec, so long peripheral in the government of Canada, a role at last appropriate to the dimensions of the province and the talents of its people. The change was overdue. It was necessary to Confederation. It alone gave Pierre Trudeau a more significant place in Canadian history than belongs to most prime ministers.

The centralization of power, which was his undoing, did not arise from any petty urge for self-aggrandizement. On the contrary, it started from a genuine intent to make Cabinet's collective responsibility for the formulation of policy more effective. The fault was not in the objective but in the means that, Trudeau thought, would achieve it. He came to office intellectually scornful of what he saw, with some justification, as the slapdash way in which governments, under Pearson and before, had made their decisions. Now there was to be the order and system required for a rational process. Issues were to be categorized and priorized. Trends were to be projected, scenarios depicted. Alternative courses of action, explored by the thorough research of experts, were to be brilliantly presented to decision-makers on flip charts and projector slides. The best solution would always be chosen, and its efficient implementation would be worked out with the charting of critical paths and the rest. The Philosopher King had arrived, trailing the paraphernalia of the 1960s fashions in "scientific" management.

It was a great nonsense. Studies were made. New agencies were set up to make more studies. There was a new jargon in which familiar issues were restated more portentously. But there were few new ideas with practical applications. The "rational" system could produce sound policies only if the options presented to the decision-makers were derived from perceptive assessments of problems. Some were, some were not. The Trudeau system had more successes than, by reaction, it has lately been given credit for. But where it went wrong, where the assessments were not perceptive, it went horribly wrong. And that was so in the crucial matter of inflation and unemployment.

The Trudeau administration inherited an active economy. Under the Pearson government, there had been strong economic growth; the unemployment inherited from Diefenbaker had been halved. This was almost maintained for the first two years of the Trudeau government. There were beginning, however, to be symptoms of cost-push inflation. Prolonged prosperity had created expectations that produced speculative price increases for such things as land and buildings. Good markets made it fairly easy for companies to raise prices and for trade unions to win higher wages. There was, in the early Trudeau years, an entirely correct concern to arrest inflation before it got out of hand.

But how? The solution proposed was what governments had long been supposed to do about the old kind of inflation discussed in the economics textbooks, "too much money chasing too few goods." You cut down the money. You "cool" the economy by tight fiscal and monetary policies. This would "squeeze out the fat." It would temporarily reduce output and employment. But, according to the scenario presented to the Cabinet for decision-making, the pain would not be prolonged. In the fall of 1970 the Department of Finance was claiming, on the evidence of its econometric model, that a moderately "tough" fiscal and monetary policy would result in growing output and employment in 1971.

I didn't believe it. I redrew the kinds of charts we had used in the 1962 election campaign to demonstrate the gap between potential and actual output and employment in the Diefenbaker "wasted years." An October 1970 memorandum, which I vainly hoped Jean Marchand could use to shift his colleagues' opinions, argued that "on present indications, it is quite possible that by mid-1972 the economic performance of the preceding two years or so will be about as bad as that of June 1962, when economic performance last provided the main theme of the opposition attack in a general election. In that election the government lost, to a previously weak opposition, 45 per cent of the seats it had won four years earlier; its strength in the House of Commons fell from 208 in 1958 to 116 in 1962."

In the event, the economic performance was indeed poor, and the Trudeau government in 1972 held only 1 per cent more of the popular vote than Diefenbaker had in 1962. But with the quirks of the electoral system, its loss of seats – starting from the less elevated point of 155 in 1968 – was 30 per cent, to 109.

In 1970, however, my attempt at a political warning was no more effective than the substantive arguments that I tried to make. Those did not fit the Trudeau scheme. The "rational" process required that issues should be categorized for consideration and decision. In this style of thinking, there was a box called "economic policy," and another called "social policy." If this distinction was sound, economic policy had to be settled first, because it determined the gross national product, the size of the pie. Social policy was what you did afterwards, to affect the distribution of the pie.

To me, this was an old-fashioned notion, fatal to effective policies for contemporary problems. I do not mean that the Trudeau government was reactionary in its social policy as such. On the contrary, its unemployment insurance reform, perhaps influenced by bad conscience about the amount of unemployment, was a measure of radical redistribution – in some particulars, too much so.

My objection to the government's approach was that the separation of economic and social issues into boxes falsified both. A letter written for Marchand to send to Trudeau, in March 1969, made the fundamental point: "The first requirement of social justice is that there should be enough jobs. That is a basic economic issue, but it is also the primary social issue."

Within its economic policy box, the government saw a simple choice. In the short run, it was between more inflation and more unemployment. In the longer run, inflation would discourage the market economy, make us internationally uncompetitive, and cause heavy unemployment. Therefore the short-run choice of more unemployment was the better from every viewpoint. "Spare the rod, spoil the child" quickly became the Ottawa attitude.

Whether they were partly or wholly wrong, the ideas that shaped the economic policies of the Trudeau government were certainly not new. In my view, they were fundamentally mistaken. In our kind of society, an efficient and innovative economy requires two legs. One is the market; there is no other process through which the energies and ideas of many free people can emerge in products and services that satisfy the community's requirements as well as its physical and human resources, its knowledge and inventiveness and enterprise, make possible. The second leg, however, is no less crucial. It is a social contract, largely implicit, but explicitly reflected in government policies for fairness both in opportunities – which requires high employment – and in rewards – which requires effectively progressive taxation of wealth and incomes.

My objection to the course taken by the Trudeau government was that it breached the social contract. When the seasonally adjusted rate of unemployment had risen to the then great height of 6 per cent, Mr Trudeau's logical defence of his policy was that he was quite prepared to see unemployment rise further if it was necessary to stop inflation. He thereby destroyed any possibility of public confidence and consent in the only policies that were likely in fact to demobilize the forces of cost-push inflation.

Those forces were deep-seated. They would not be overcome by the moderate and temporary increase in unemployment that the conventional wisdom of Ottawa at first predicted. It seemed to me that the monetarist policy would turn out to be not a bottle of medicine but an alcoholic binge. It would become severe and prolonged. In the process the economy would be stultified, its efficiency reduced and its development impaired, our capacity to win more export trade inhibited at what should have been the critical time for us to adapt to the new world economy that had emerged from the postwar recovery. There would be a devastating shake-out of business and an appalling increase in unemployment before Mr Trudeau, perhaps, wrestled inflation to the ground. And if the social contract was not only breached but set aside for a long time, it would also be a long time further before confidence was restored to the point that would make it possible to turn to effective policies for operating a buoyant, high-employment economy without inflation.

The conclusion of this long book is not the place to make my case for alternative economic policies. In 1970, however, it led me to advocate budgetary and monetary measures different from those that were in fact implemented. I urged that the government should promptly act on most of the recommendations of the Carter Royal Commission on Taxation. In particular, capital gains should be taxed exactly like income. In addition to its equity, that would weaken the speculative urge that was a major factor in bidding up costs and prices. In the same spirit, tax reform should end the legal laxity regarding the expenses that a corporation could deduct from its income for taxation.

If I were writing similar memoranda now, I would suggest much larger changes in corporation law and taxation, in order to prevent the massive distortion of a competitive economy that has come about through the paper entrepreneurship of corporate concentration. In 1970, however, I was focusing on the more immediate requirements of the social contract. It was necessary to secure enough equity, as between the tax treatment of capital and of incomes, for the public at large to accept, and therefore for trade union organizers to be unable to resist, the government's credentials on behalf of restraint in income increases. In that event, there was a large body of common sense for the government to rely on, and it would not have to plan to dissipate the common sense by inducing unemployment. It could follow a somewhat more expansionist budgetary and monetary policy than the Department of Finance and others were recommending.

This, I recognized, would result in some depreciation in the exchange value of the Canadian dollar. It was at about par with the us dollar, and the Department of Finance projection was that it would remain there. I commented: "That has no merit. Indeed, it really is ridiculous to suppose that the Canadian economy can operate at full employment unless the Canadian dollar normally is appreciably (say, 10 per cent) cheaper than

the US dollar. So what virtue is there in policies that keep it higher now?"
In more informal discussions, I used to say then (1970) that there was
nothing the country needed so much as a good 90-cent dollar.

By that November, however, I was beginning a memorandum to Jean
Marchand, about an impending Cabinet discussion of economic policy,
with a despairing section on "The battle that we can't win." Bitterly, it
said "the predominant economics of the Cabinet are those of Mr Glad-
stone, and the value of the dollar is more important than jobs." With the
benefit of hindsight, it can fairly be argued that if in the 1970s there had
been acceptance of a lower exchange rate – recognition, I put it, that "a
rate much above 90″ is " an escape from reality into a make-believe
world" – then not only would we have had less unemployment, but the
exchange rate of the 1980s would not have had to fall so far as it did.

In 1970, I could see only worse times ahead. We seemed to be going
backwards. In the Pearson years we had fumbled, but we had been
feeling our way towards adapting government to the new society. Within the institutions of co-operative federalism essential to Canada, we had
begun also to establish what I summarized as the sense of social contract
required for a modern democracy. We were moving, slowly but clearly,
to a more equal society. It was on that basis, I thought, that we could
sustain steady economic development appropriate to the society. But it
could not be done by the methods of 1970.

My special regret, of course, concerned the manpower programs that
we had put in place and the regional development programs that I had
thought might take hold. Both had been designed for the kind of economy that I had believed to be our future. Neither could do much good in
a stagnant economy with high unemployment. The best of manpower
counselling will not put many people into better jobs if jobs are not
available. There is little point in training people when people who already have the relevant skills cannot get work. Few people can be
usefully helped to move from areas of heavy unemployment when there
are only areas of somewhat less unemployment to move to. No sensible
programs will diversify much economic growth to the more peripheral
regions when little growth is taking place in the more prosperous areas.
A cold economic climate will stunt even the best devised of community
development projects. It seemed, by late 1970, that the work of the
previous few years had been wasted.

I was too fond of Jean Marchand, with whom I had shared that work,
for it to be easy to leave him. I could understand that his concern for
Quebec in Confederation could outweigh – though only with much
emotional conflict – his unhappiness with an economic policy that ran
counter to all his background and his instincts. But, much as I appreciated the importance of saving Quebec for Confederation, I could not

reconcile myself to the policies that involved me more directly. Early in 1971, I made up my mind to leave Ottawa. I thought about returning to journalism or to private business, or undertaking a new venture into university life. In doing none of those, I was influenced by Allan Mac-Eachen and by Gerry Regan, who in 1970 had become Premier of Nova Scotia. They convinced me that there was a difficult and important job to do there. They were right. I never regretted the decision to move to Nova Scotia, which I did in September 1971. And as events in Ottawa unfolded, I became increasingly sure that there would have been no happiness in staying. I do not, however, see reason for despair. Progress is made in fits and starts. We might have done better in the 1960s, and others can do so in future. In some important ways, we were on the right lines. Believing that, I expect that they will be taken up again. If so, perhaps this account of our efforts will be some help.

Index